LIVING·ROOM

LIVING·ROOM

MATSUNAGA·SAN

3

Keiko Iwashita

MATSUNAGA SAN

LIVING-ROOM

Contents

Story

Family circumstances have wrested Meeko from an ordinary family life into her uncle's boarding house, where she must learn to live with rather unusual adult housemates. What's more, the oldest of the bunch, Matsunaga-san, is a little scary. However, contrary to his appearance, he watches out for Meeko and helps her get used to her new life, and Meeko finds herself increasingly drawn to him. Swept up in the moment after an accidental kiss, Meeko confesses her feelings! She manages to cover it up, but her love for him only grows. ♥ Unfortunately, Meeko's bubble is burst when Matsunaga-san tells her "You're like family to me"... Or so she thinks, until he says, "I want to worry about you." With a single meaningful line, Meeko's heart is thrown yet again into a whirlwind of confusion and hope...!

MATSUNAGA SAN

Let's introduce the people living at my boarding house!

Uncle   Sabako

Characters

Miko Sonoda

A 17-year-old high school girl.
Only knows how to cook curry.
Pining for Matsunaga-san.

Jun Matsunaga

A designer who works from home.
27 years old.
Sharp-tongued but caring.

Kentaro Suzuki
A bartender.
Girl-crazy (?)

Asako Onuki
A nail artist.
Like a big sister.

Ryo Hojo
A quiet
college student.
Doesn't have
a girlfriend.

Akane Hattori
An enigma.
Actually has
a boyfriend.

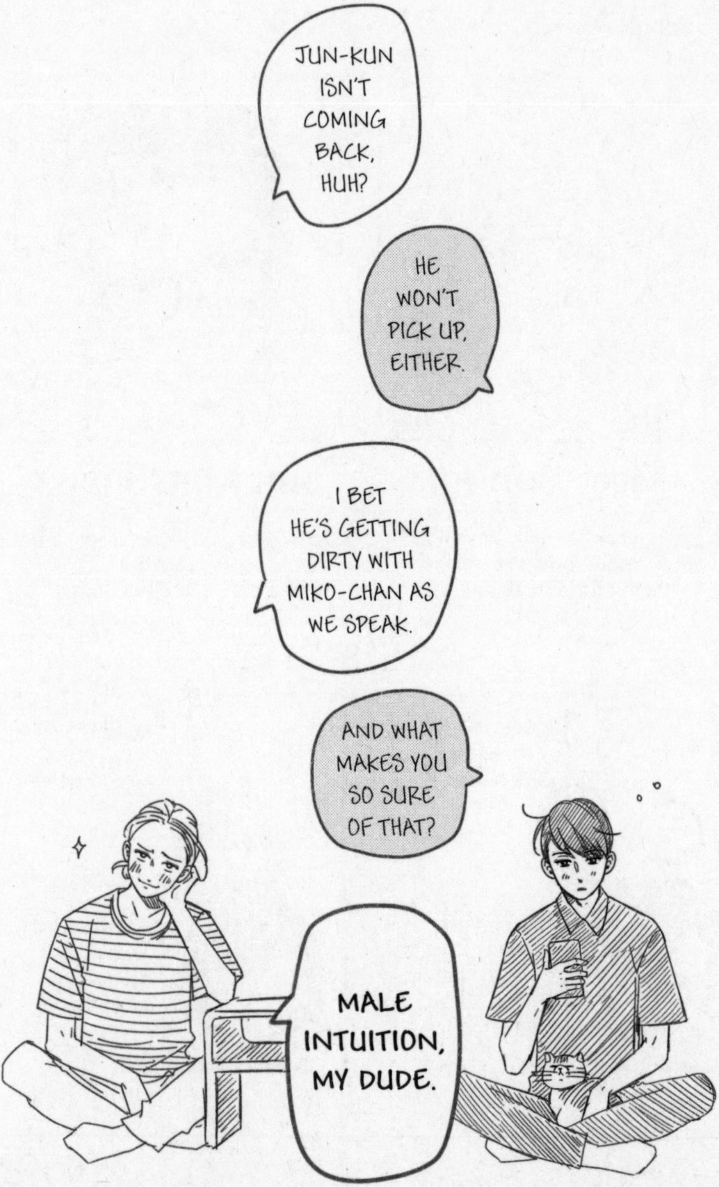
JUN-KUN ISN'T COMING BACK, HUH?
HE WON'T PICK UP, EITHER.
I BET HE'S GETTING DIRTY WITH MIKO-CHAN AS WE SPEAK.
AND WHAT MAKES YOU SO SURE OF THAT?
MALE INTUITION, MY DUDE.

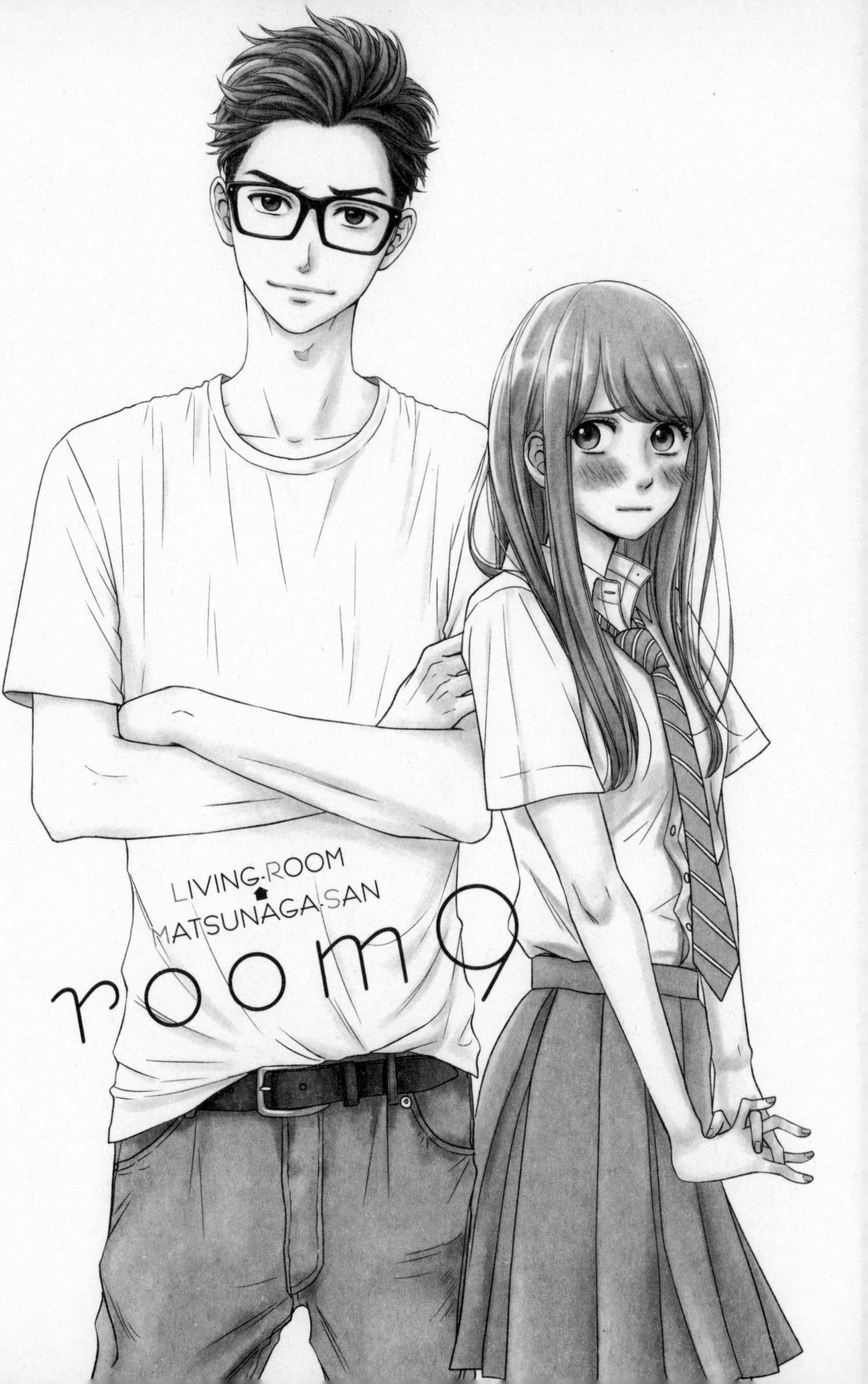

LIVING-ROOM MATSUNAGA-SAN
room9

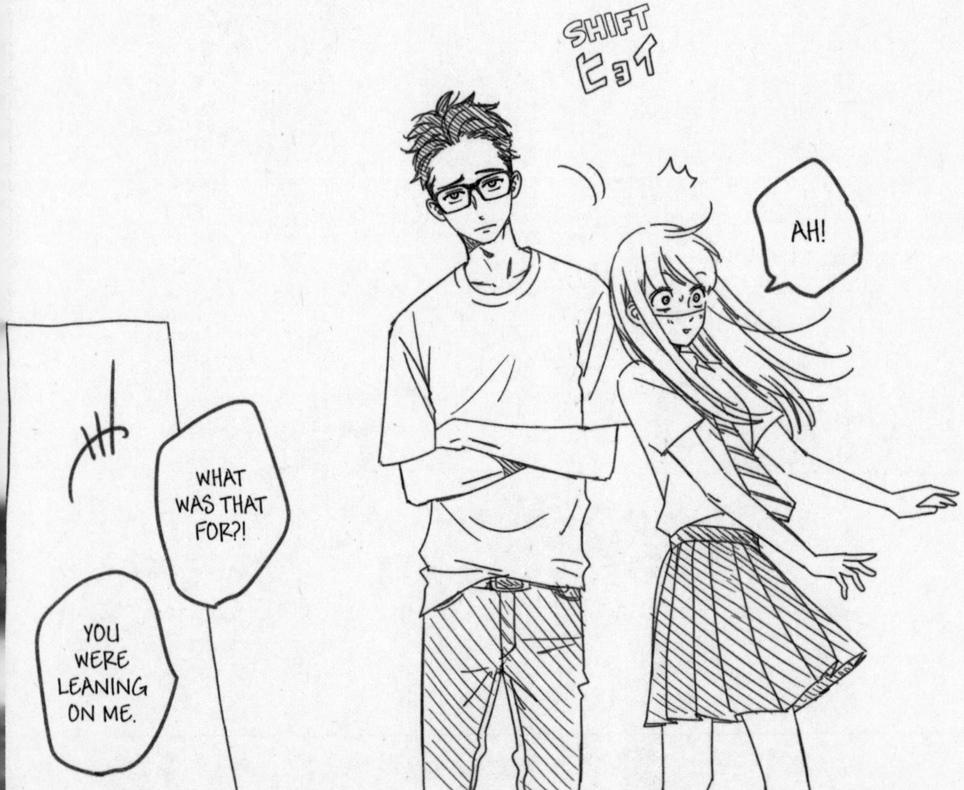
SHIFT
ヒョイ
AH!
WHAT WAS THAT FOR?!
YOU WERE LEANING ON ME.

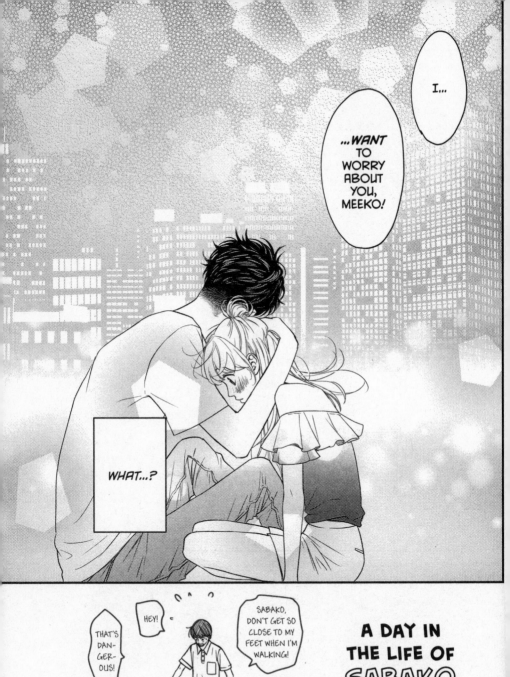

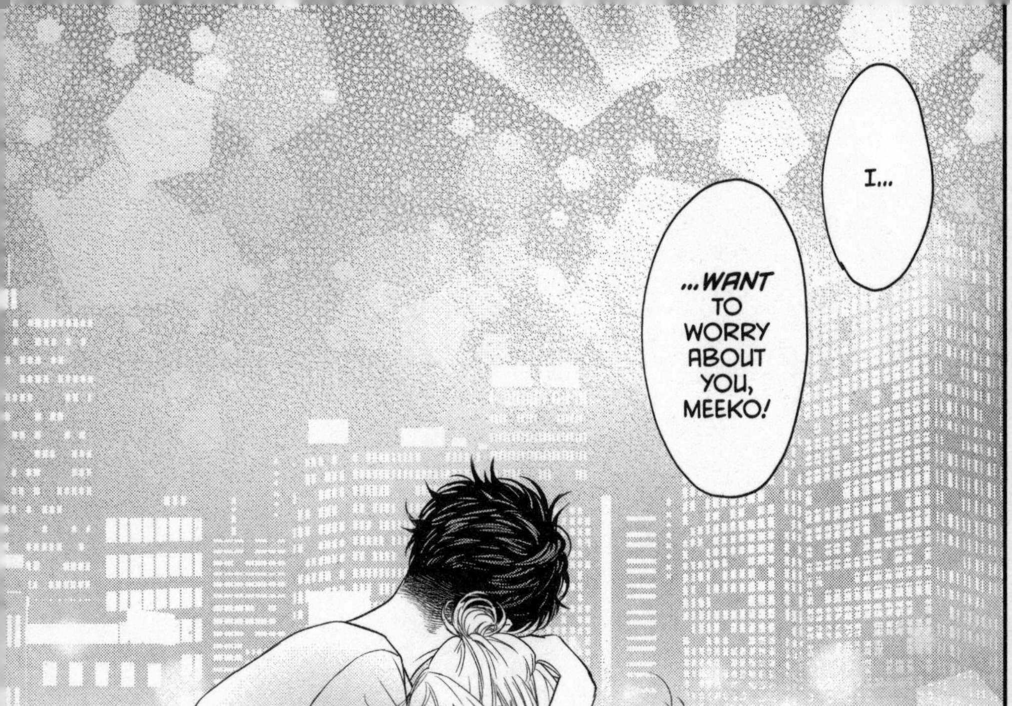
I...
...WANT TO WORRY ABOUT YOU, MEEKO!
WHAT...?

A DAY IN THE LIFE OF SABAKO

WITH RYO-KUN

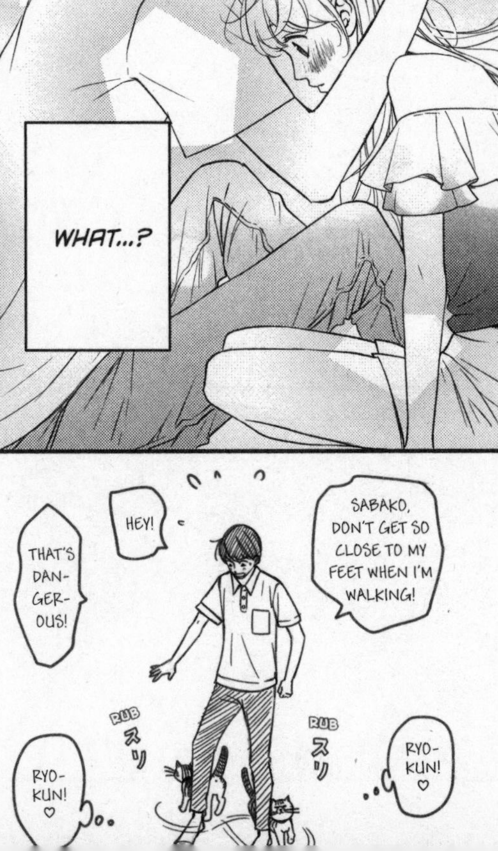
SABAKO, DON'T GET SO CLOSE TO MY FEET WHEN I'M WALKING!
HEY!
THAT'S DAN-GER-OUS!
RUB スリ
RYO-KUN! ♡
RUB スリ
RYO-KUN! ♡

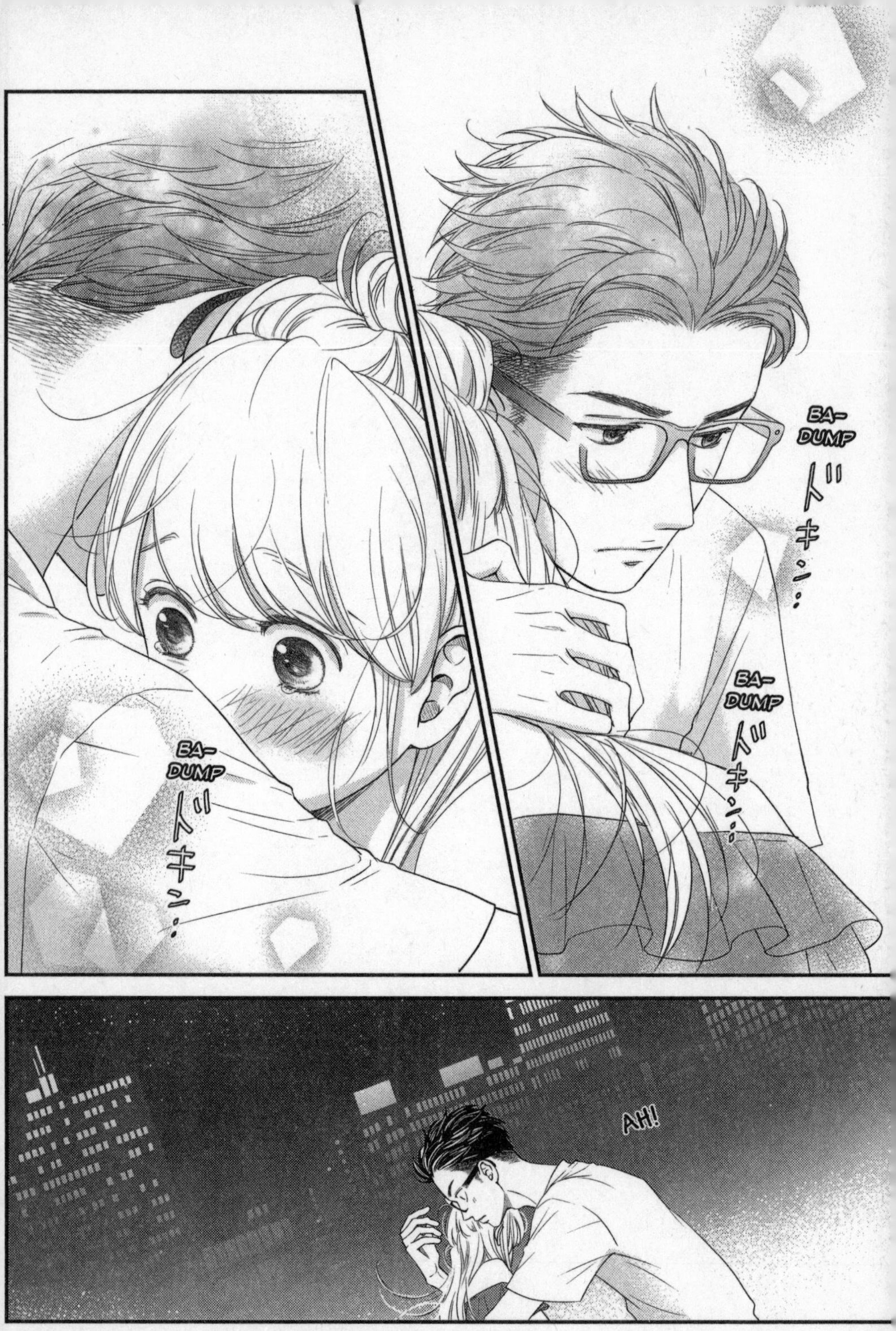
BA-DUMP
ドキン…
BA-DUMP
ドキン…
BA-DUMP
ドキン…
AH!

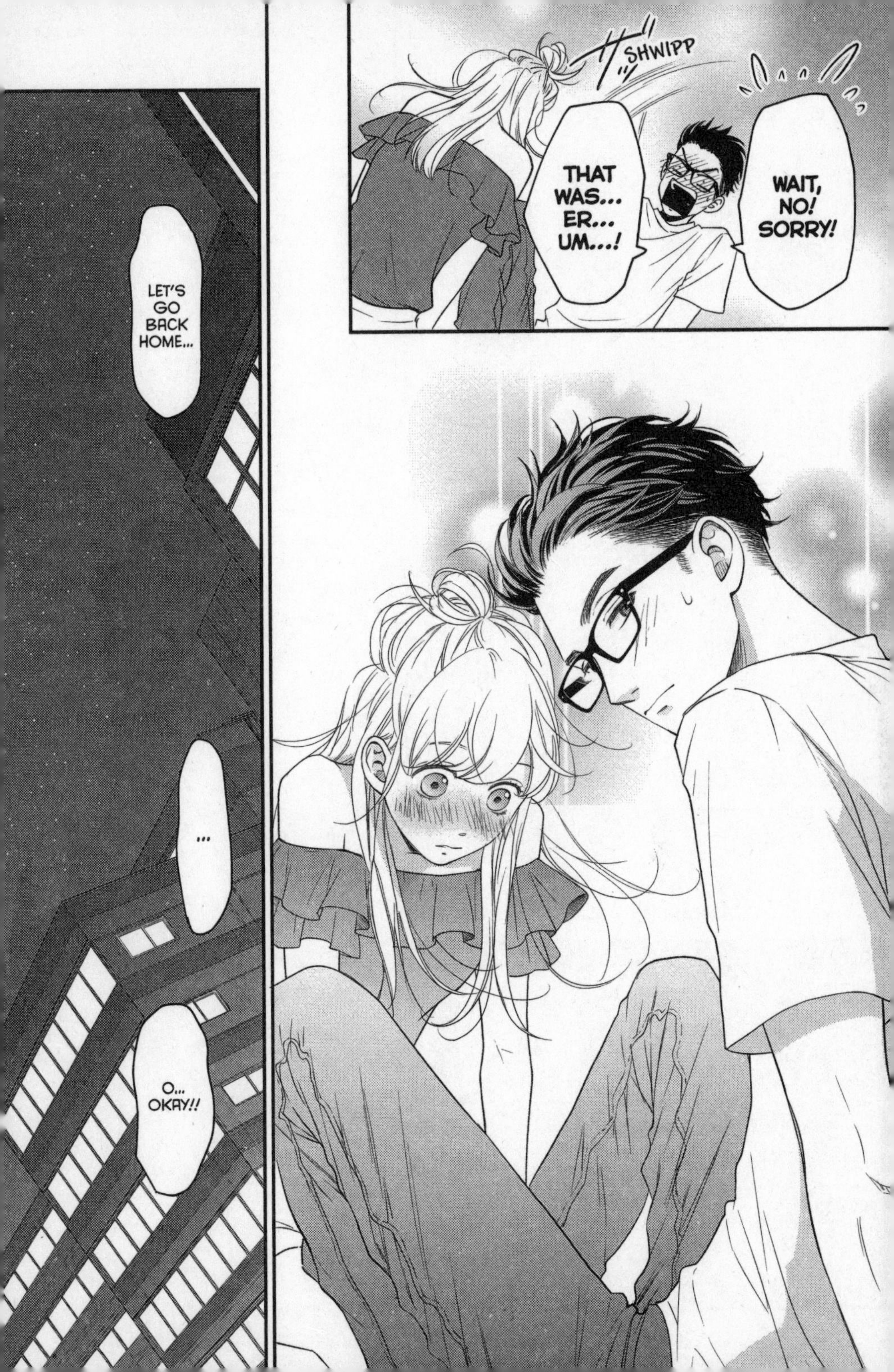
WAIT, NO! SORRY!
SHWIPP
THAT WAS... ER... UM...!
LET'S GO BACK HOME...
...
O... OKAY!!

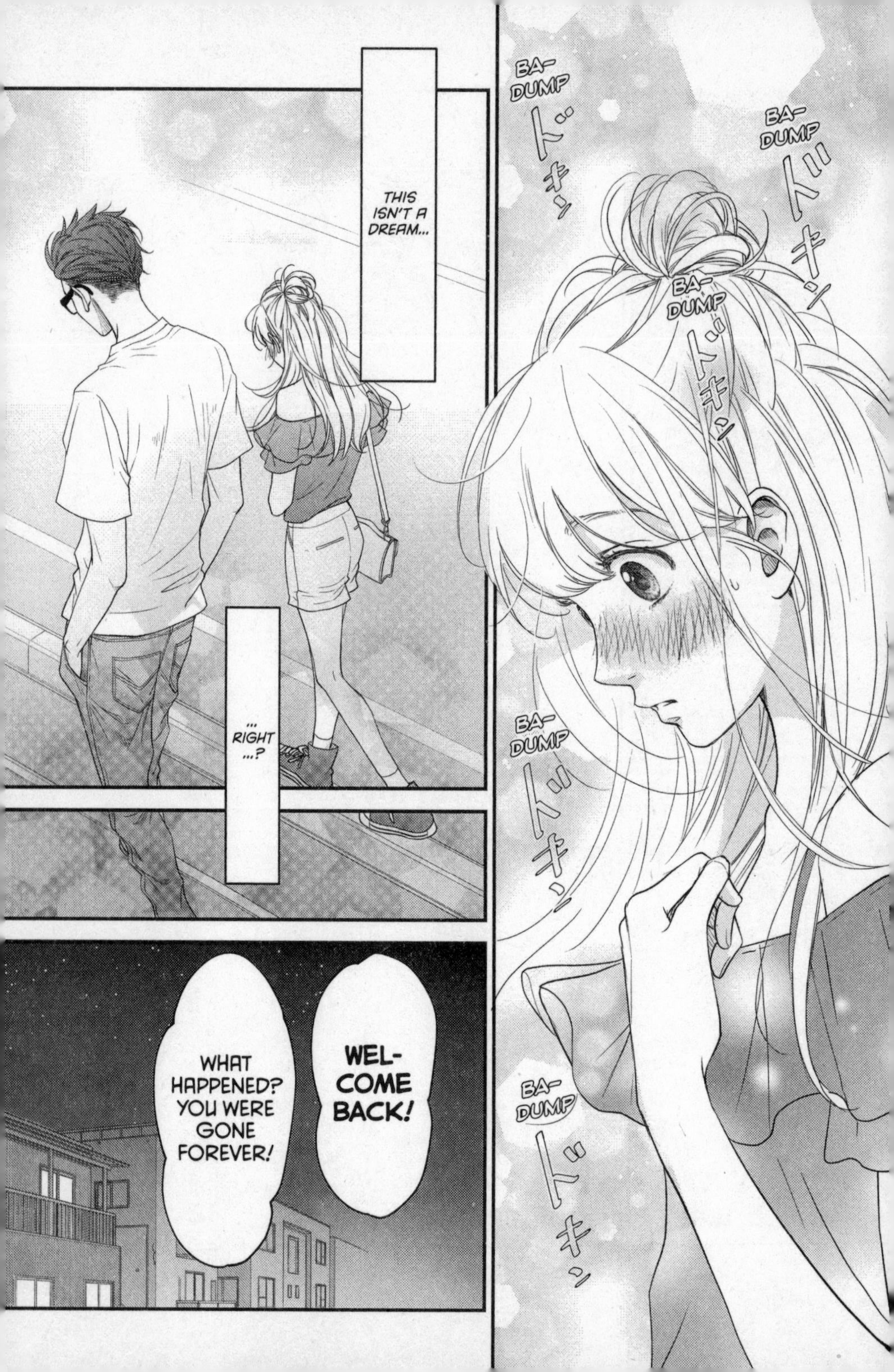
BA-DUMP
BA-DUMP
BA-DUMP
BA-DUMP
BA-DUMP
THIS ISN'T A DREAM...
...RIGHT...?
WEL-COME BACK!
WHAT HAPPENED? YOU WERE GONE FOREVER!

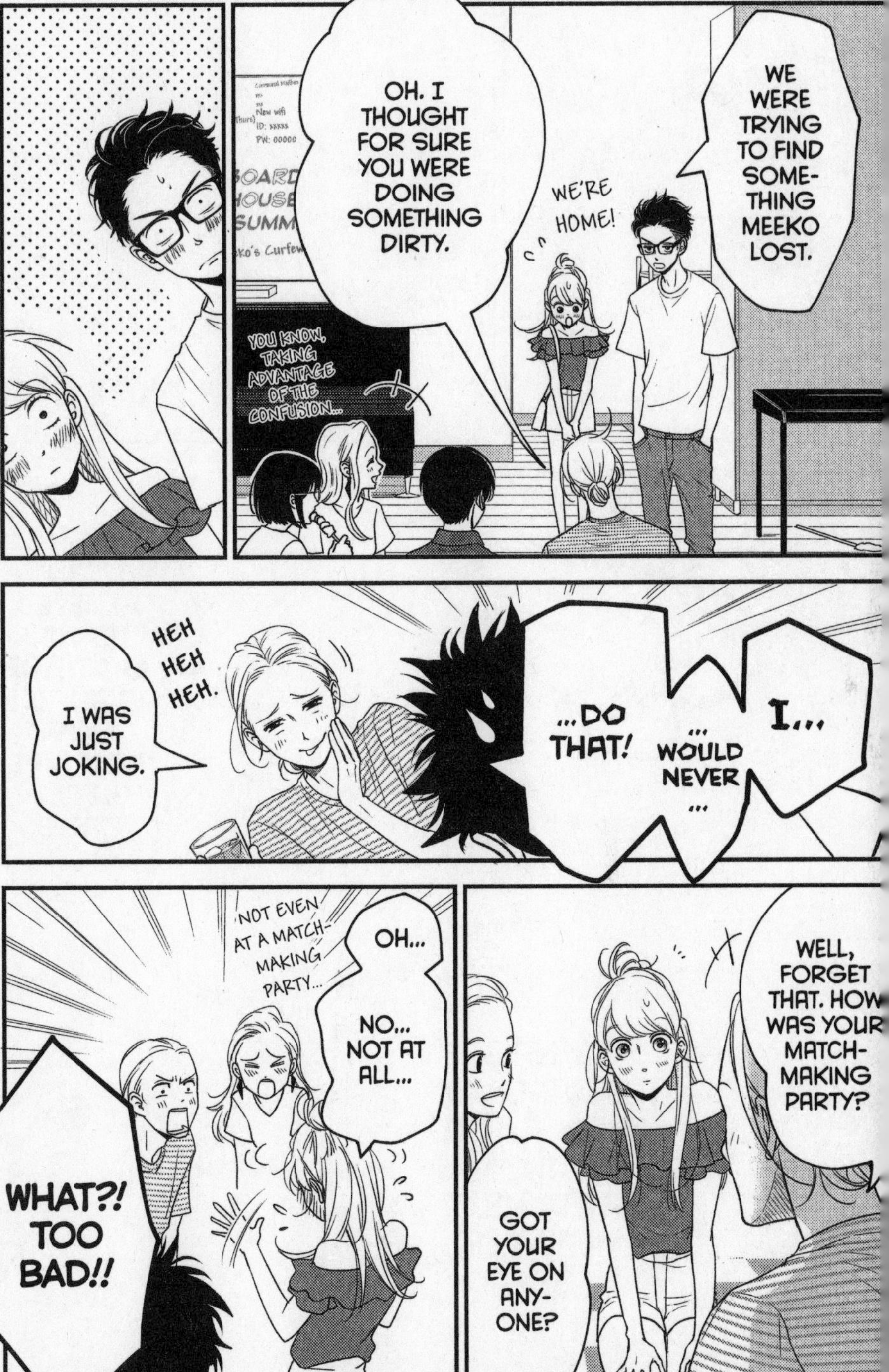
WE WERE TRYING TO FIND SOME-THING MEEKO LOST.
WE'RE HOME!
OH. I THOUGHT FOR SURE YOU WERE DOING SOMETHING DIRTY.
YOU KNOW, TAKING ADVANTAGE OF THE CONFUSION...
I...
...WOULD NEVER...
...DO THAT!
HEH HEH HEH.
I WAS JUST JOKING.
WELL, FORGET THAT. HOW WAS YOUR MATCH-MAKING PARTY?
GOT YOUR EYE ON ANY-ONE?
OH...
NO... NOT AT ALL...
NOT EVEN AT A MATCH-MAKING PARTY...
WHAT?! TOO BAD!!

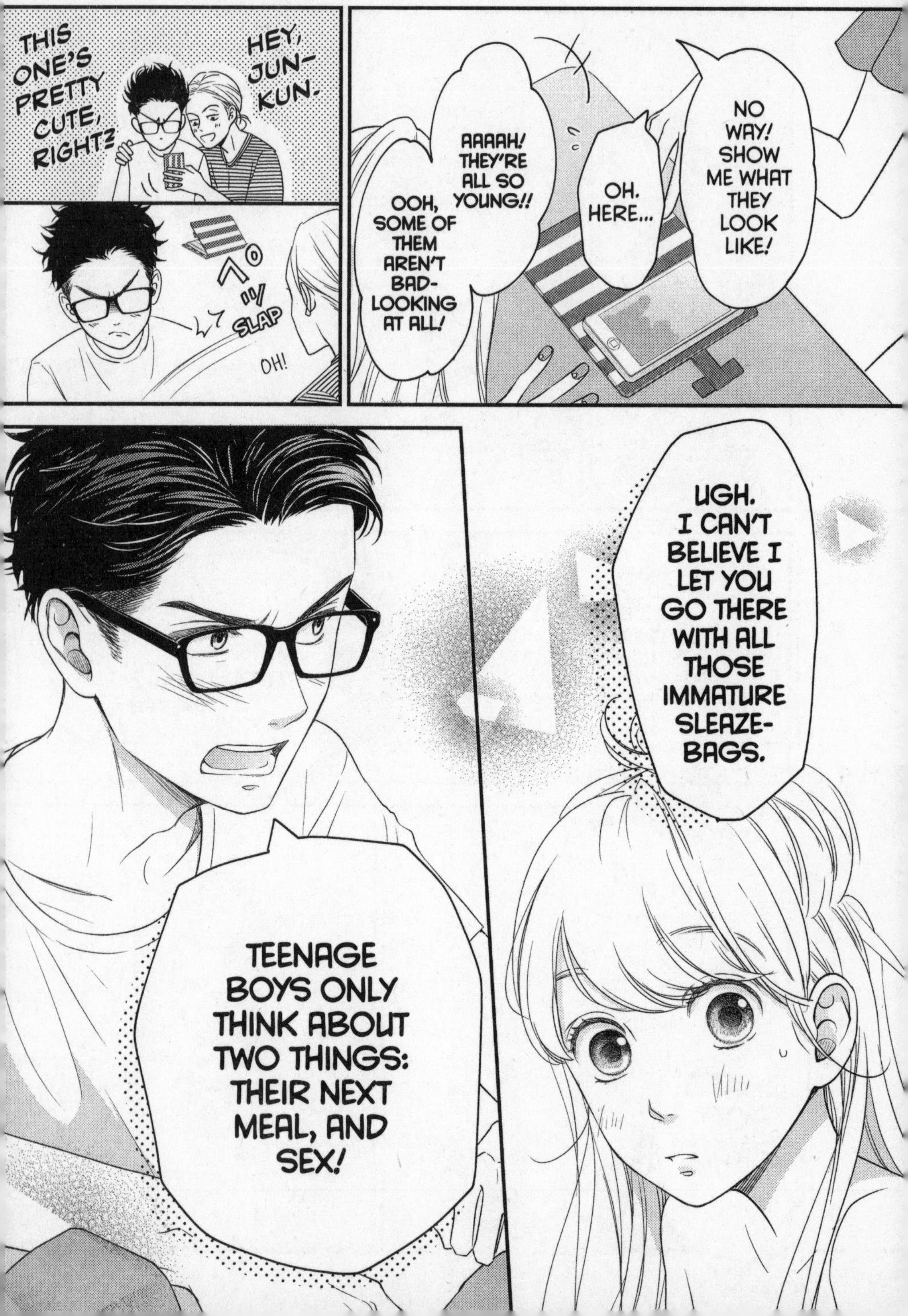
NO WAY! SHOW ME WHAT THEY LOOK LIKE!
OH. HERE...
AAAAH! THEY'RE ALL SO YOUNG!!
OOH, SOME OF THEM AREN'T BAD-LOOKING AT ALL!
HEY, JUN-KUN.
THIS ONE'S PRETTY CUTE, RIGHT?
SLAP
OH!
UGH. I CAN'T BELIEVE I LET YOU GO THERE WITH ALL THOSE IMMATURE SLEAZE-BAGS.
TEENAGE BOYS ONLY THINK ABOUT TWO THINGS: THEIR NEXT MEAL, AND SEX!

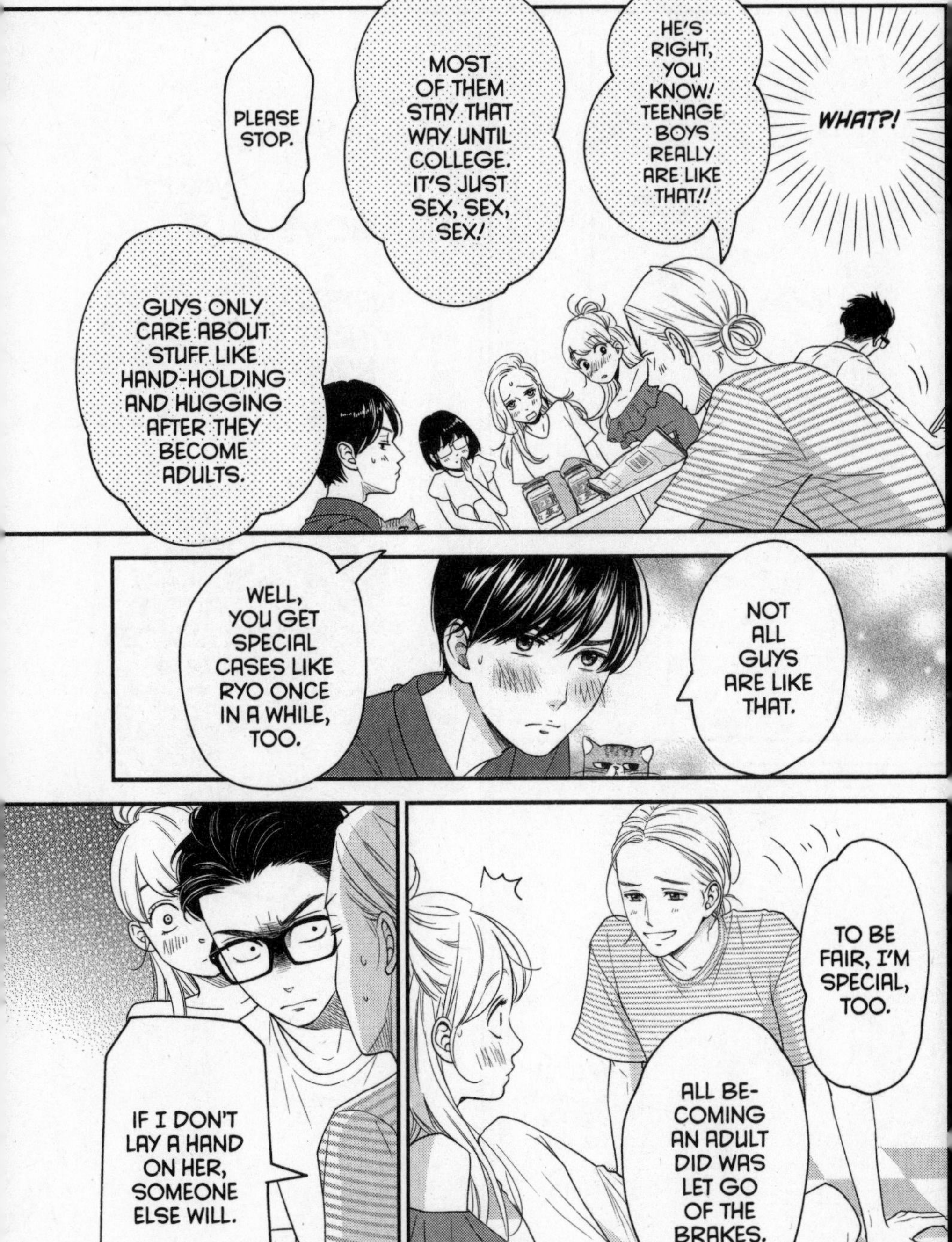
WHAT?!
HE'S RIGHT, YOU KNOW! TEENAGE BOYS REALLY ARE LIKE THAT!!
MOST OF THEM STAY THAT WAY UNTIL COLLEGE. IT'S JUST SEX, SEX, SEX!
PLEASE STOP.
GUYS ONLY CARE ABOUT STUFF LIKE HAND-HOLDING AND HUGGING AFTER THEY BECOME ADULTS.
NOT ALL GUYS ARE LIKE THAT.
WELL, YOU GET SPECIAL CASES LIKE RYO ONCE IN A WHILE, TOO.
TO BE FAIR, I'M SPECIAL, TOO.
ALL BE-COMING AN ADULT DID WAS LET GO OF THE BRAKES.
IF I DON'T LAY A HAND ON HER, SOMEONE ELSE WILL.

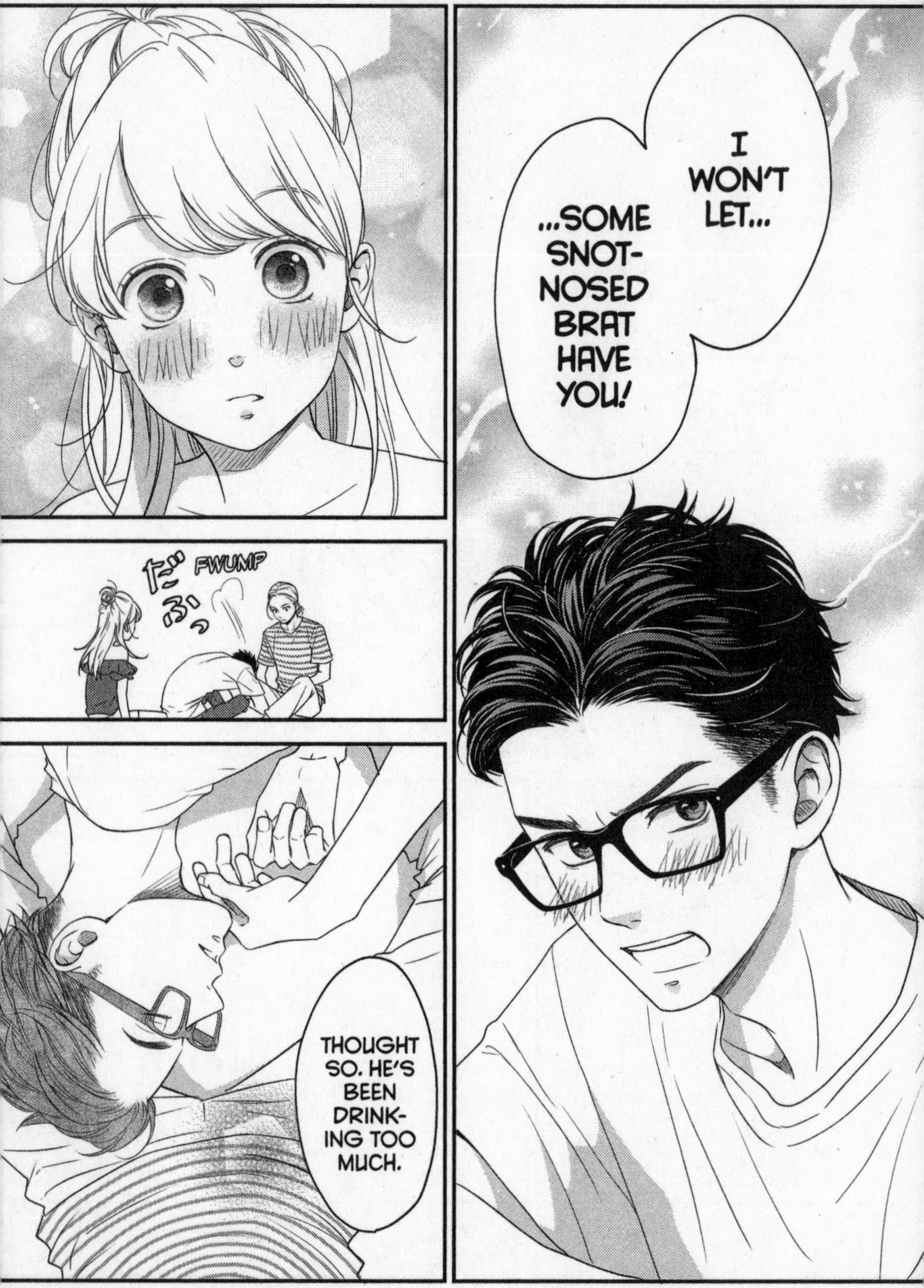
I WON'T LET...
...SOME SNOT-NOSED BRAT HAVE YOU!
だふっ
FWUMP
THOUGHT SO. HE'S BEEN DRINKING TOO MUCH.

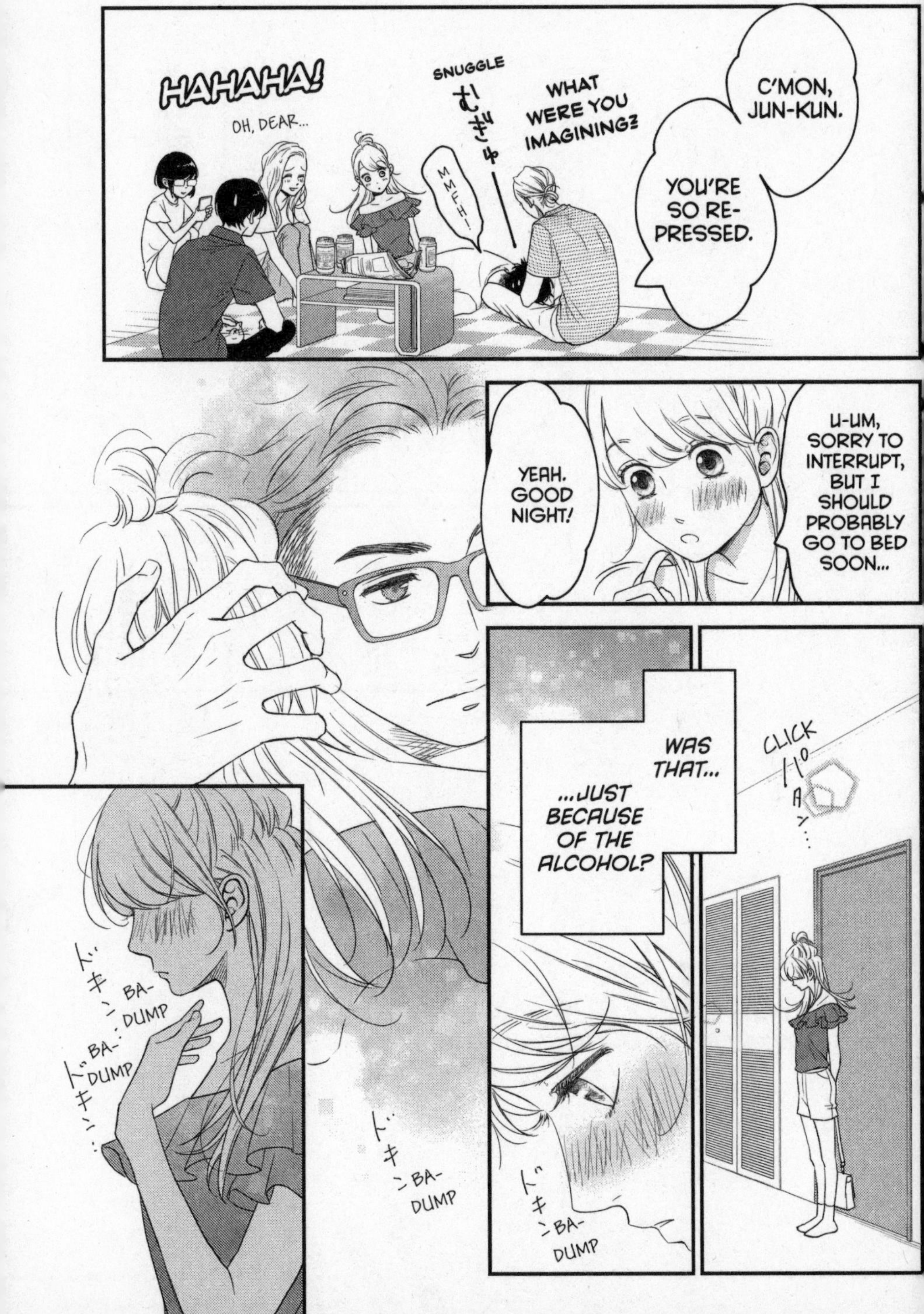
C'MON, JUN-KUN.
YOU'RE SO RE-PRESSED.
WHAT WERE YOU IMAGINING?
SNUGGLE
MMFH!
OH, DEAR...
HAHAHA!
U-UM, SORRY TO INTERRUPT, BUT I SHOULD PROBABLY GO TO BED SOON...
YEAH. GOOD NIGHT!
CLICK
WAS THAT...
...JUST BECAUSE OF THE ALCOHOL?
BA-DUMP
BA-DUMP
BA-DUMP
BA-DUMP

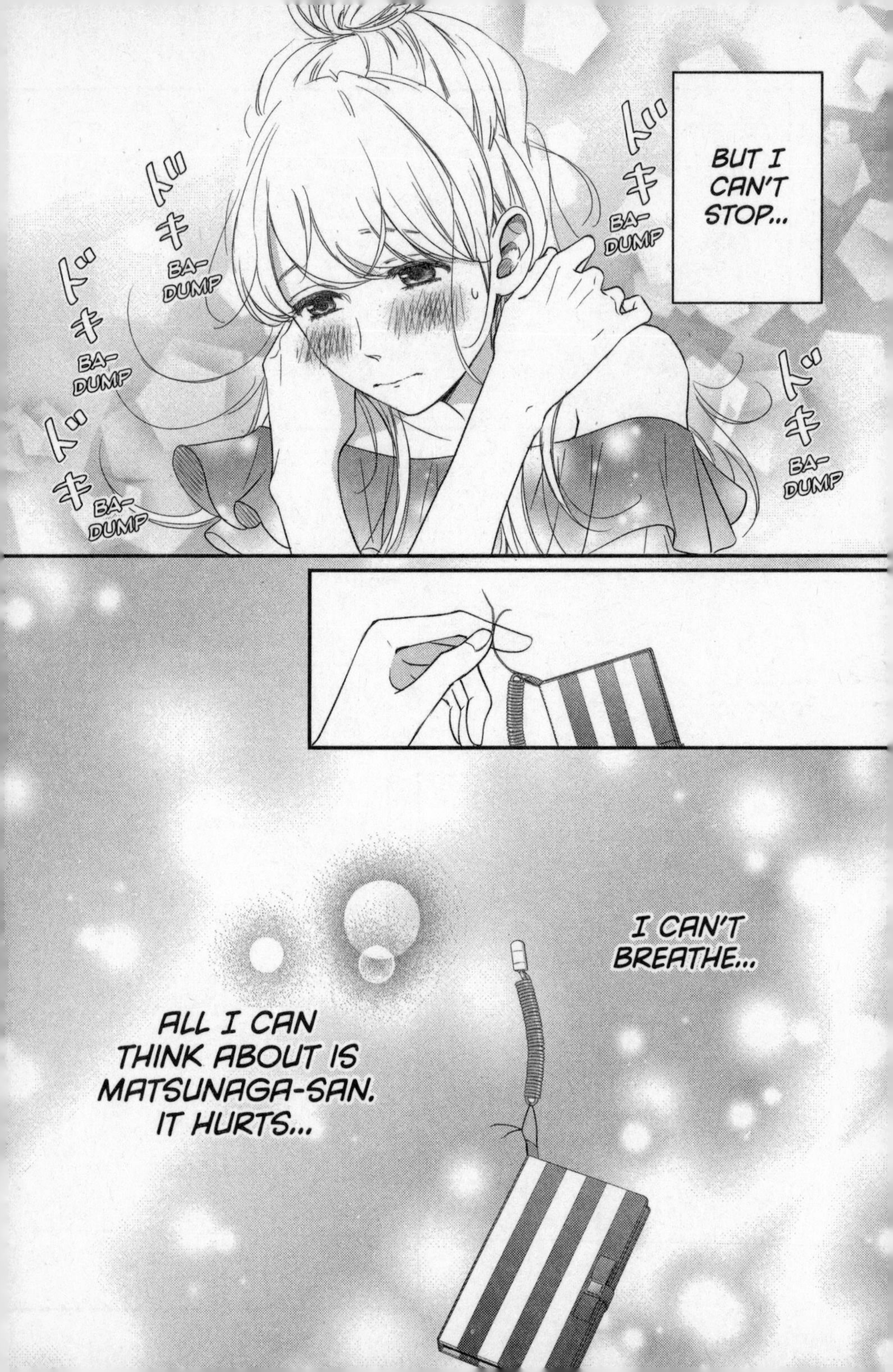
BUT I CAN'T STOP...
ドキ BA-DUMP
ドキ BA-DUMP
ドキ BA-DUMP
ドキ BA-DUMP
ドキ BA-DUMP
I CAN'T BREATHE...
ALL I CAN THINK ABOUT IS MATSUNAGA-SAN. IT HURTS...

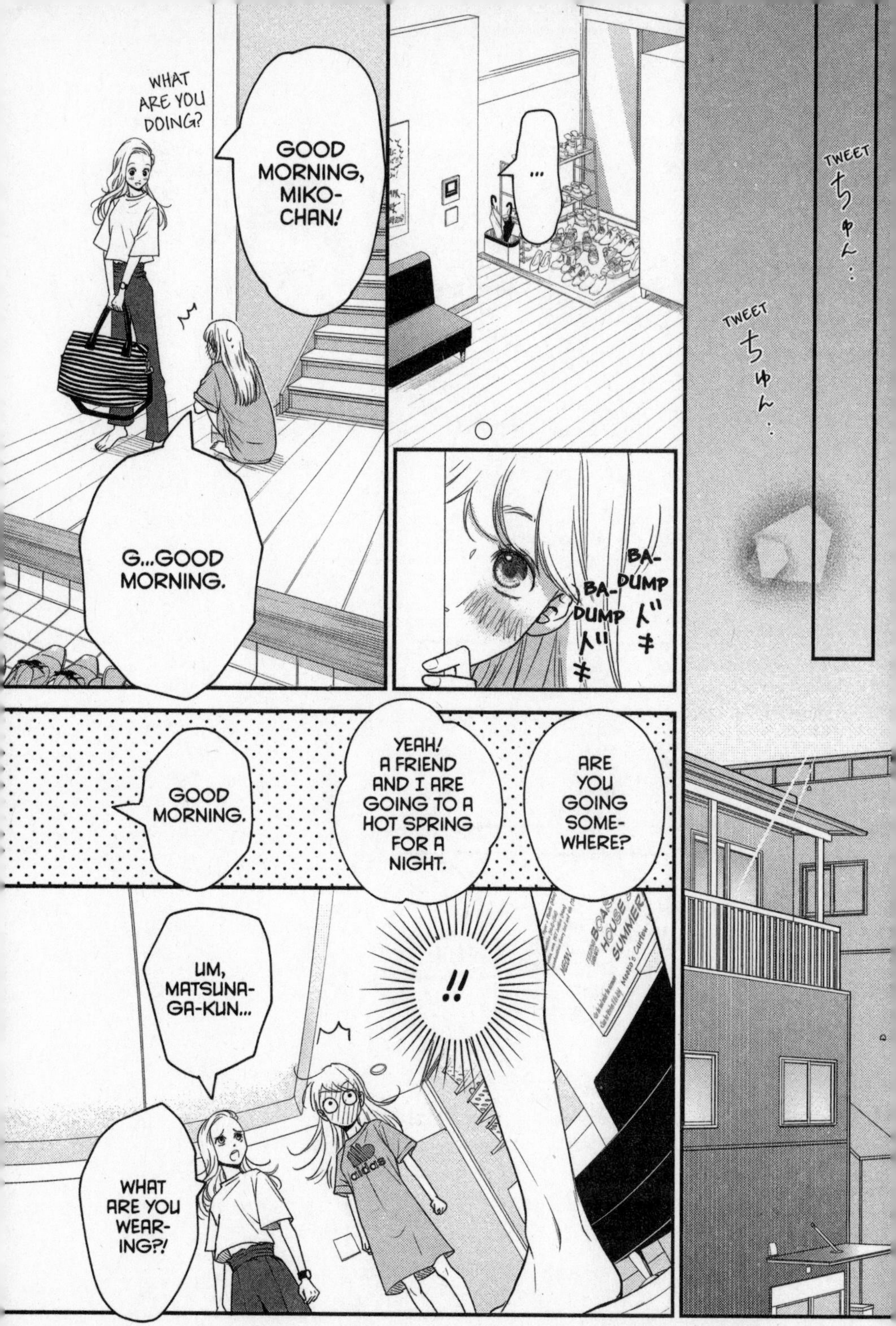
TWEET
ちゅん‥
TWEET
ちゅん‥
…
BA-DUMP ドキ
BA-DUMP ドキ
WHAT ARE YOU DOING?
GOOD MORNING, MIKO-CHAN!
G...GOOD MORNING.
ARE YOU GOING SOMEWHERE?
YEAH! A FRIEND AND I ARE GOING TO A HOT SPRING FOR A NIGHT.
GOOD MORNING.
!!
UM, MATSUNAGA-KUN...
WHAT ARE YOU WEARING?!

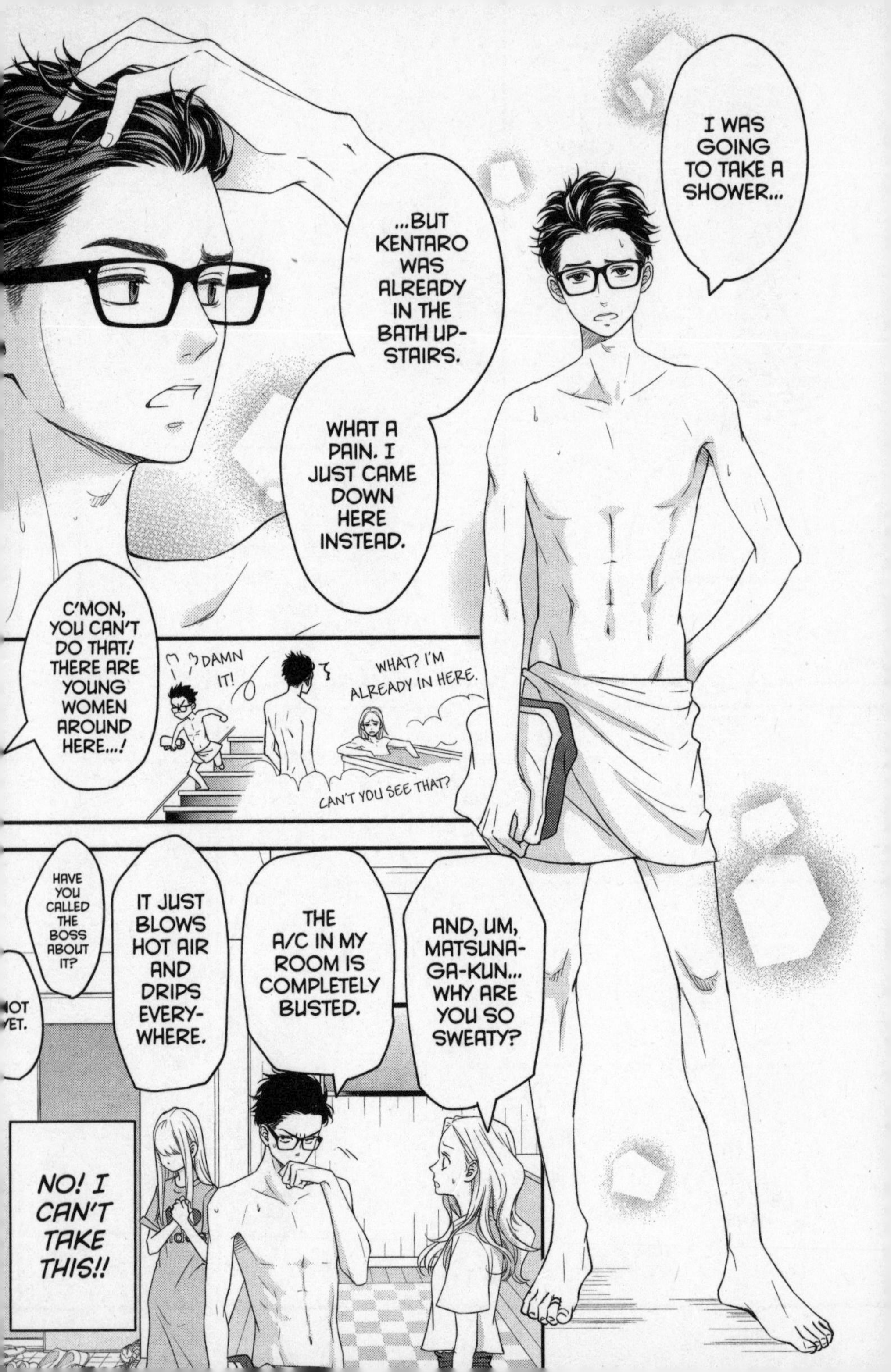
I WAS GOING TO TAKE A SHOWER...
...BUT KENTARO WAS ALREADY IN THE BATH UP-STAIRS.
WHAT A PAIN. I JUST CAME DOWN HERE INSTEAD.
C'MON, YOU CAN'T DO THAT! THERE ARE YOUNG WOMEN AROUND HERE...!
WHAT? I'M ALREADY IN HERE.
CAN'T YOU SEE THAT?
DAMN IT!
AND, UM, MATSUNAGA-KUN... WHY ARE YOU SO SWEATY?
THE A/C IN MY ROOM IS COMPLETELY BUSTED.
IT JUST BLOWS HOT AIR AND DRIPS EVERY-WHERE.
HAVE YOU CALLED THE BOSS ABOUT IT?
NO! I CAN'T TAKE THIS!!

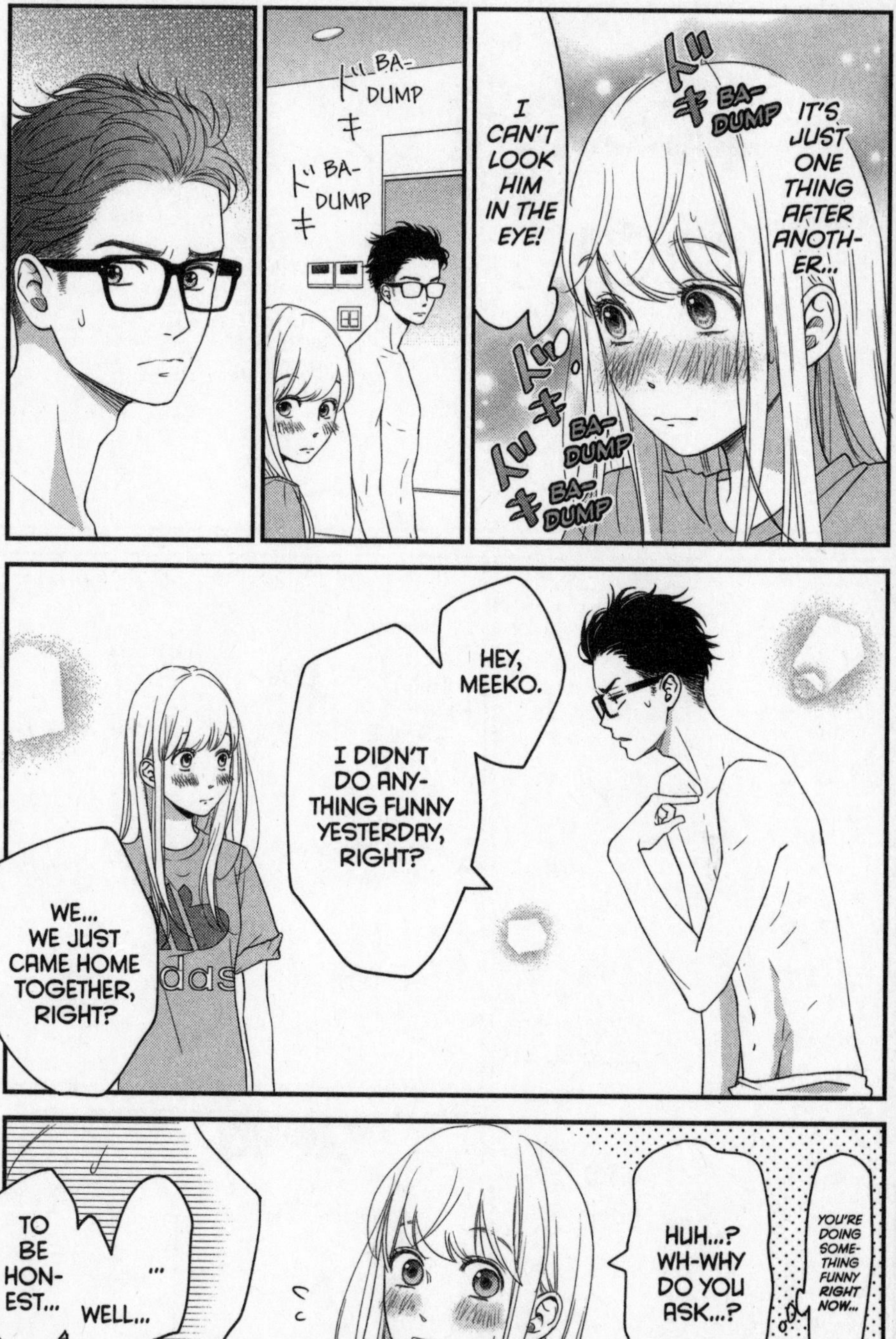
ドキ BA-DUMP
IT'S JUST ONE THING AFTER ANOTHER...
I CAN'T LOOK HIM IN THE EYE!
ドキ BA-DUMP
ドキ BA-DUMP
ドキ BA-DUMP
ドキ BA-DUMP
HEY, MEEKO.
I DIDN'T DO ANYTHING FUNNY YESTERDAY, RIGHT?
WE... WE JUST CAME HOME TOGETHER, RIGHT?
YOU'RE DOING SOMETHING FUNNY RIGHT NOW...
HUH...? WH-WHY DO YOU ASK...?
...
WELL...
TO BE HONEST...

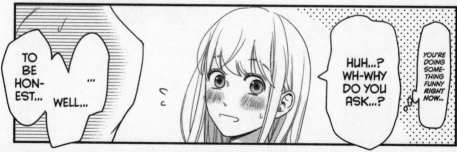

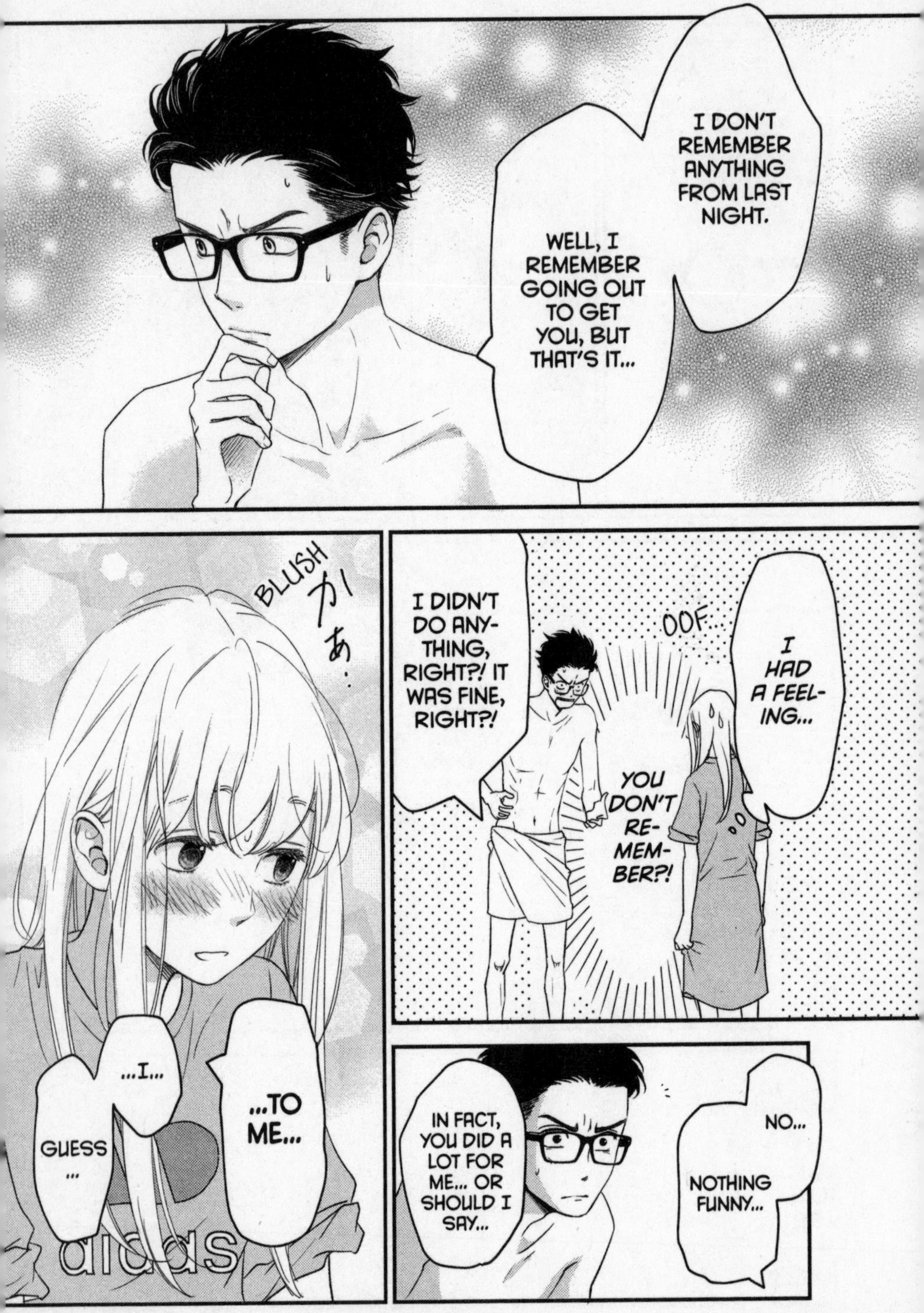

I DON'T REMEMBER ANYTHING FROM LAST NIGHT.
WELL, I REMEMBER GOING OUT TO GET YOU, BUT THAT'S IT...
I HAD A FEEL-ING...
OOF
YOU DON'T RE-MEM-BER?!
I DIDN'T DO ANY-THING, RIGHT?! IT WAS FINE, RIGHT?!
NO...
NOTHING FUNNY...
IN FACT, YOU DID A LOT FOR ME... OR SHOULD I SAY...
BLUSH
かあ…
...TO ME...
...I...
GUESS ...

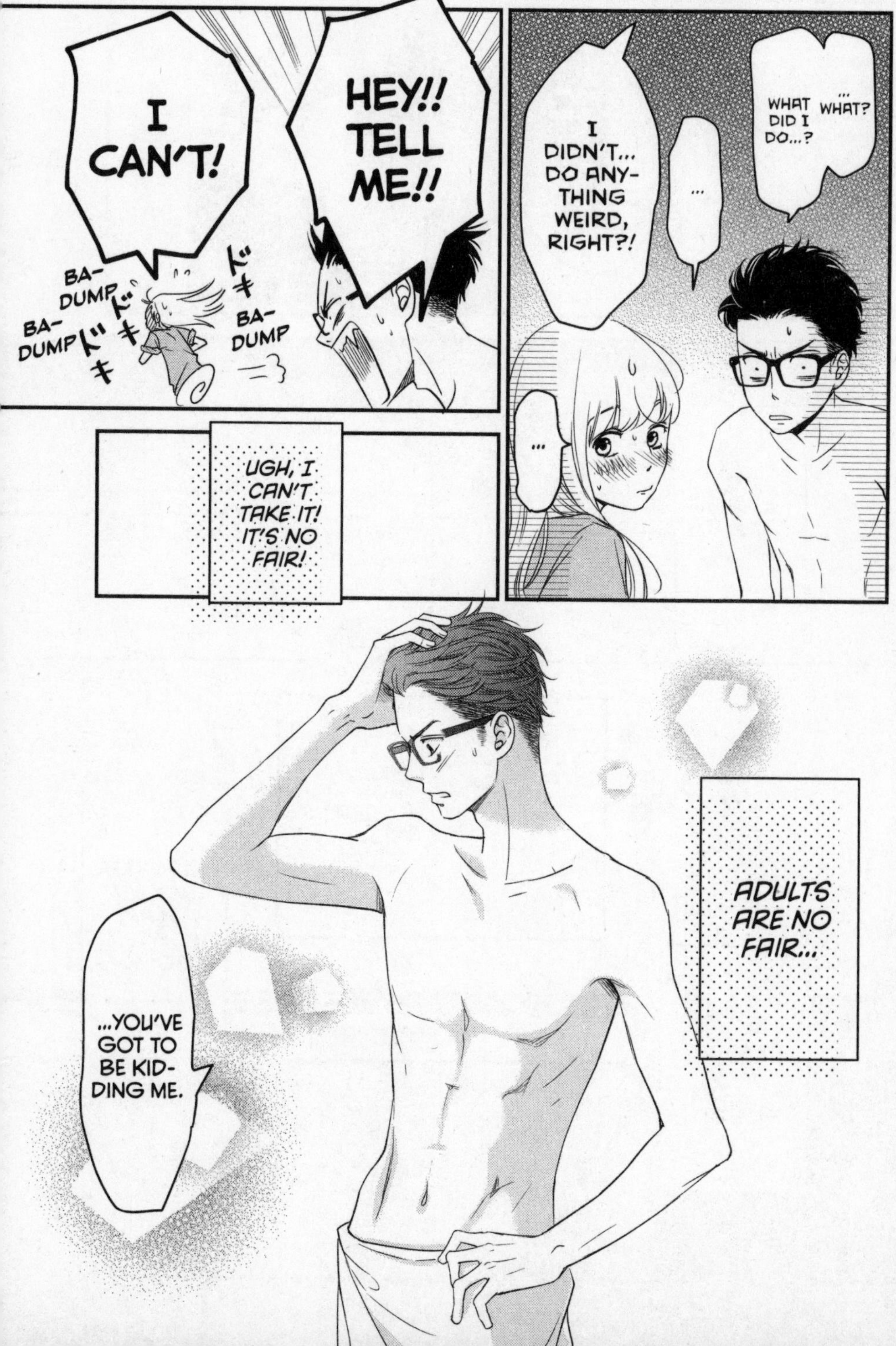

... WHAT?
WHAT DID I DO...?
...
I DIDN'T... DO ANYTHING WEIRD, RIGHT?!
...
HEY!! TELL ME!!
I CAN'T!
BA-DUMP ドキ
BA-DUMP ドキ
BA-DUMP ドキ
UGH, I CAN'T TAKE IT! IT'S NO FAIR!
ADULTS ARE NO FAIR...
...YOU'VE GOT TO BE KIDDING ME.

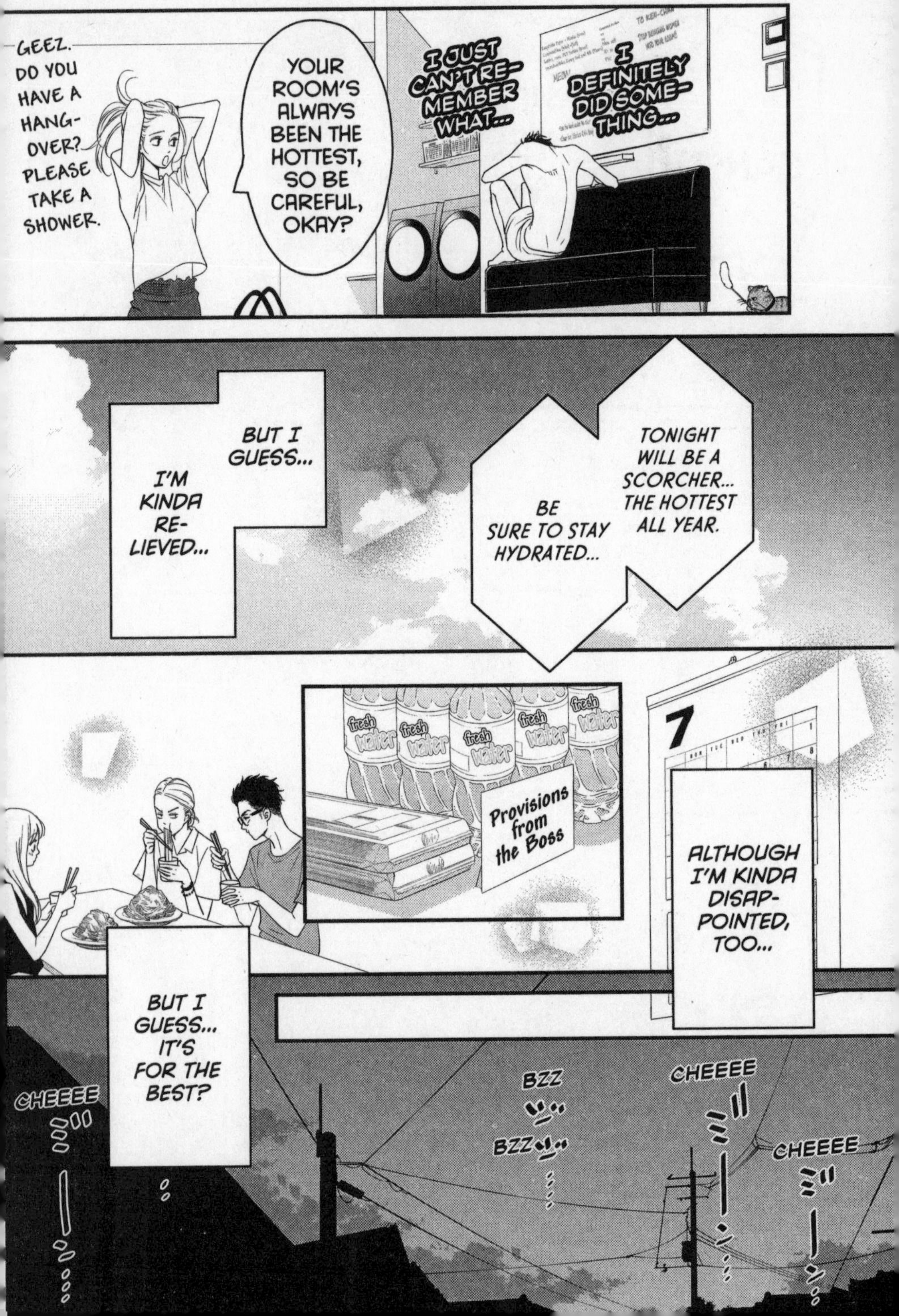
I DEFINITELY DID SOME-THING...
I JUST CAN'T RE-MEMBER WHAT...
YOUR ROOM'S ALWAYS BEEN THE HOTTEST, SO BE CAREFUL, OKAY?
GEEZ. DO YOU HAVE A HANG-OVER? PLEASE TAKE A SHOWER.
TONIGHT WILL BE A SCORCHER... THE HOTTEST ALL YEAR.
BE SURE TO STAY HYDRATED...
BUT I GUESS...
I'M KINDA RE-LIEVED...
7
ALTHOUGH I'M KINDA DISAP-POINTED, TOO...
fresh water
Provisions from the Boss
BUT I GUESS... IT'S FOR THE BEST?
CHEEEE
CHEEEE
BZZ
BZZ
CHEEEE

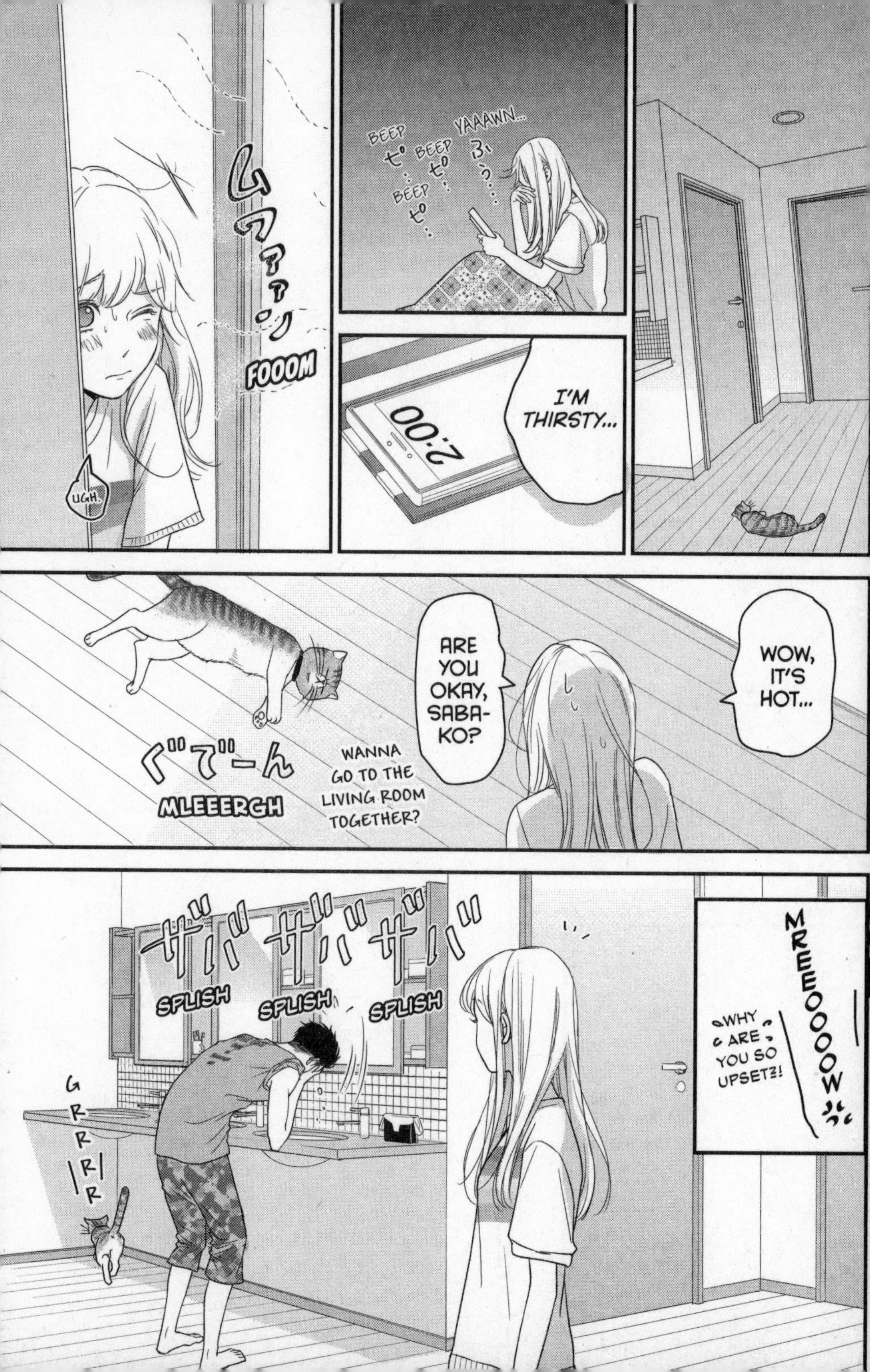
BEEP
ぴ
BEEP
ぴ
BEEP
ぴ
YAAAWN...
I'M THIRSTY...
ムワァァン
FOOOM
UGH.
WOW, IT'S HOT...
ARE YOU OKAY, SABAKO?
WANNA GO TO THE LIVING ROOM TOGETHER?
ぐでーん
MLEEERGH
MREEOOOOW
WHY ARE YOU SO UPSET?!
ザバザバザバ
SPLISH
SPLISH
SPLISH
GRRRRR

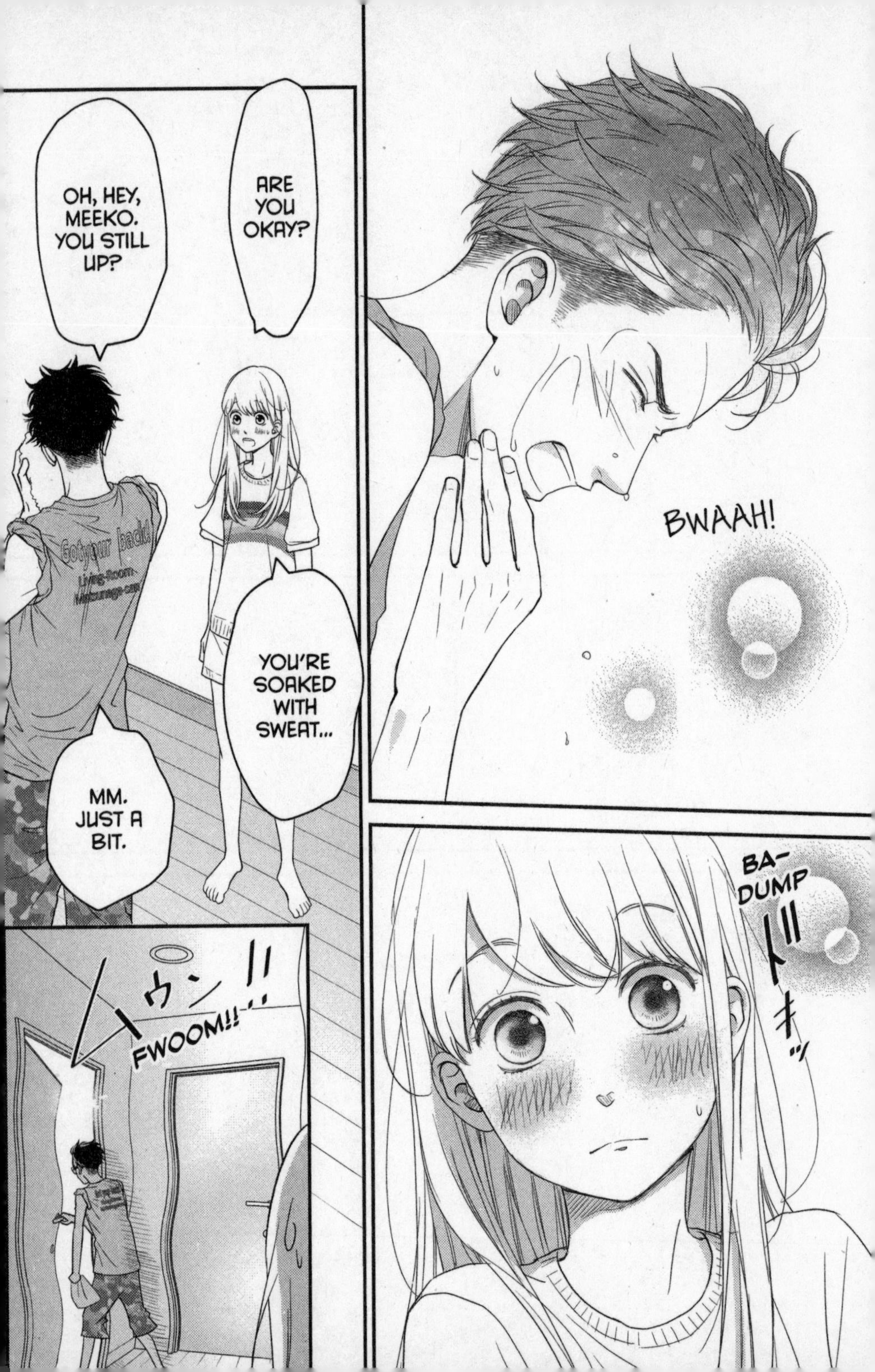
BWAAH!
BA-DUMP
ドキッ
ARE YOU OKAY?
OH, HEY, MEEKO. YOU STILL UP?
YOU'RE SOAKED WITH SWEAT...
MM. JUST A BIT.
Got your back!
Living-room Matsunaga-san
FWOOM!!

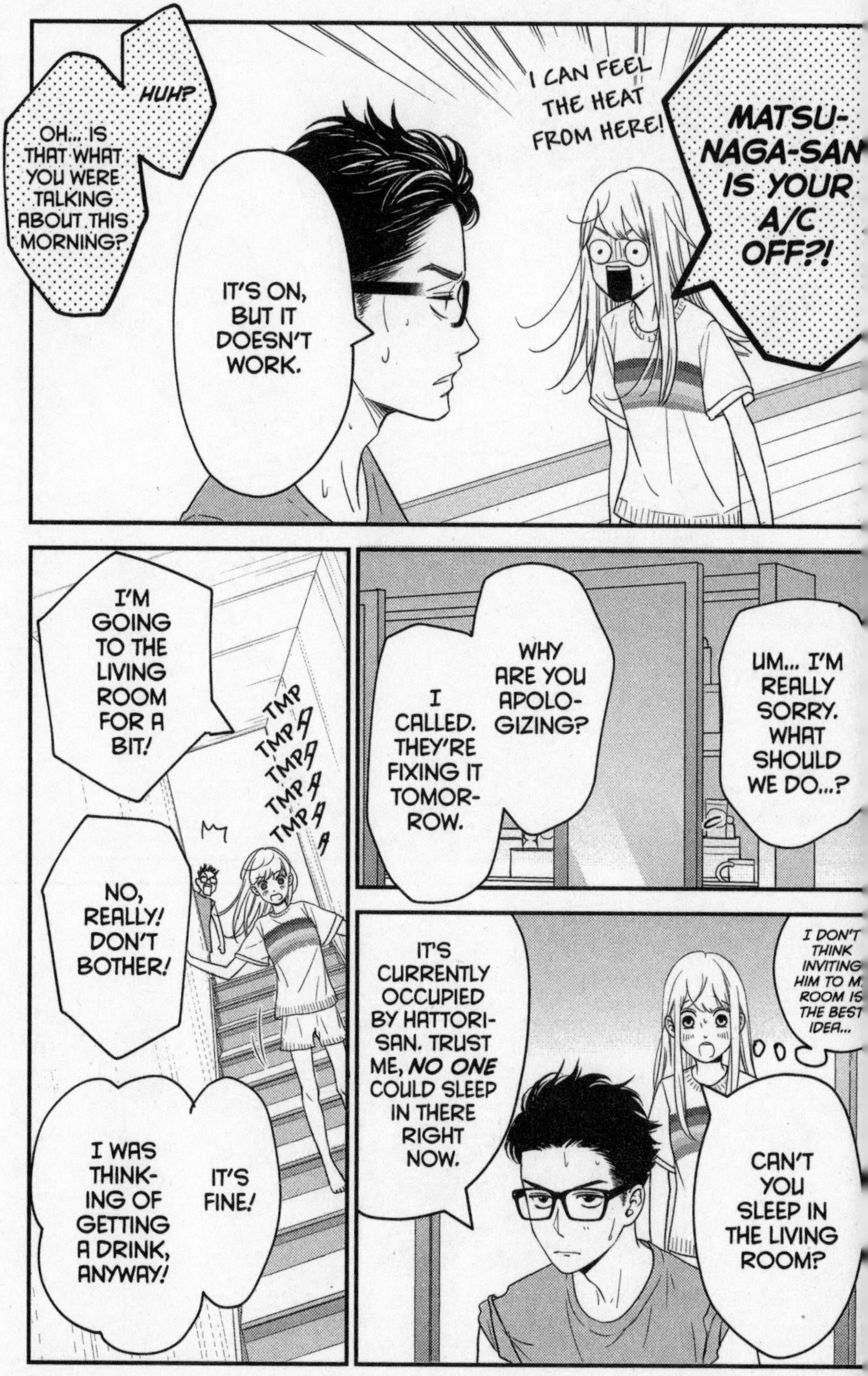
MATSUNAGA-SAN IS YOUR A/C OFF?!
I CAN FEEL THE HEAT FROM HERE!
IT'S ON, BUT IT DOESN'T WORK.
HUH?
OH... IS THAT WHAT YOU WERE TALKING ABOUT THIS MORNING?
UM... I'M REALLY SORRY. WHAT SHOULD WE DO...?
WHY ARE YOU APOLOGIZING?
I CALLED. THEY'RE FIXING IT TOMORROW.
I DON'T THINK INVITING HIM TO M ROOM IS THE BEST IDEA...
CAN'T YOU SLEEP IN THE LIVING ROOM?
IT'S CURRENTLY OCCUPIED BY HATTORI-SAN. TRUST ME, NO ONE COULD SLEEP IN THERE RIGHT NOW.
I'M GOING TO THE LIVING ROOM FOR A BIT!
TMP TMP TMP TMP TMP
NO, REALLY! DON'T BOTHER!
IT'S FINE!
I WAS THINKING OF GETTING A DRINK, ANYWAY!

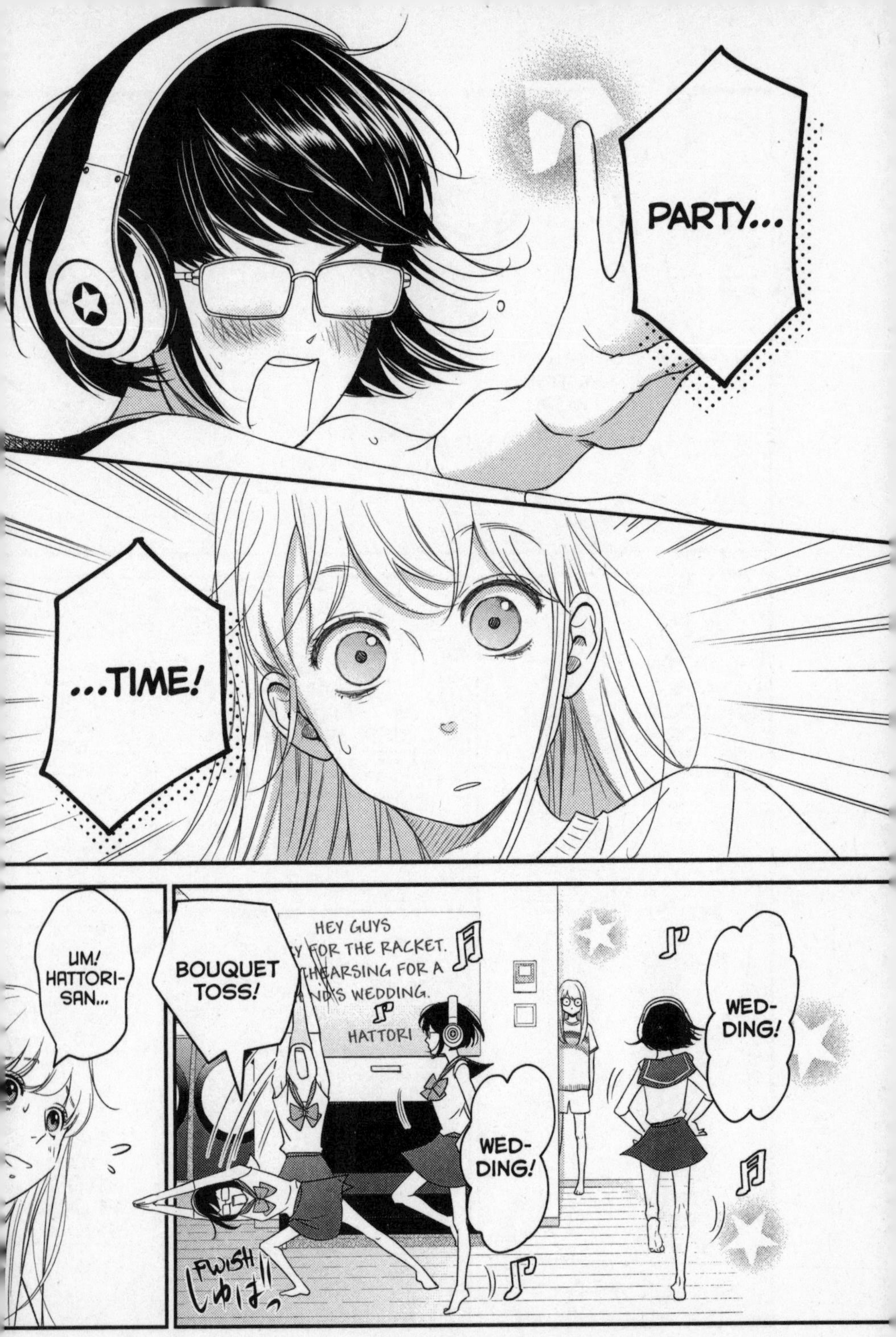
PARTY...
...TIME!
WED-DING!
HEY GUYS
FOR THE RACKET.
WEDDING.
HATTORI
WED-DING!
BOUQUET TOSS!
FWISH
UM! HATTORI-SAN...

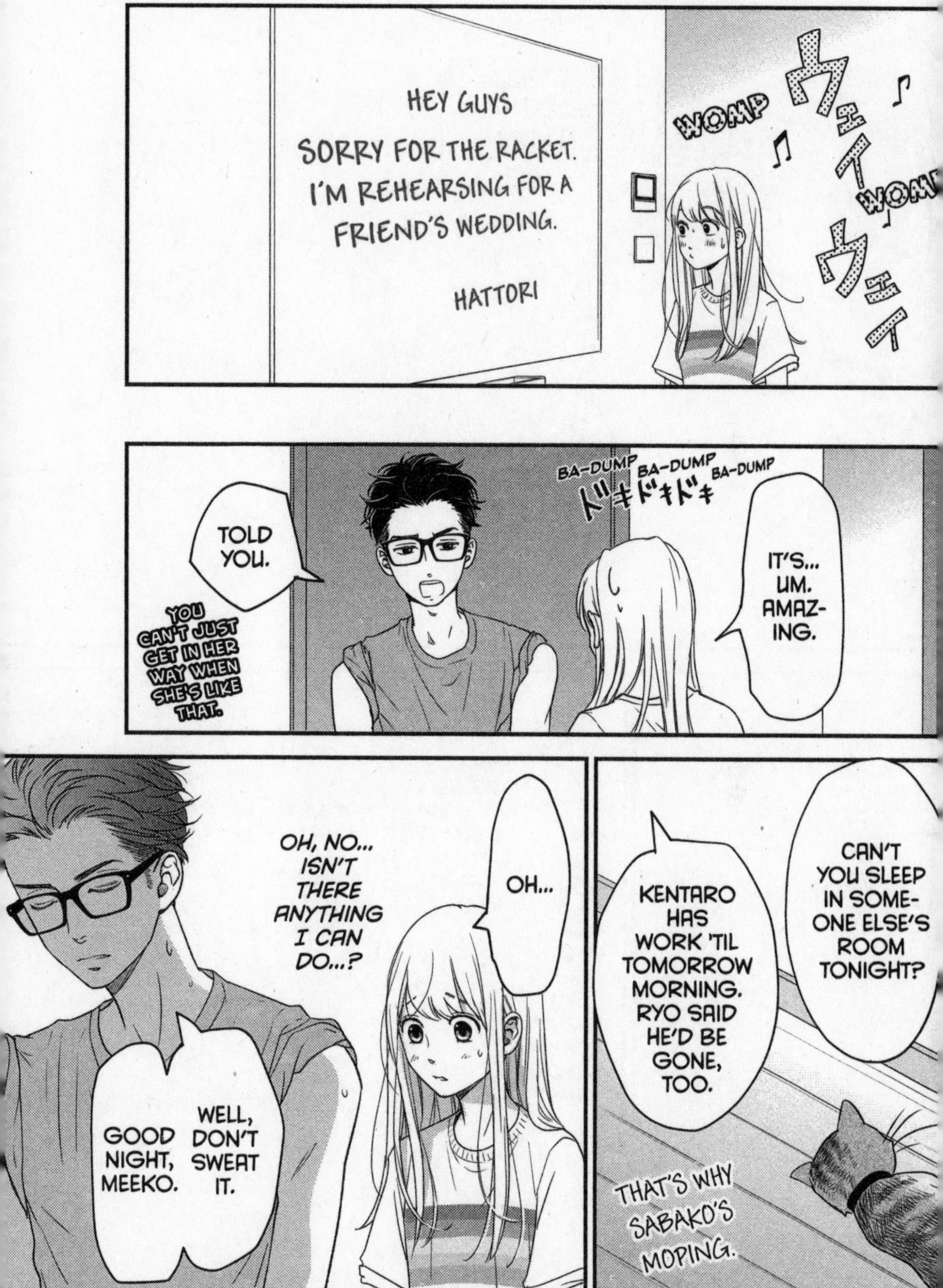

WOMP
WOMP
HEY GUYS
SORRY FOR THE RACKET.
I'M REHEARSING FOR A FRIEND'S WEDDING.
HATTORI
BA-DUMP BA-DUMP BA-DUMP
ドキドキドキ
IT'S... UM. AMAZ-ING.
TOLD YOU.
YOU CAN'T JUST GET IN HER WAY WHEN SHE'S LIKE THAT.
CAN'T YOU SLEEP IN SOME-ONE ELSE'S ROOM TONIGHT?
KENTARO HAS WORK 'TIL TOMORROW MORNING. RYO SAID HE'D BE GONE, TOO.
THAT'S WHY SABAKO'S MOPING.
OH...
OH, NO... ISN'T THERE ANYTHING I CAN DO...?
WELL, DON'T SWEAT IT.
GOOD NIGHT, MEEKO.

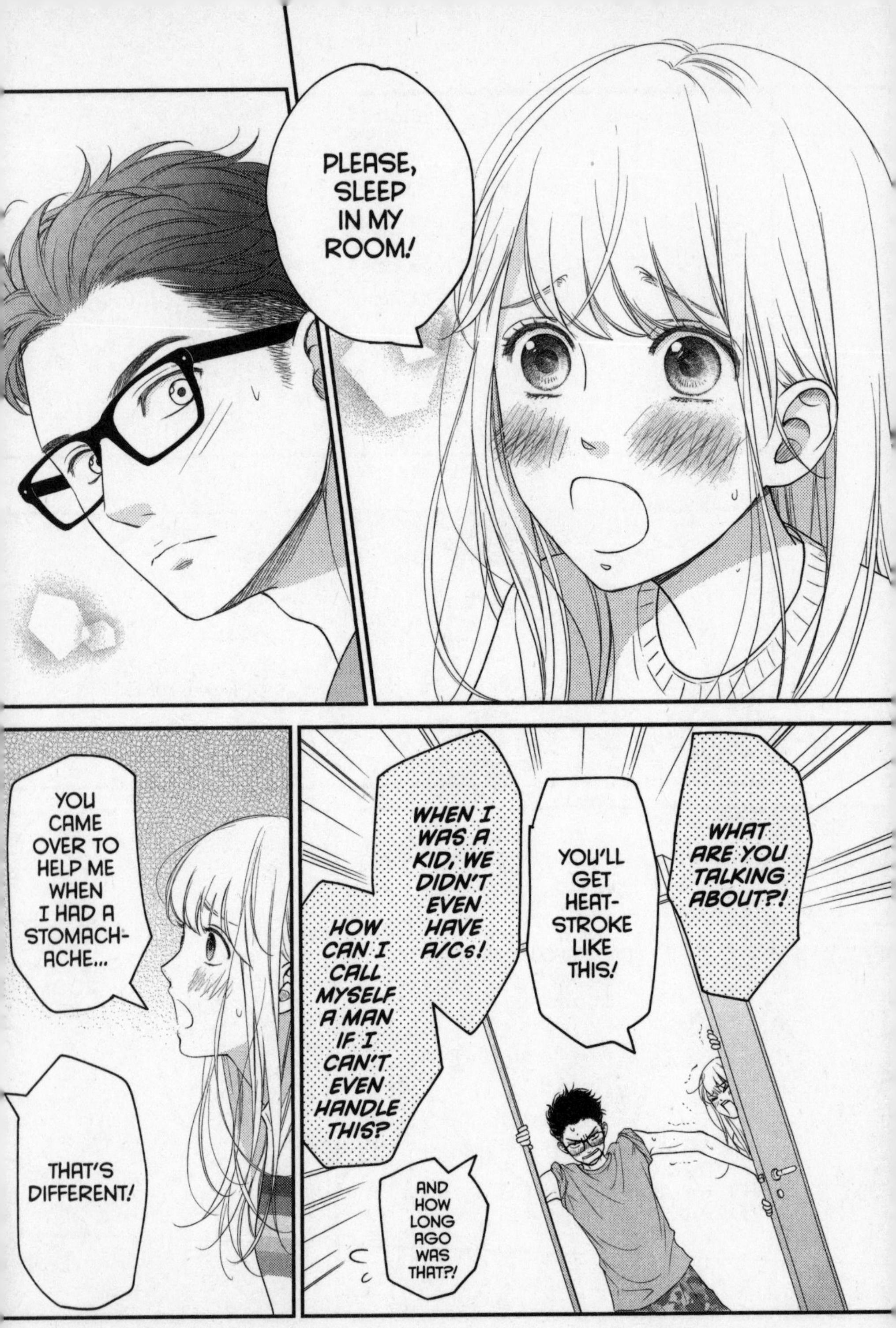
PLEASE, SLEEP IN MY ROOM!
WHAT ARE YOU TALKING ABOUT?!
YOU'LL GET HEAT-STROKE LIKE THIS!
WHEN I WAS A KID, WE DIDN'T EVEN HAVE A/Cs!
HOW CAN I CALL MYSELF A MAN IF I CAN'T EVEN HANDLE THIS?
AND HOW LONG AGO WAS THAT?!
YOU CAME OVER TO HELP ME WHEN I HAD A STOMACH-ACHE...
THAT'S DIFFERENT!

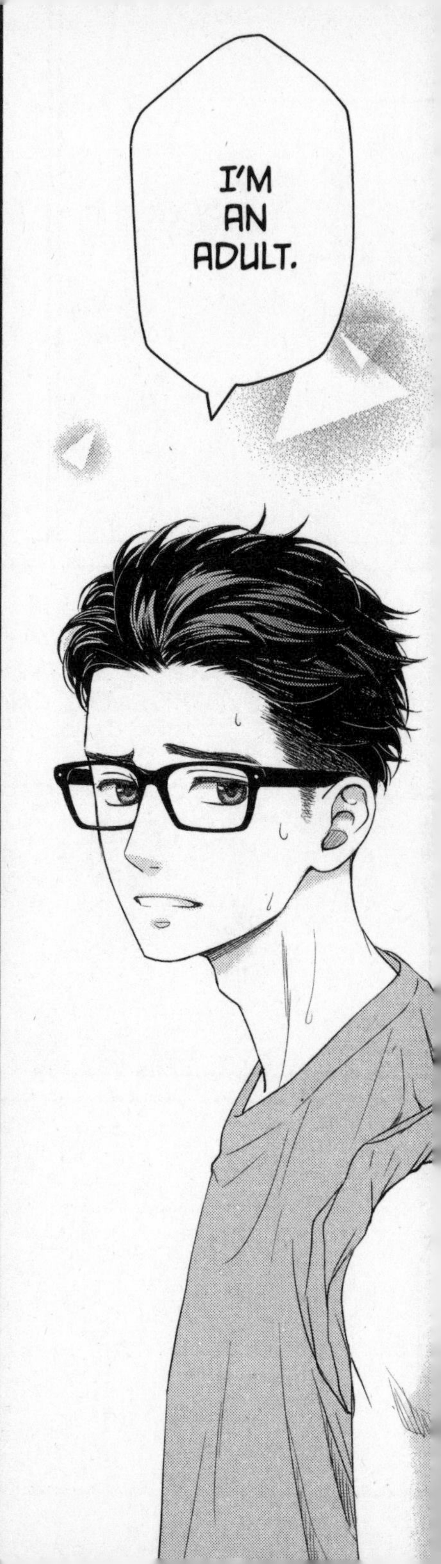
I'M AN ADULT.

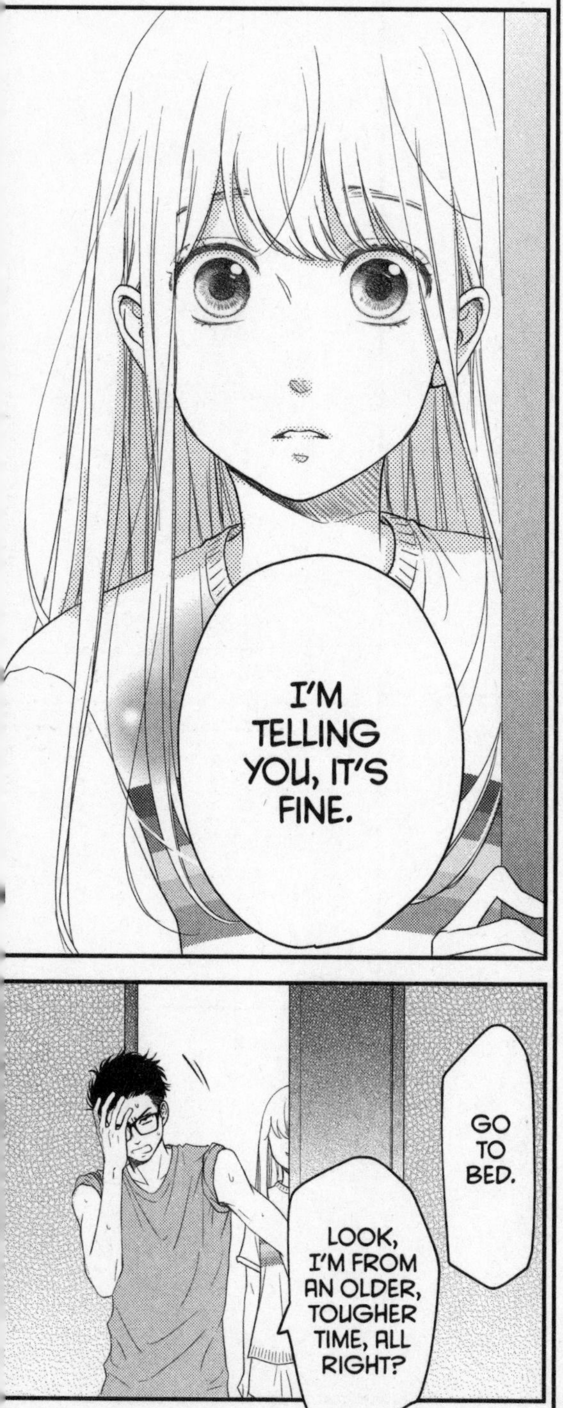
I'M TELLING YOU, IT'S FINE.
GO TO BED.
LOOK, I'M FROM AN OLDER, TOUGHER TIME, ALL RIGHT?

CLICK...

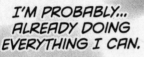

I'M PROBABLY...
ALREADY DOING
EVERYTHING I CAN.

"I WANT TO WORRY ABOUT YOU!"

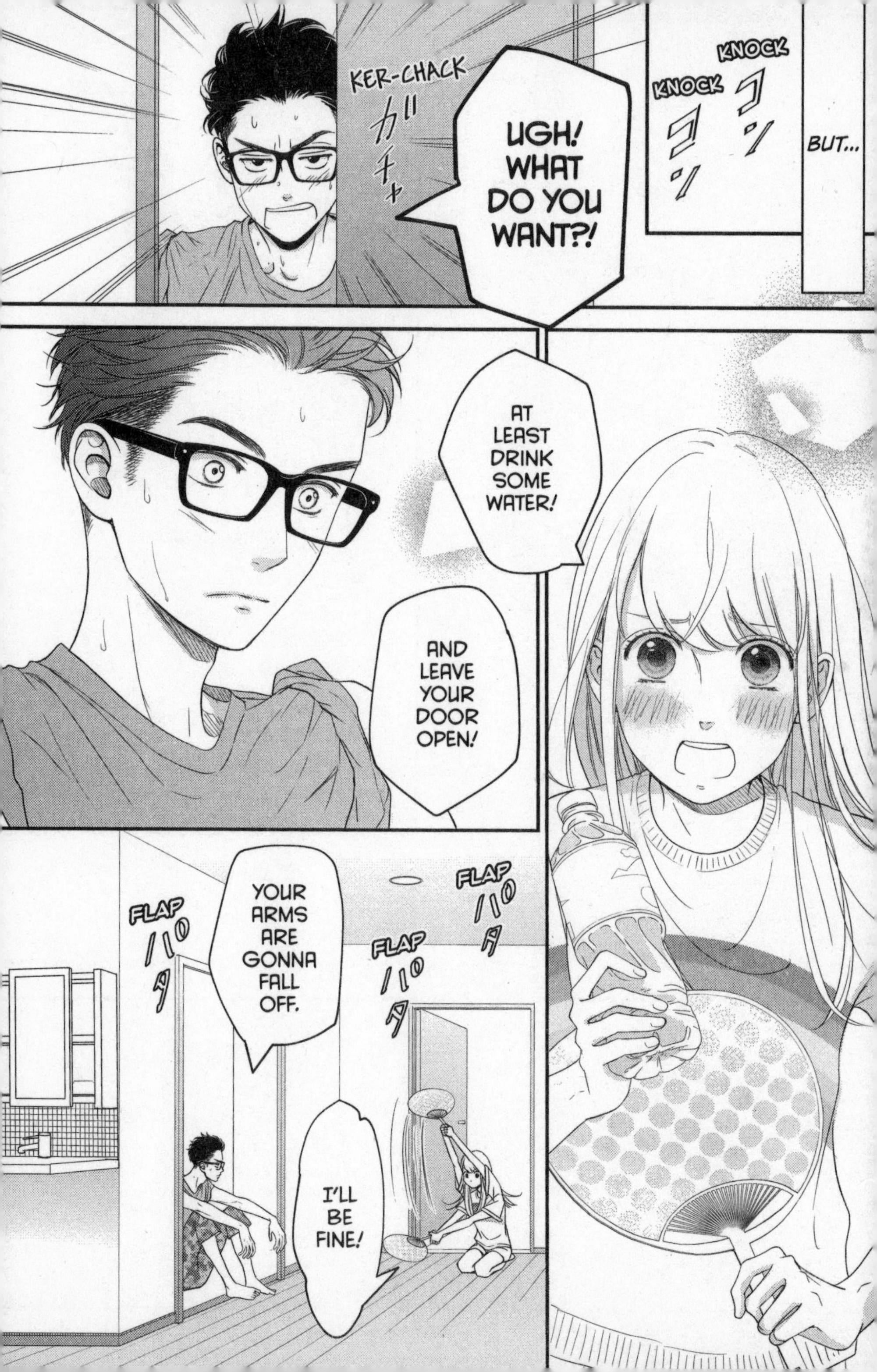
KNOCK
KNOCK
BUT...
KER-CHACK
UGH! WHAT DO YOU WANT?!
AT LEAST DRINK SOME WATER!
AND LEAVE YOUR DOOR OPEN!
FLAP
FLAP
YOUR ARMS ARE GONNA FALL OFF.
FLAP
I'LL BE FINE!

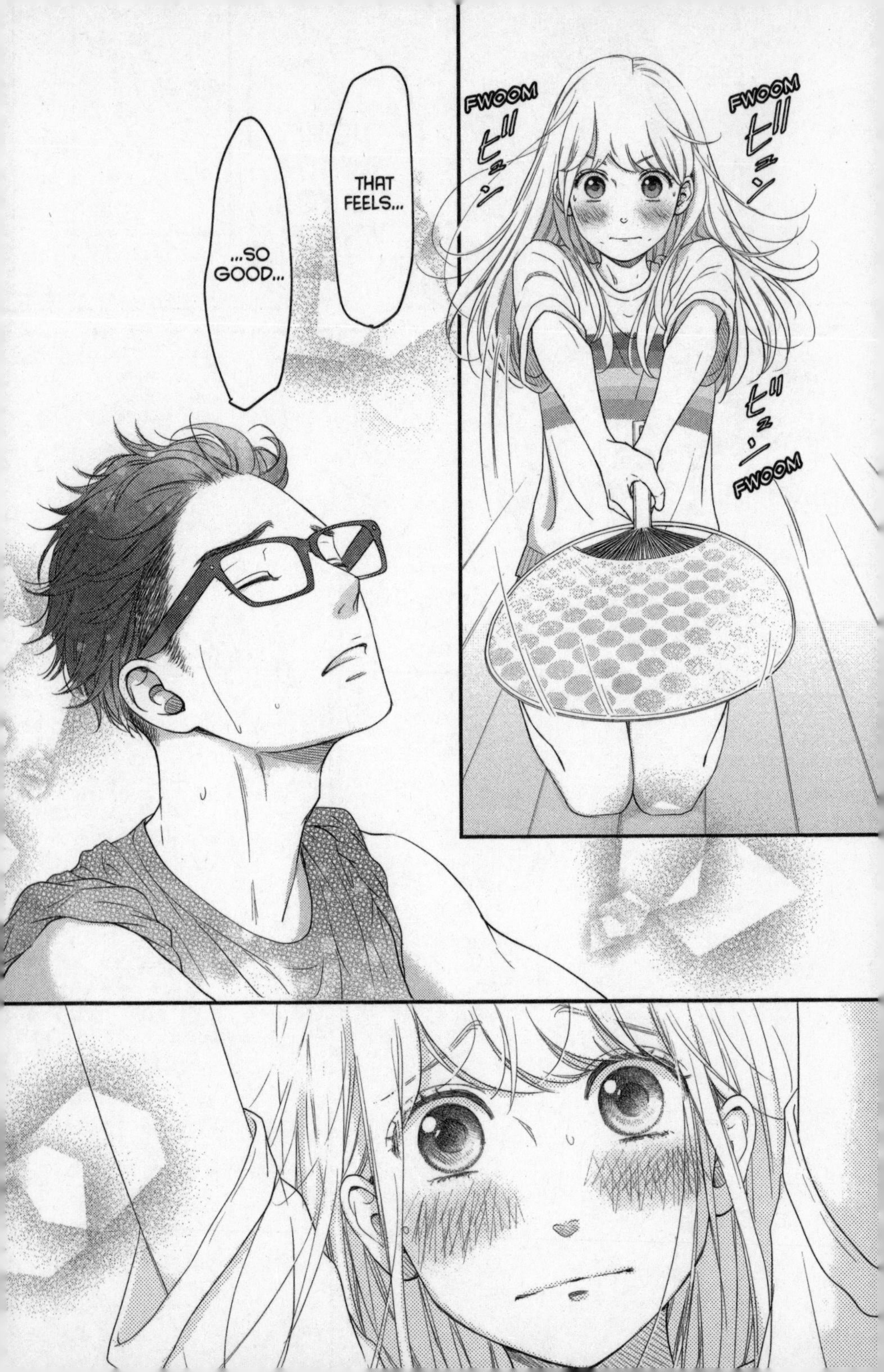
FWOOM
FWOOM
FWOOM
THAT FEELS...
...SO GOOD...

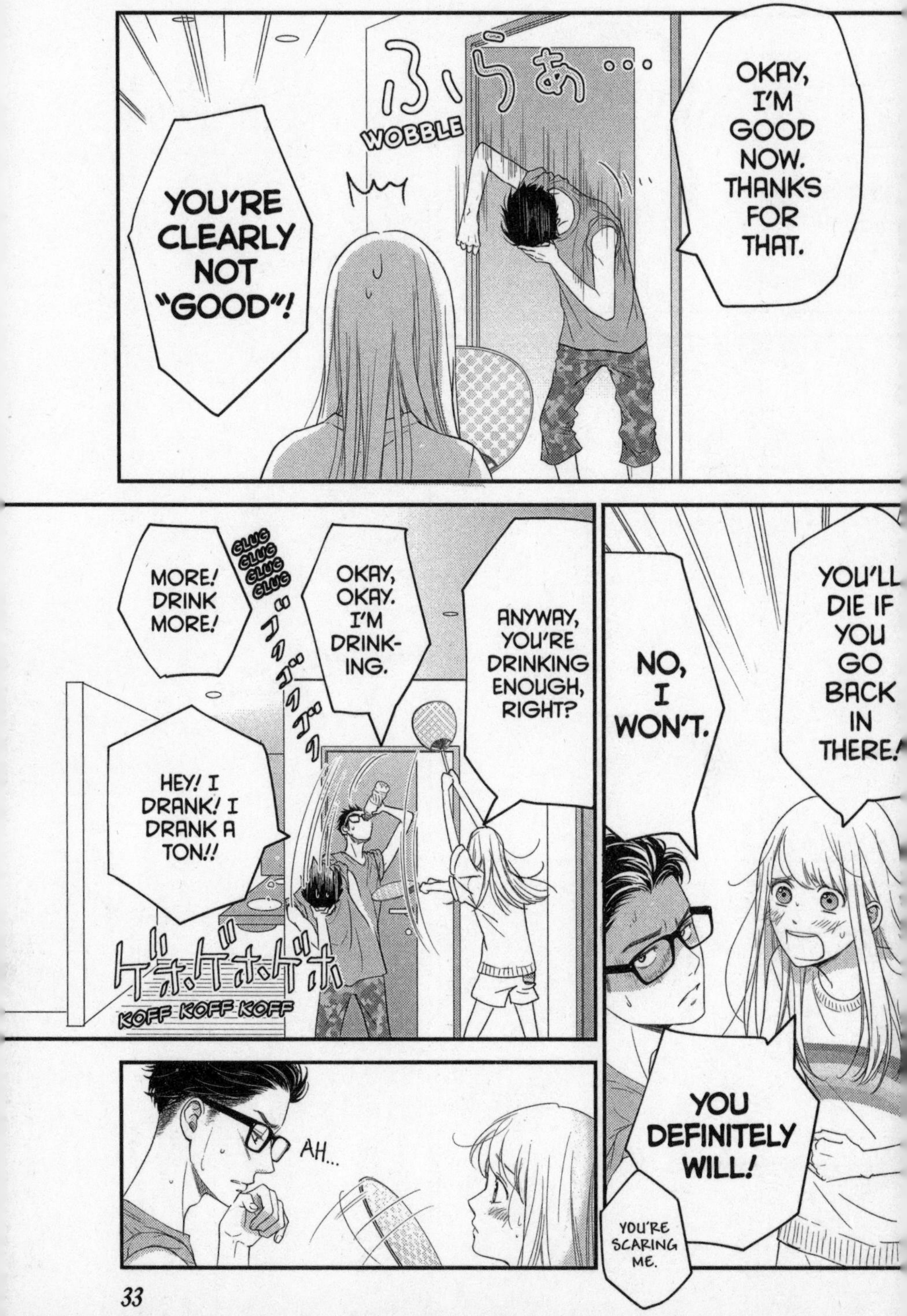
OKAY, I'M GOOD NOW. THANKS FOR THAT.
ふらぁ…
WOBBLE
YOU'RE CLEARLY NOT "GOOD"!
YOU'LL DIE IF YOU GO BACK IN THERE!
NO, I WON'T.
YOU DEFINITELY WILL!
YOU'RE SCARING ME.
ANYWAY, YOU'RE DRINKING ENOUGH, RIGHT?
OKAY, OKAY. I'M DRINK-ING.
GLUG GLUG GLUG GLUG
MORE! DRINK MORE!
HEY! I DRANK! I DRANK A TON!!
KOFF KOFF KOFF
AH...

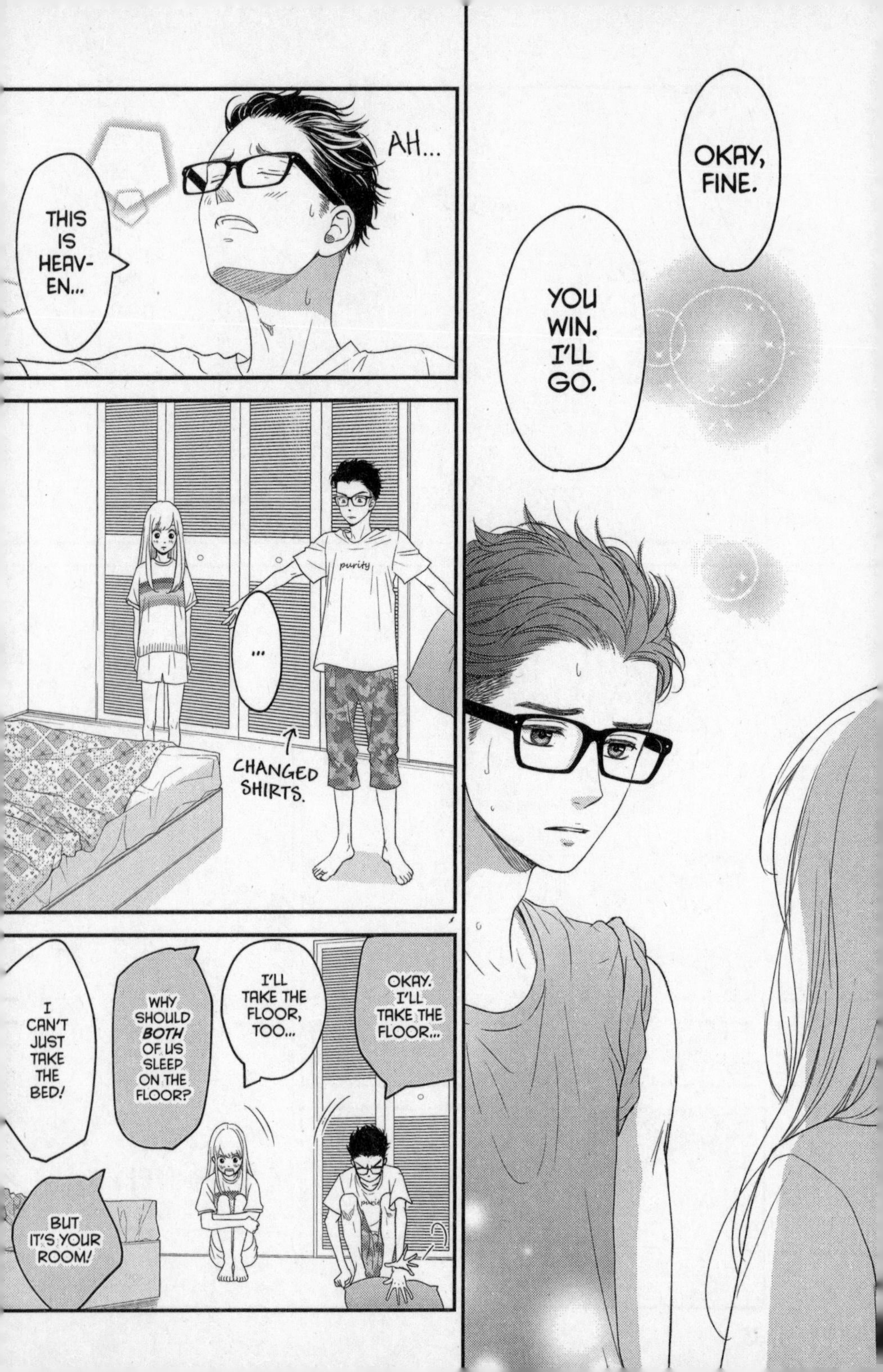
OKAY, FINE.
YOU WIN. I'LL GO.
AH...
THIS IS HEAVEN...
...
CHANGED SHIRTS.
OKAY. I'LL TAKE THE FLOOR...
I'LL TAKE THE FLOOR, TOO...
WHY SHOULD *BOTH* OF US SLEEP ON THE FLOOR?
I CAN'T JUST TAKE THE BED!
BUT IT'S YOUR ROOM!

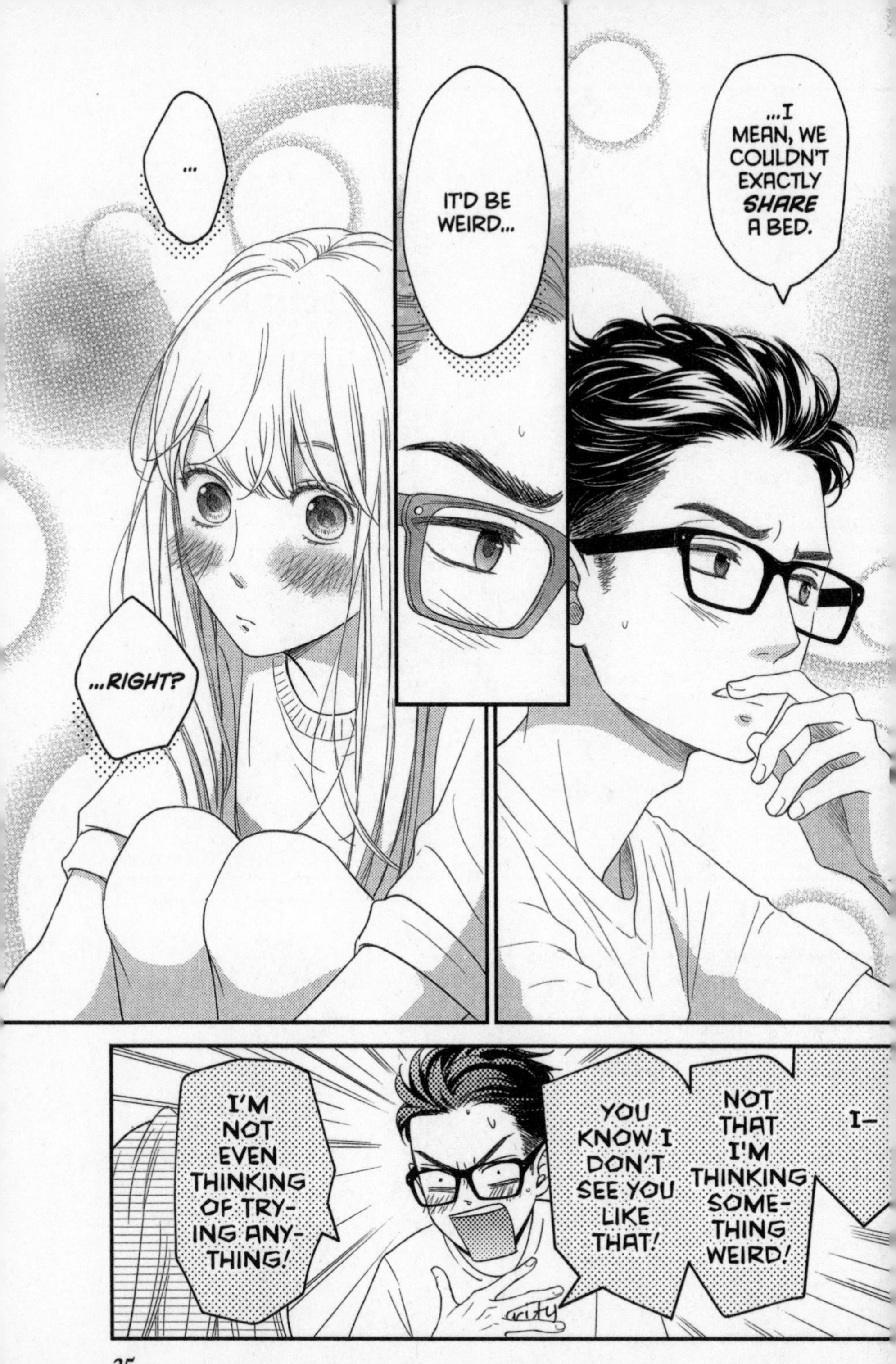
...I MEAN, WE COULDN'T EXACTLY *SHARE* A BED.
IT'D BE WEIRD...
...
...RIGHT?
I—
NOT THAT I'M THINKING SOME-THING WEIRD!
YOU KNOW I DON'T SEE YOU LIKE THAT!
I'M NOT EVEN THINKING OF TRY-ING ANY-THING!

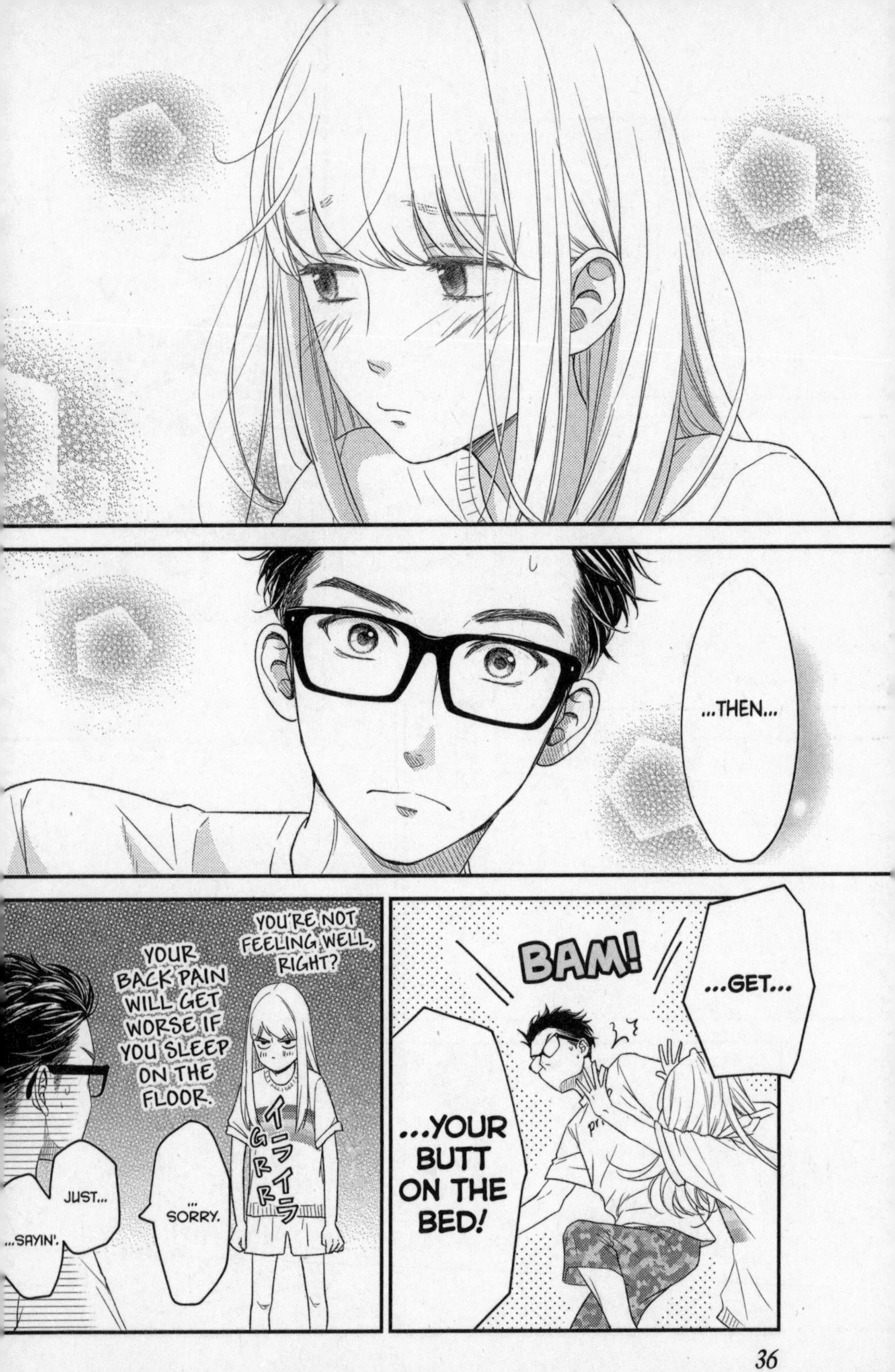
...THEN...
...GET...
BAM!
...YOUR BUTT ON THE BED!
YOU'RE NOT FEELING WELL, RIGHT?
YOUR BACK PAIN WILL GET WORSE IF YOU SLEEP ON THE FLOOR.
イライラ
GRR
... SORRY.
JUST...
...SAYIN'.

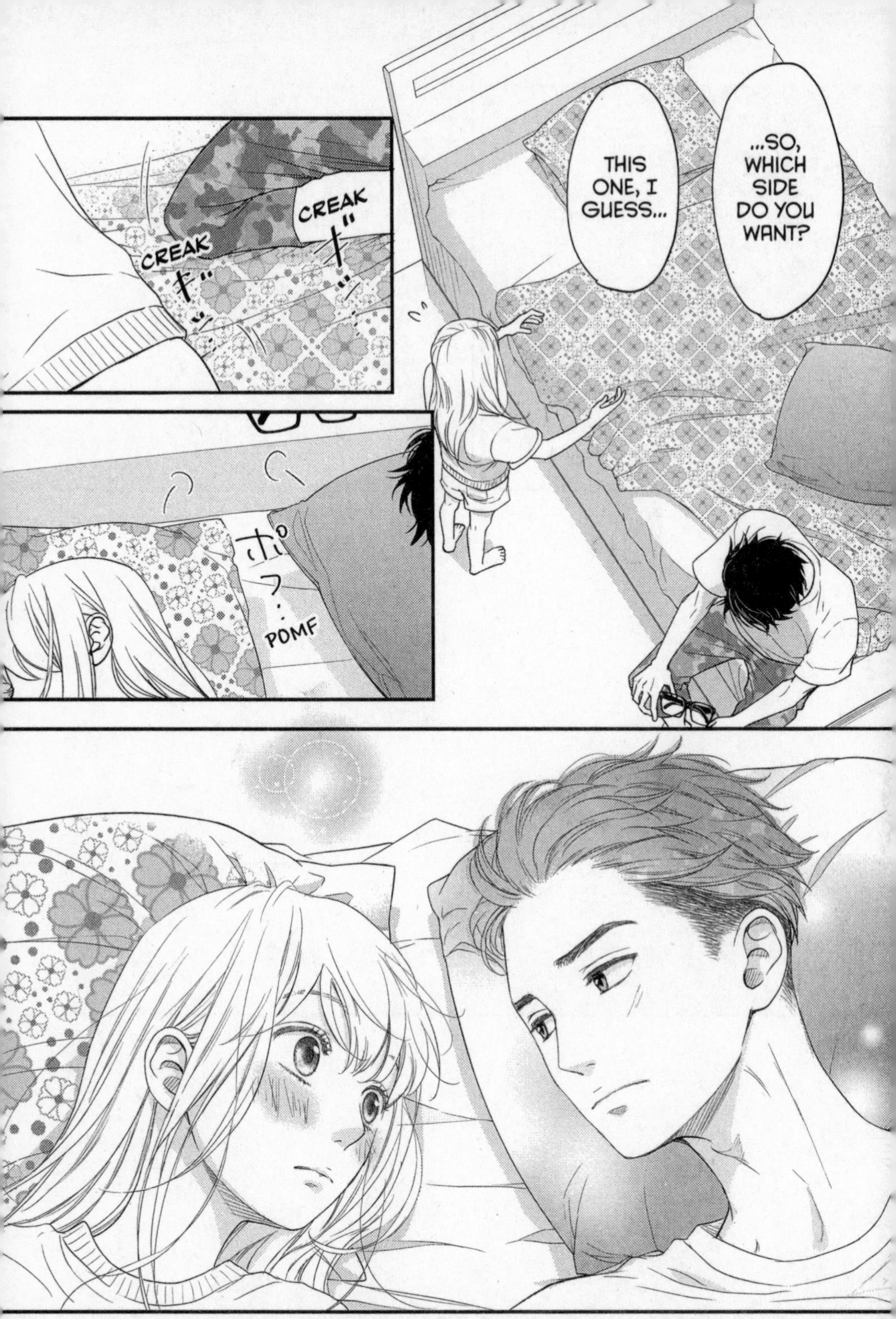
...SO, WHICH SIDE DO YOU WANT?
THIS ONE, I GUESS...
CREAK
CREAK
POMF

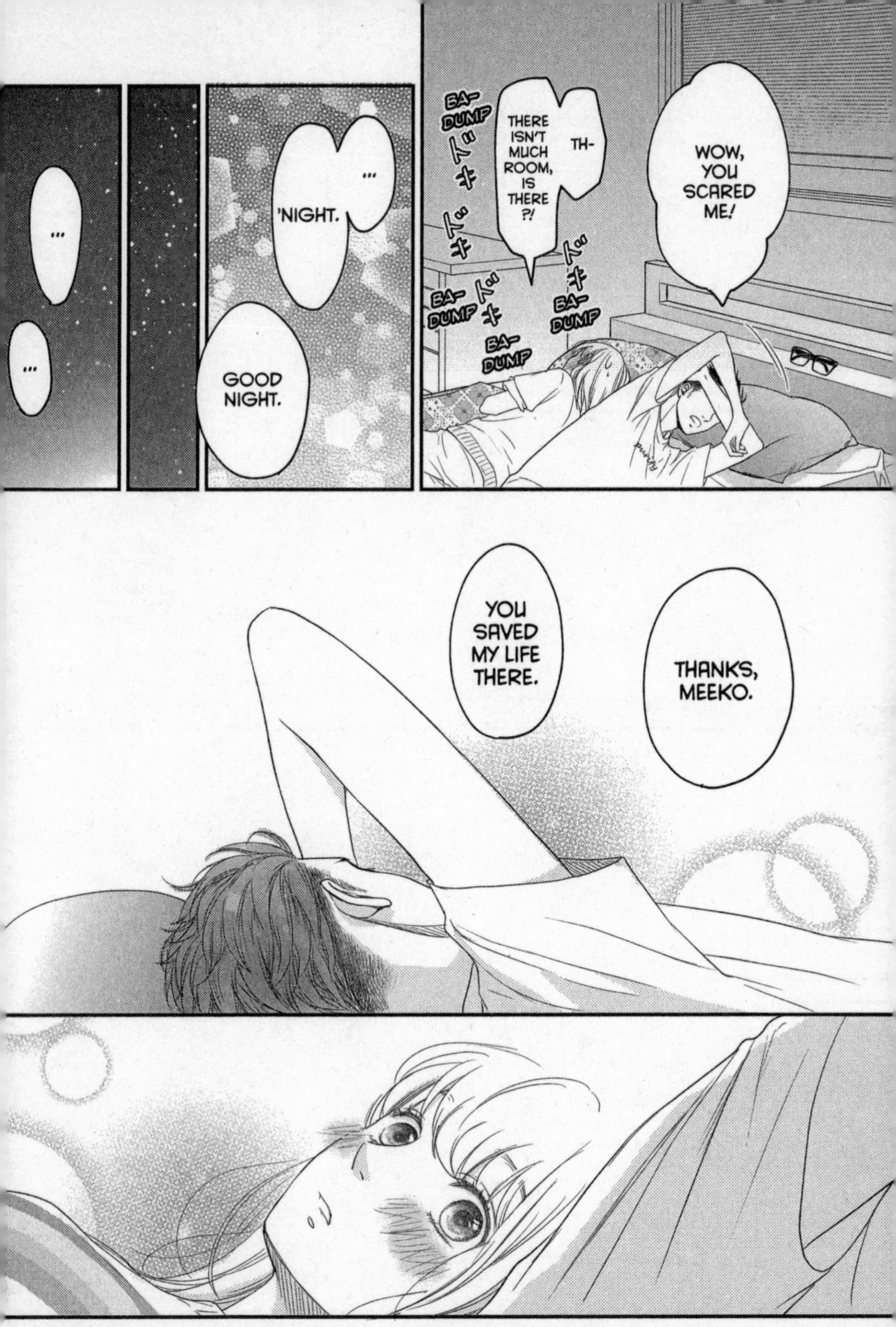
WOW, YOU SCARED ME!
TH-
THERE ISN'T MUCH ROOM, IS THERE?!
BA-DUMP
BA-DUMP
BA-DUMP
BA-DUMP
...
'NIGHT.
GOOD NIGHT.
...
...
THANKS, MEEKO.
YOU SAVED MY LIFE THERE.

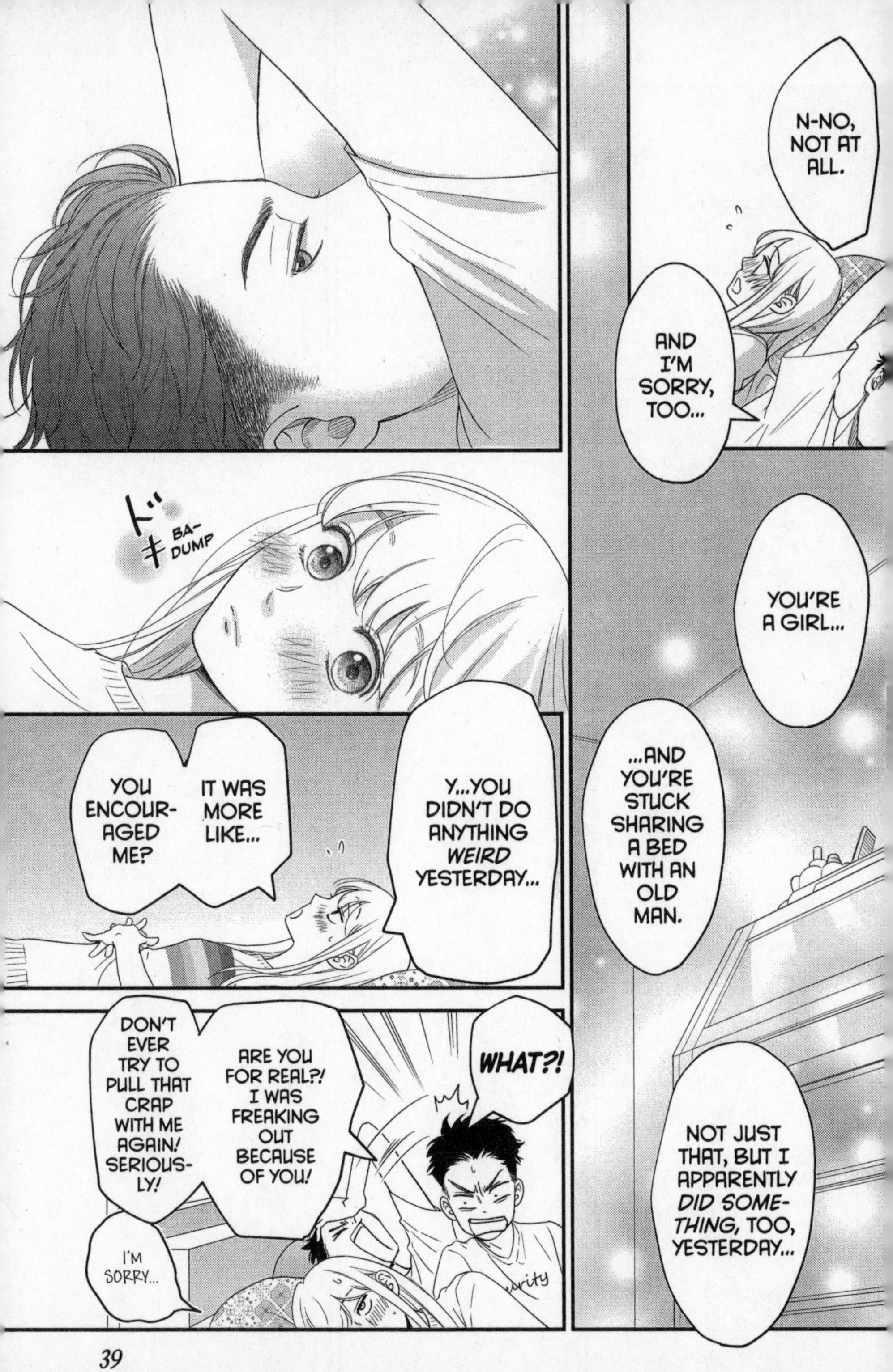
N-NO, NOT AT ALL.
AND I'M SORRY, TOO...
YOU'RE A GIRL...
...AND YOU'RE STUCK SHARING A BED WITH AN OLD MAN.
NOT JUST THAT, BUT I APPARENTLY *DID SOMETHING*, TOO, YESTERDAY...
ドキ
BA-DUMP
Y...YOU DIDN'T DO ANYTHING *WEIRD* YESTERDAY...
IT WAS MORE LIKE...
YOU ENCOURAGED ME?
WHAT?!
ARE YOU FOR REAL?! I WAS FREAKING OUT BECAUSE OF YOU!
DON'T EVER TRY TO PULL THAT CRAP WITH ME AGAIN! SERIOUSLY!
I'M SORRY...

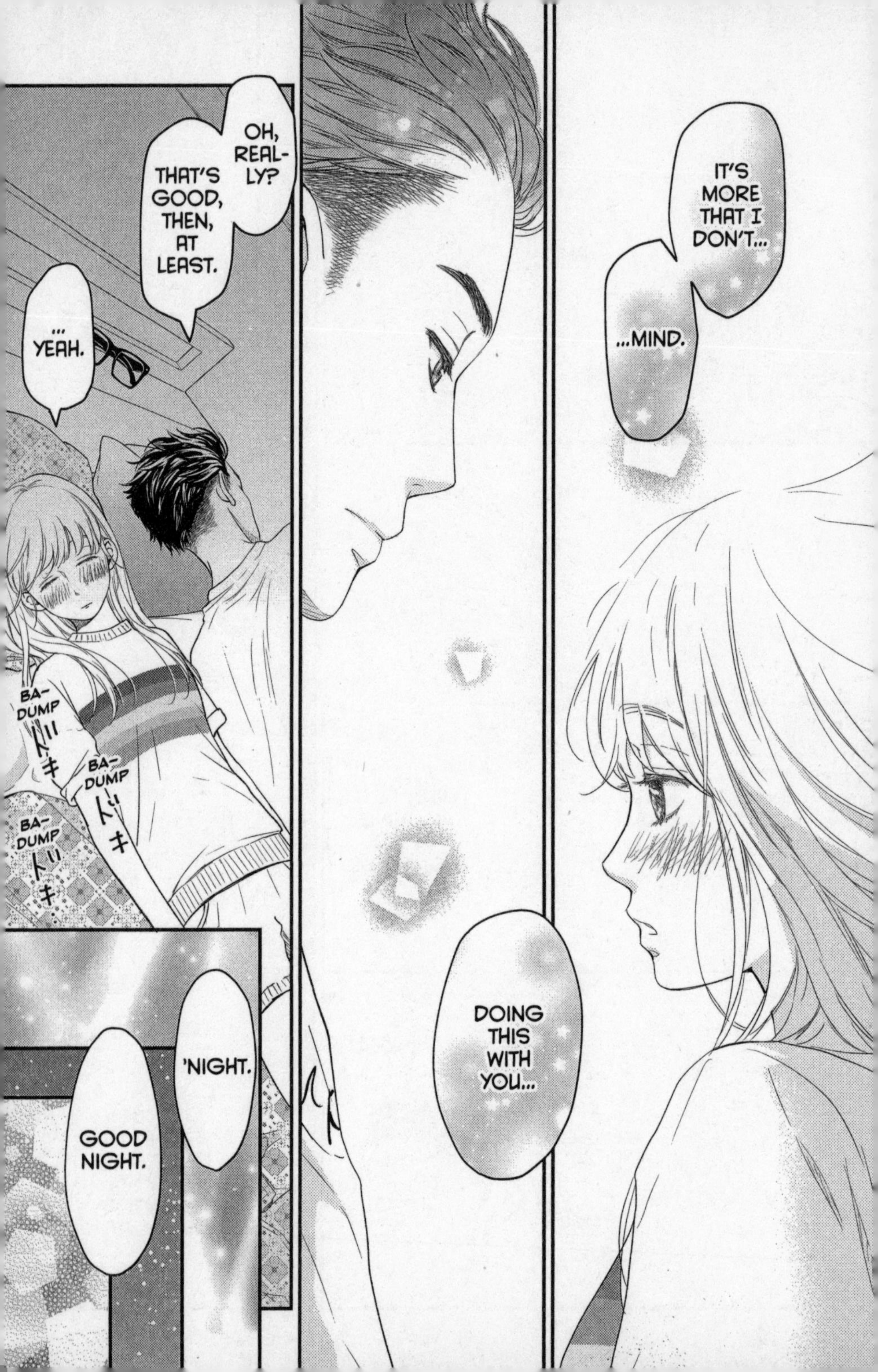
IT'S MORE THAT I DON'T...
...MIND.
DOING THIS WITH YOU...
OH, REALLY?
THAT'S GOOD, THEN, AT LEAST.
...YEAH.
BA-DUMP ドキ
BA-DUMP ドキ
BA-DUMP ドキ
'NIGHT.
GOOD NIGHT.

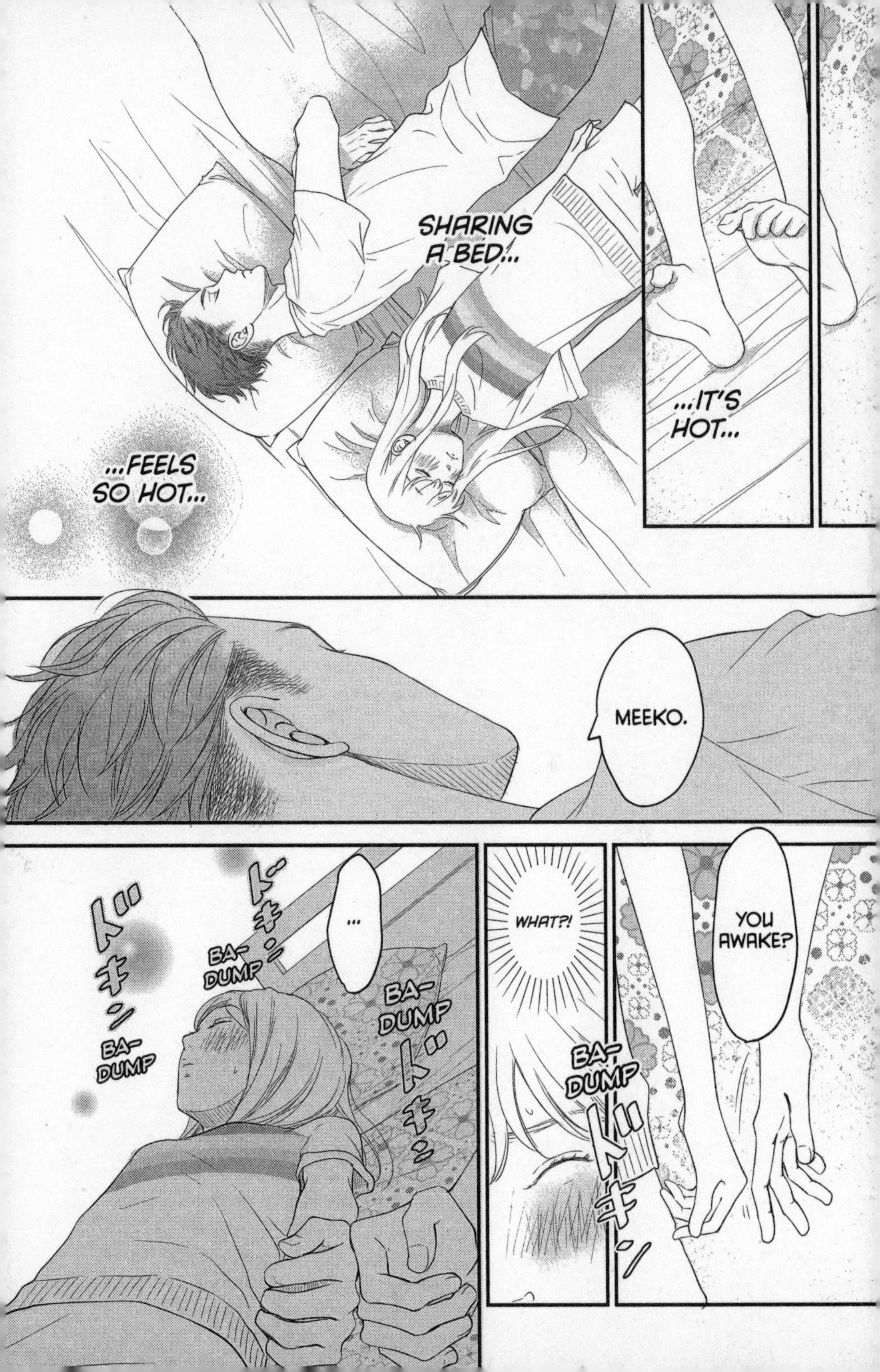
...IT'S HOT...
SHARING A BED...
...FEELS SO HOT...
MEEKO.
YOU AWAKE?
BA-DUMP
WHAT?!
...
BA-DUMP
BA-DUMP
BA-DUMP

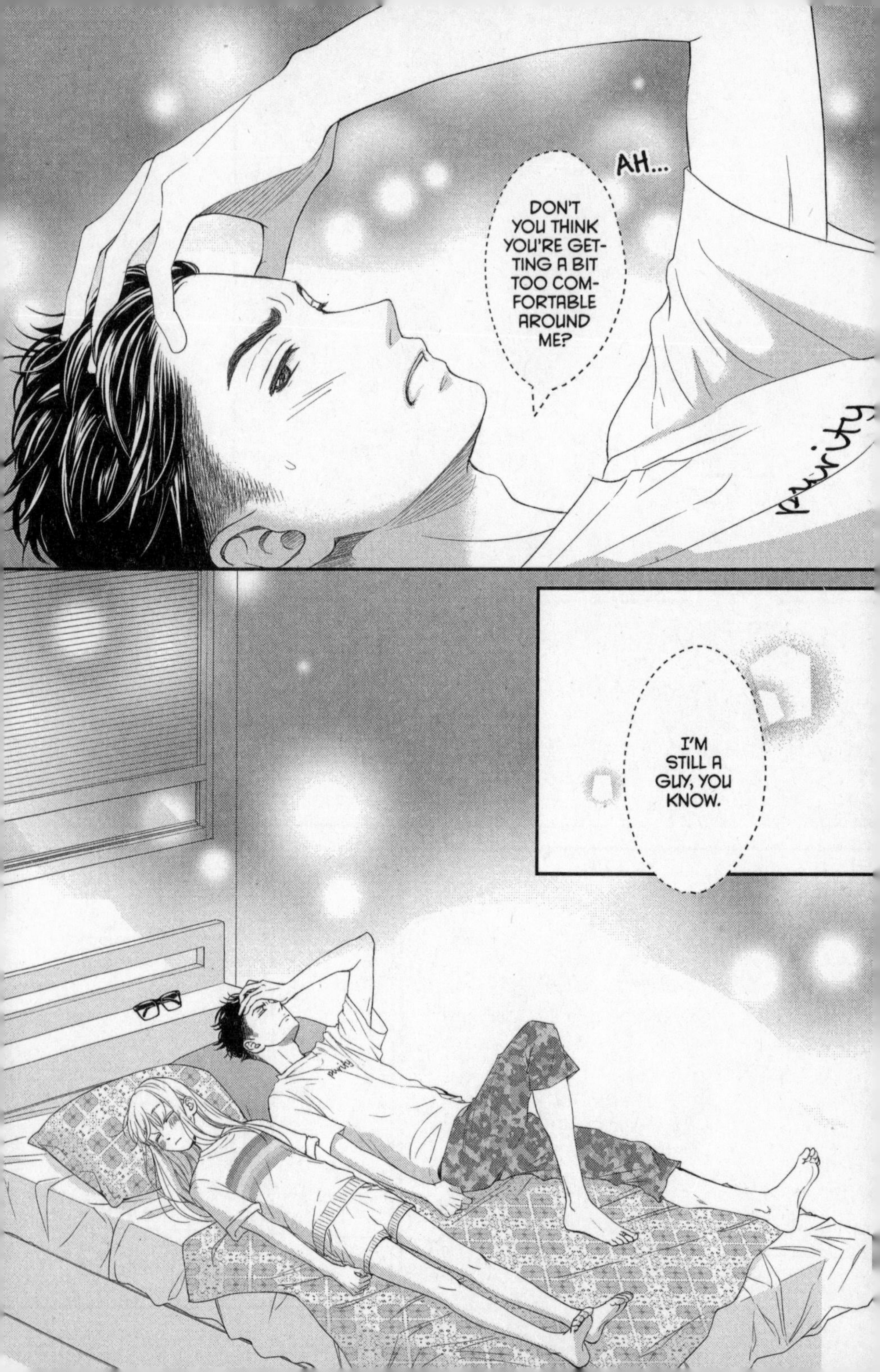
AH...
DON'T YOU THINK YOU'RE GETTING A BIT TOO COMFORTABLE AROUND ME?
purity
I'M STILL A GUY, YOU KNOW.

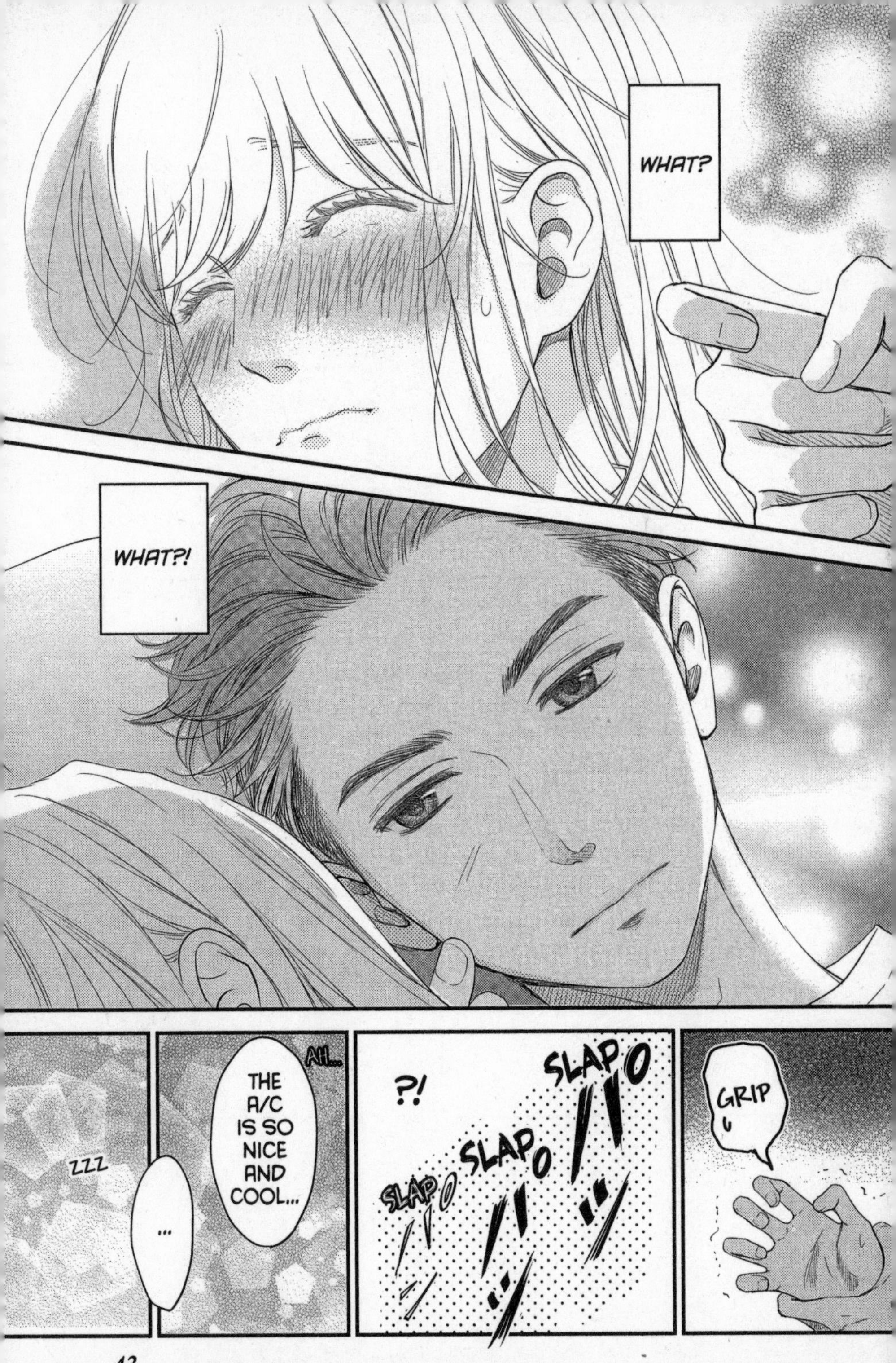
WHAT?
WHAT?!
GRIP
SLAP
?!
SLAP
SLAP
AH...
THE A/C IS SO NICE AND COOL...
...
ZZZ

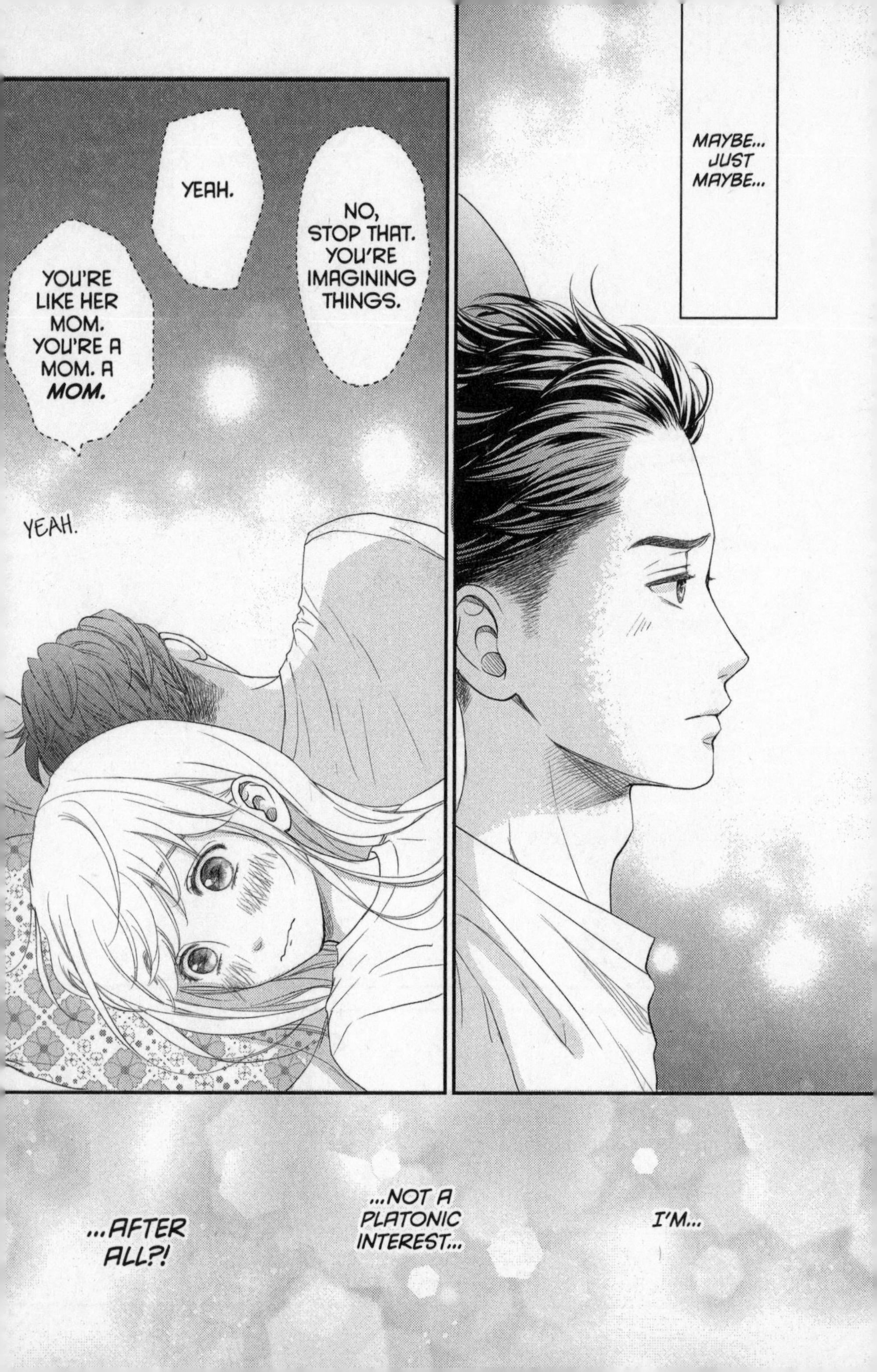
MAYBE... JUST MAYBE...
NO, STOP THAT. YOU'RE IMAGINING THINGS.
YEAH.
YOU'RE LIKE HER MOM. YOU'RE A MOM. A **MOM.**
YEAH.
I'M...
...NOT A PLATONIC INTEREST...
...AFTER ALL?!

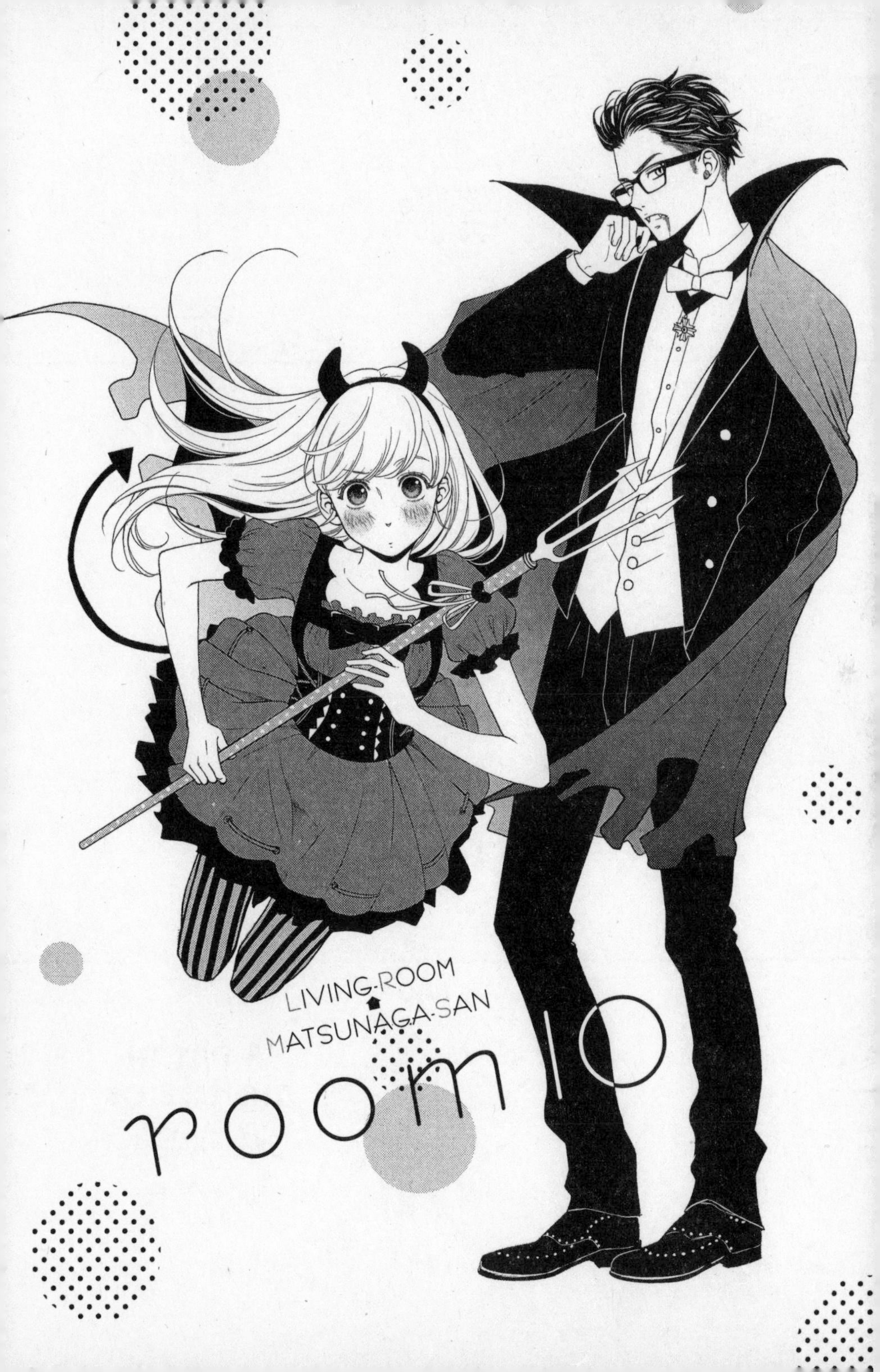
LIVING-ROOM MATSUNAGA-SAN
room 10

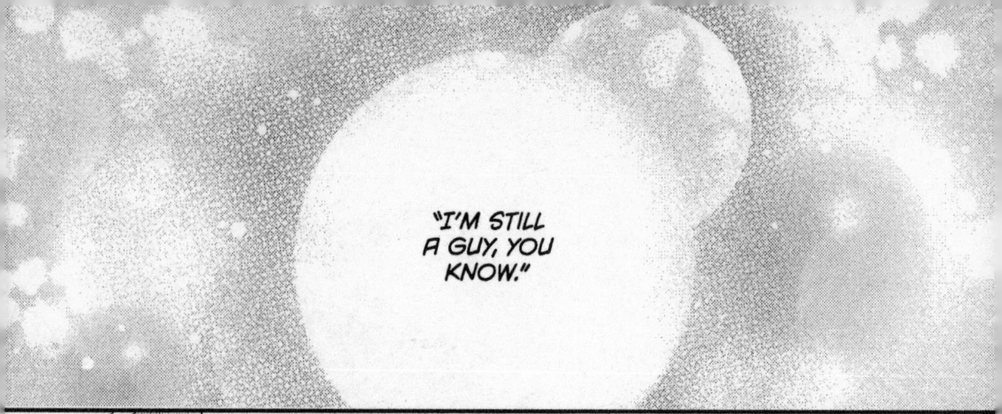
"I'M STILL A GUY, YOU KNOW."

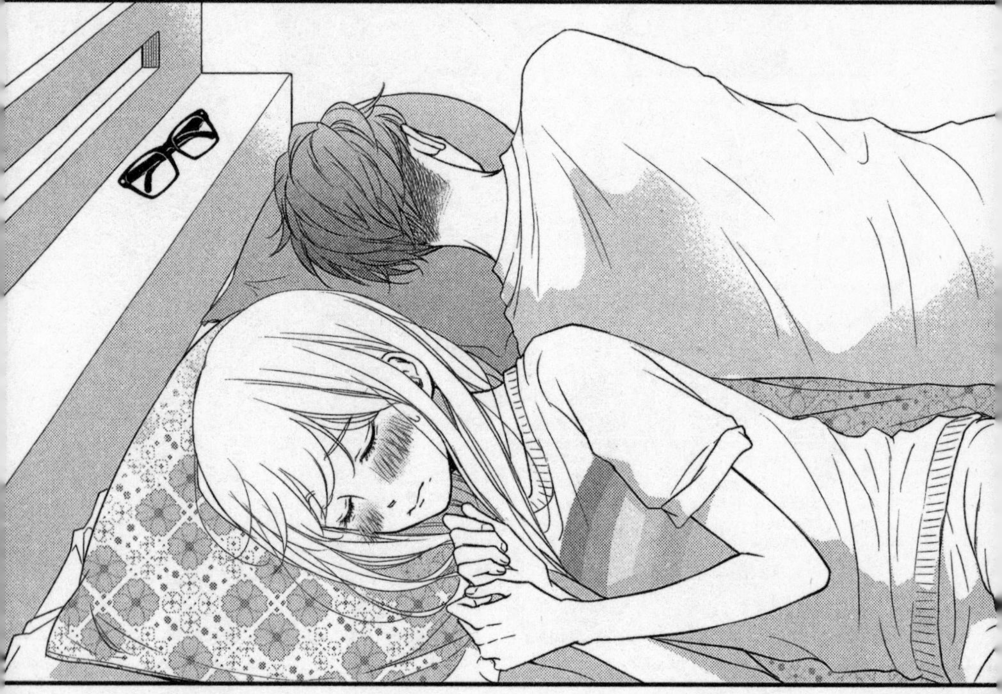

A DAY IN THE LIFE OF SABAKO

WITH ASAKO-SAN

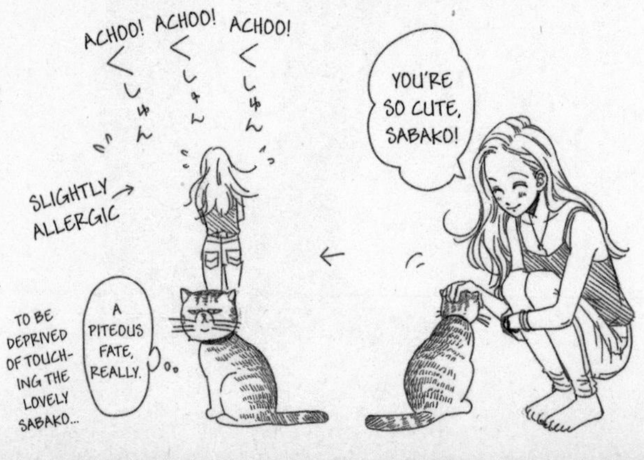
YOU'RE SO CUTE, SABAKO!
ACHOO! くしゅん
ACHOO! くしゅん
ACHOO! くしゅん
SLIGHTLY ALLERGIC
A PITEOUS FATE, REALLY.
TO BE DEPRIVED OF TOUCHING THE LOVELY SABAKO...

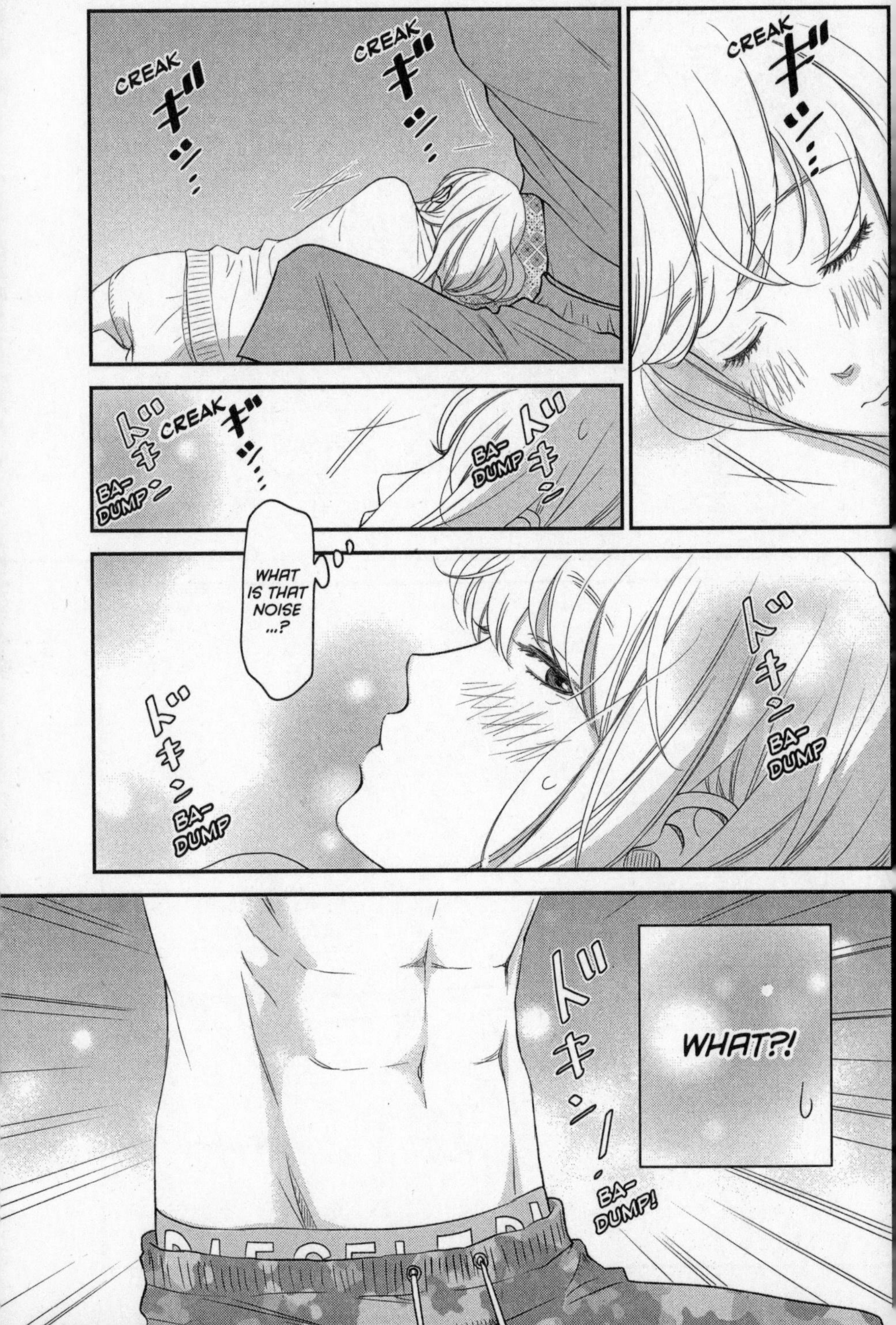
CREAK
CREAK
CREAK
BA-DUMP
CREAK
BA-DUMP
WHAT IS THAT NOISE ...?
BA-DUMP
BA-DUMP
WHAT?!
BA-DUMP!

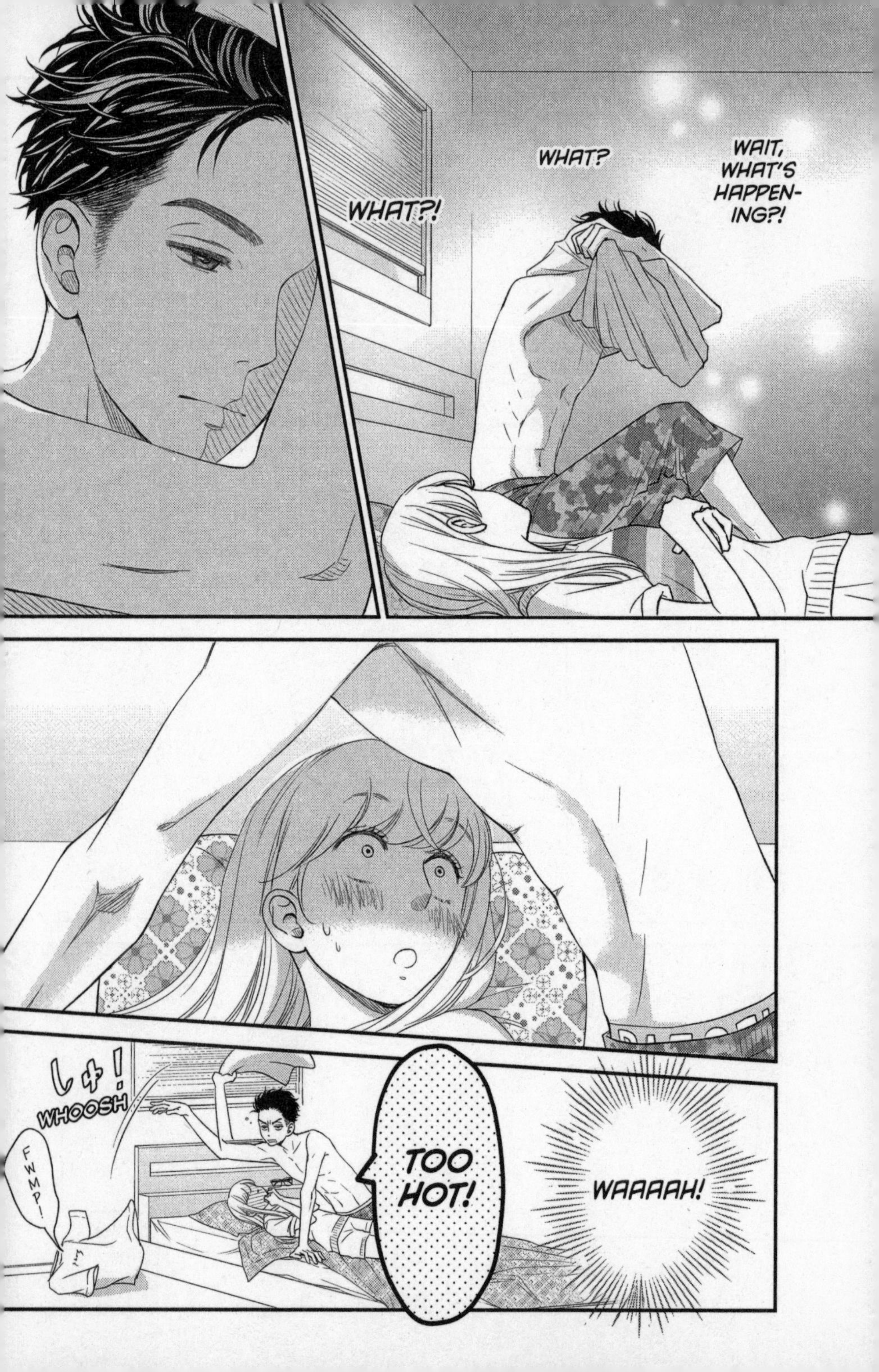
WAIT, WHAT'S HAPPENING?!
WHAT?
WHAT?!
WAAAAH!
TOO HOT!
しゅ!
WHOOSH
FWMP!

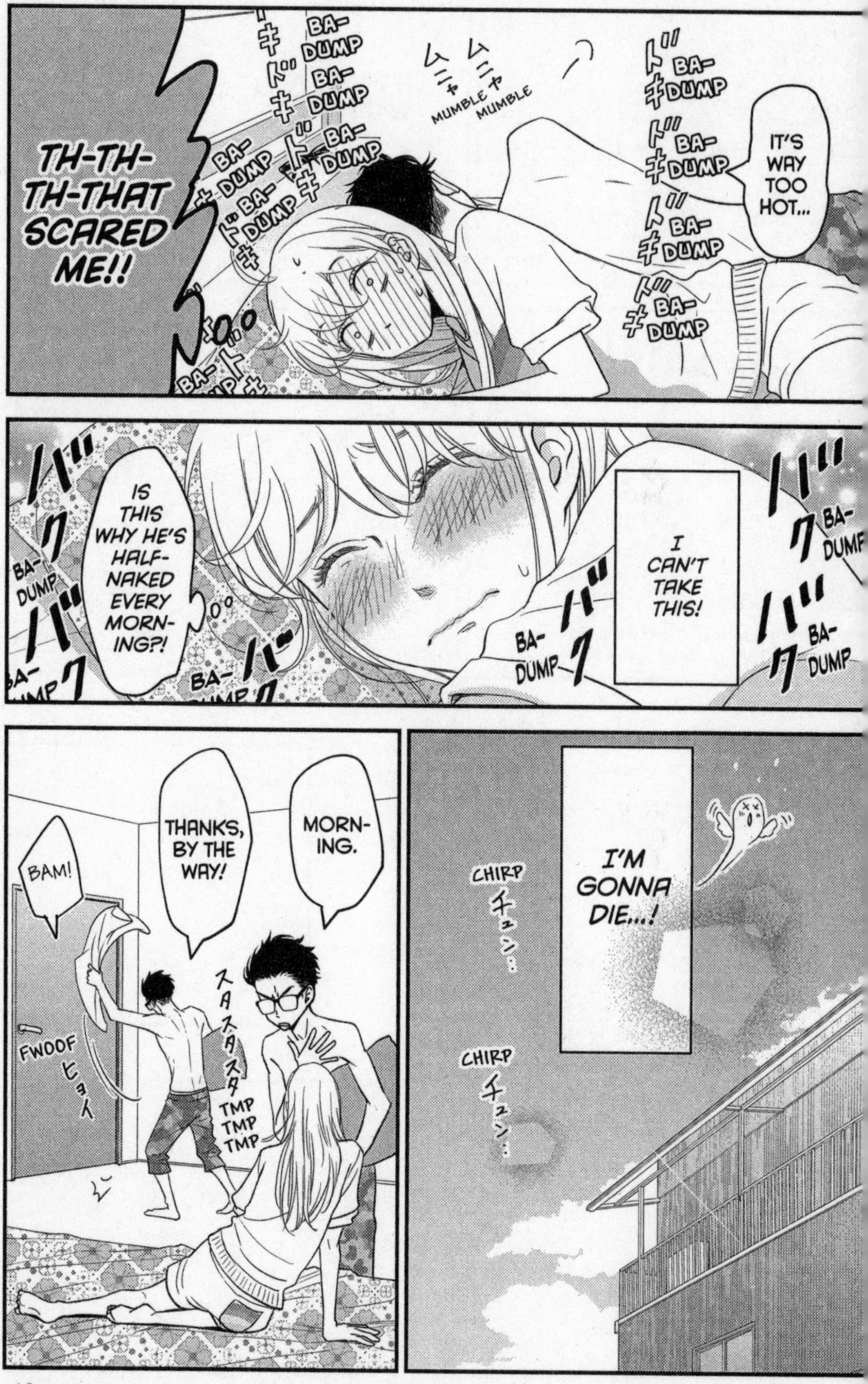
IT'S WAY TOO HOT...
BA-DUMP BA-DUMP BA-DUMP BA-DUMP
MUMBLE MUMBLE
BA-DUMP BA-DUMP BA-DUMP BA-DUMP
TH-TH-TH-THAT SCARED ME!!
I CAN'T TAKE THIS!
BA-DUMP BA-DUMP BA-DUMP
IS THIS WHY HE'S HALF-NAKED EVERY MORNING?!
BA-DUMP
I'M GONNA DIE...!
CHIRP
CHIRP
MORNING.
THANKS, BY THE WAY!
TMP TMP TMP
BAM!
FWOOF

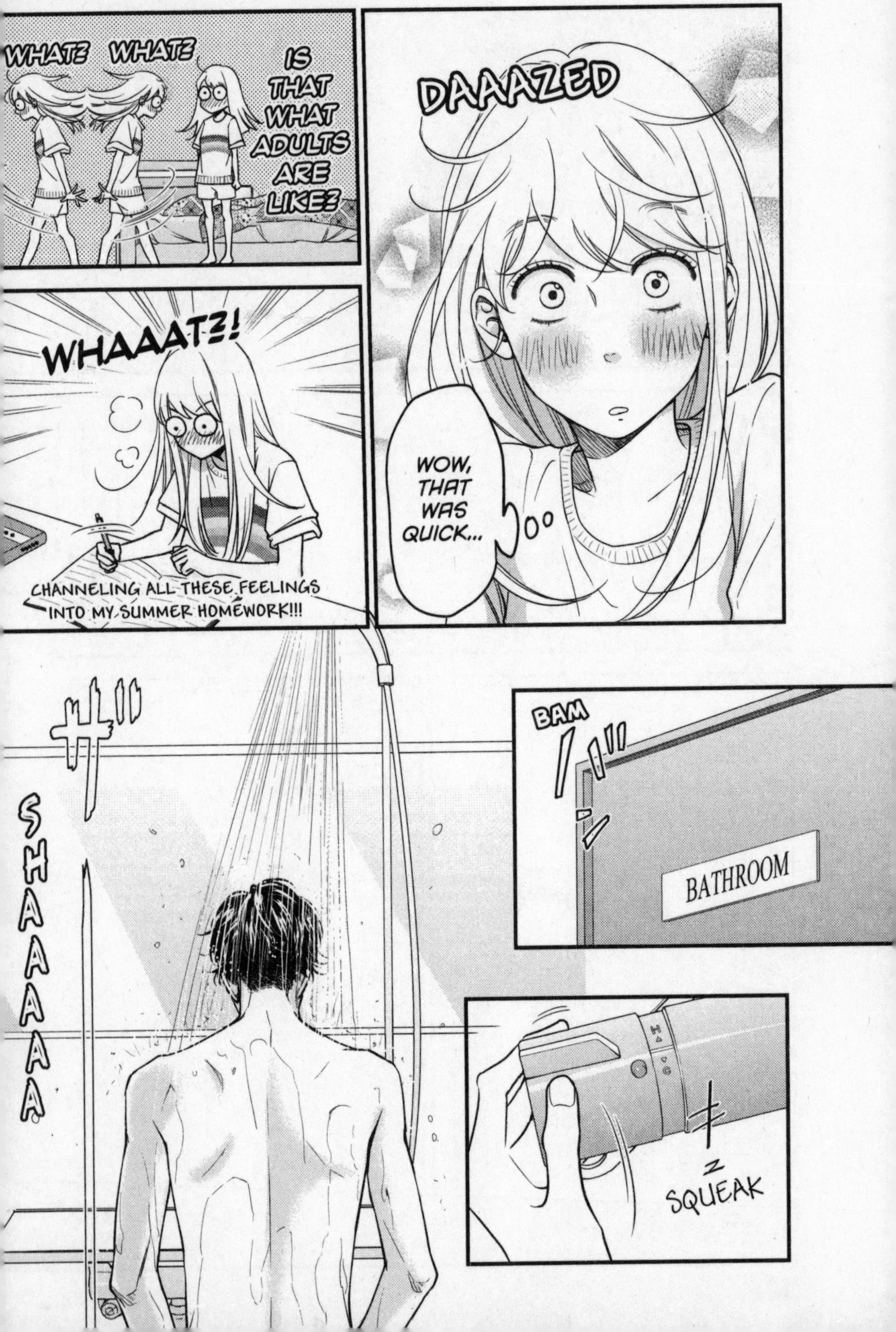
DAAAZED
WOW, THAT WAS QUICK...
IS THAT WHAT ADULTS ARE LIKE?
WHAT? WHAT?
WHAAAT?!
CHANNELING ALL THESE FEELINGS INTO MY SUMMER HOMEWORK!!!
BAM
BATHROOM
SQUEAK
SHAAAAAA

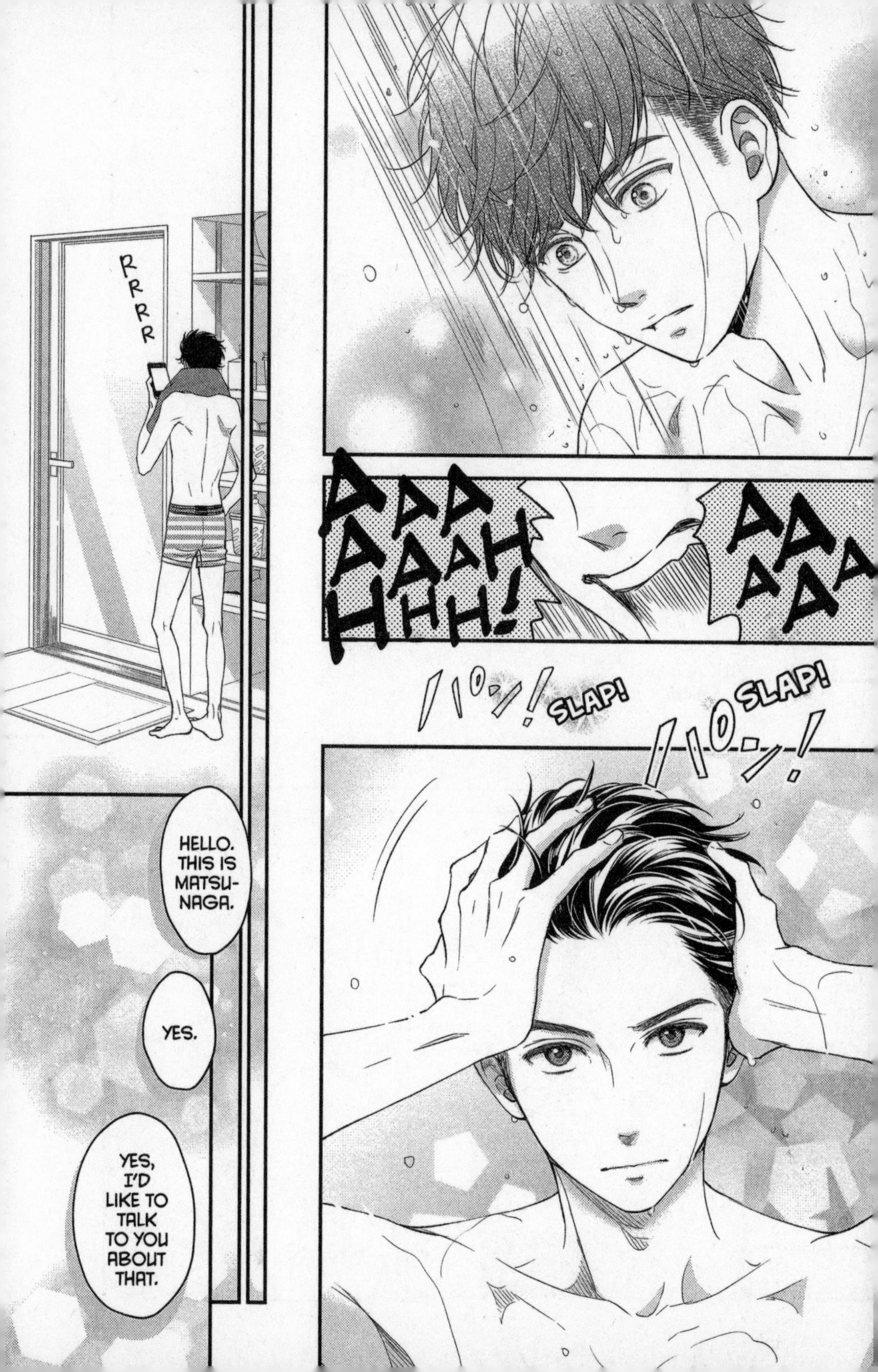

AAAAAAA
AAAAAAHHHH!
SLAP!
SLAP!
RRRR
HELLO. THIS IS MATSU-NAGA.
YES.
YES, I'D LIKE TO TALK TO YOU ABOUT THAT.

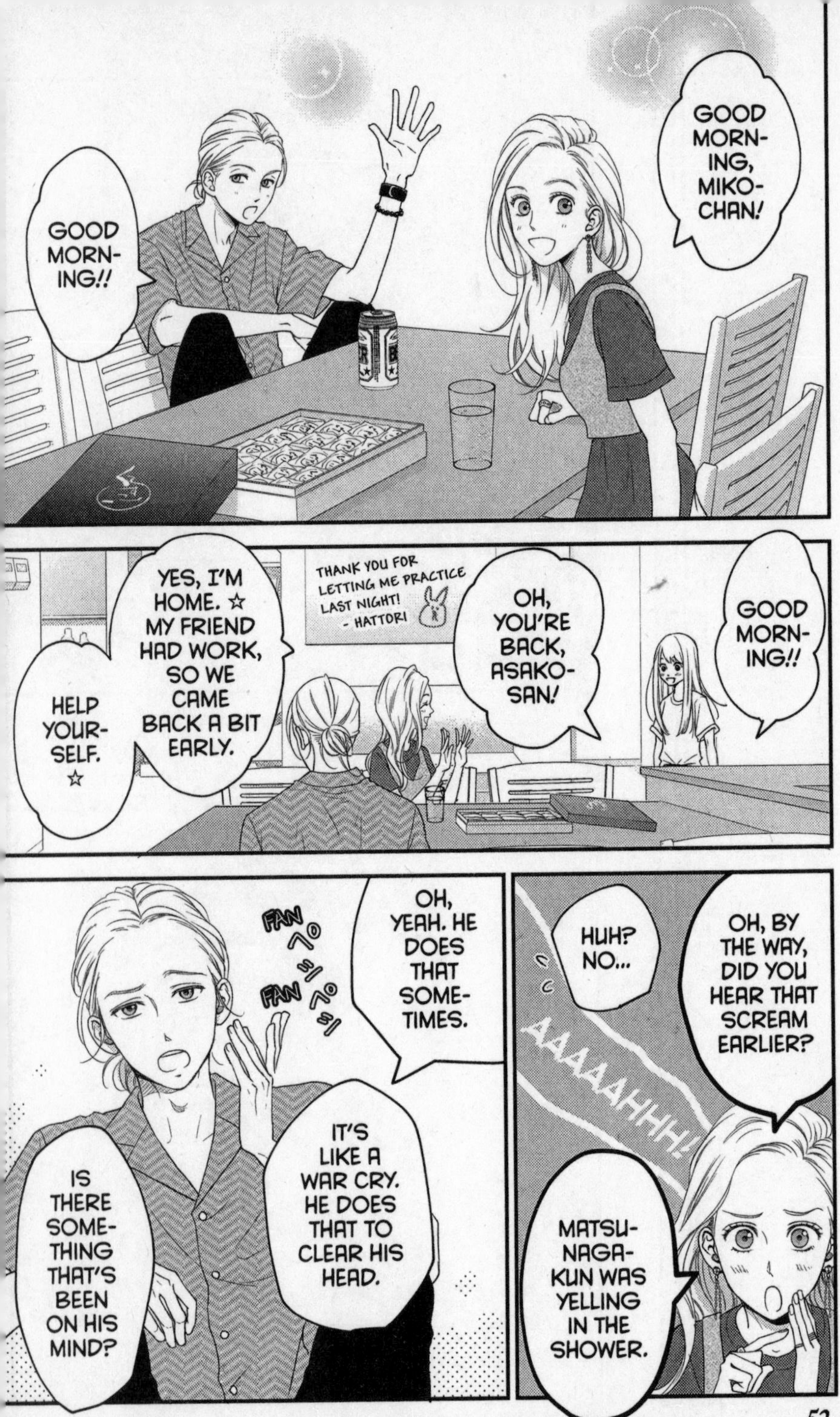
GOOD MORNING, MIKO-CHAN!
GOOD MORNING!!
GOOD MORNING!!
OH, YOU'RE BACK, ASAKO-SAN!
THANK YOU FOR LETTING ME PRACTICE LAST NIGHT! - HATTORI
YES, I'M HOME. ☆ MY FRIEND HAD WORK, SO WE CAME BACK A BIT EARLY.
HELP YOURSELF. ☆
OH, BY THE WAY, DID YOU HEAR THAT SCREAM EARLIER?
HUH? NO...
AAAAAAHHH!
MATSUNAGA-KUN WAS YELLING IN THE SHOWER.
OH, YEAH. HE DOES THAT SOMETIMES.
FAN
FAN
IT'S LIKE A WAR CRY. HE DOES THAT TO CLEAR HIS HEAD.
IS THERE SOMETHING THAT'S BEEN ON HIS MIND?

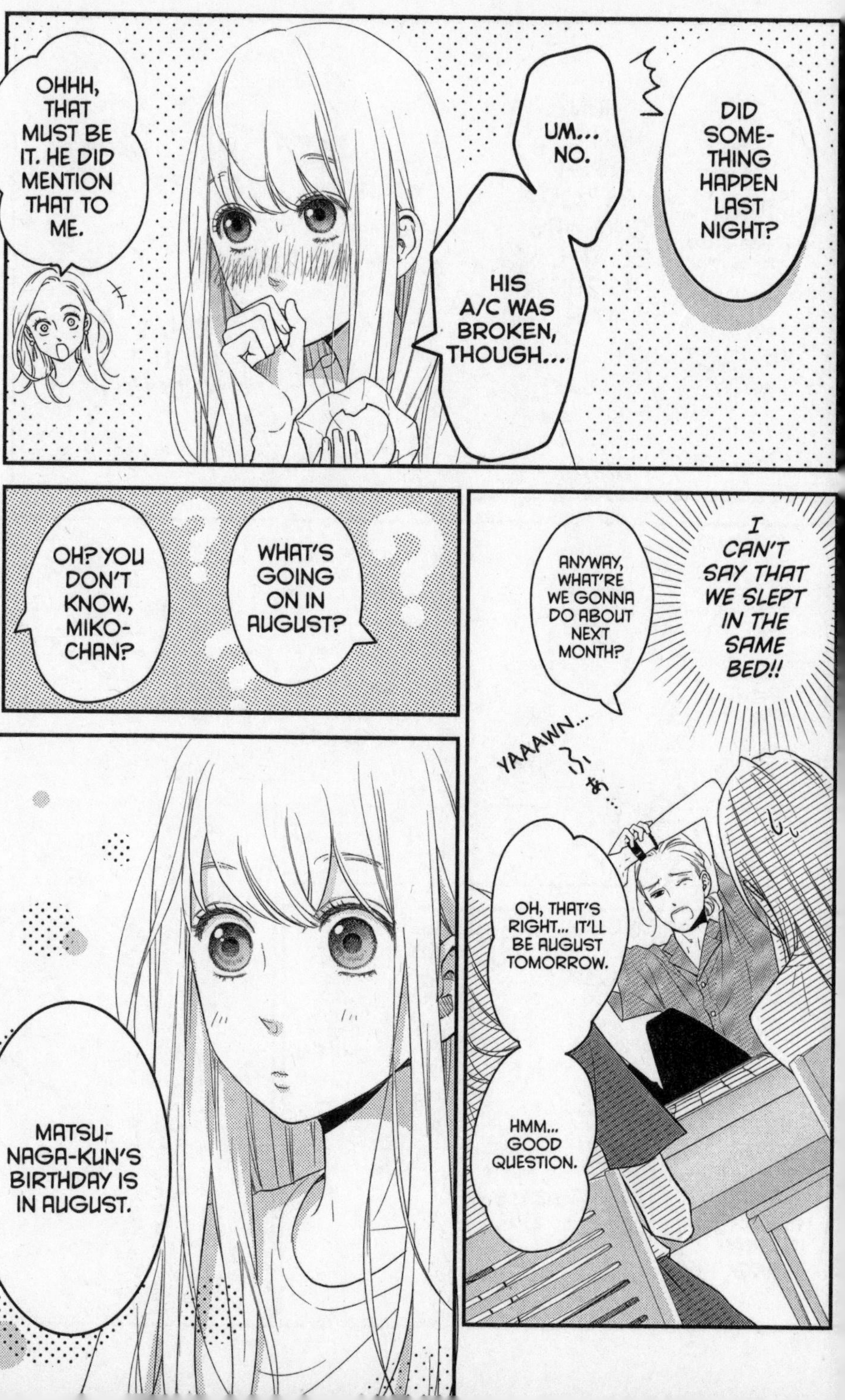
DID SOME-THING HAPPEN LAST NIGHT?
UM... NO.
HIS A/C WAS BROKEN, THOUGH...
OHHH, THAT MUST BE IT. HE DID MENTION THAT TO ME.
I CAN'T SAY THAT WE SLEPT IN THE SAME BED!!
ANYWAY, WHAT'RE WE GONNA DO ABOUT NEXT MONTH?
YAAAWN...
OH, THAT'S RIGHT... IT'LL BE AUGUST TOMORROW.
HMM... GOOD QUESTION.
WHAT'S GOING ON IN AUGUST?
OH? YOU DON'T KNOW, MIKO-CHAN?
MATSU-NAGA-KUN'S BIRTHDAY IS IN AUGUST.

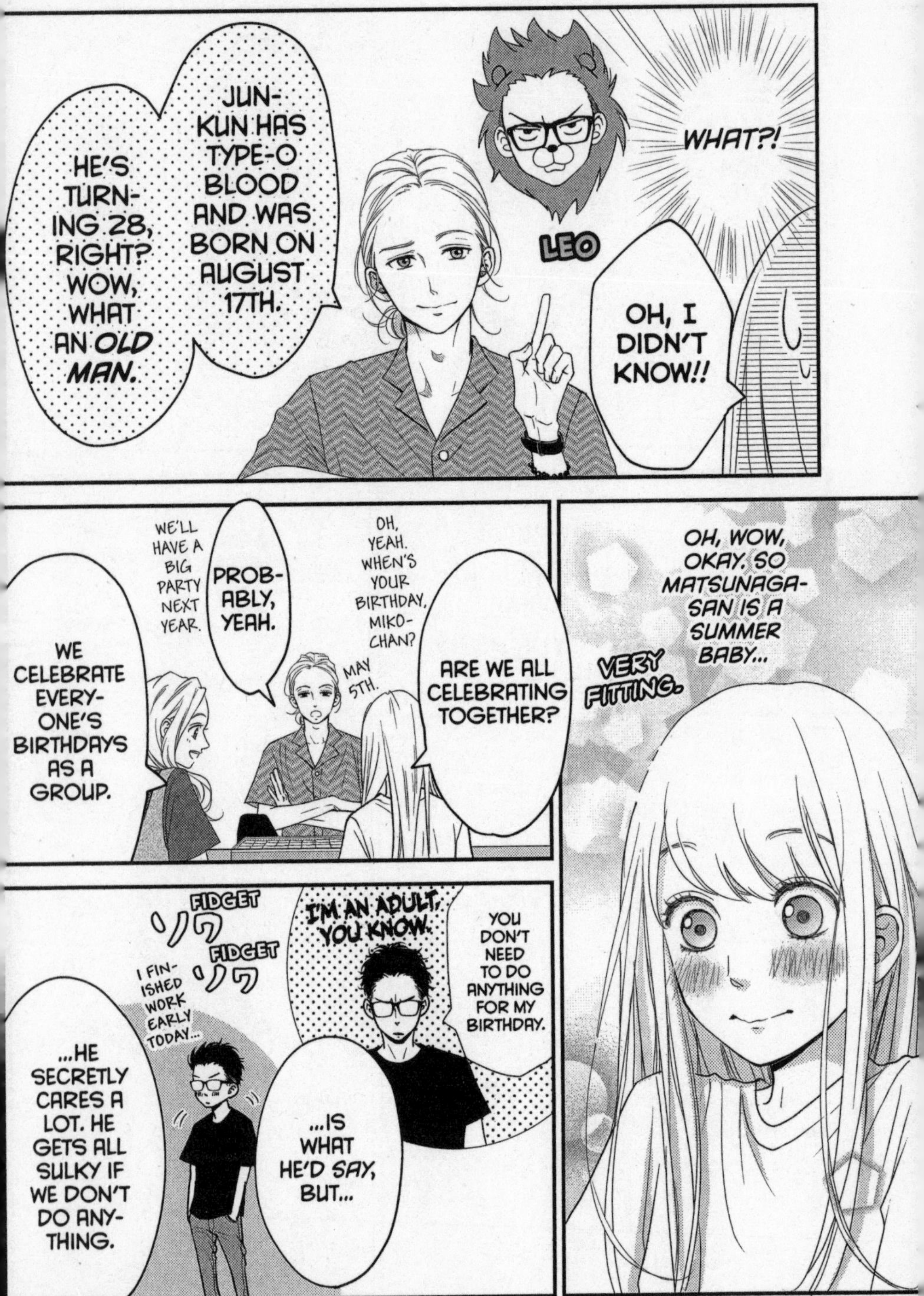
WHAT?!
LEO
OH, I DIDN'T KNOW!!
JUN-KUN HAS TYPE-O BLOOD AND WAS BORN ON AUGUST 17TH.
HE'S TURNING 28, RIGHT? WOW, WHAT AN *OLD MAN.*
OH, WOW, OKAY. SO MATSUNAGA-SAN IS A SUMMER BABY...
VERY FITTING.
ARE WE ALL CELEBRATING TOGETHER?
OH, YEAH. WHEN'S YOUR BIRTHDAY, MIKO-CHAN?
MAY 5TH.
PROBABLY, YEAH.
WE'LL HAVE A BIG PARTY NEXT YEAR.
WE CELEBRATE EVERYONE'S BIRTHDAYS AS A GROUP.
YOU DON'T NEED TO DO ANYTHING FOR MY BIRTHDAY.
I'M AN ADULT, YOU KNOW.
...IS WHAT HE'D *SAY*, BUT...
FIDGET ソワ
FIDGET ソワ
I FINISHED WORK EARLY TODAY...
...HE SECRETLY CARES A LOT. HE GETS ALL SULKY IF WE DON'T DO ANYTHING.

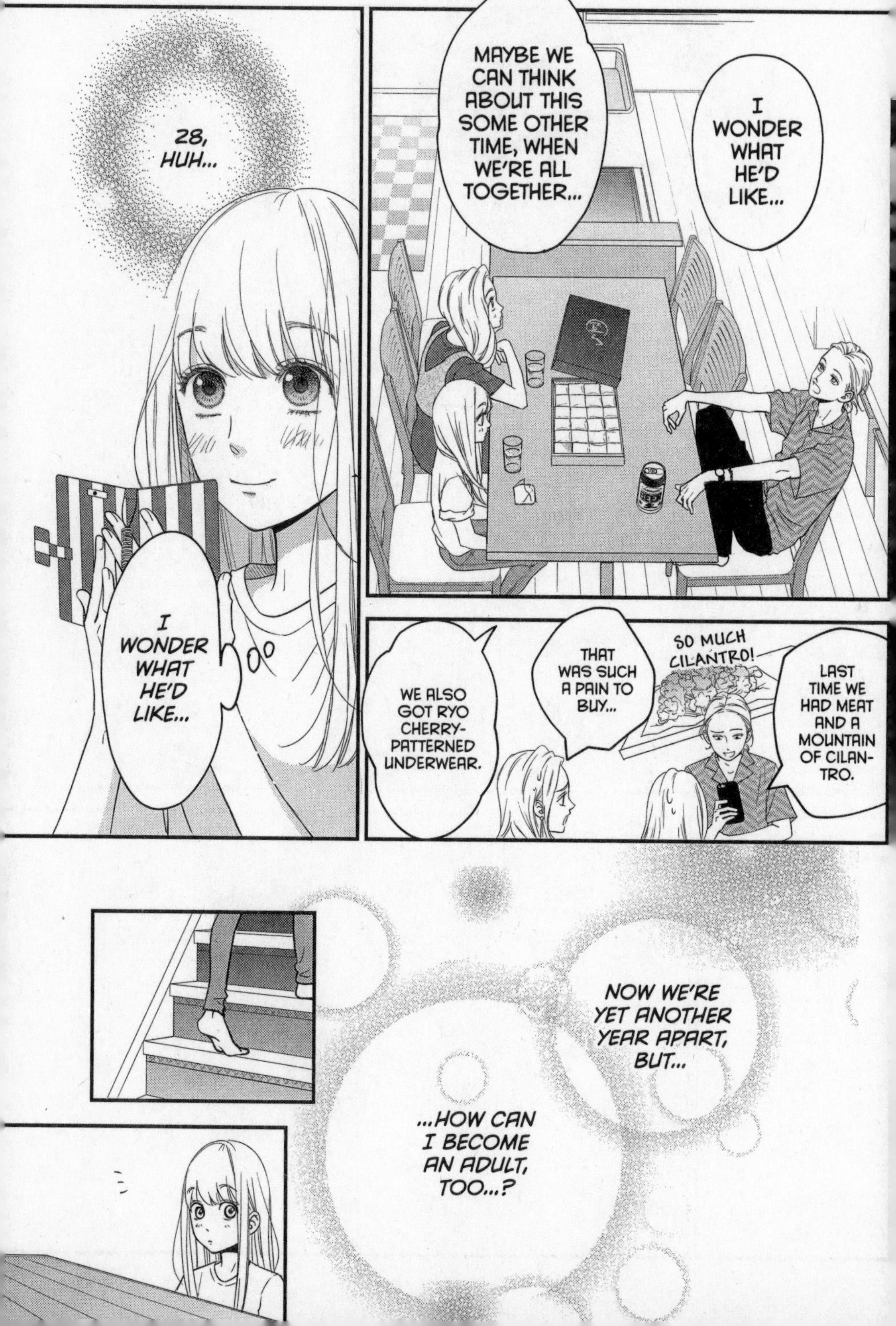
I WONDER WHAT HE'D LIKE...
MAYBE WE CAN THINK ABOUT THIS SOME OTHER TIME, WHEN WE'RE ALL TOGETHER...
LAST TIME WE HAD MEAT AND A MOUNTAIN OF CILAN-TRO.
SO MUCH CILANTRO!
THAT WAS SUCH A PAIN TO BUY...
WE ALSO GOT RYO CHERRY-PATTERNED UNDERWEAR.
28, HUH...
I WONDER WHAT HE'D LIKE...
NOW WE'RE YET ANOTHER YEAR APART, BUT...
...HOW CAN I BECOME AN ADULT, TOO...?

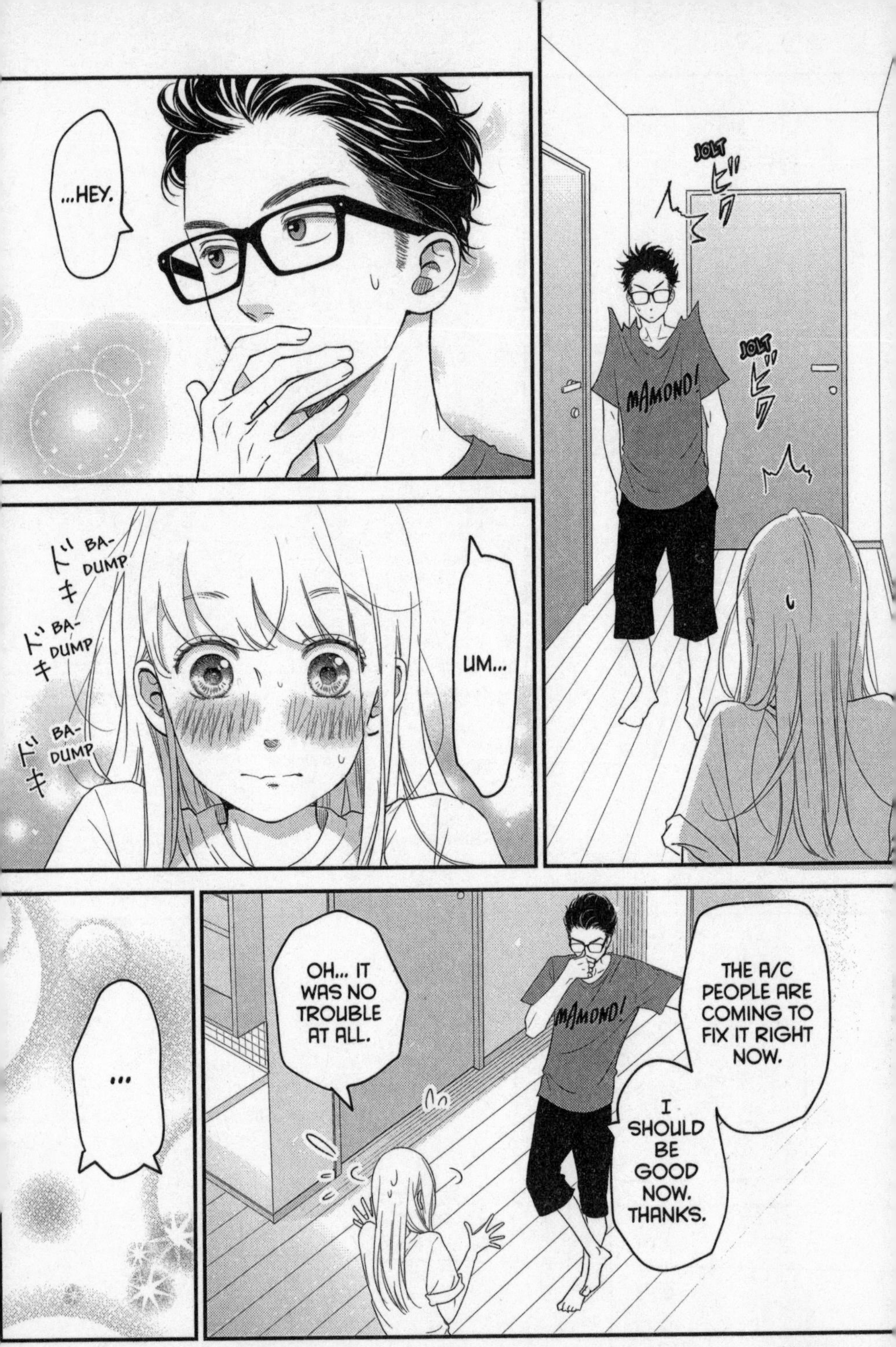
JOLT
ビク
JOLT
ビク
MAMOND!
...HEY.
UM...
BA-DUMP
ドキ
BA-DUMP
ドキ
BA-DUMP
ドキ
THE A/C PEOPLE ARE COMING TO FIX IT RIGHT NOW.
I SHOULD BE GOOD NOW. THANKS.
MAMOND!
OH... IT WAS NO TROUBLE AT ALL.
...

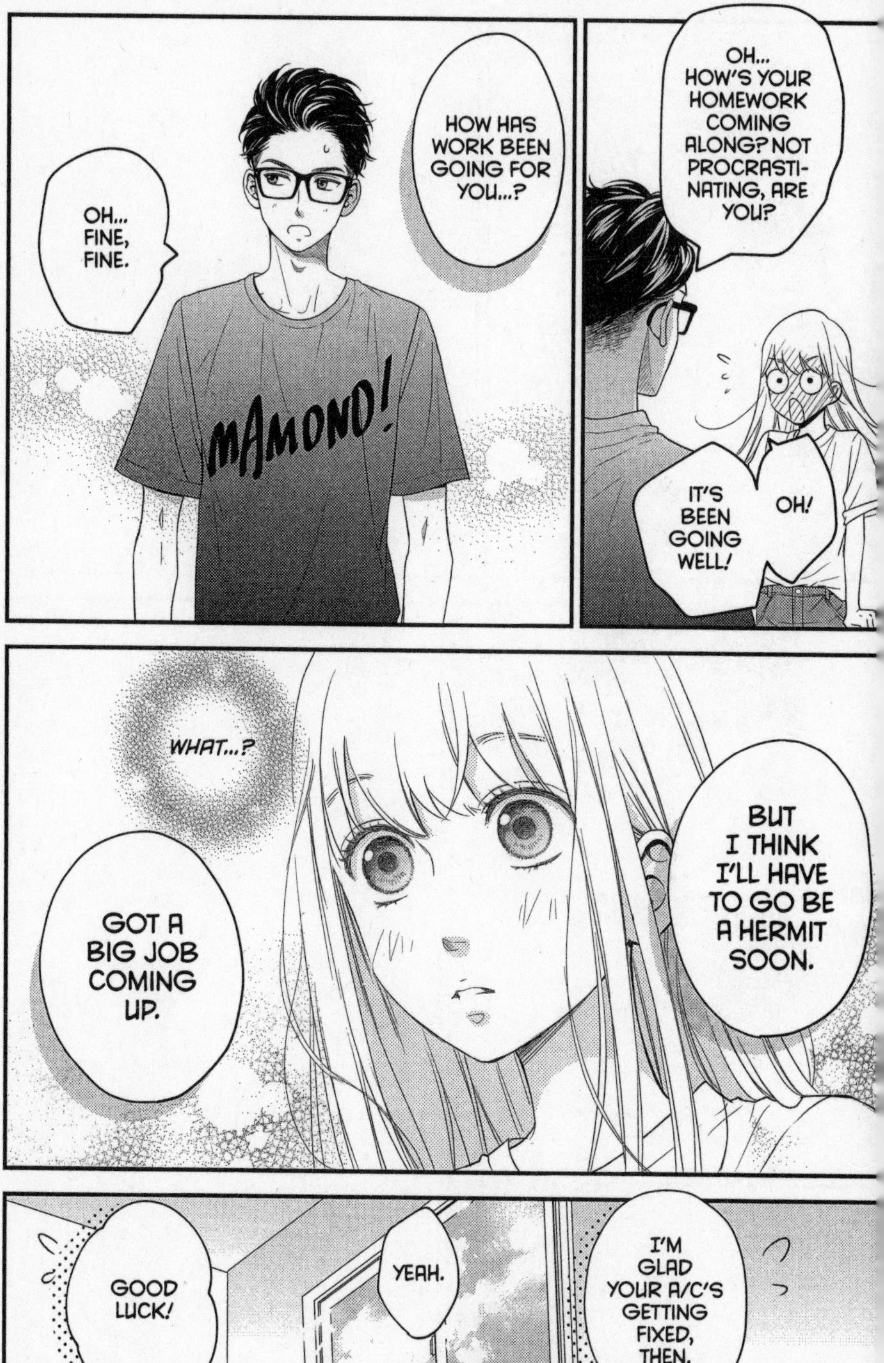
OH... HOW'S YOUR HOMEWORK COMING ALONG? NOT PROCRASTI-NATING, ARE YOU?
OH!
IT'S BEEN GOING WELL!
HOW HAS WORK BEEN GOING FOR YOU...?
OH... FINE, FINE.
MAMONO!
BUT I THINK I'LL HAVE TO GO BE A HERMIT SOON.
WHAT...?
GOT A BIG JOB COMING UP.
I'M GLAD YOUR A/C'S GETTING FIXED, THEN.
YEAH.
GOOD LUCK!

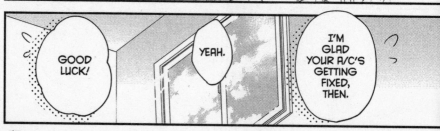

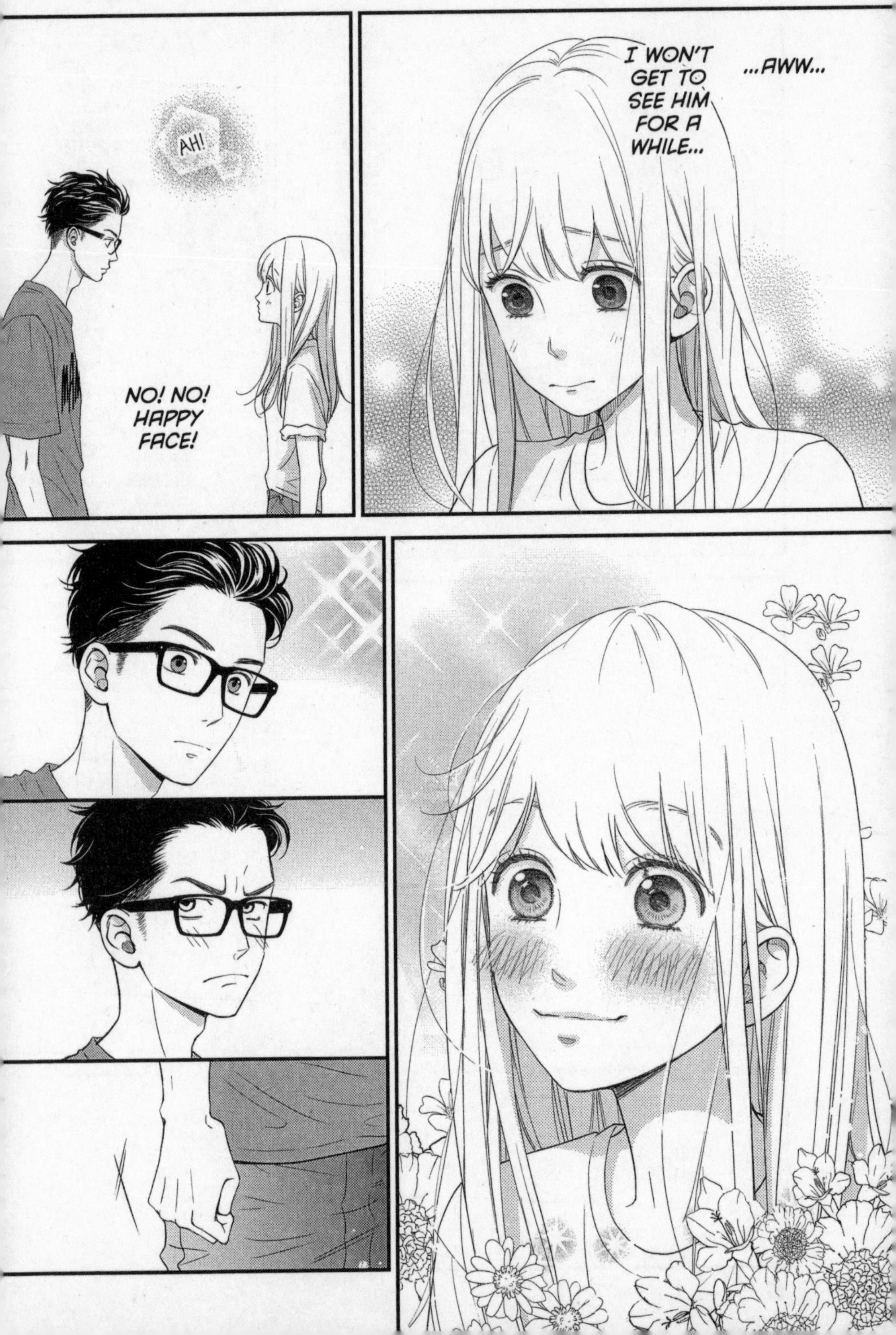
...AWW...
I WON'T GET TO SEE HIM FOR A WHILE...
AH!
NO! NO! HAPPY FACE!

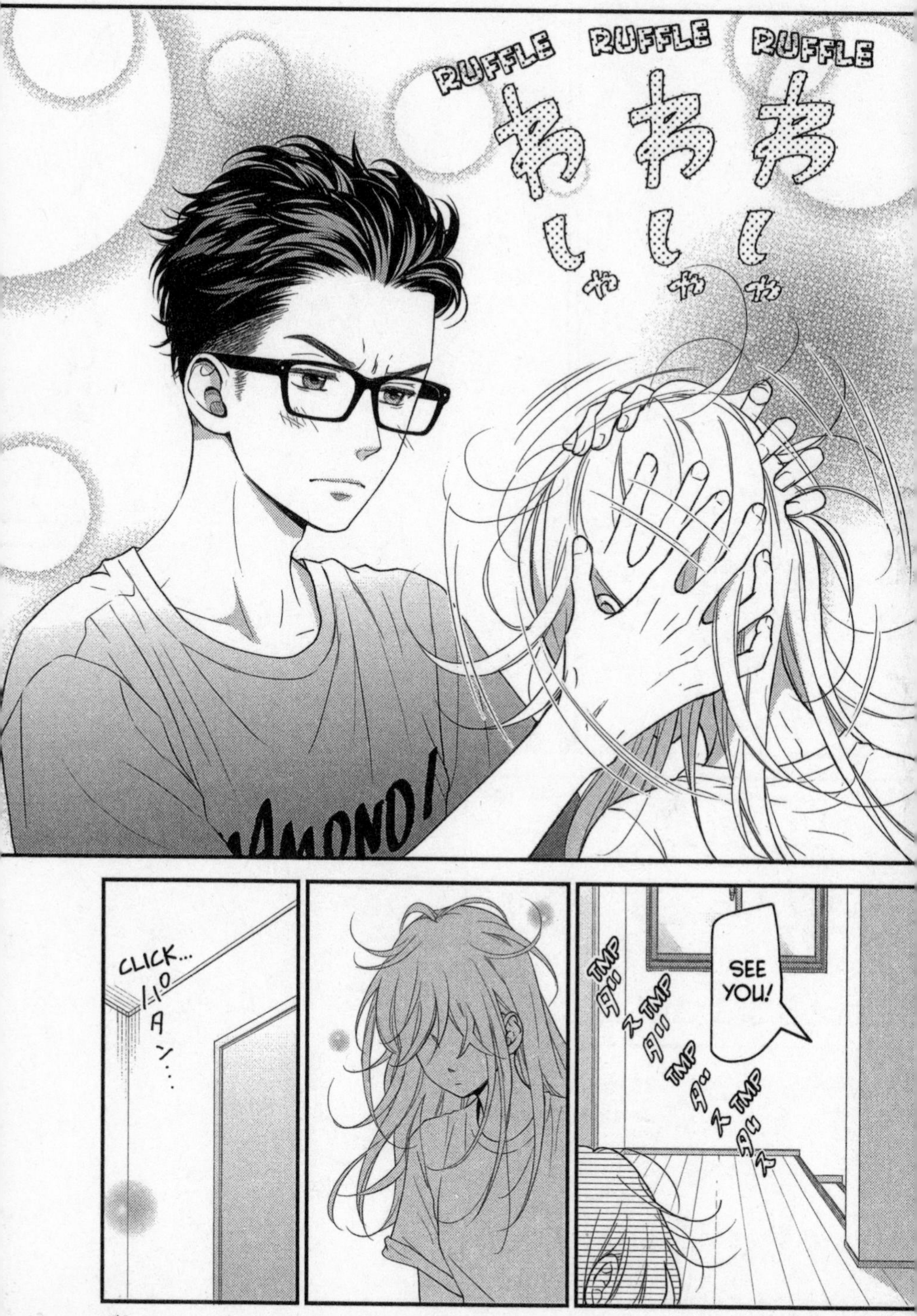
RUFFLE RUFFLE RUFFLE
わしゃわしゃわしゃ
SEE YOU!
TMP TMP TMP TMP
ダッダッダッダッ
CLICK...
パタン...

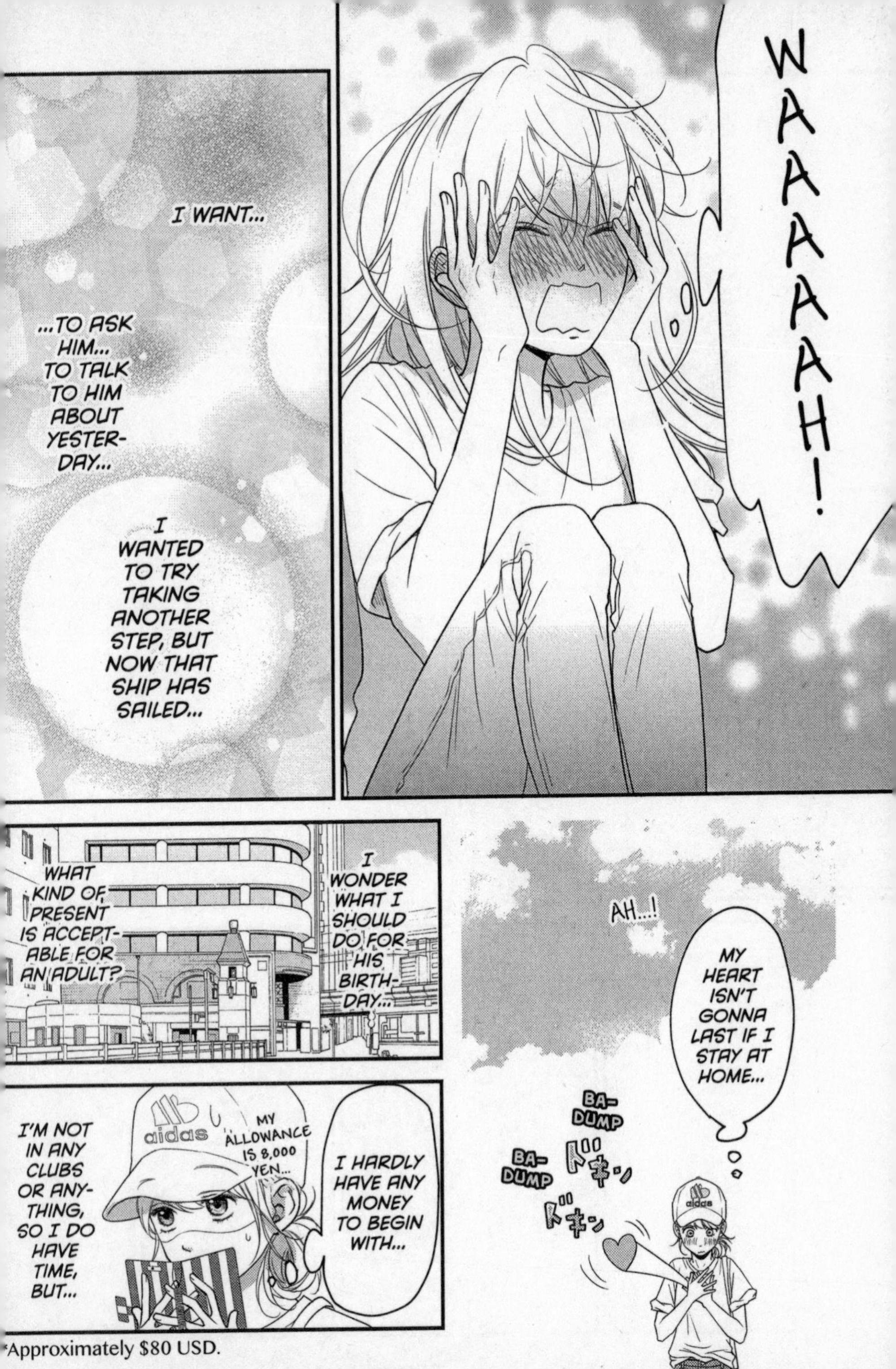
WAAAAAH!
I WANT...
...TO ASK HIM... TO TALK TO HIM ABOUT YESTERDAY...
I WANTED TO TRY TAKING ANOTHER STEP, BUT NOW THAT SHIP HAS SAILED...
AH...!
MY HEART ISN'T GONNA LAST IF I STAY AT HOME...
BA-DUMP
ドキン
BA-DUMP
ドキン
I WONDER WHAT I SHOULD DO FOR HIS BIRTHDAY...
WHAT KIND OF PRESENT IS ACCEPTABLE FOR AN ADULT?
I HARDLY HAVE ANY MONEY TO BEGIN WITH...
MY ALLOWANCE IS 8,000 YEN...
I'M NOT IN ANY CLUBS OR ANYTHING, SO I DO HAVE TIME, BUT...

*Approximately $80 USD.

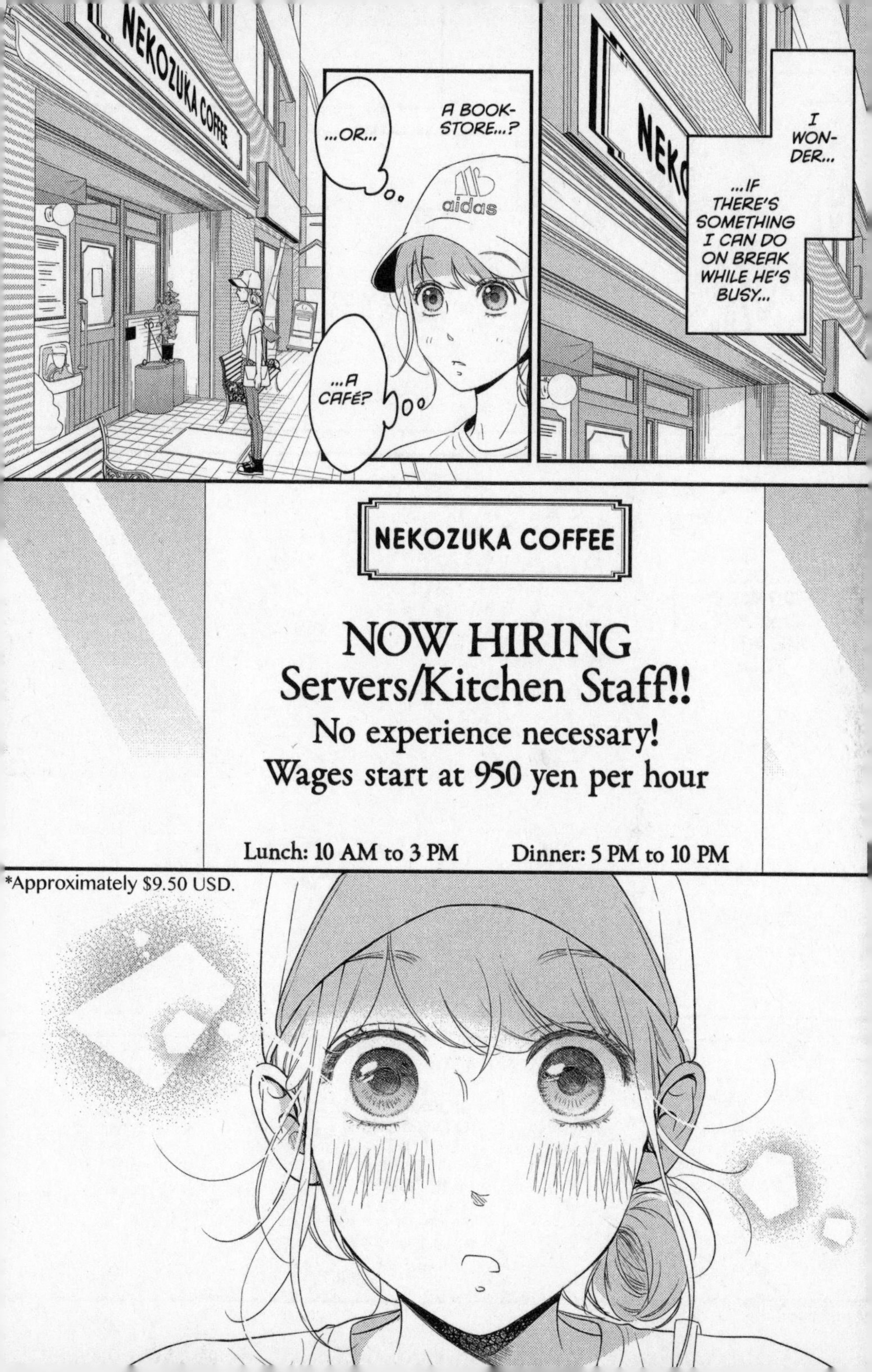
NEKO
I WONDER...
...IF THERE'S SOMETHING I CAN DO ON BREAK WHILE HE'S BUSY...
A BOOK-STORE...?
...OR...
...A CAFÉ?
aidas
NEKOZUKA COFFEE
NEKOZUKA COFFEE
NOW HIRING
Servers/Kitchen Staff!!
No experience necessary!
Wages start at 950 yen per hour
Lunch: 10 AM to 3 PM
Dinner: 5 PM to 10 PM

*Approximately $9.50 USD.

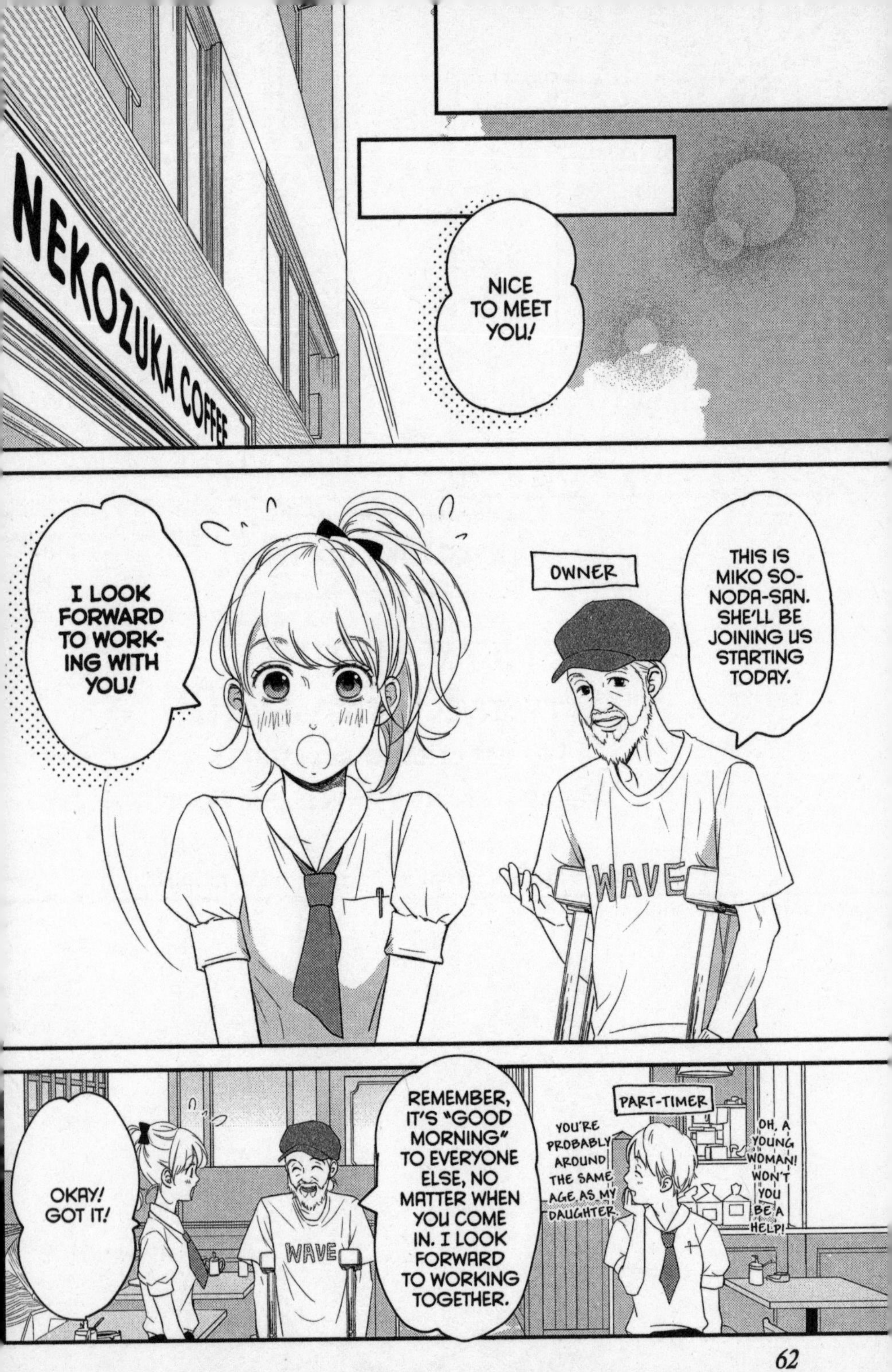
NEKOZUKA COFFEE
NICE TO MEET YOU!
THIS IS MIKO SONODA-SAN. SHE'LL BE JOINING US STARTING TODAY.
OWNER
I LOOK FORWARD TO WORKING WITH YOU!
PART-TIMER
OH, A YOUNG WOMAN! WON'T YOU BE A HELP!
YOU'RE PROBABLY AROUND THE SAME AGE AS MY DAUGHTER.
REMEMBER, IT'S "GOOD MORNING" TO EVERYONE ELSE, NO MATTER WHEN YOU COME IN. I LOOK FORWARD TO WORKING TOGETHER.
OKAY! GOT IT!

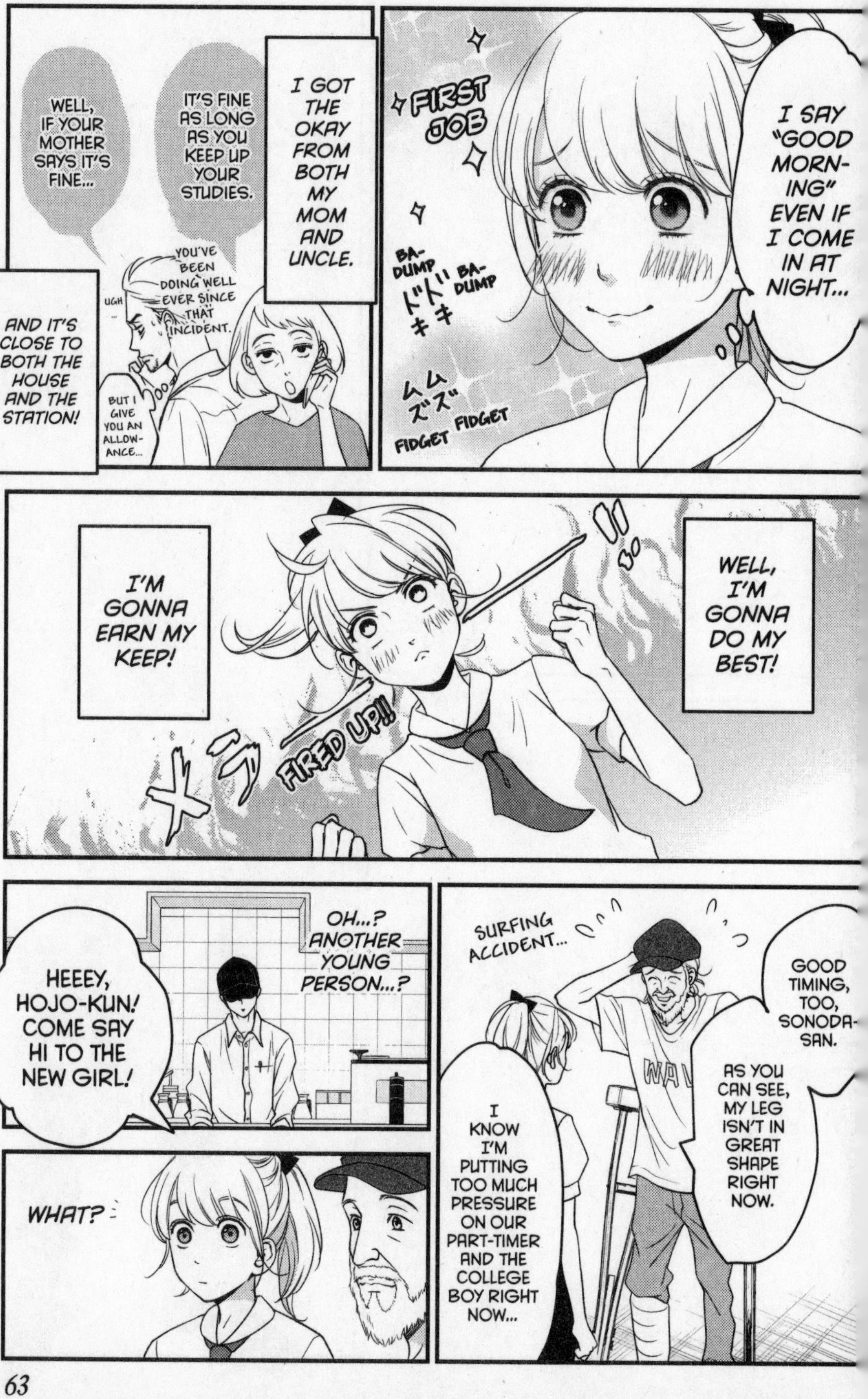

I SAY "GOOD MORNING" EVEN IF I COME IN AT NIGHT...
FIRST JOB
ドキドキ
BA-DUMP BA-DUMP
ムズムズ
FIDGET FIDGET
I GOT THE OKAY FROM BOTH MY MOM AND UNCLE.
IT'S FINE AS LONG AS YOU KEEP UP YOUR STUDIES.
WELL, IF YOUR MOTHER SAYS IT'S FINE...
YOU'VE BEEN DOING WELL EVER SINCE THAT INCIDENT.
UGH...
BUT I GIVE YOU AN ALLOWANCE...
AND IT'S CLOSE TO BOTH THE HOUSE AND THE STATION!
WELL, I'M GONNA DO MY BEST!
メラ
FIRED UP!!
I'M GONNA EARN MY KEEP!
GOOD TIMING, TOO, SONODA-SAN.
SURFING ACCIDENT...
AS YOU CAN SEE, MY LEG ISN'T IN GREAT SHAPE RIGHT NOW.
I KNOW I'M PUTTING TOO MUCH PRESSURE ON OUR PART-TIMER AND THE COLLEGE BOY RIGHT NOW...
OH...? ANOTHER YOUNG PERSON...?
HEEEY, HOJO-KUN! COME SAY HI TO THE NEW GIRL!
WHAT?

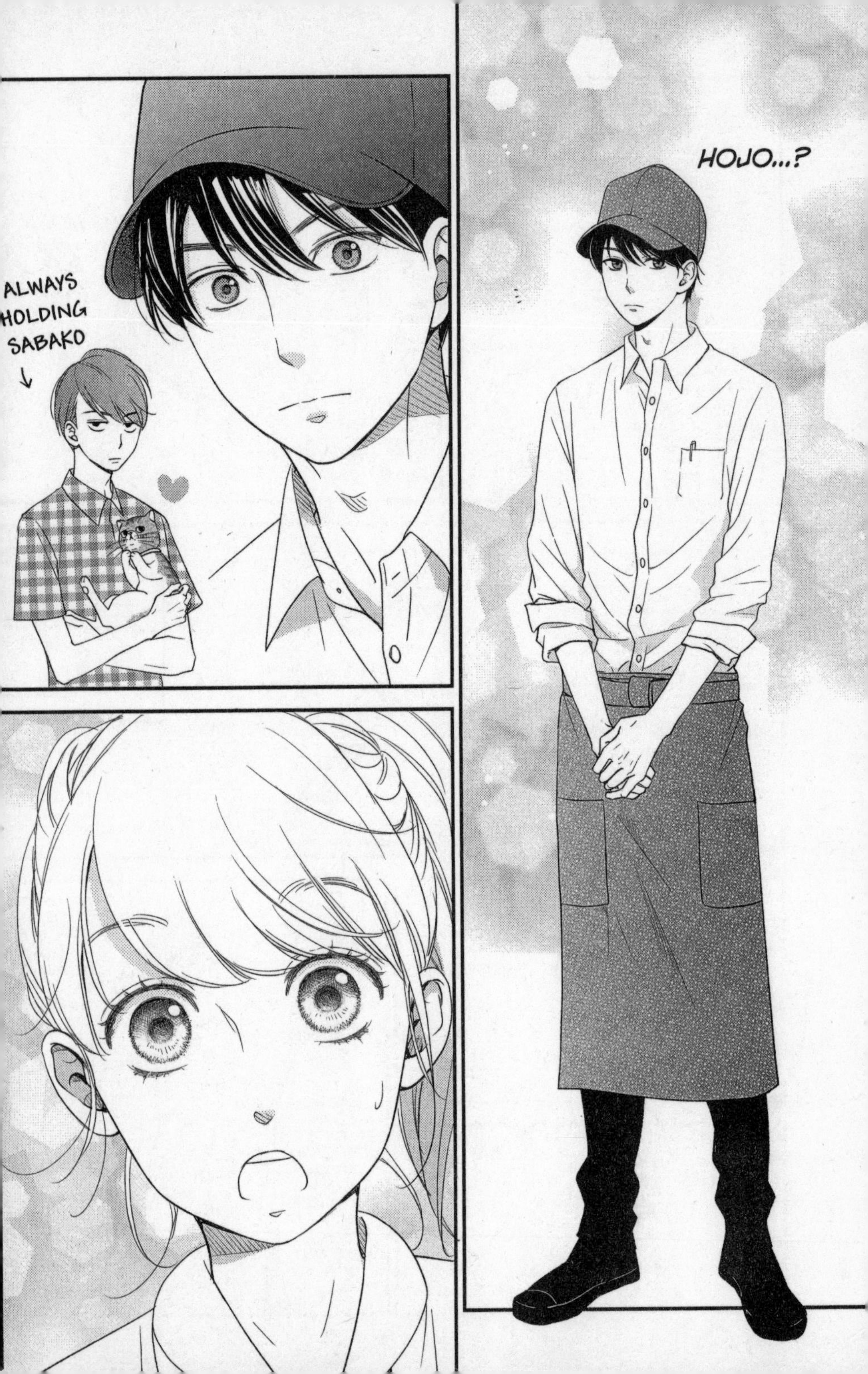
HOJO...?
ALWAYS HOLDING SABAKO

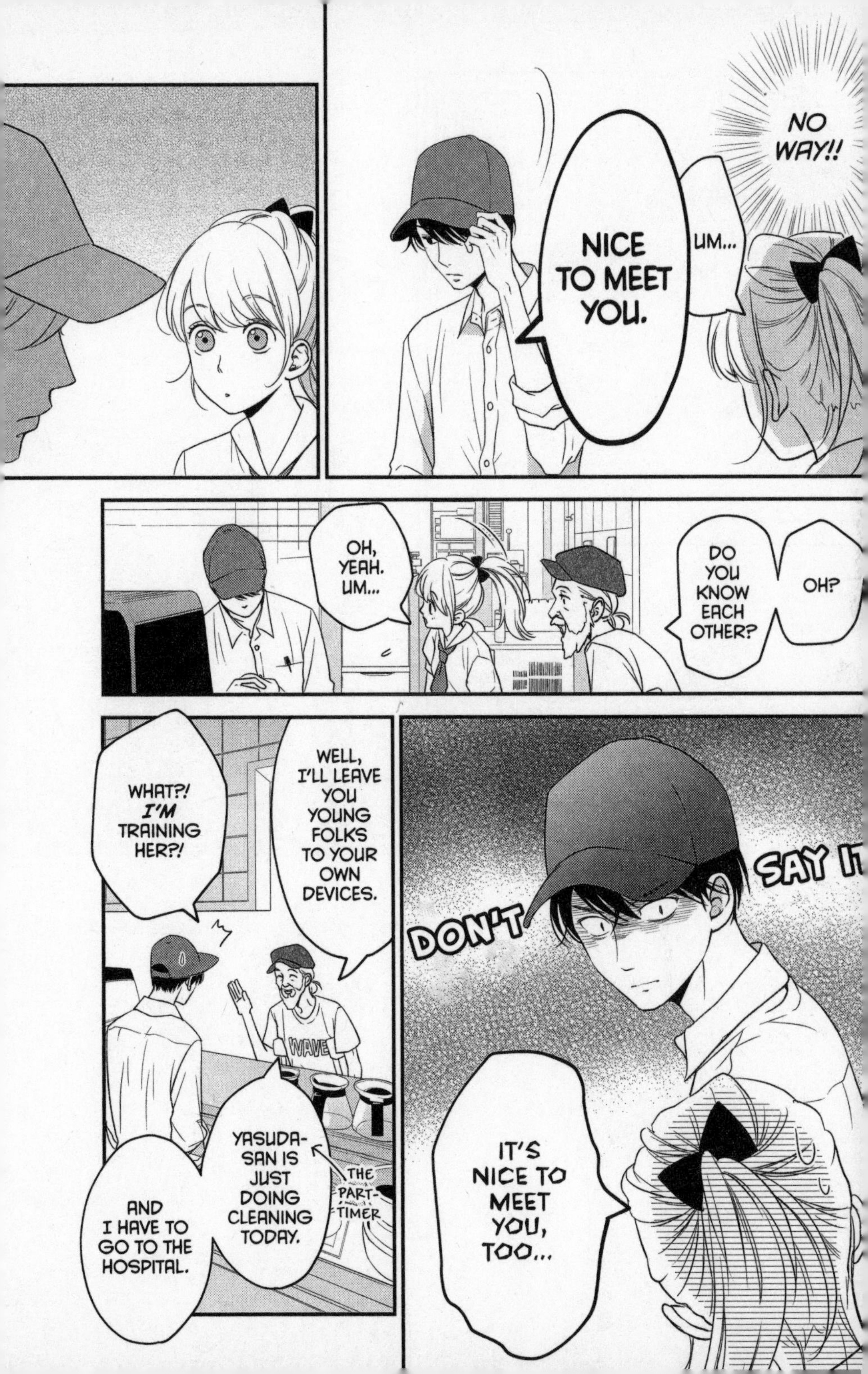
NO WAY!!
UM...
NICE TO MEET YOU.
OH?
DO YOU KNOW EACH OTHER?
OH, YEAH. UM...
SAY IT
DON'T
IT'S NICE TO MEET YOU, TOO...
WELL, I'LL LEAVE YOU YOUNG FOLKS TO YOUR OWN DEVICES.
WHAT?! *I'M* TRAINING HER?!
YASUDA-SAN IS JUST DOING CLEANING TODAY.
THE PART-TIMER
AND I HAVE TO GO TO THE HOSPITAL.

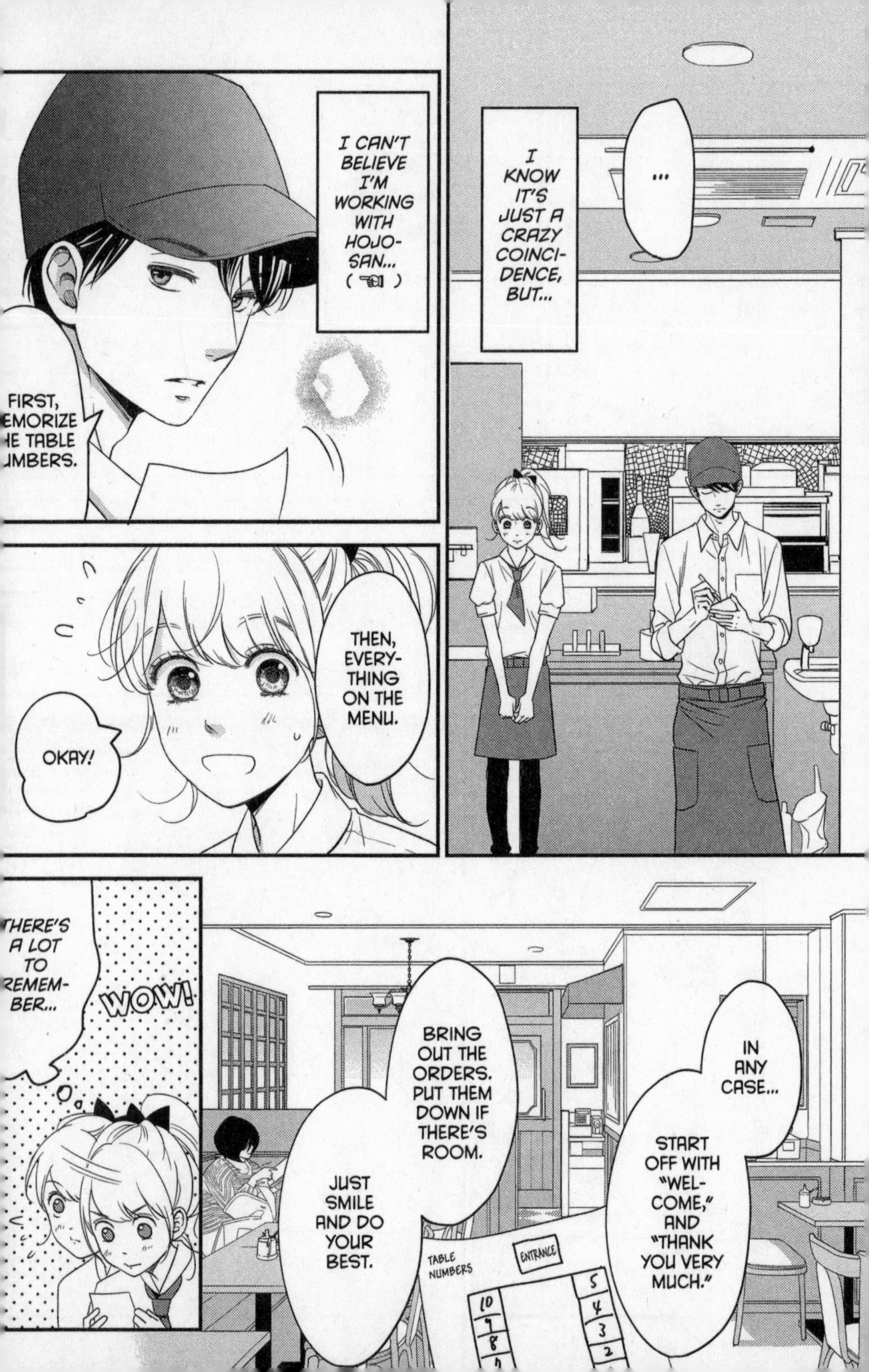
...
I KNOW IT'S JUST A CRAZY COINCIDENCE, BUT...
I CAN'T BELIEVE I'M WORKING WITH HOJO-SAN... (☜)
FIRST, EMORIZE IE TABLE JMBERS.
THEN, EVERYTHING ON THE MENU.
OKAY!
IN ANY CASE...
START OFF WITH "WELCOME," AND "THANK YOU VERY MUCH."
BRING OUT THE ORDERS. PUT THEM DOWN IF THERE'S ROOM.
JUST SMILE AND DO YOUR BEST.
TABLE NUMBERS
ENTRANCE
10 9 8 5 4 3 2
WOW!
THERE'S A LOT TO REMEM-BER...

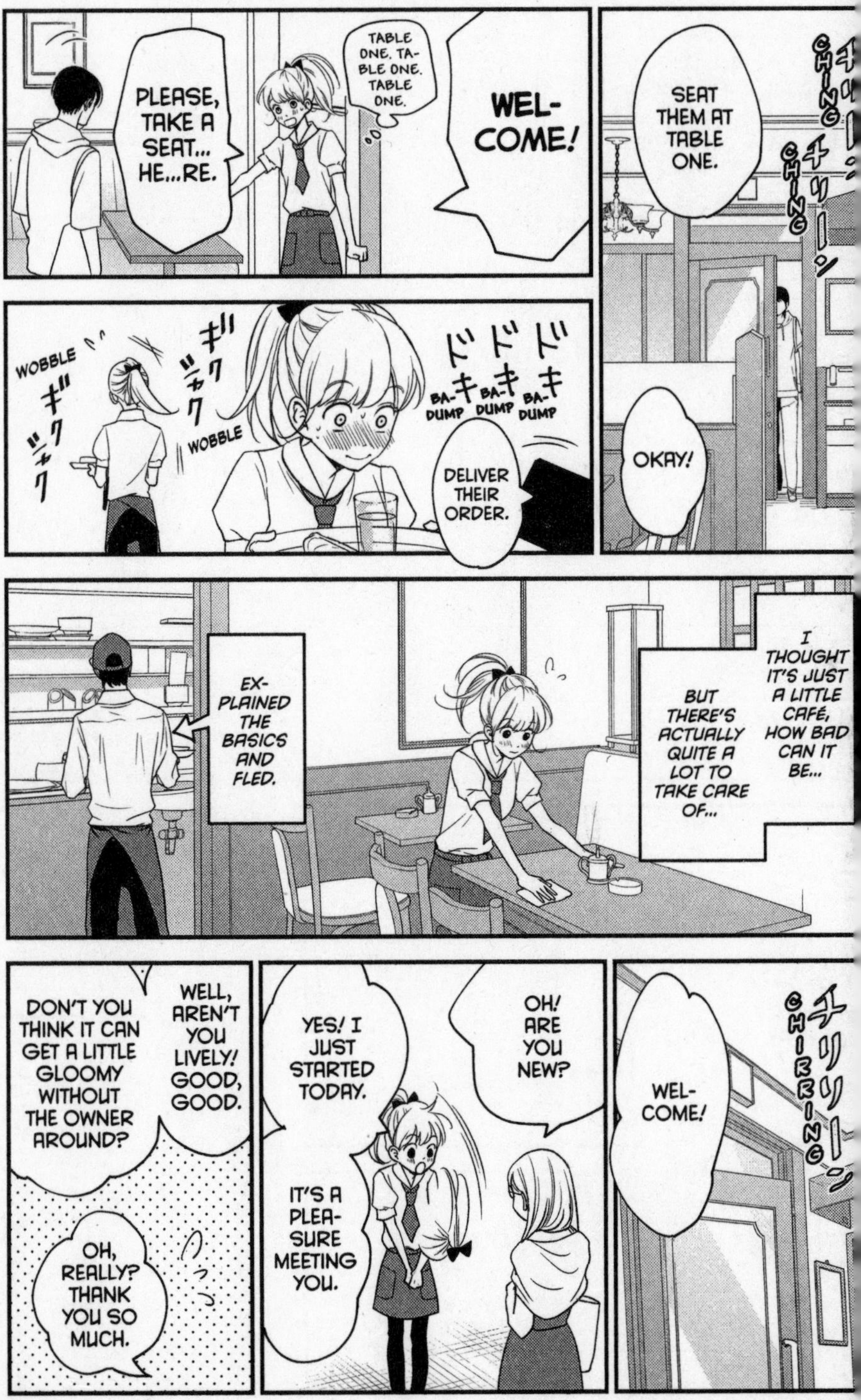
CHING
CHING
SEAT THEM AT TABLE ONE.
OKAY!
WEL-COME!
TABLE ONE. TA-BLE ONE. TABLE ONE.
PLEASE, TAKE A SEAT... HE...RE.
DELIVER THEIR ORDER.
ドキ BA-DUMP
ドキ BA-DUMP
ドキ BA-DUMP
ギクシャク WOBBLE
ギクシャク WOBBLE
I THOUGHT IT'S JUST A LITTLE CAFÉ, HOW BAD CAN IT BE...
BUT THERE'S ACTUALLY QUITE A LOT TO TAKE CARE OF...
EX-PLAINED THE BASICS AND FLED.
CHIRRING
WEL-COME!
OH! ARE YOU NEW?
YES! I JUST STARTED TODAY.
IT'S A PLEA-SURE MEETING YOU.
WELL, AREN'T YOU LIVELY! GOOD, GOOD.
DON'T YOU THINK IT CAN GET A LITTLE GLOOMY WITHOUT THE OWNER AROUND?
OH, REALLY? THANK YOU SO MUCH.

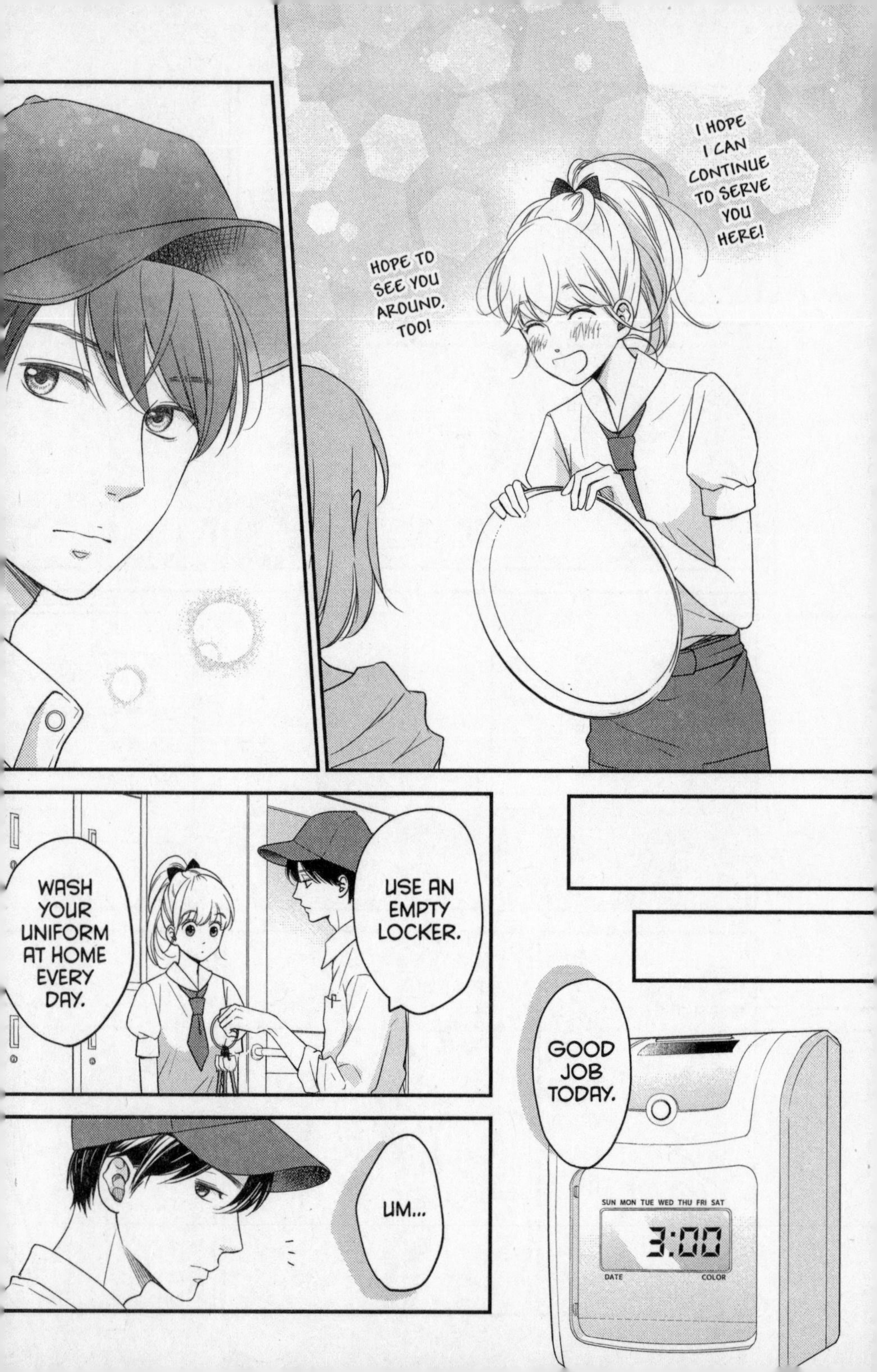
I HOPE I CAN CONTINUE TO SERVE YOU HERE!
HOPE TO SEE YOU AROUND, TOO!
GOOD JOB TODAY.
SUN MON TUE WED THU FRI SAT
3:00
DATE
COLOR
USE AN EMPTY LOCKER.
WASH YOUR UNIFORM AT HOME EVERY DAY.
UM...

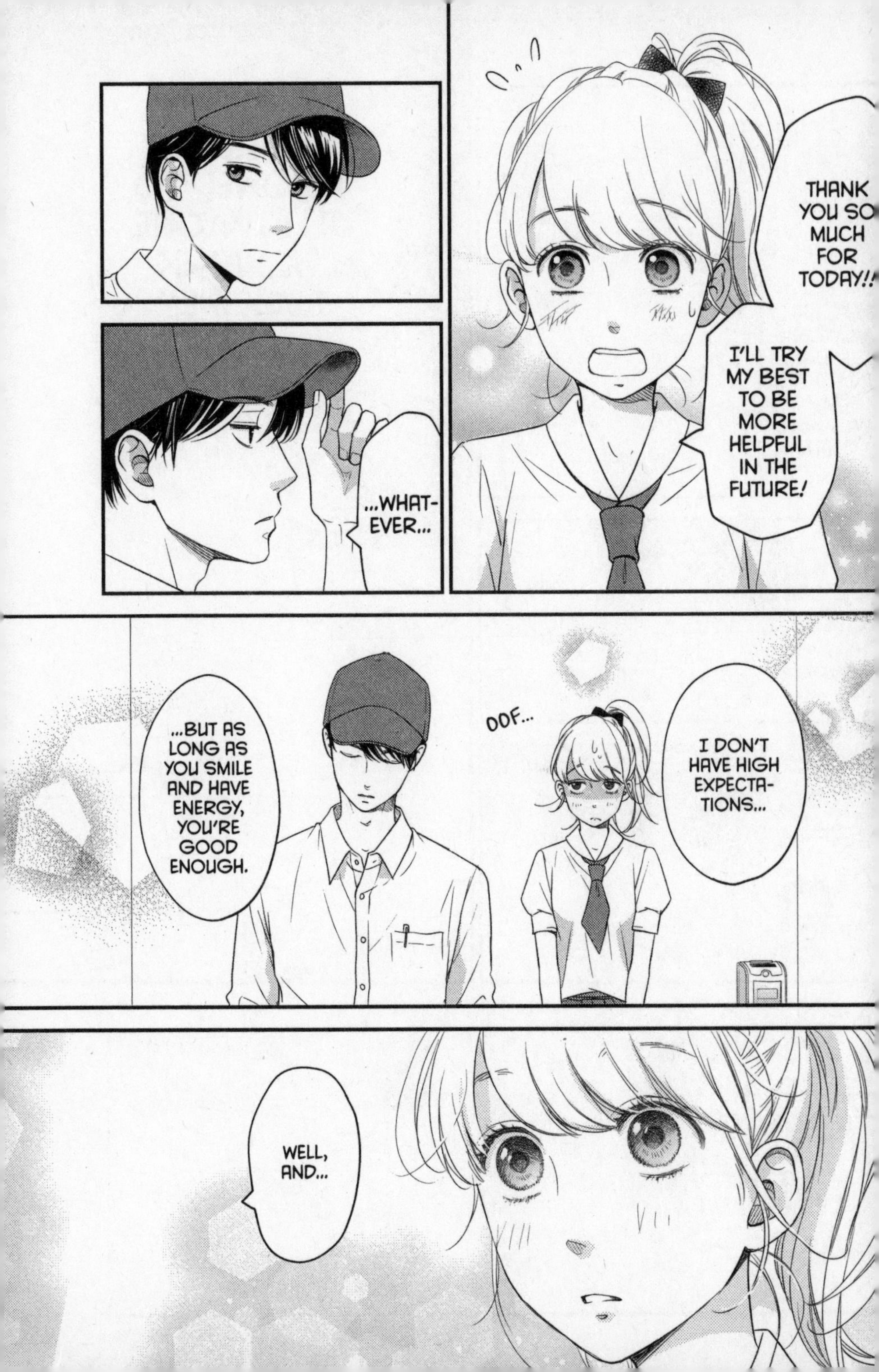
THANK YOU SO MUCH FOR TODAY!!
I'LL TRY MY BEST TO BE MORE HELPFUL IN THE FUTURE!
...WHATEVER...
I DON'T HAVE HIGH EXPECTATIONS...
OOF...
...BUT AS LONG AS YOU SMILE AND HAVE ENERGY, YOU'RE GOOD ENOUGH.
WELL, AND...

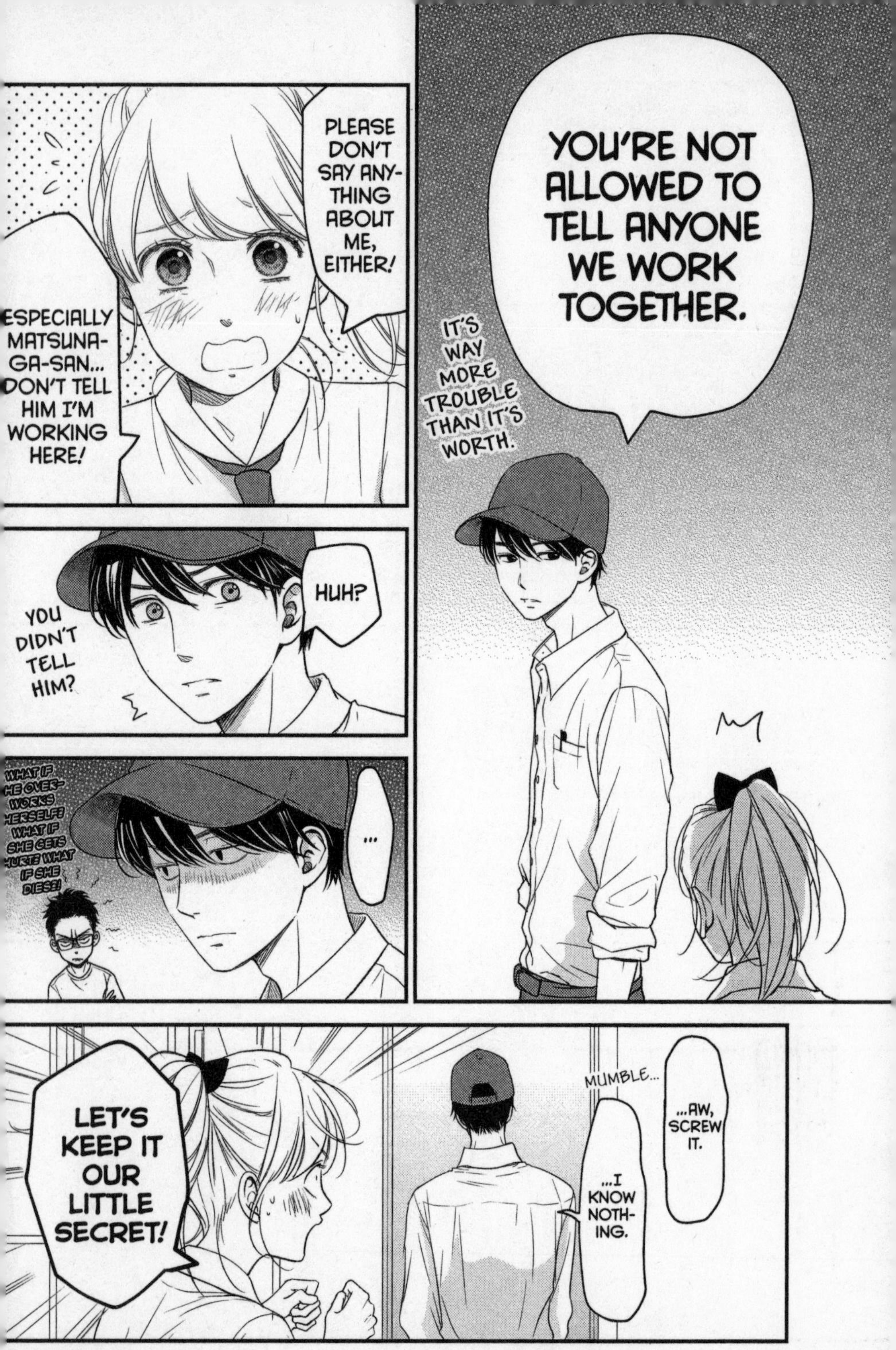
YOU'RE NOT ALLOWED TO TELL ANYONE WE WORK TOGETHER.
IT'S WAY MORE TROUBLE THAN IT'S WORTH.
PLEASE DON'T SAY ANY-THING ABOUT ME, EITHER!
ESPECIALLY MATSUNAGA-SAN... DON'T TELL HIM I'M WORKING HERE!
HUH?
YOU DIDN'T TELL HIM?
...
WHAT IF HE OVER-WORKS HERSELF? WHAT IF SHE GETS HURT? WHAT IF SHE DIES?!
...AW, SCREW IT.
MUMBLE...
...I KNOW NOTH-ING.
LET'S KEEP IT OUR LITTLE SECRET!

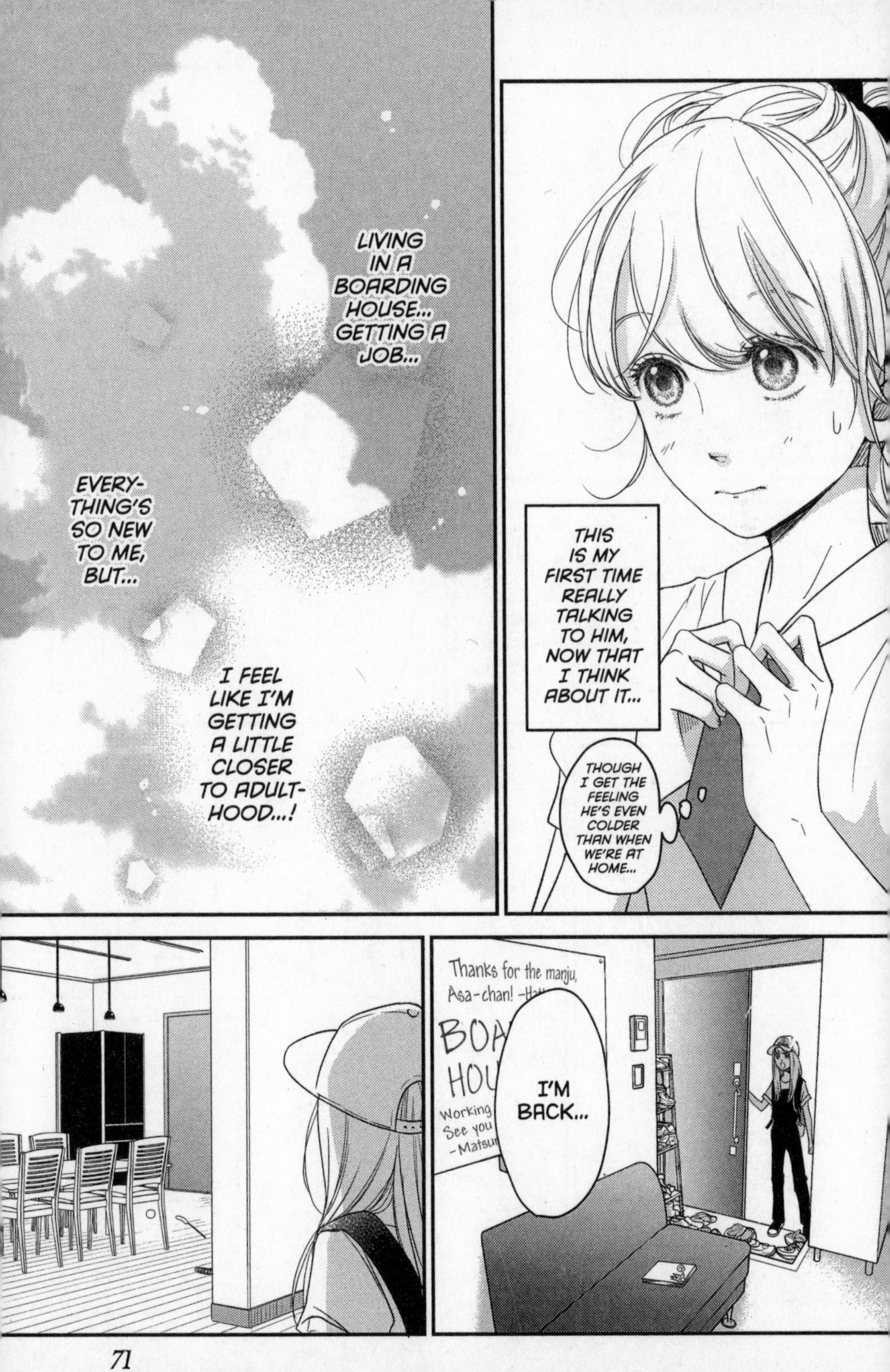
THIS IS MY FIRST TIME REALLY TALKING TO HIM, NOW THAT I THINK ABOUT IT...
THOUGH I GET THE FEELING HE'S EVEN COLDER THAN WHEN WE'RE AT HOME...
LIVING IN A BOARDING HOUSE... GETTING A JOB...
EVERY-THING'S SO NEW TO ME, BUT...
I FEEL LIKE I'M GETTING A LITTLE CLOSER TO ADULT-HOOD...!
Thanks for the manju,
Asa-chan!
I'M BACK...

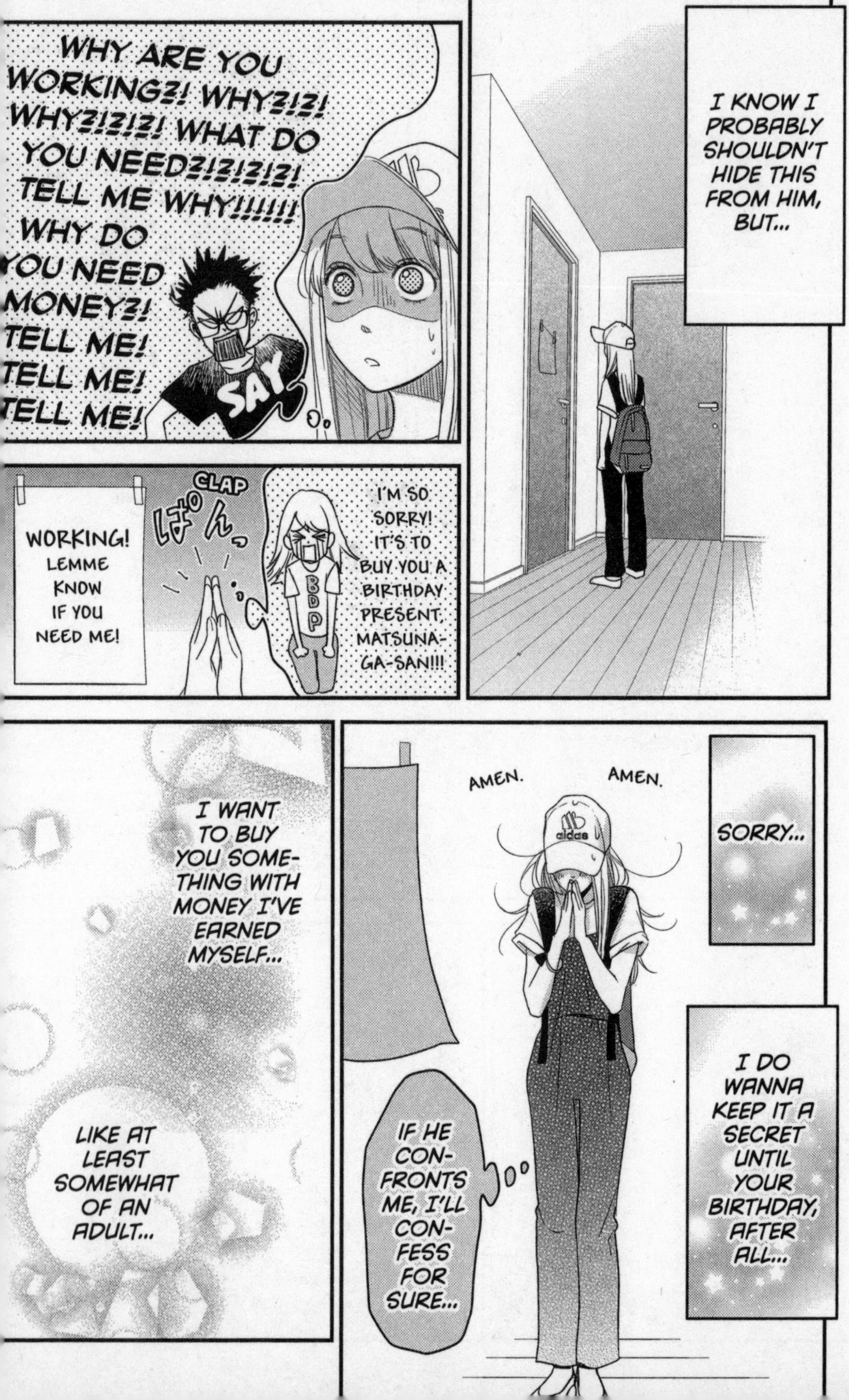
I KNOW I PROBABLY SHOULDN'T HIDE THIS FROM HIM, BUT...
WHY ARE YOU WORKING?! WHY?!?! WHY?!?!?! WHAT DO YOU NEED?!?!?!?! TELL ME WHY!!!!!! WHY DO YOU NEED MONEY?! TELL ME! TELL ME! TELL ME!
SAY
I'M SO SORRY! IT'S TO BUY YOU A BIRTHDAY PRESENT, MATSUNAGA-SAN!!!
CLAP
ぱん
WORKING! LEMME KNOW IF YOU NEED ME!
SORRY...
AMEN.
AMEN.
I DO WANNA KEEP IT A SECRET UNTIL YOUR BIRTHDAY, AFTER ALL...
IF HE CONFRONTS ME, I'LL CONFESS FOR SURE...
I WANT TO BUY YOU SOMETHING WITH MONEY I'VE EARNED MYSELF...
LIKE AT LEAST SOMEWHAT OF AN ADULT...

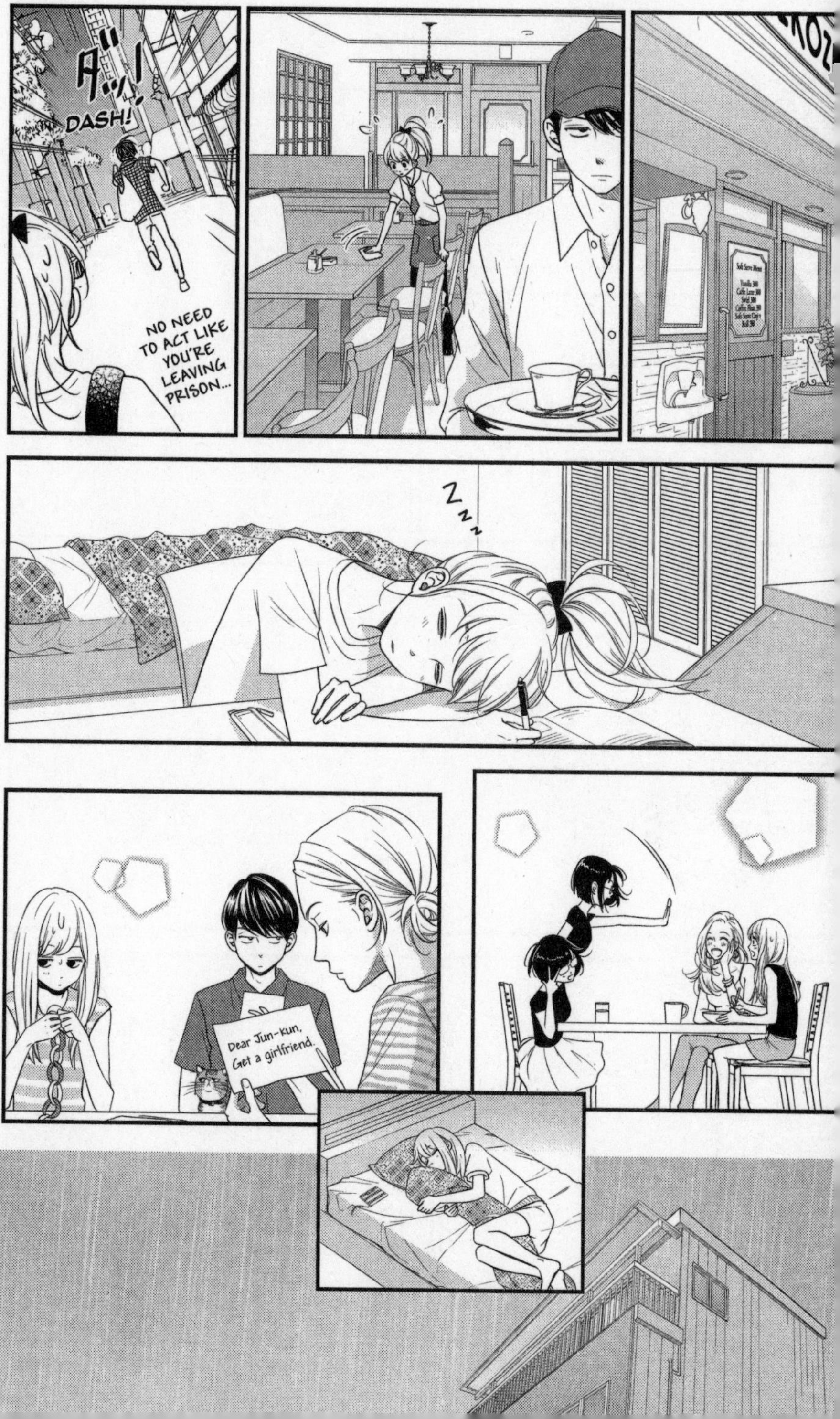
Soft Serve Menu
ダッ！
DASH!
NO NEED TO ACT LIKE YOU'RE LEAVING PRISON...
Z Z Z
Dear Jun-kun, Get a girlfriend.

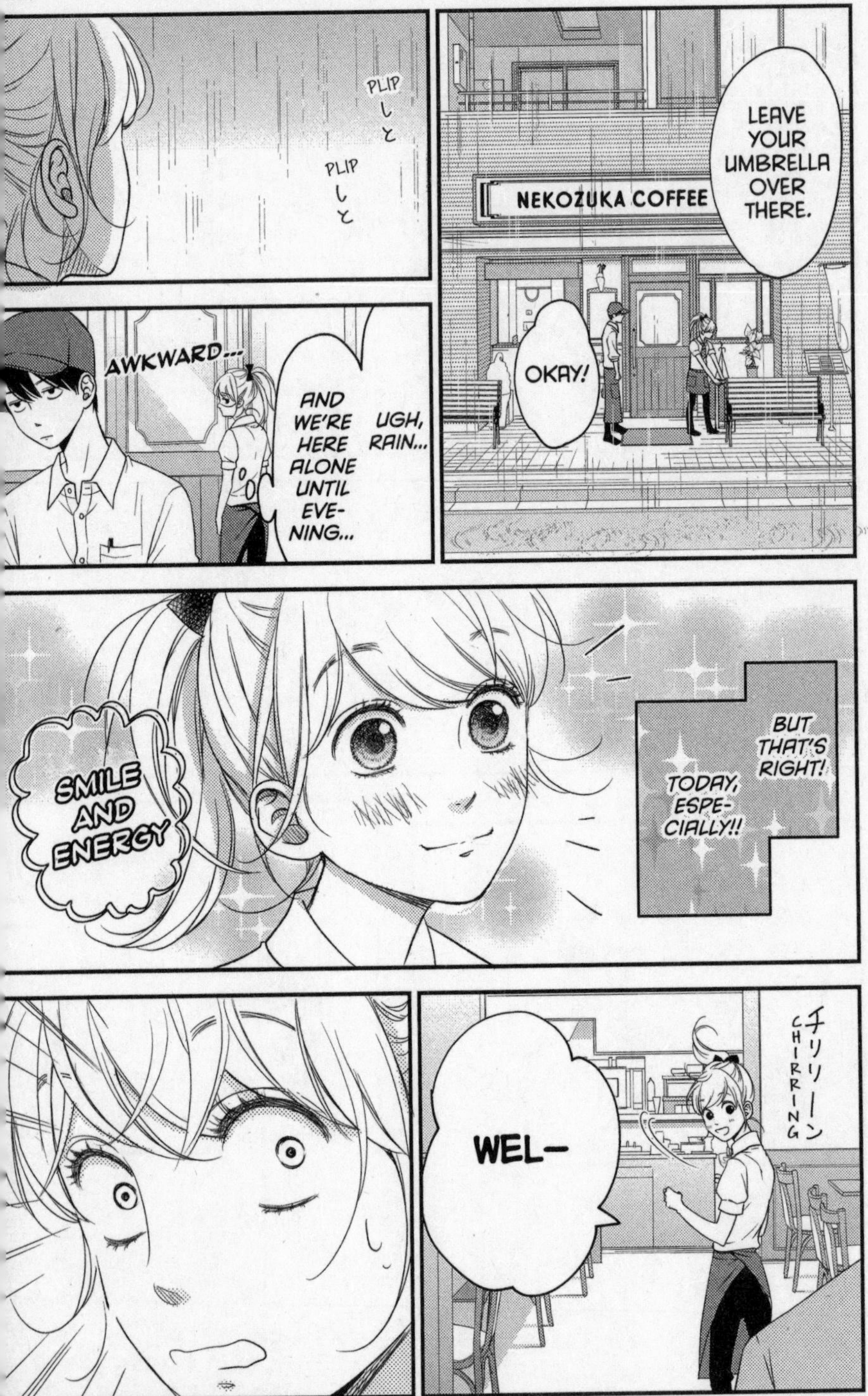
NEKOZUKA COFFEE
LEAVE YOUR UMBRELLA OVER THERE.
OKAY!
PLIP しと
PLIP しと
UGH, RAIN...
AND WE'RE HERE ALONE UNTIL EVE-NING...
AWKWARD...
BUT THAT'S RIGHT!
TODAY, ESPE-CIALLY!!
SMILE AND ENERGY
チリリーン CHIRRING
WEL-

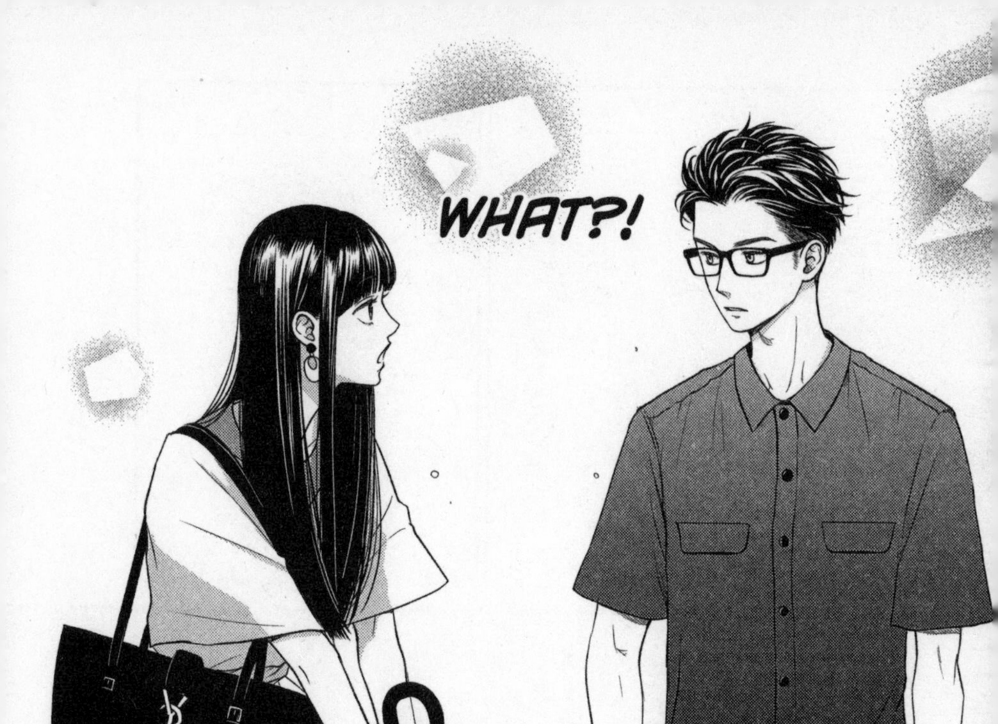
WHAT?!
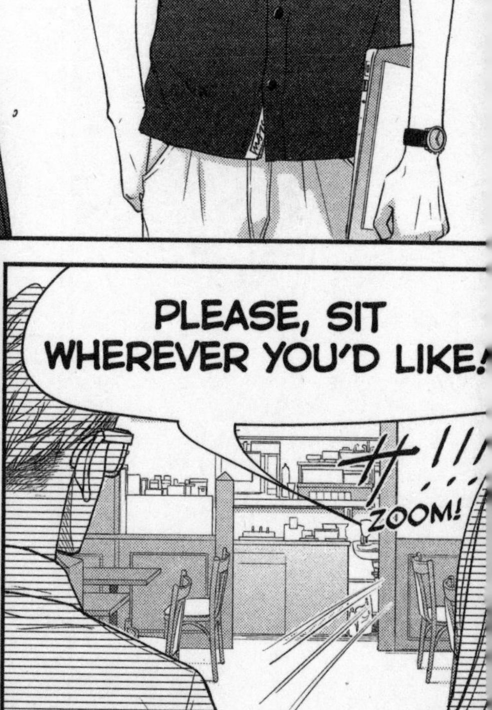
PLEASE, SIT WHEREVER YOU'D LIKE!
ZOOM!
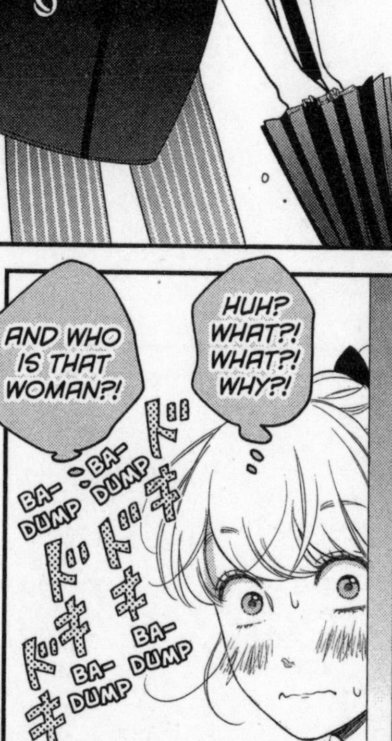
HUH? WHAT?! WHAT?! WHY?!
AND WHO IS THAT WOMAN?!
BA-DUMP
BA-DUMP
BA-DUMP
BA-DUMP

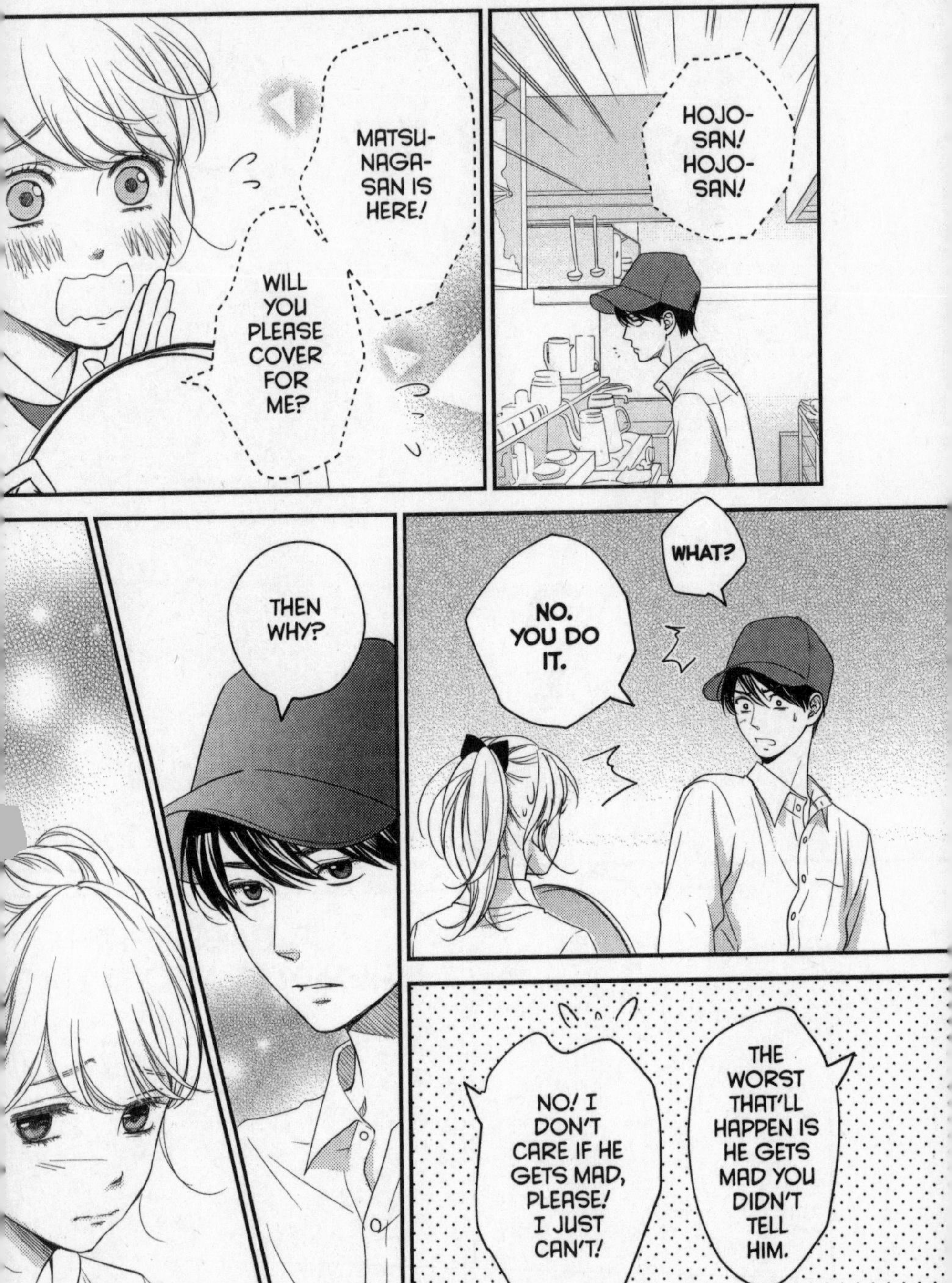
HOJO-SAN! HOJO-SAN!
MATSUNAGA-SAN IS HERE!
WILL YOU PLEASE COVER FOR ME?
WHAT?
NO. YOU DO IT.
THE WORST THAT'LL HAPPEN IS HE GETS MAD YOU DIDN'T TELL HIM.
NO! I DON'T CARE IF HE GETS MAD, PLEASE! I JUST CAN'T!
THEN WHY?

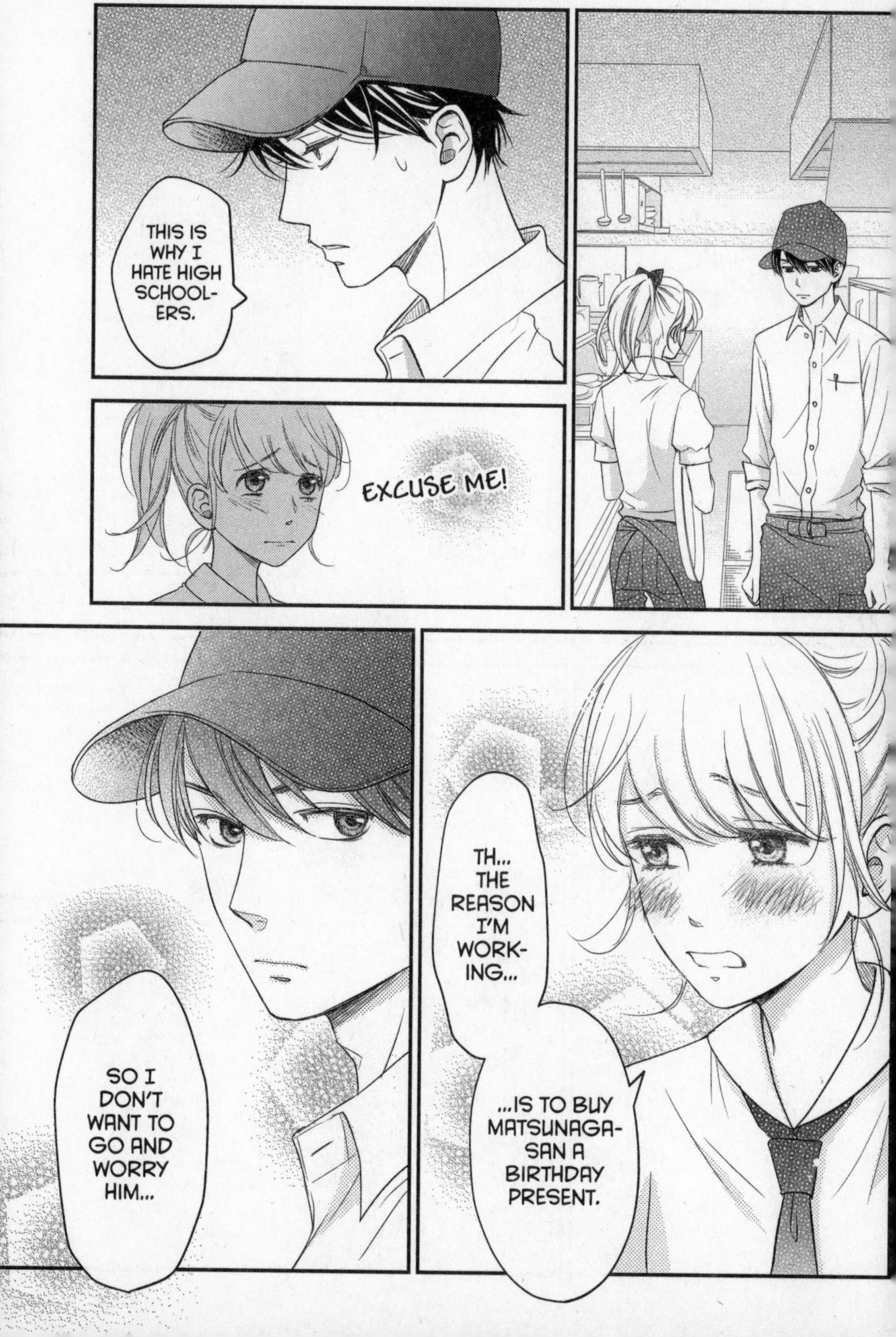
THIS IS WHY I HATE HIGH SCHOOL-ERS.
EXCUSE ME!
TH... THE REASON I'M WORK-ING...
...IS TO BUY MATSUNAGA-SAN A BIRTHDAY PRESENT.
SO I DON'T WANT TO GO AND WORRY HIM...

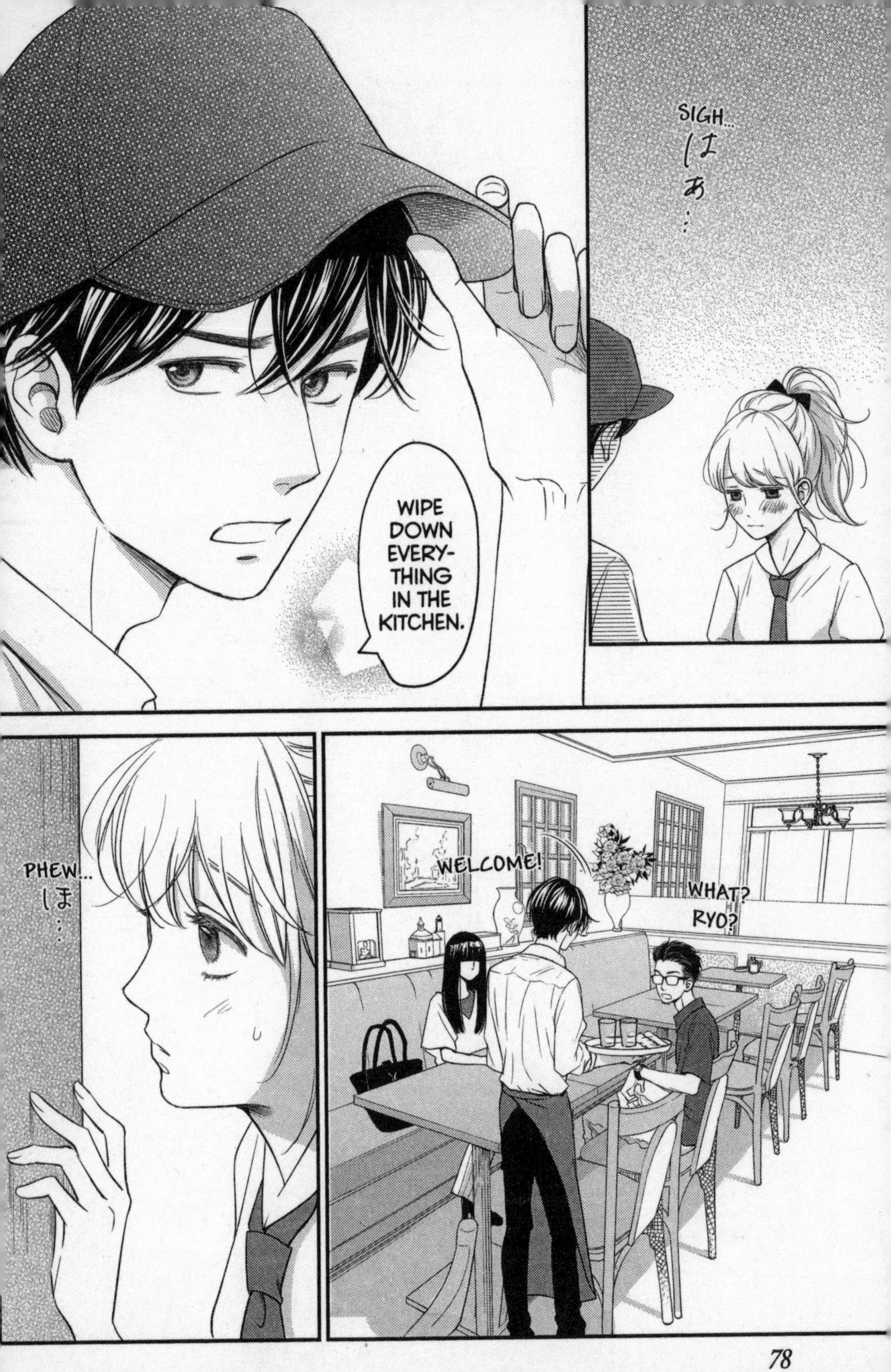
SIGH...
はあ...
WIPE DOWN EVERY-THING IN THE KITCHEN.
WELCOME!
WHAT? RYO?
PHEW...
ほ...

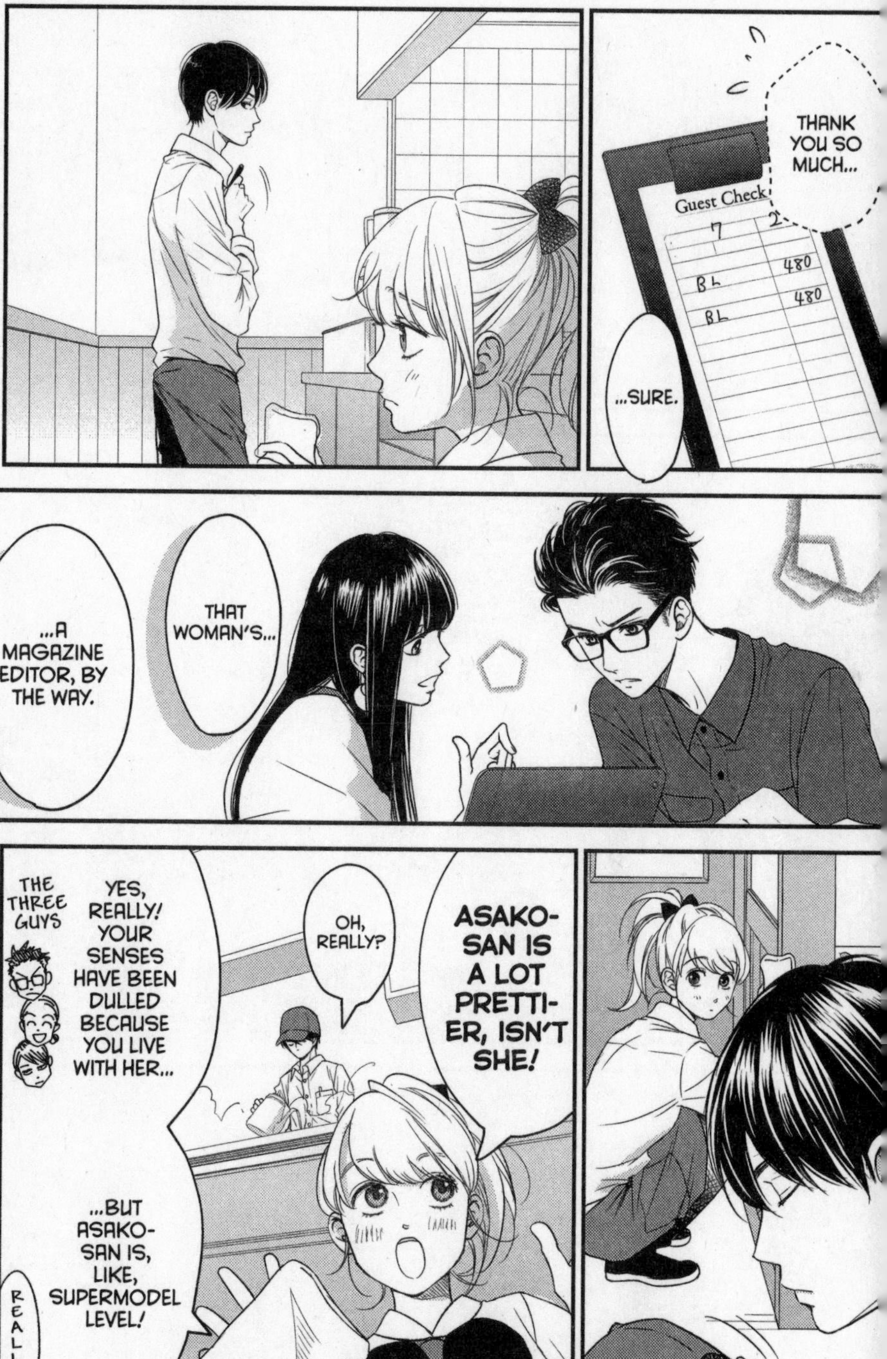
THANK YOU SO MUCH...
Guest Check
7
2
480
BL
480
BL
...SURE.
THAT WOMAN'S...
...A MAGAZINE EDITOR, BY THE WAY.
ASAKO-SAN IS A LOT PRETTIER, ISN'T SHE!
OH, REALLY?
YES, REALLY! YOUR SENSES HAVE BEEN DULLED BECAUSE YOU LIVE WITH HER...
THE THREE GUYS
...BUT ASAKO-SAN IS, LIKE, SUPERMODEL LEVEL!
REALLY?

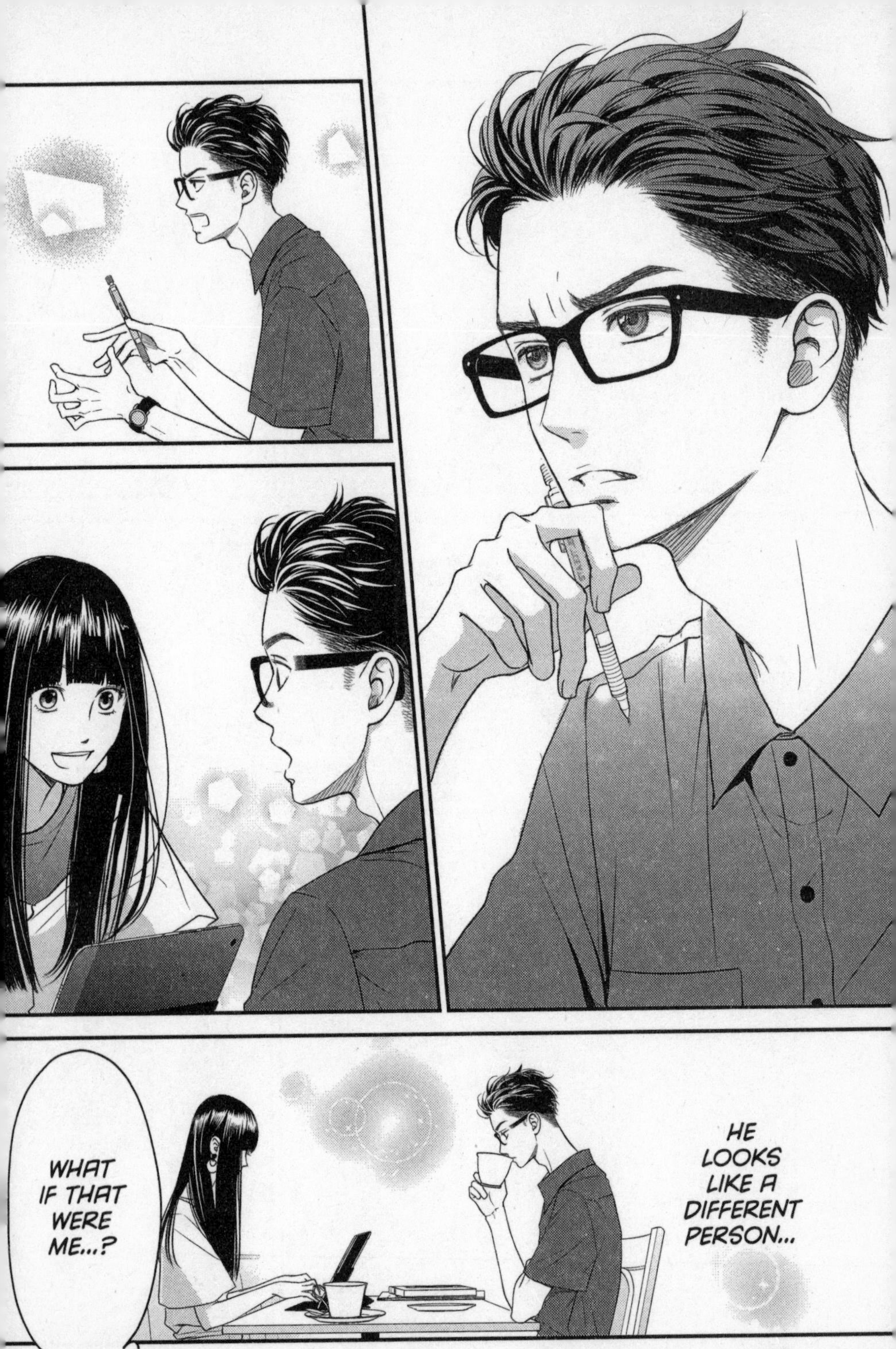
HE LOOKS LIKE A DIFFERENT PERSON...
WHAT IF THAT WERE ME...?

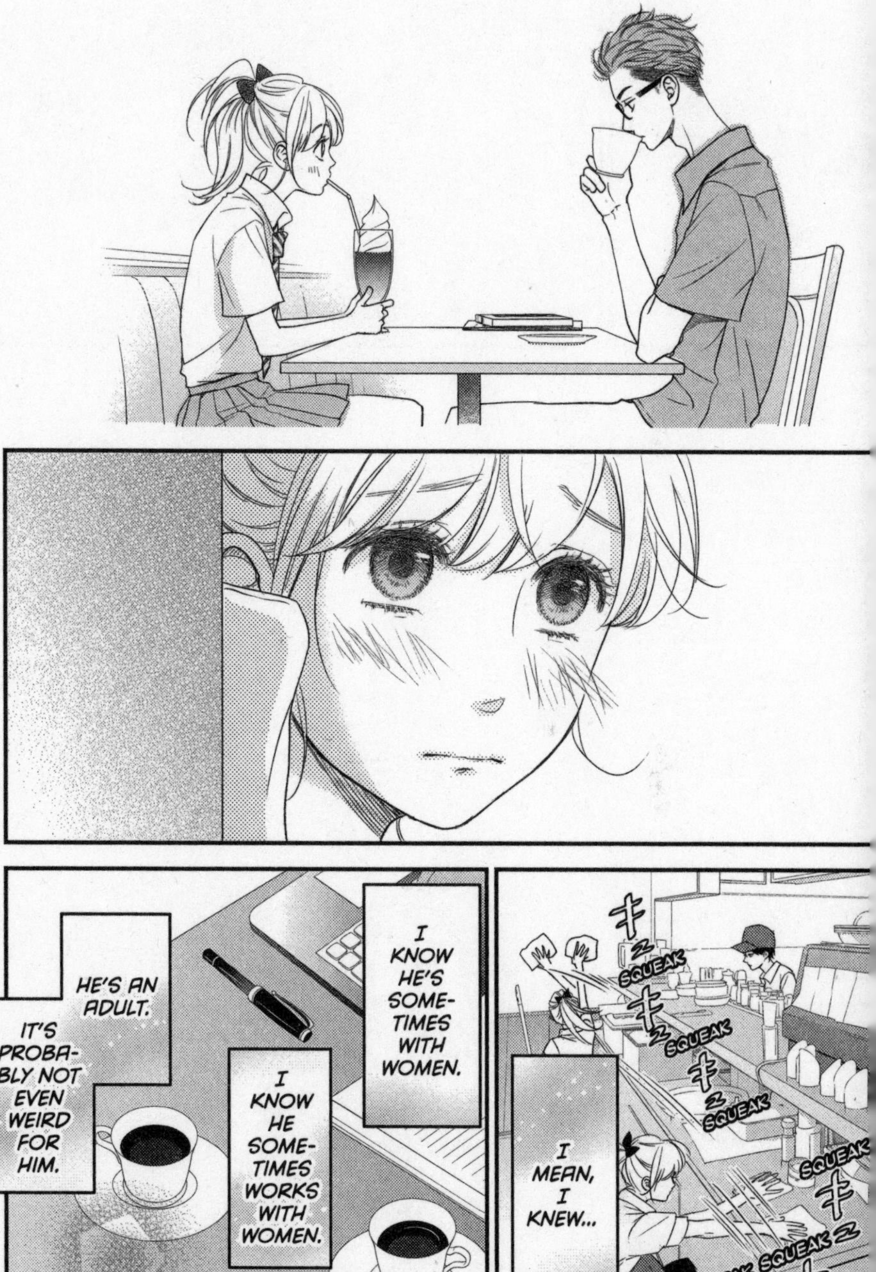
SQUEAK
SQUEAK
SQUEAK
SQUEAK
SQUEAK SQUEAK
SQUEAK
I MEAN, I KNEW...
I KNOW HE'S SOMETIMES WITH WOMEN.
I KNOW HE SOMETIMES WORKS WITH WOMEN.
HE'S AN ADULT.
IT'S PROBABLY NOT EVEN WEIRD FOR HIM.

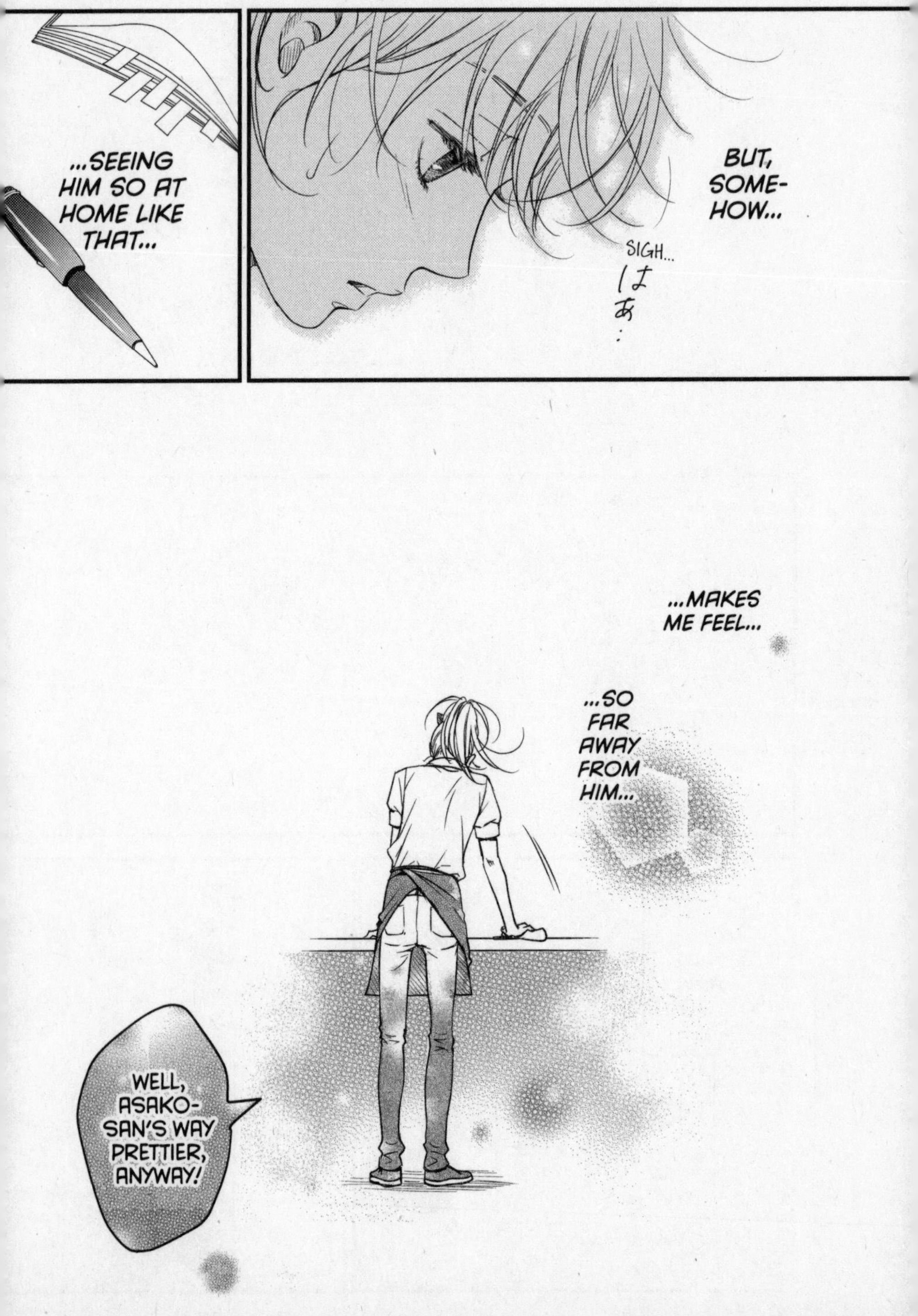
BUT, SOME-HOW...
SIGH...
はあ…
...SEEING HIM SO AT HOME LIKE THAT...
...MAKES ME FEEL...
...SO FAR AWAY FROM HIM...
WELL, ASAKO-SAN'S WAY PRETTIER, ANYWAY!

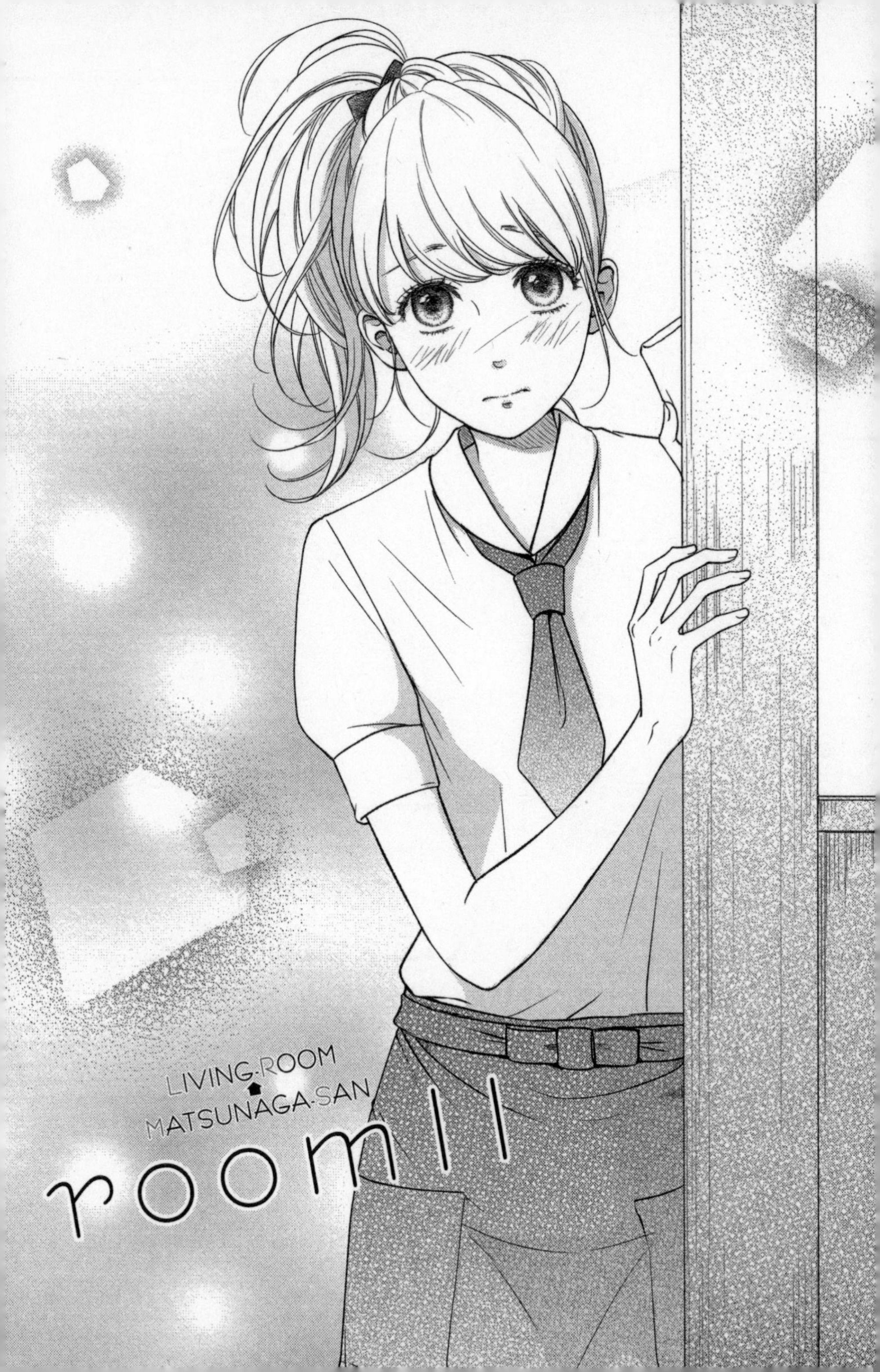
LIVING-ROOM MATSUNAGA-SAN
room11

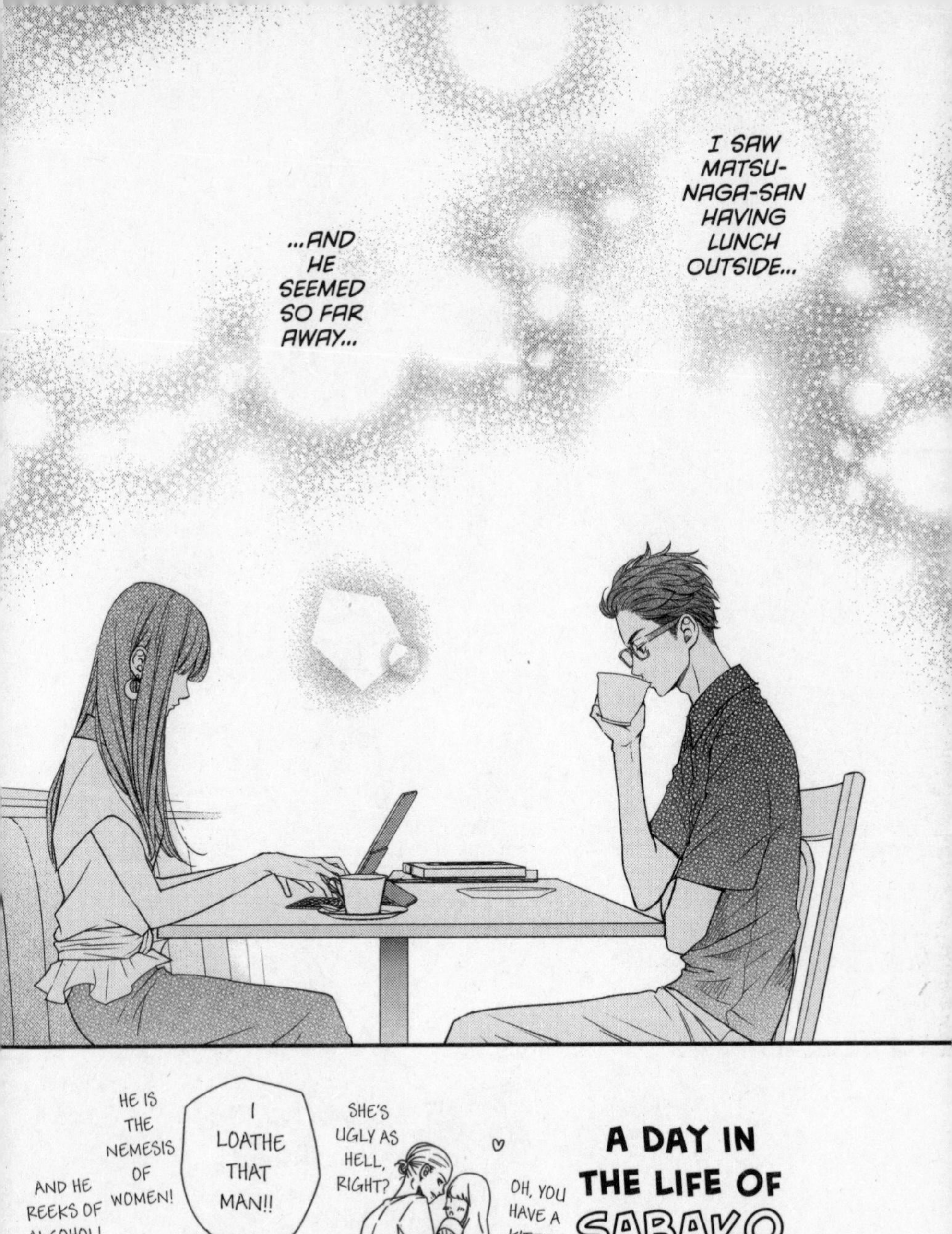
I SAW MATSU-NAGA-SAN HAVING LUNCH OUTSIDE...
...AND HE SEEMED SO FAR AWAY...

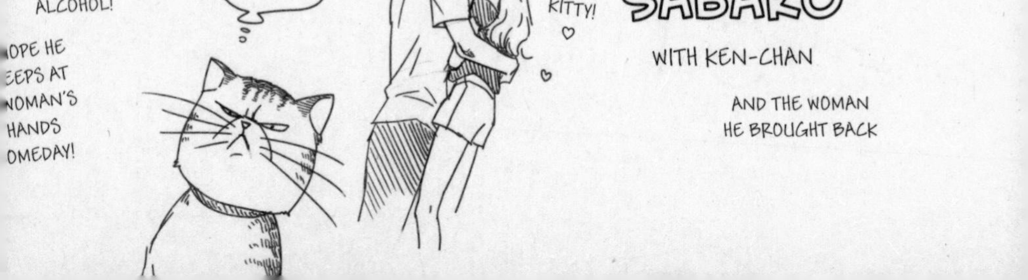
A DAY IN THE LIFE OF SABAKO
WITH KEN-CHAN
AND THE WOMAN HE BROUGHT BACK
OH, YOU HAVE A KITTY!
SHE'S UGLY AS HELL, RIGHT?
I LOATHE THAT MAN!!
HE IS THE NEMESIS OF WOMEN!
AND HE REEKS OF ALCOHOL!
OPE HE EEPS AT OMAN'S HANDS OMEDAY!

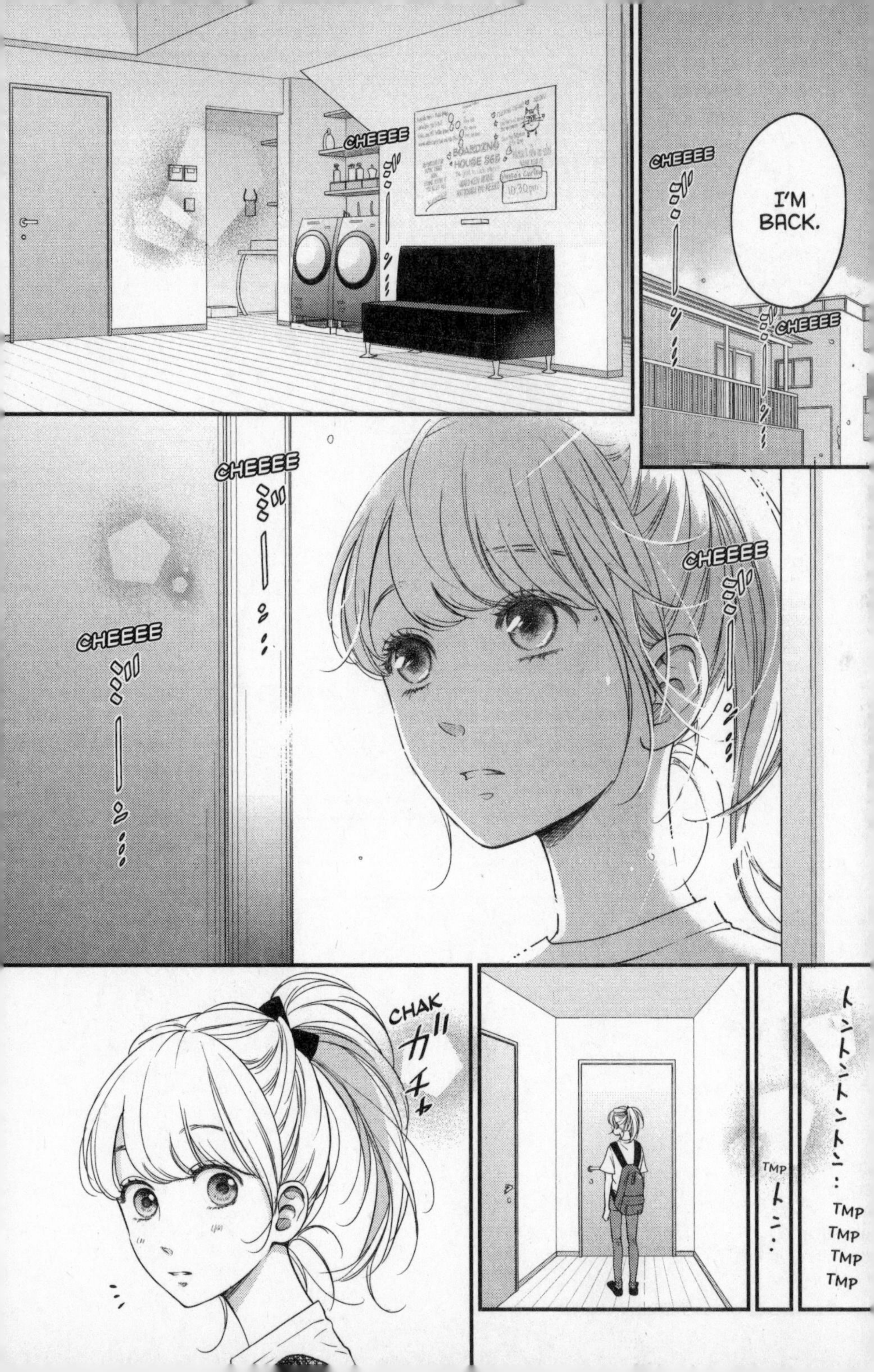
I'M BACK.
CHEEEE
CHEEEE
CHEEEE
CHEEEE
CHEEEE
CHEEEE
トントントン…
TMP
TMP
TMP
TMP
トン…
TMP
CHAK
ガチャ

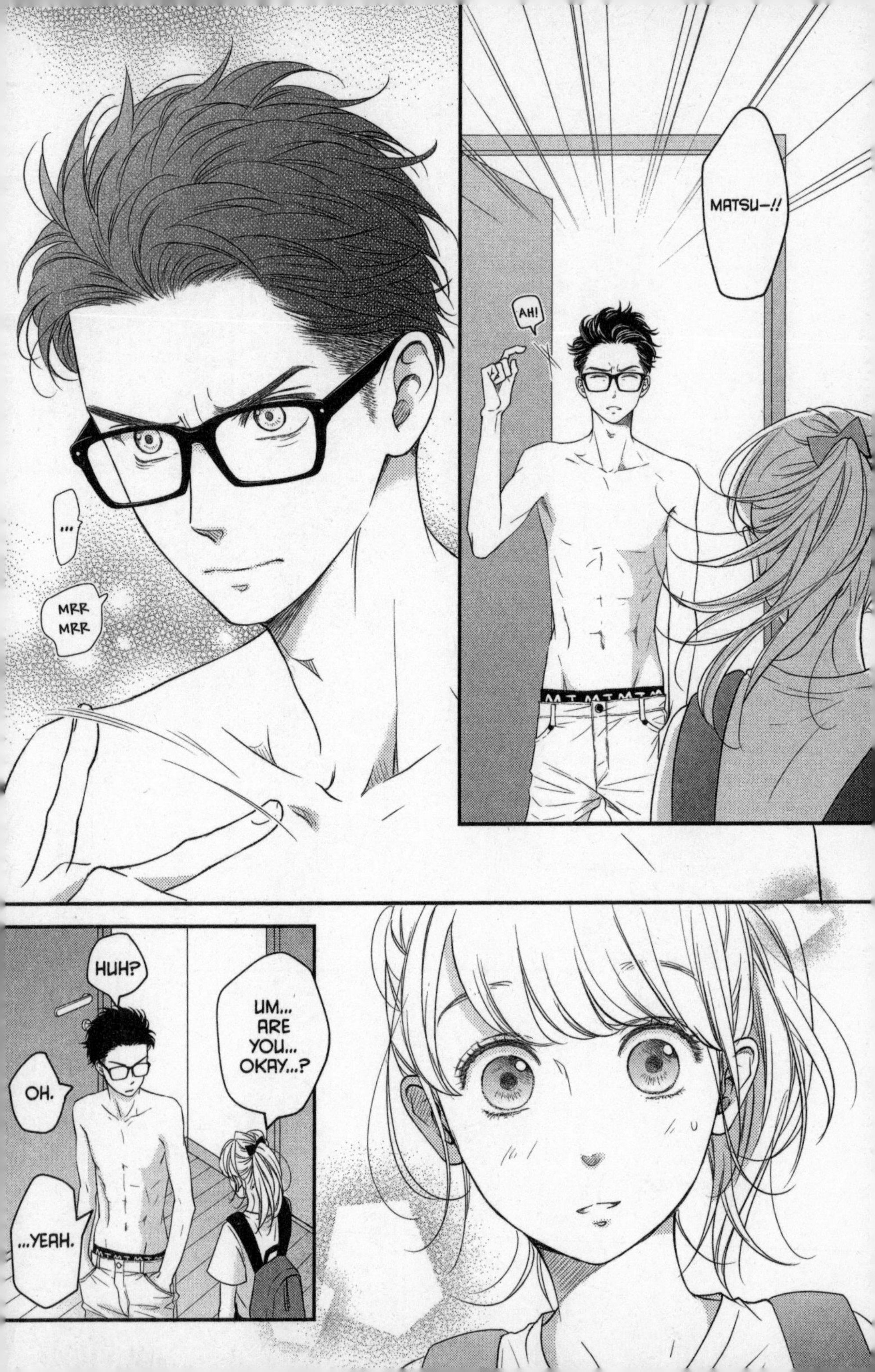
MATSU-!!
AH!
...
MRR MRR
UM... ARE YOU... OKAY...?
HUH?
OH.
...YEAH.

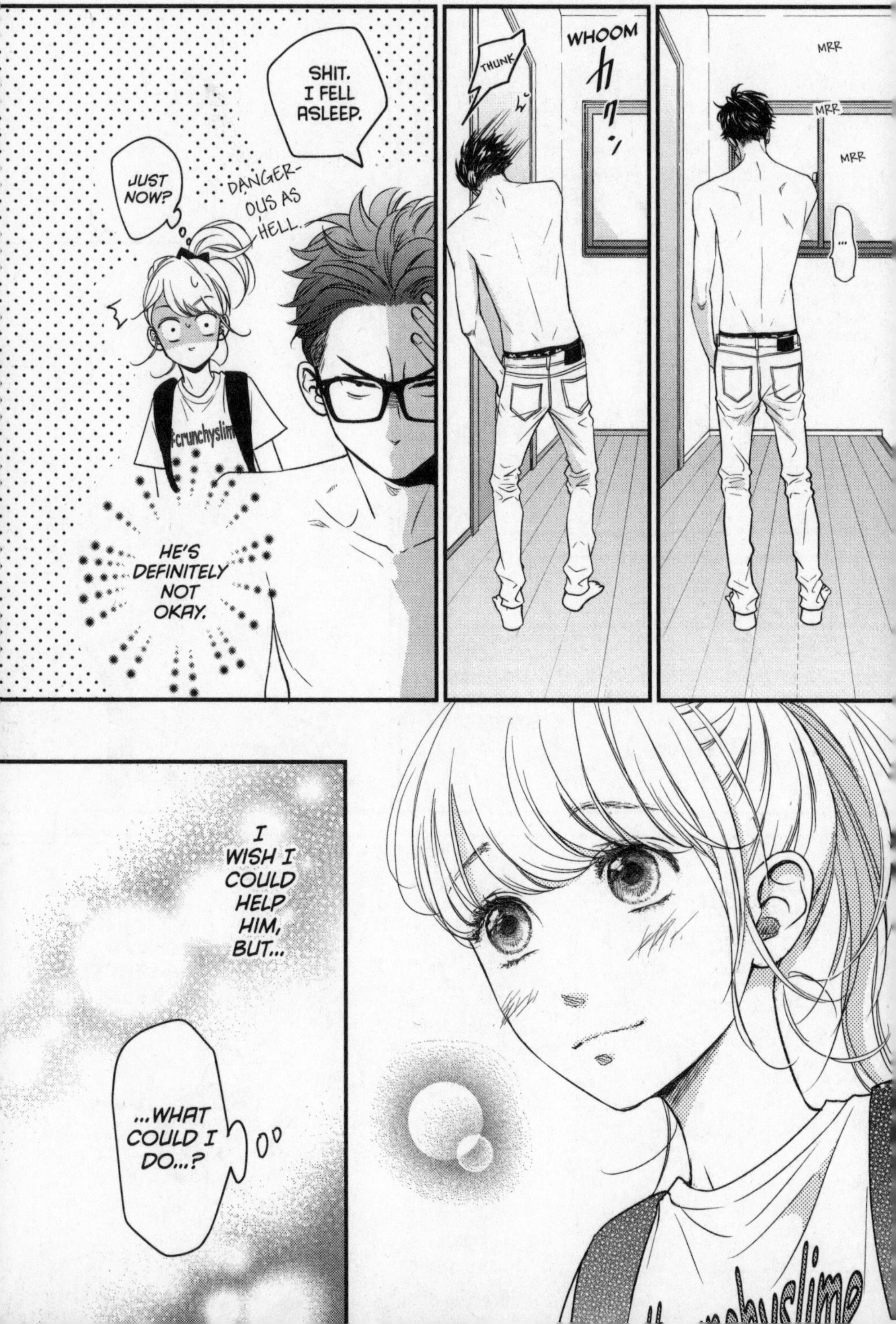
MRR
MRR
MRR
...
THUNK
WHOOM
SHIT. I FELL ASLEEP.
DANGER-OUS AS HELL.
JUST NOW?
HE'S DEFINITELY NOT OKAY.
I WISH I COULD HELP HIM, BUT...
...WHAT COULD I DO...?

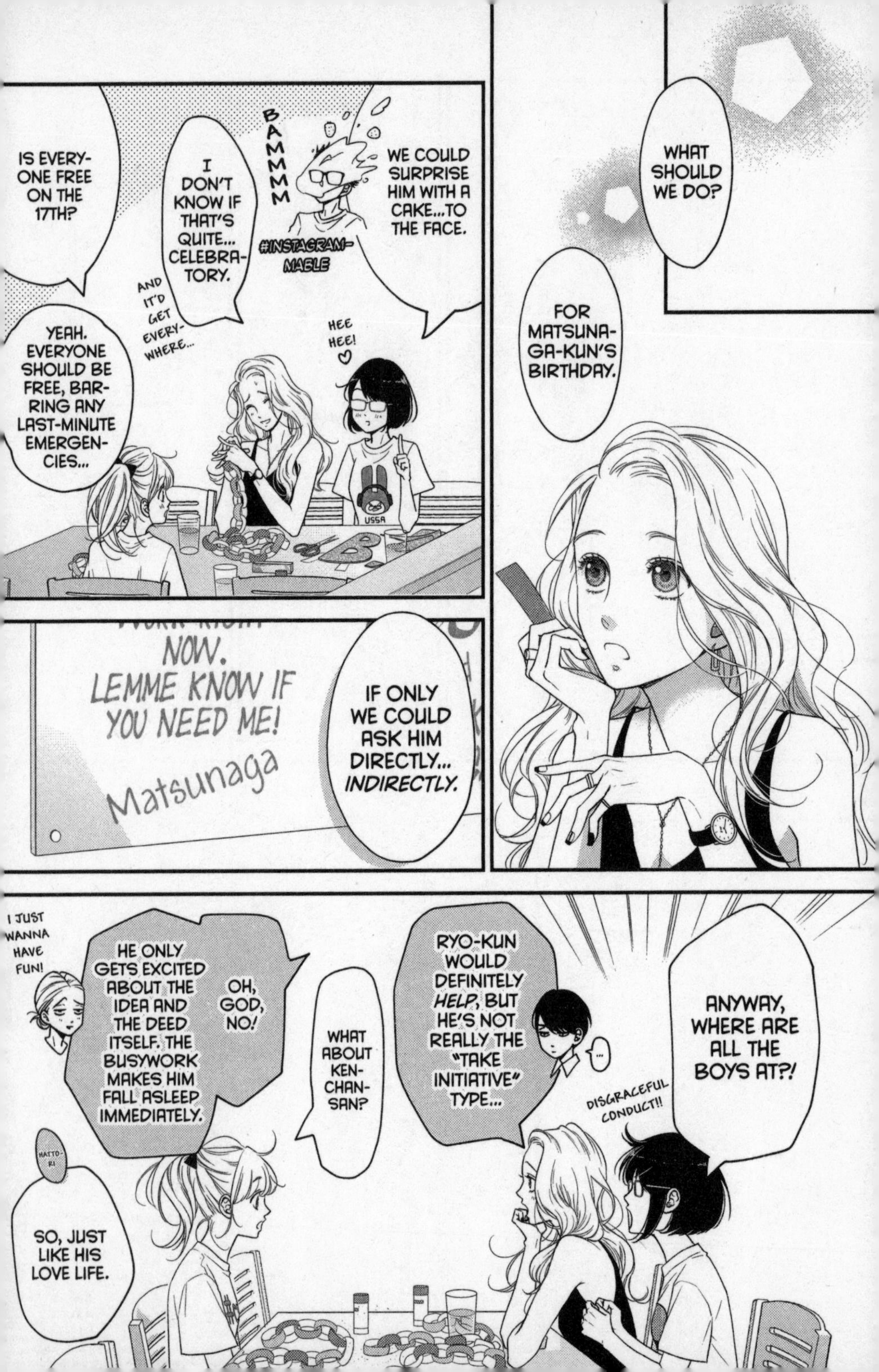
WHAT SHOULD WE DO?
FOR MATSUNAGA-KUN'S BIRTHDAY.
WE COULD SURPRISE HIM WITH A CAKE...TO THE FACE.
BAMMMM
#INSTAGRAMMABLE
I DON'T KNOW IF THAT'S QUITE... CELEBRATORY.
AND IT'D GET EVERYWHERE...
IS EVERYONE FREE ON THE 17TH?
HEE HEE! ♡
YEAH. EVERYONE SHOULD BE FREE, BARRING ANY LAST-MINUTE EMERGENCIES...
IF ONLY WE COULD ASK HIM DIRECTLY... *INDIRECTLY.*
NOW. LEMME KNOW IF YOU NEED ME!
Matsunaga
ANYWAY, WHERE ARE ALL THE BOYS AT?!
DISGRACEFUL CONDUCT!!
...
RYO-KUN WOULD DEFINITELY *HELP*, BUT HE'S NOT REALLY THE "TAKE INITIATIVE" TYPE...
WHAT ABOUT KEN-CHAN-SAN?
OH, GOD, NO!
HE ONLY GETS EXCITED ABOUT THE IDEA AND THE DEED ITSELF. THE BUSYWORK MAKES HIM FALL ASLEEP IMMEDIATELY.
I JUST WANNA HAVE FUN!
HATTORI
SO, JUST LIKE HIS LOVE LIFE.

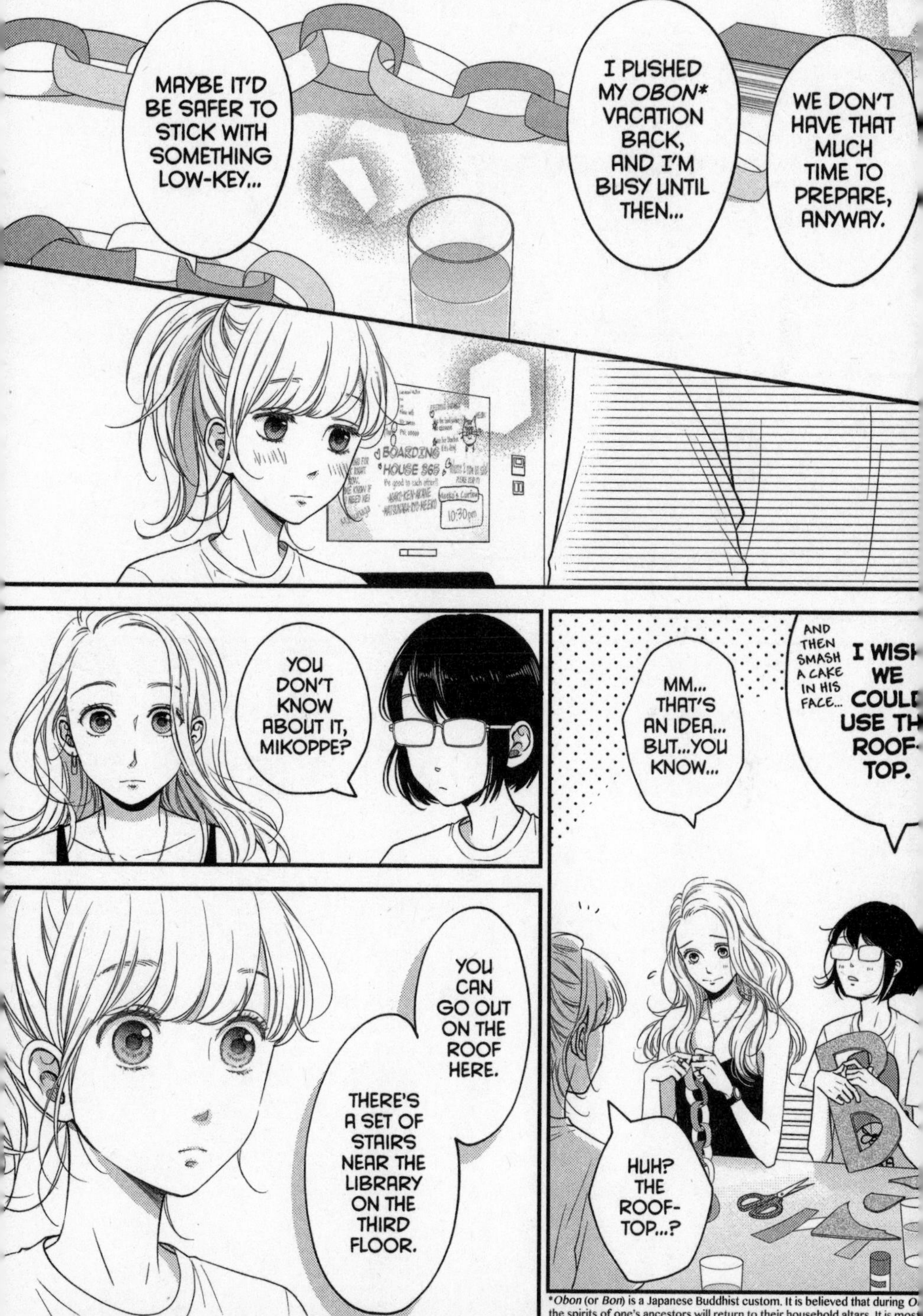
WE DON'T HAVE THAT MUCH TIME TO PREPARE, ANYWAY.
I PUSHED MY *OBON** VACATION BACK, AND I'M BUSY UNTIL THEN...
MAYBE IT'D BE SAFER TO STICK WITH SOMETHING LOW-KEY...
I WISH WE COULD USE THE ROOF-TOP.
AND THEN SMASH A CAKE IN HIS FACE...
MM... THAT'S AN IDEA... BUT...YOU KNOW...
HUH? THE ROOF-TOP...?
YOU DON'T KNOW ABOUT IT, MIKOPPE?
YOU CAN GO OUT ON THE ROOF HERE.
THERE'S A SET OF STAIRS NEAR THE LIBRARY ON THE THIRD FLOOR.

**Obon* (or *Bon*) is a Japanese Buddhist custom. It is believed that during *O*[illegible] the spirits of one's ancestors will return to their household altars. It is mos[illegible] commonly celebrated around August 15th, but there are some regional differences due to the shift from the lunar to the Gregorian calendar.

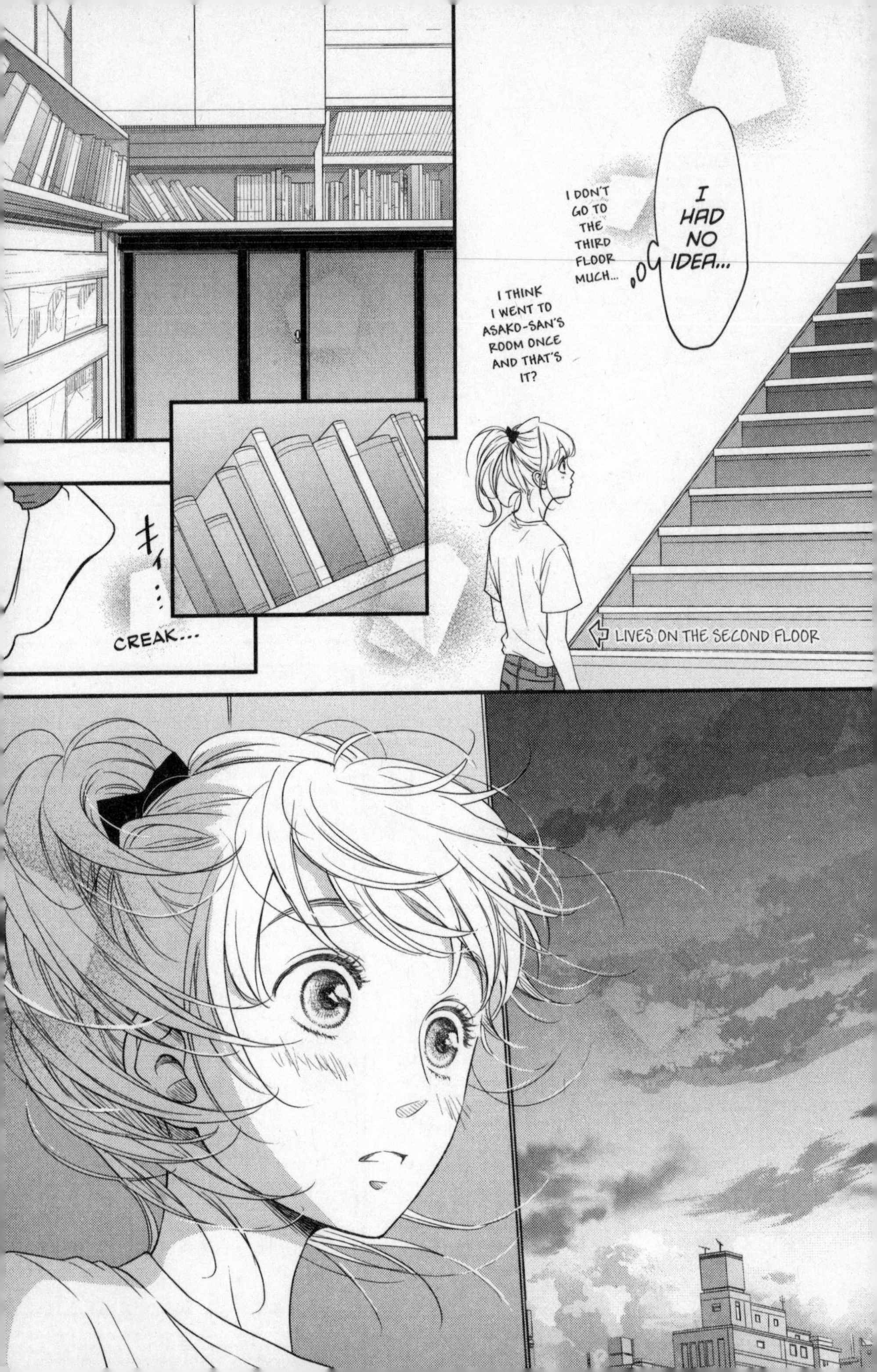
I HAD NO IDEA...
I DON'T GO TO THE THIRD FLOOR MUCH...
I THINK I WENT TO ASAKO-SAN'S ROOM ONCE AND THAT'S IT?
LIVES ON THE SECOND FLOOR
キィ…
CREAK...

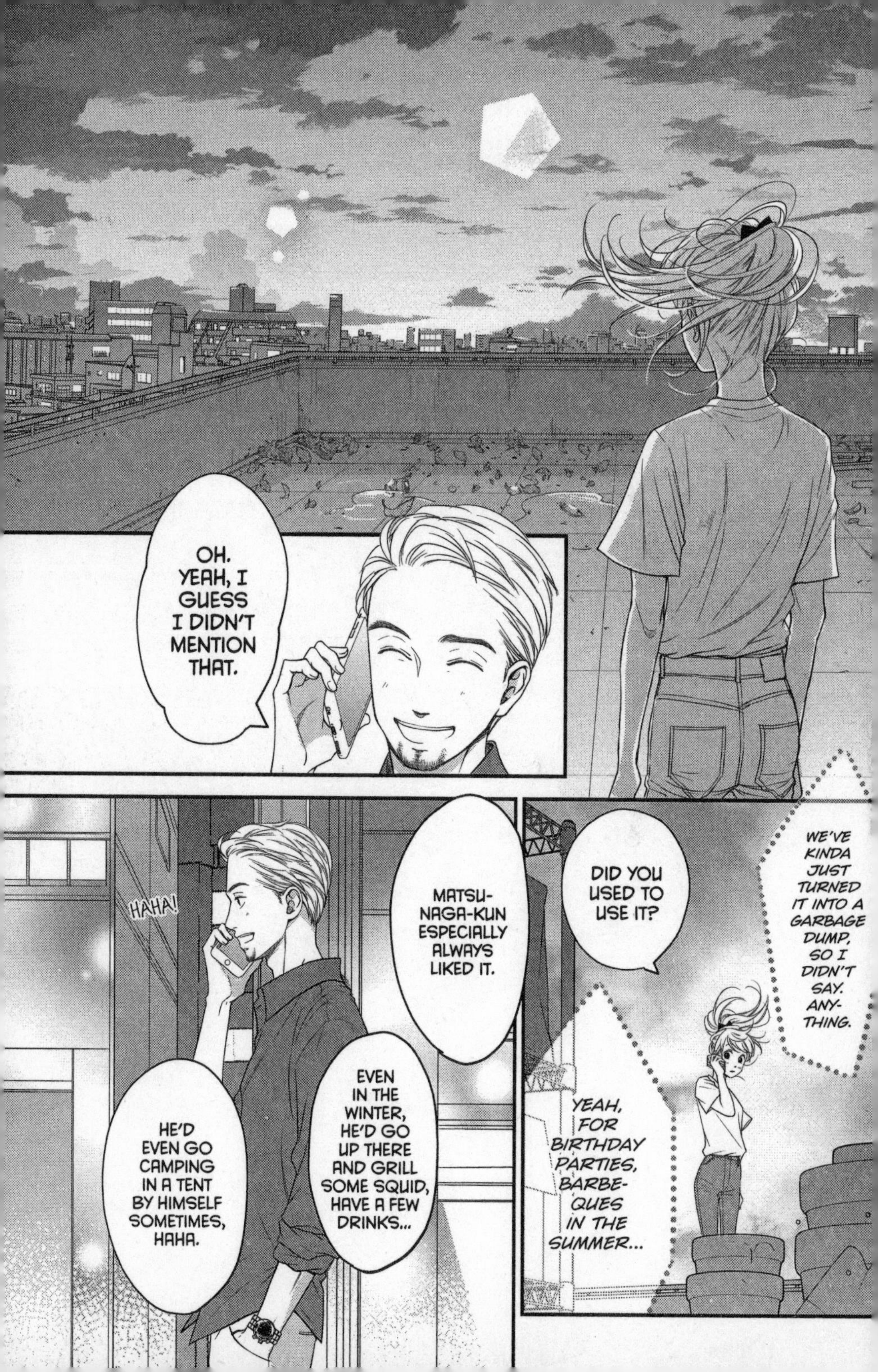
OH. YEAH, I GUESS I DIDN'T MENTION THAT.
WE'VE KINDA JUST TURNED IT INTO A GARBAGE DUMP, SO I DIDN'T SAY. ANY-THING.
DID YOU USED TO USE IT?
YEAH, FOR BIRTHDAY PARTIES, BARBE-QUES IN THE SUMMER...
MATSU-NAGA-KUN ESPECIALLY ALWAYS LIKED IT.
HAHA!
EVEN IN THE WINTER, HE'D GO UP THERE AND GRILL SOME SQUID, HAVE A FEW DRINKS...
HE'D EVEN GO CAMPING IN A TENT BY HIMSELF SOMETIMES, HAHA.

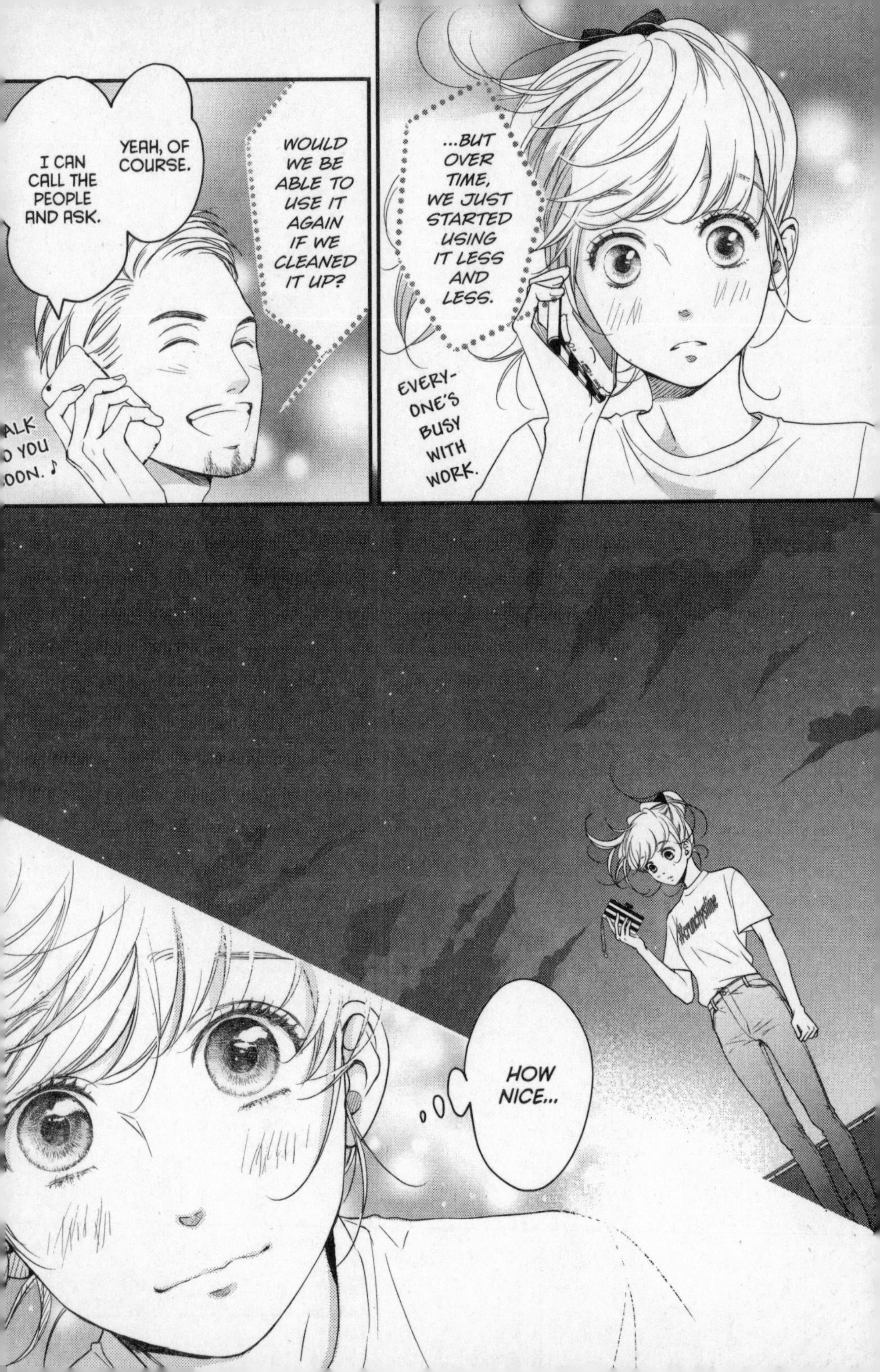
...BUT OVER TIME, WE JUST STARTED USING IT LESS AND LESS.
EVERY-ONE'S BUSY WITH WORK.
WOULD WE BE ABLE TO USE IT AGAIN IF WE CLEANED IT UP?
YEAH, OF COURSE.
I CAN CALL THE PEOPLE AND ASK.
HOW NICE...

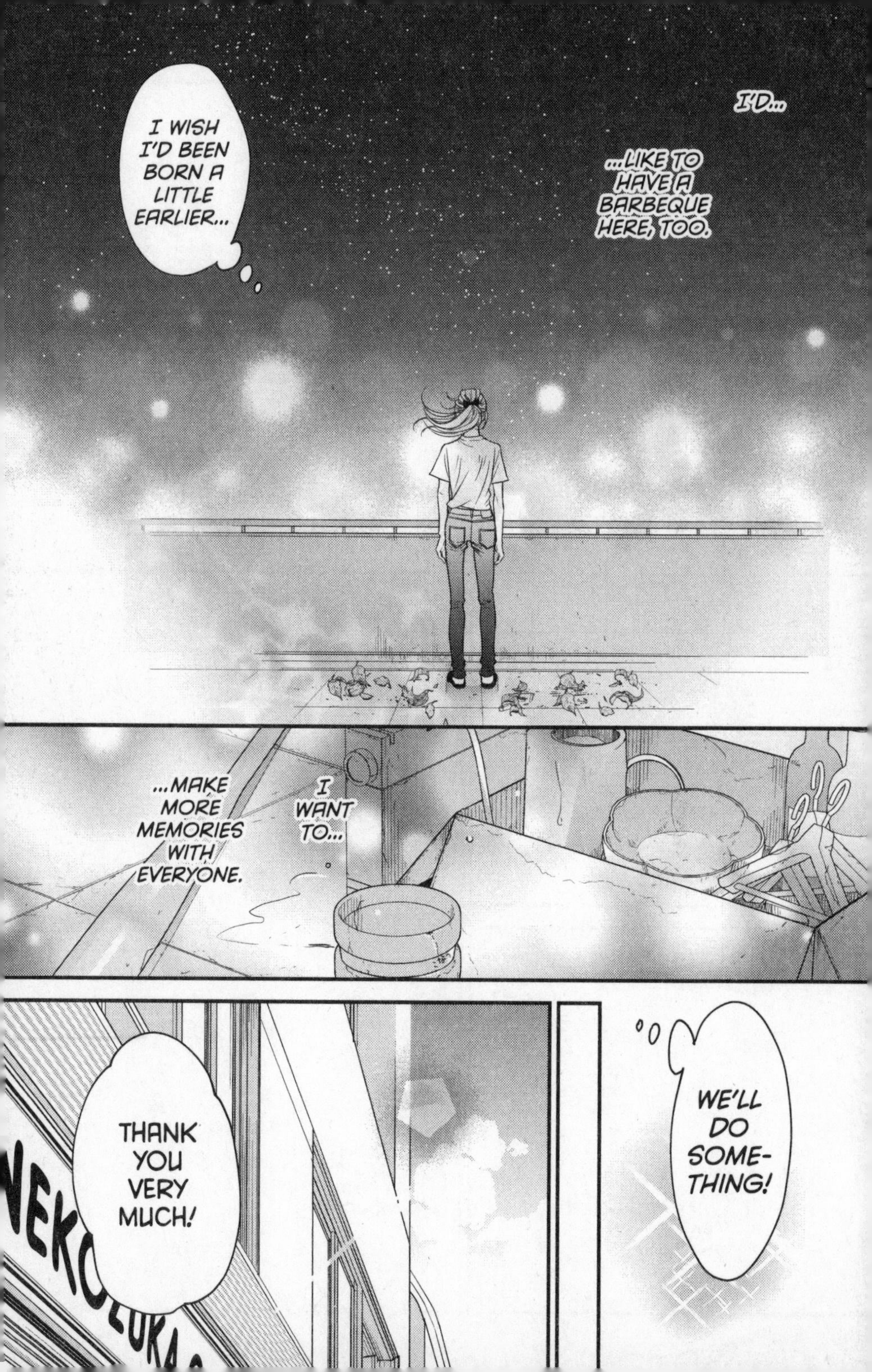
I'D...
...LIKE TO HAVE A BARBEQUE HERE, TOO.
I WISH I'D BEEN BORN A LITTLE EARLIER...
I WANT TO...
...MAKE MORE MEMORIES WITH EVERYONE.
WE'LL DO SOME-THING!
THANK YOU VERY MUCH!

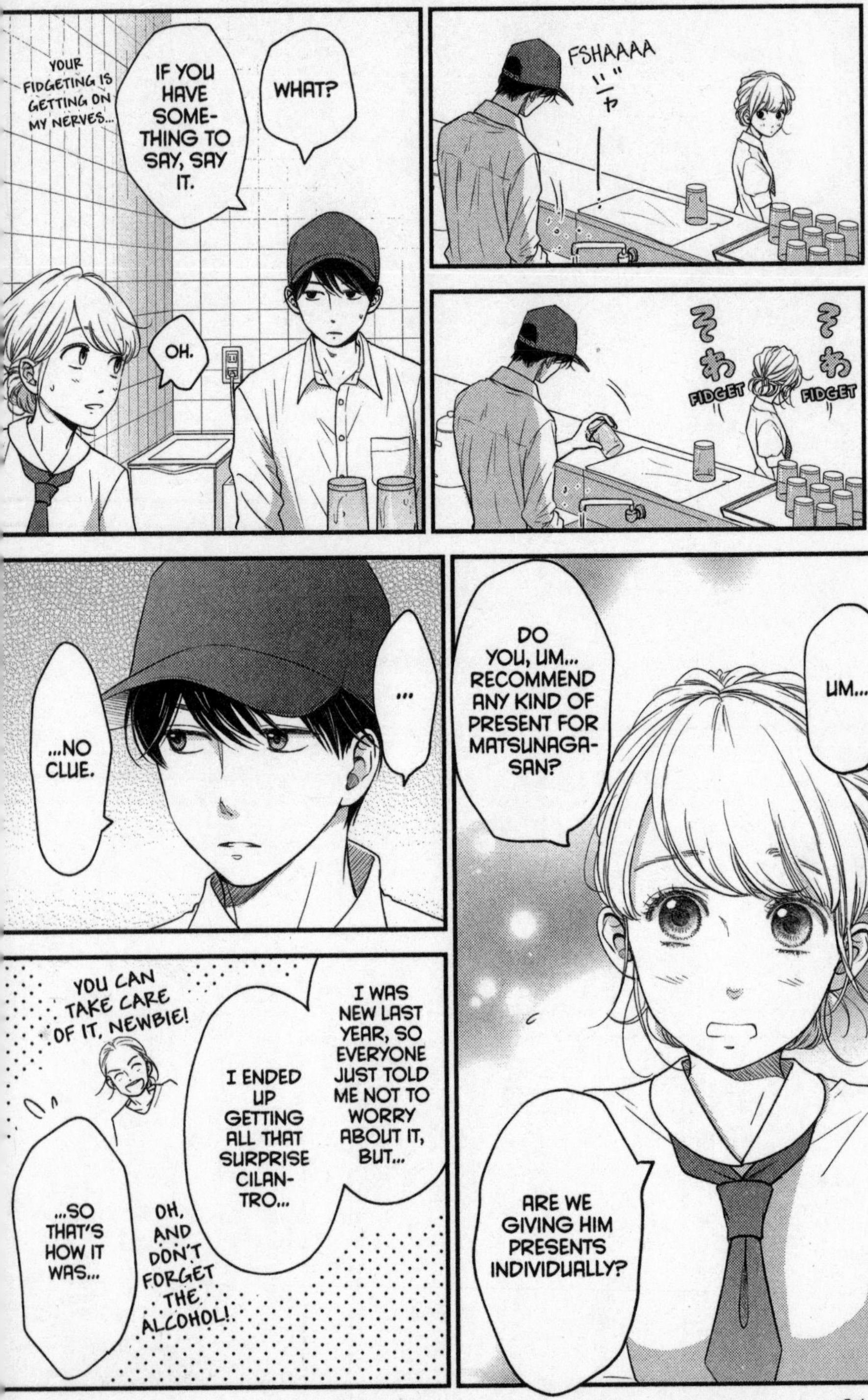
FSHAAAA
ジャ
そわ FIDGET
そわ FIDGET
WHAT?
IF YOU HAVE SOME-THING TO SAY, SAY IT.
YOUR FIDGETING IS GETTING ON MY NERVES...
OH.
UM...
DO YOU, UM... RECOMMEND ANY KIND OF PRESENT FOR MATSUNAGA-SAN?
ARE WE GIVING HIM PRESENTS INDIVIDUALLY?
...
...NO CLUE.
I WAS NEW LAST YEAR, SO EVERYONE JUST TOLD ME NOT TO WORRY ABOUT IT, BUT...
I ENDED UP GETTING ALL THAT SURPRISE CILAN-TRO...
YOU CAN TAKE CARE OF IT, NEWBIE!
OH, AND DON'T FORGET THE ALCOHOL!
...SO THAT'S HOW IT WAS...

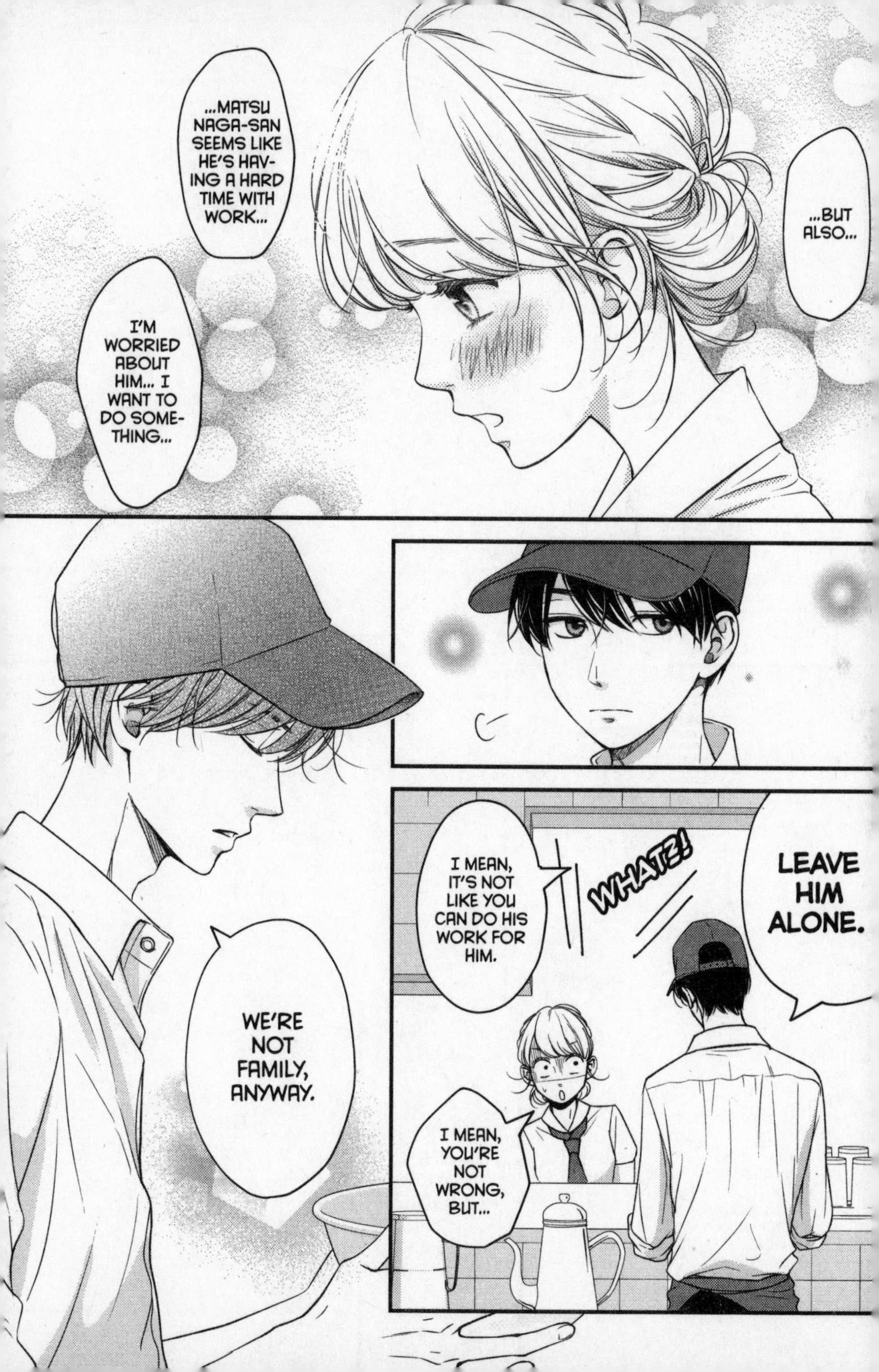
...MATSU NAGA-SAN SEEMS LIKE HE'S HAV- ING A HARD TIME WITH WORK...
I'M WORRIED ABOUT HIM... I WANT TO DO SOME- THING...
...BUT ALSO...
LEAVE HIM ALONE.
WHAT?!
I MEAN, IT'S NOT LIKE YOU CAN DO HIS WORK FOR HIM.
I MEAN, YOU'RE NOT WRONG, BUT...
WE'RE NOT FAMILY, ANYWAY.

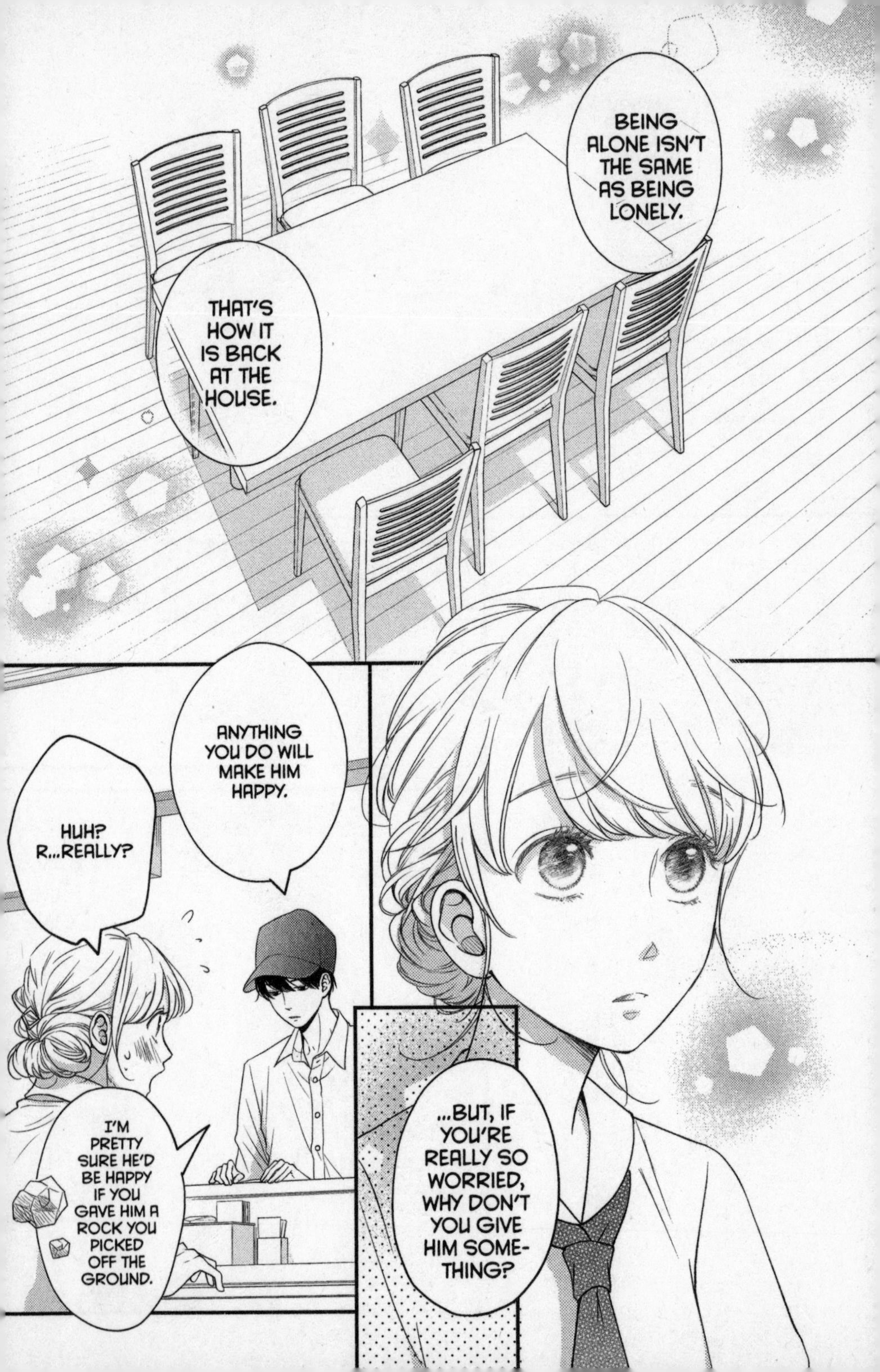
BEING ALONE ISN'T THE SAME AS BEING LONELY.
THAT'S HOW IT IS BACK AT THE HOUSE.
...BUT, IF YOU'RE REALLY SO WORRIED, WHY DON'T YOU GIVE HIM SOME-THING?
ANYTHING YOU DO WILL MAKE HIM HAPPY.
HUH? R...REALLY?
I'M PRETTY SURE HE'D BE HAPPY IF YOU GAVE HIM A ROCK YOU PICKED OFF THE GROUND.

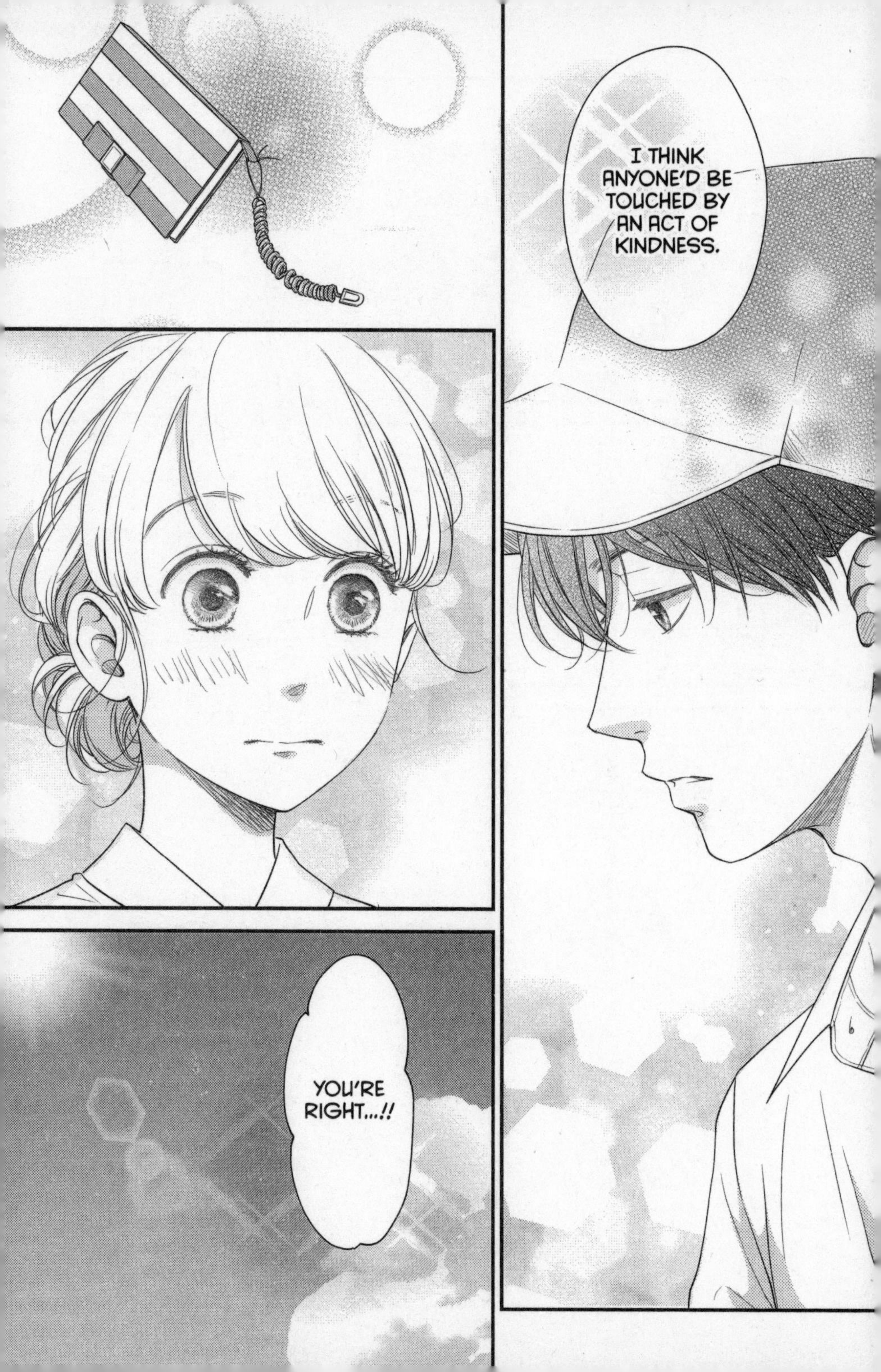
I THINK ANYONE'D BE TOUCHED BY AN ACT OF KINDNESS.
YOU'RE RIGHT...!!

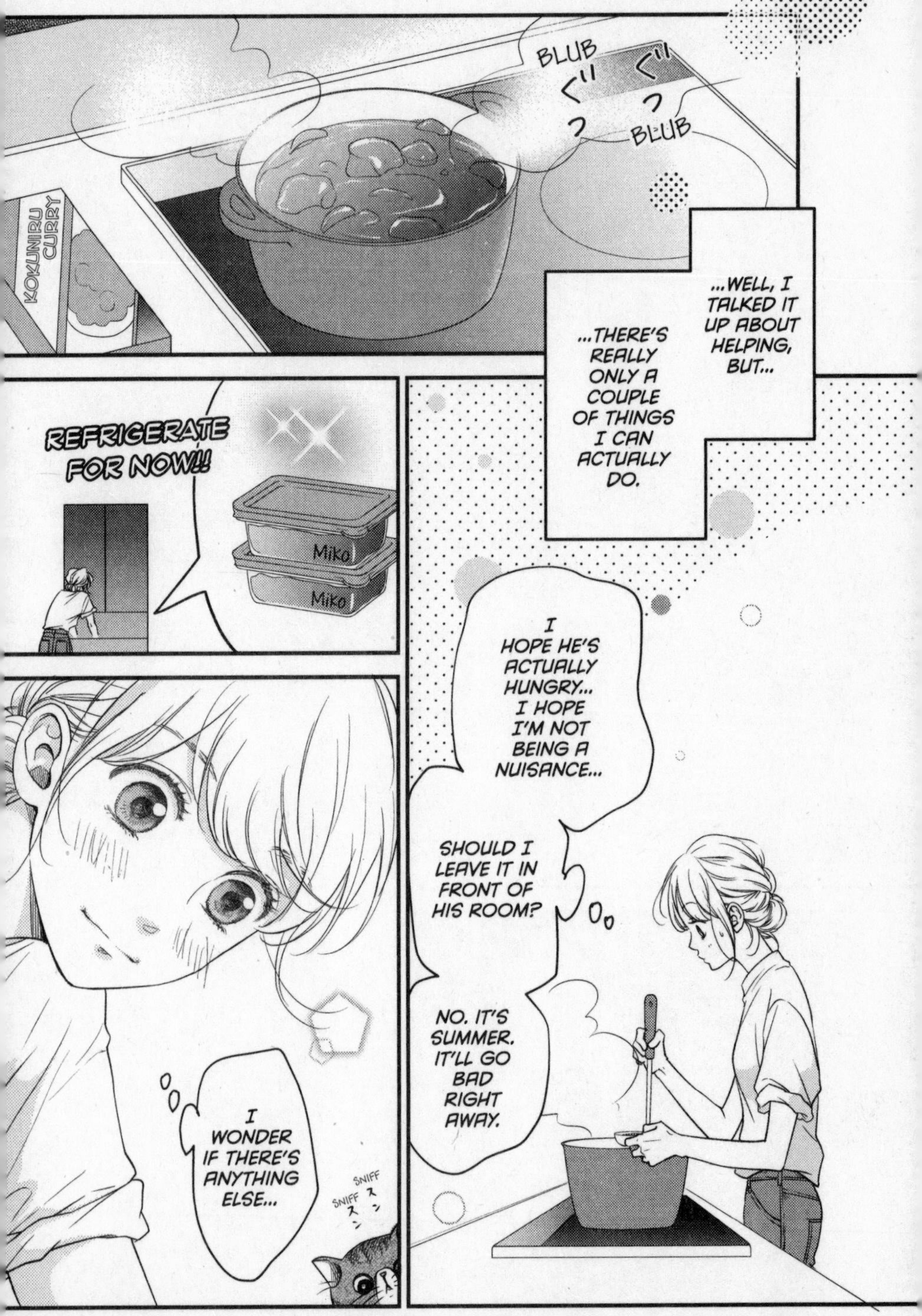
BLUB
ぐつ
ぐつ
BLUB
KOKUNIRU CURRY
...WELL, I TALKED IT UP ABOUT HELPING, BUT...
...THERE'S REALLY ONLY A COUPLE OF THINGS I CAN ACTUALLY DO.
I HOPE HE'S ACTUALLY HUNGRY... I HOPE I'M NOT BEING A NUISANCE...
SHOULD I LEAVE IT IN FRONT OF HIS ROOM?
NO. IT'S SUMMER. IT'LL GO BAD RIGHT AWAY.
REFRIGERATE FOR NOW!!
Miko
Miko
I WONDER IF THERE'S ANYTHING ELSE...
SNIFF
スン
SNIFF
スン

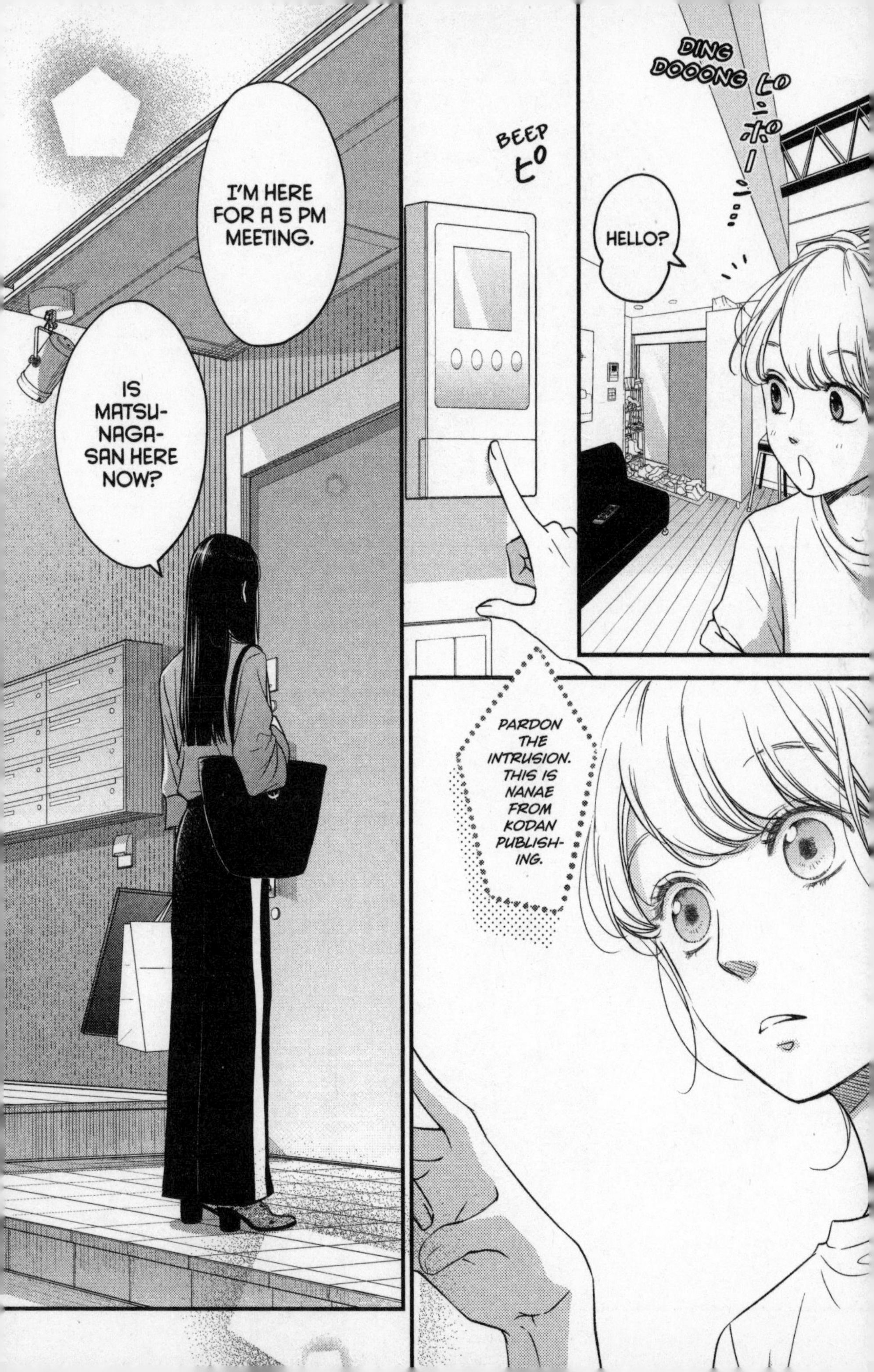

DING DOOONG
HELLO?
BEEP
PARDON THE INTRUSION. THIS IS NANAE FROM KODAN PUBLISHING.
I'M HERE FOR A 5 PM MEETING.
IS MATSUNAGA-SAN HERE NOW?

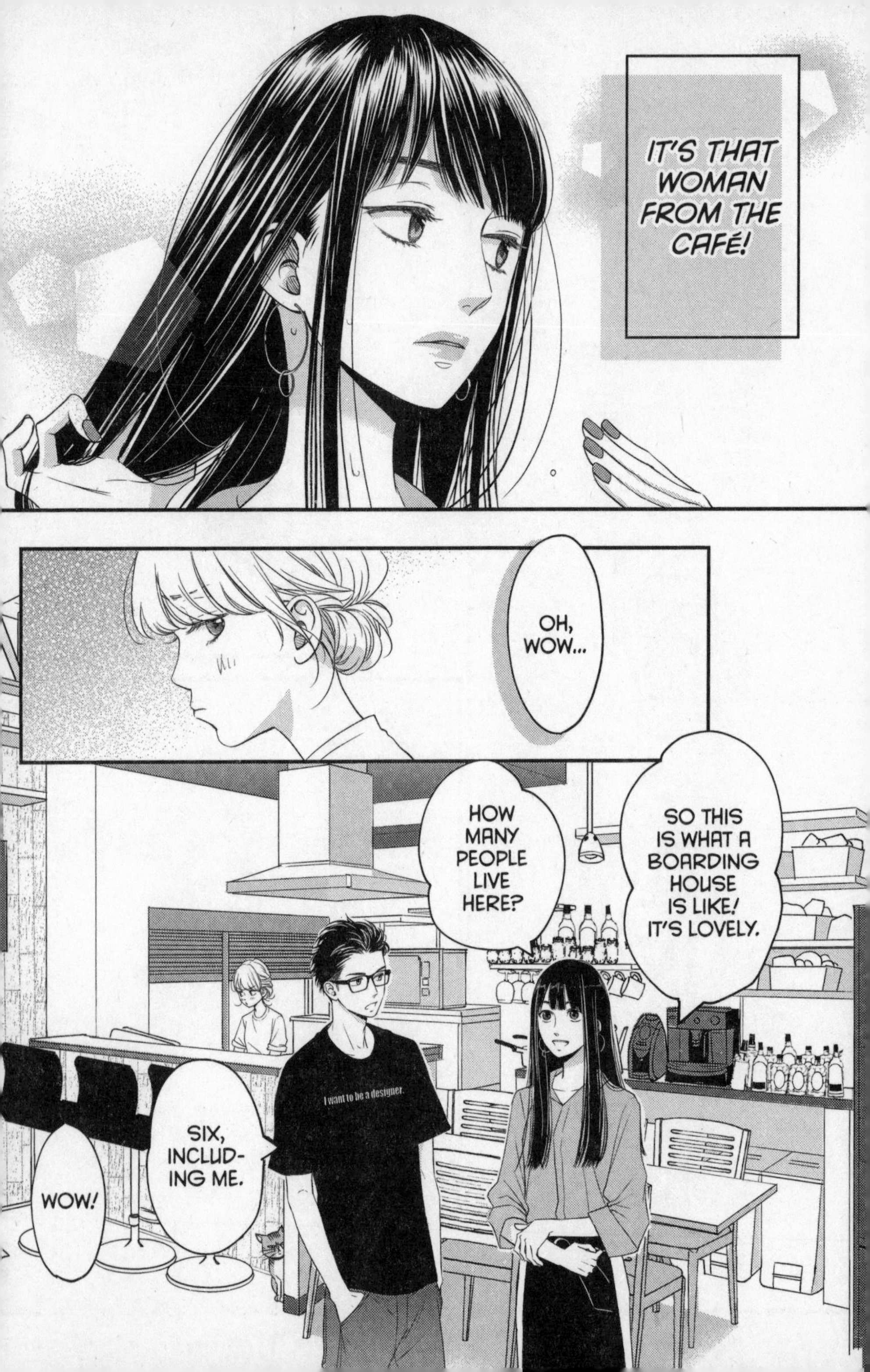
IT'S THAT WOMAN FROM THE CAFÉ!
OH, WOW...
SO THIS IS WHAT A BOARDING HOUSE IS LIKE! IT'S LOVELY.
HOW MANY PEOPLE LIVE HERE?
I want to be a designer.
SIX, INCLUD-ING ME.
WOW!

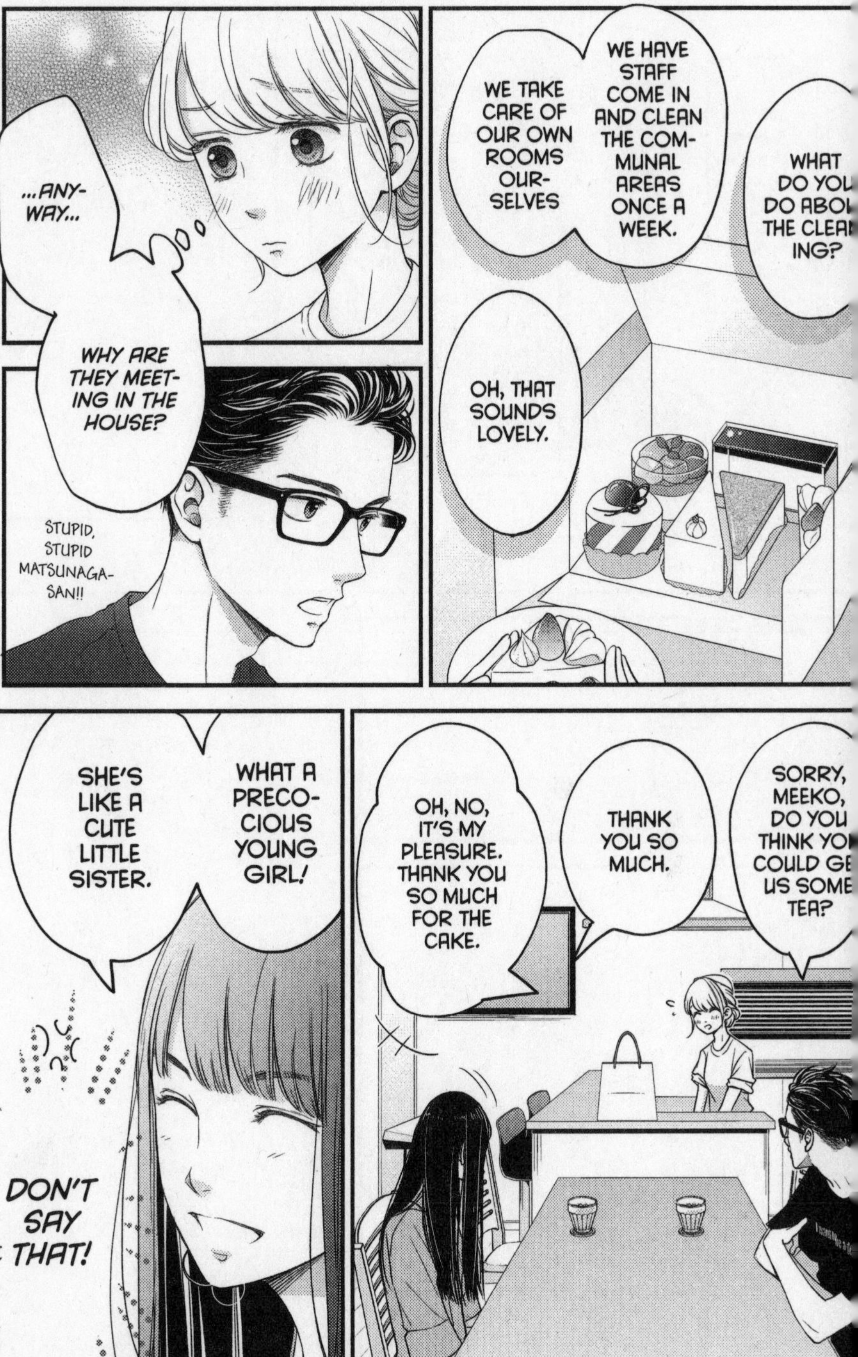
WHAT DO YOU DO ABOL THE CLEAI ING?
WE HAVE STAFF COME IN AND CLEAN THE COMMUNAL AREAS ONCE A WEEK.
WE TAKE CARE OF OUR OWN ROOMS OURSELVES
OH, THAT SOUNDS LOVELY.
...ANYWAY...
WHY ARE THEY MEETING IN THE HOUSE?
STUPID, STUPID MATSUNAGA-SAN!!
SORRY, MEEKO, DO YOU THINK YO COULD GE US SOME TEA?
THANK YOU SO MUCH.
OH, NO, IT'S MY PLEASURE. THANK YOU SO MUCH FOR THE CAKE.
WHAT A PRECOCIOUS YOUNG GIRL!
SHE'S LIKE A CUTE LITTLE SISTER.
DON'T SAY THAT!

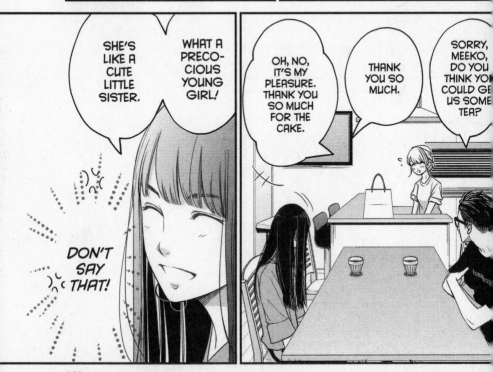

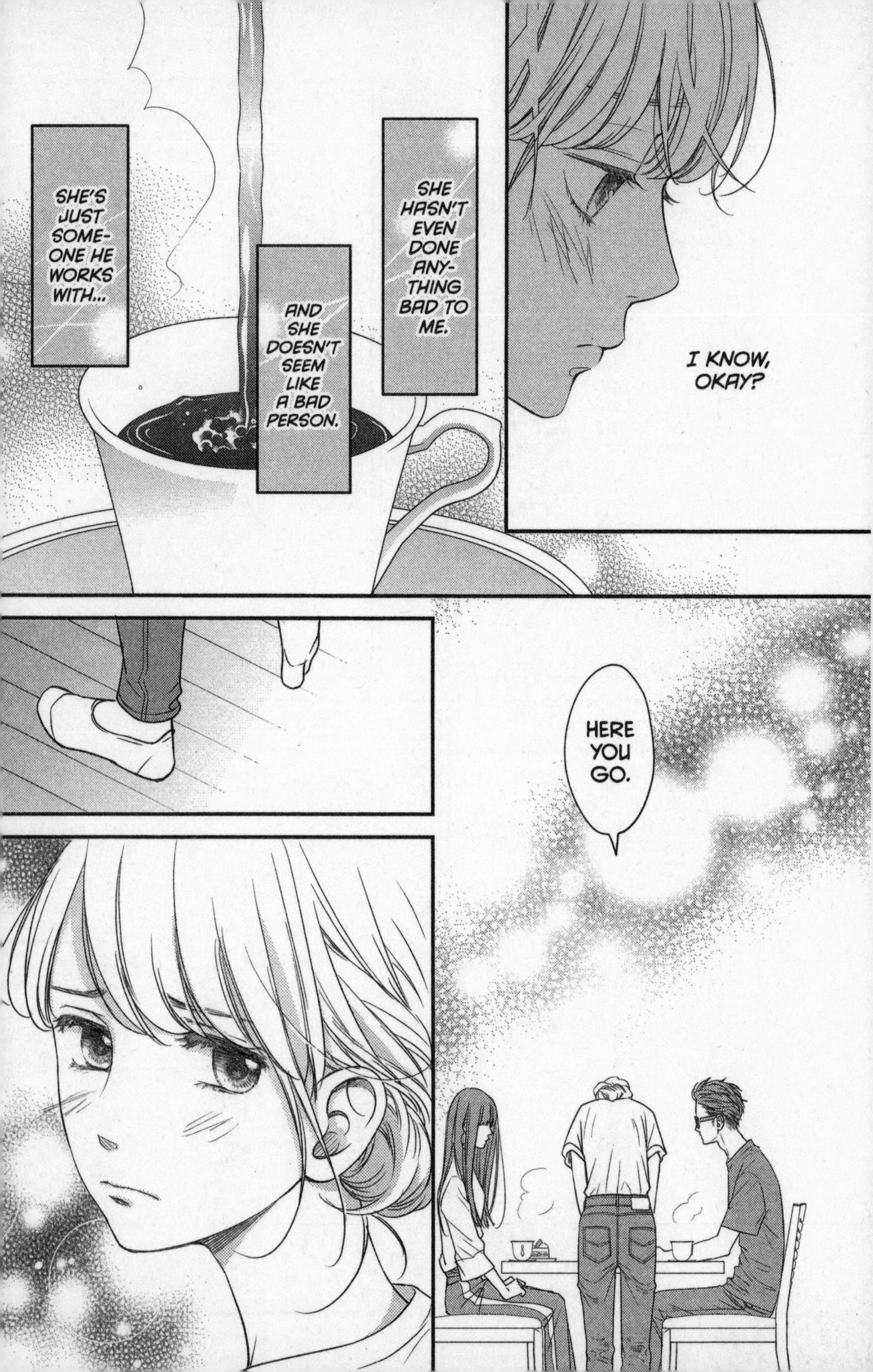
I KNOW, OKAY?
SHE HASN'T EVEN DONE ANY-THING BAD TO ME.
AND SHE DOESN'T SEEM LIKE A BAD PERSON.
SHE'S JUST SOME-ONE HE WORKS WITH...
HERE YOU GO.

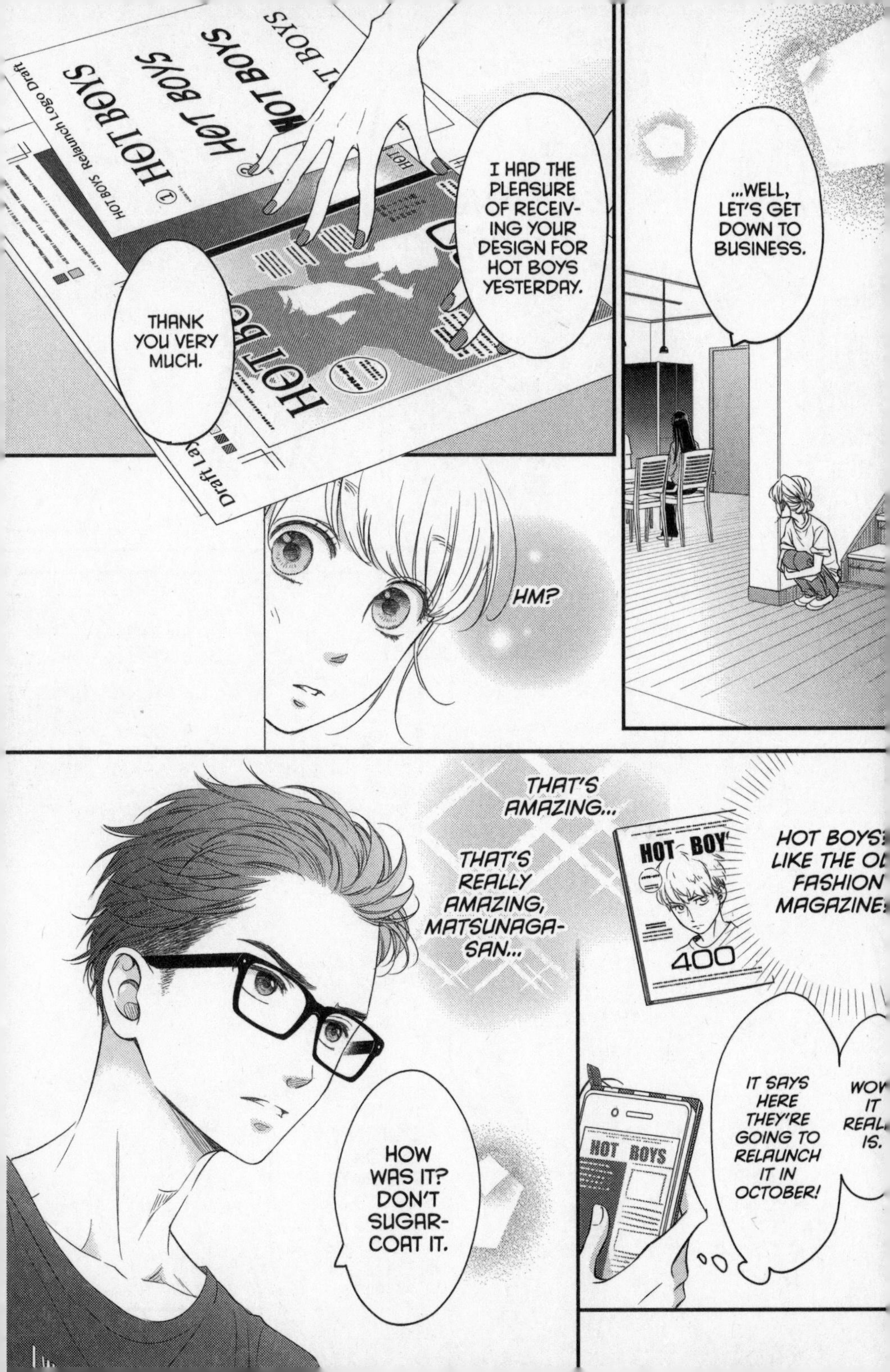
...WELL, LET'S GET DOWN TO BUSINESS.
I HAD THE PLEASURE OF RECEIVING YOUR DESIGN FOR HOT BOYS YESTERDAY.
THANK YOU VERY MUCH.
HOT BOYS
HOT BOYS Relaunch Logo Draft
Draft Lay
HM?
HOT BOYS: LIKE THE OL FASHION MAGAZINE
HOT BOY
400
WOW IT REAL IS.
IT SAYS HERE THEY'RE GOING TO RELAUNCH IT IN OCTOBER!
HOT BOYS
THAT'S AMAZING...
THAT'S REALLY AMAZING, MATSUNAGA-SAN...
HOW WAS IT? DON'T SUGARCOAT IT.

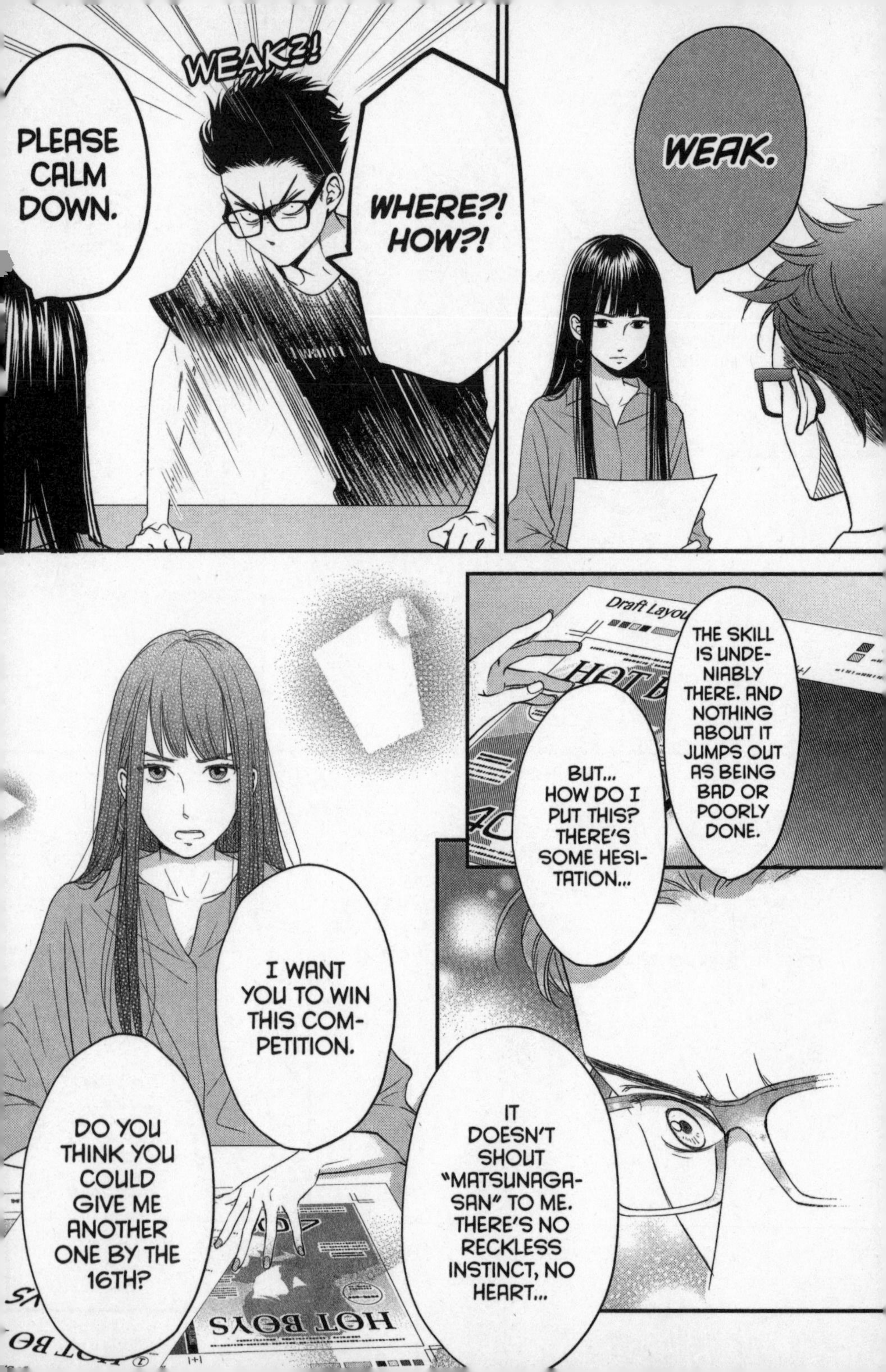
WEAK.
WEAK?!
WHERE?! HOW?!
PLEASE CALM DOWN.
THE SKILL IS UNDENIABLY THERE. AND NOTHING ABOUT IT JUMPS OUT AS BEING BAD OR POORLY DONE.
BUT... HOW DO I PUT THIS? THERE'S SOME HESITATION...
IT DOESN'T SHOUT "MATSUNAGA-SAN" TO ME. THERE'S NO RECKLESS INSTINCT, NO HEART...
I WANT YOU TO WIN THIS COMPETITION.
DO YOU THINK YOU COULD GIVE ME ANOTHER ONE BY THE 16TH?

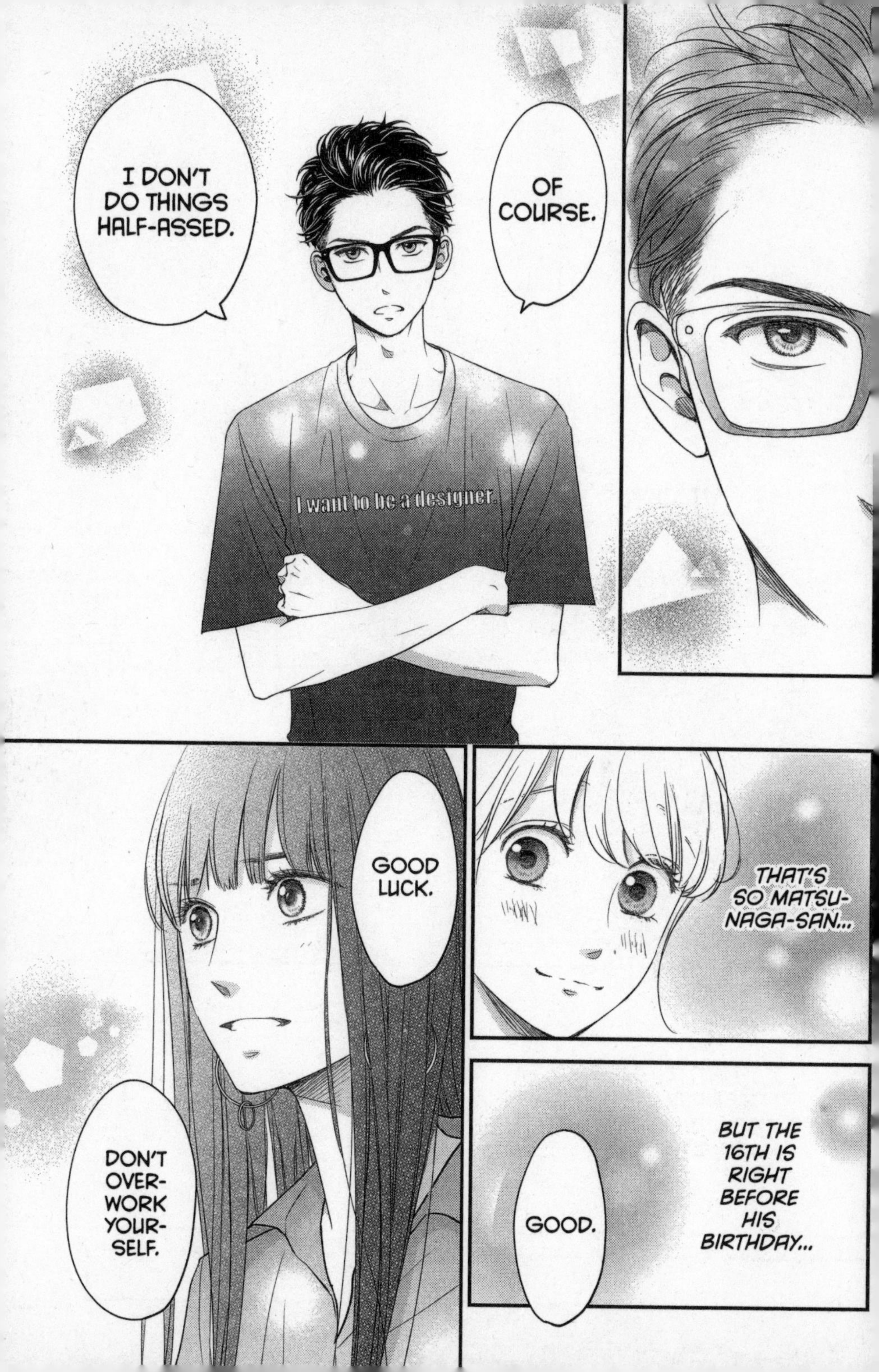
OF COURSE.
I DON'T DO THINGS HALF-ASSED.
I want to be a designer.
THAT'S SO MATSU-NAGA-SAN...
BUT THE 16TH IS RIGHT BEFORE HIS BIRTHDAY...
GOOD.
GOOD LUCK.
DON'T OVER-WORK YOUR-SELF.

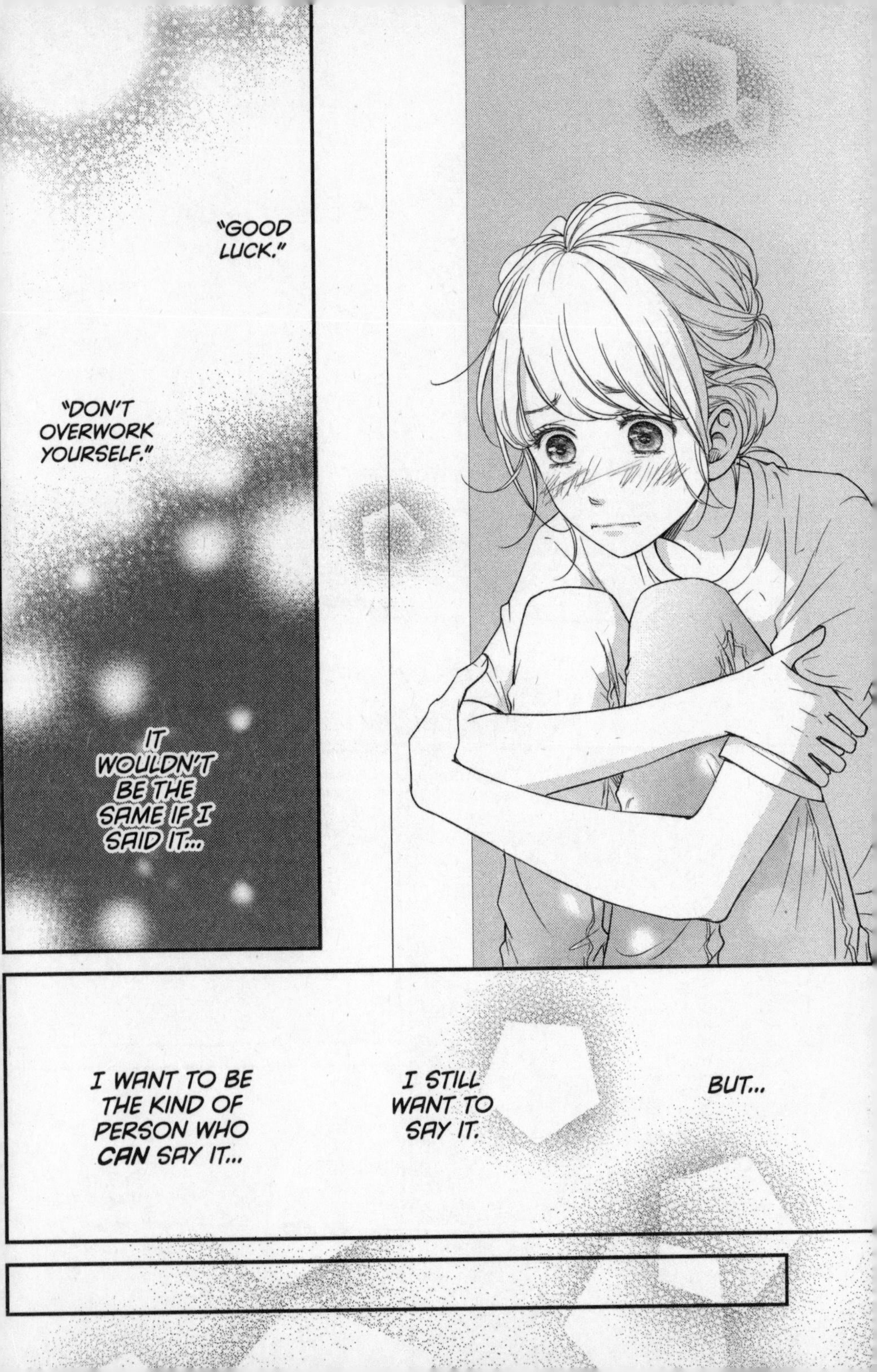
"GOOD LUCK."
"DON'T OVERWORK YOURSELF."
IT WOULDN'T BE THE SAME IF I SAID IT...
BUT...
I STILL WANT TO SAY IT.
I WANT TO BE THE KIND OF PERSON WHO CAN SAY IT...

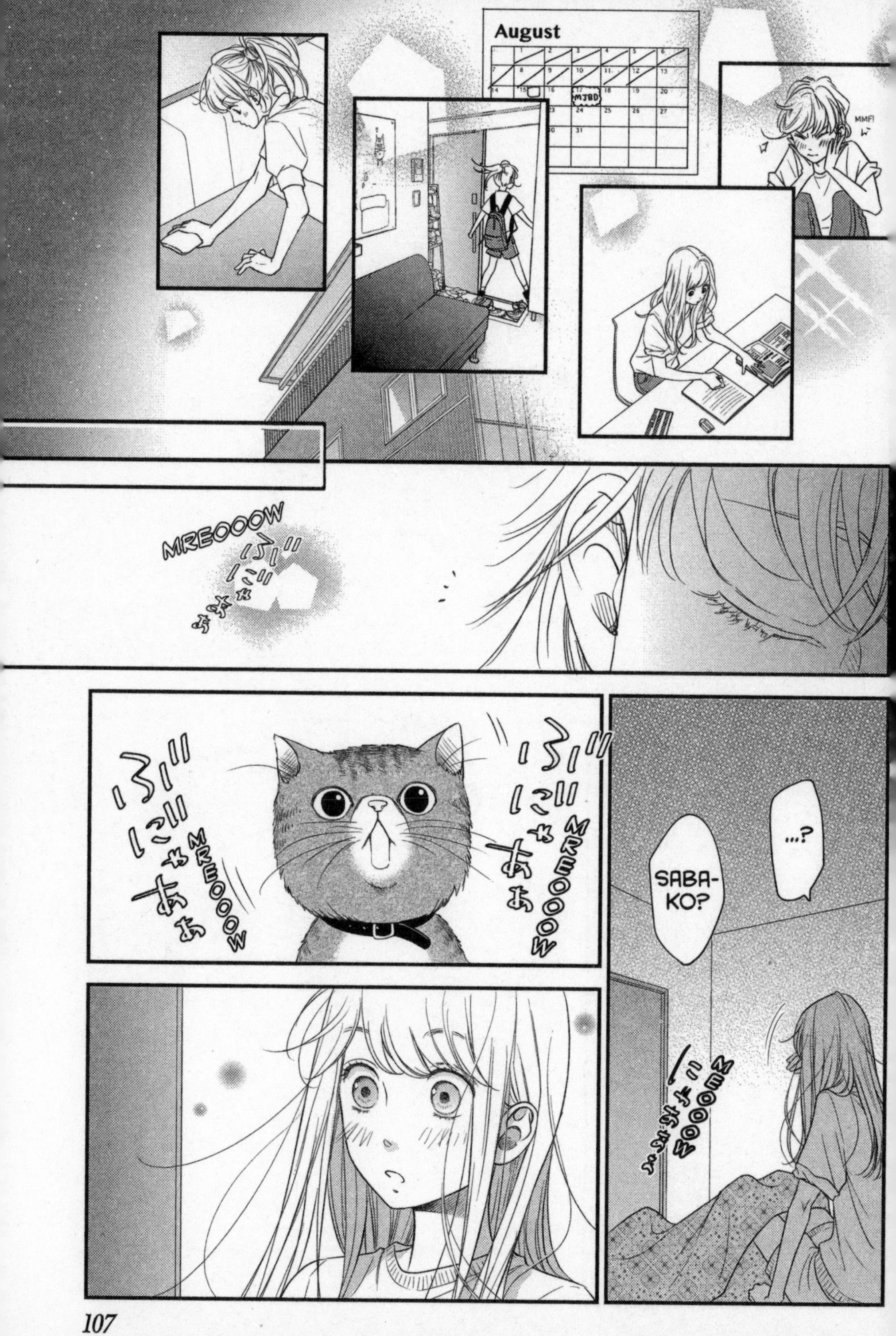
MMF!
August
MJBD
MREOOOW
ふにゃあ
...?
SABAKO?
MREOOOW!!
ふにゃあ
MREOOOW
ふにゃあ
MREOOOW
ふにゃあ

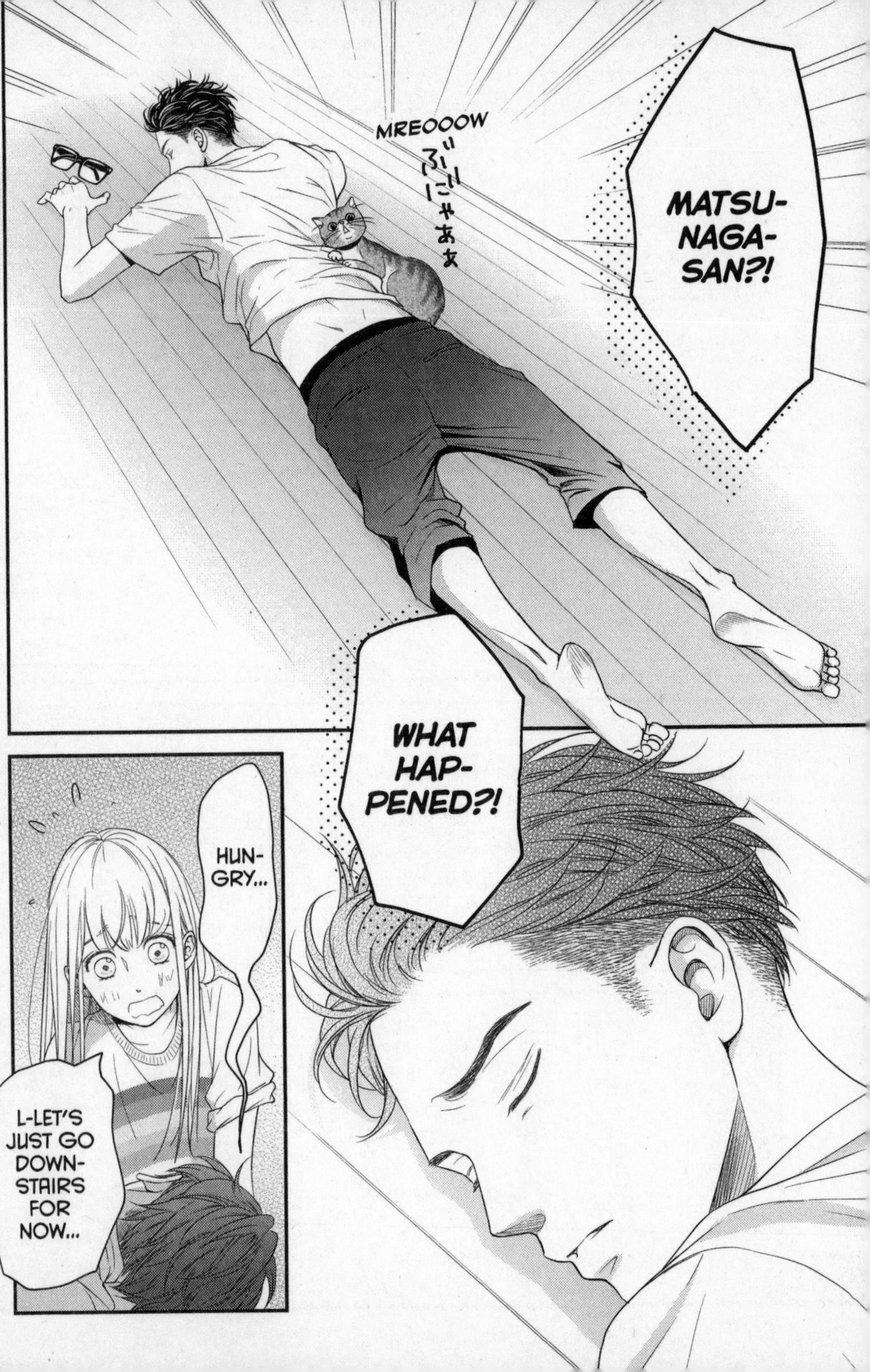
MATSUNAGA-SAN?!
MREOOOW
ぶにゃあぁ
WHAT HAPPENED?!
HUNGRY...
L-LET'S JUST GO DOWNSTAIRS FOR NOW...

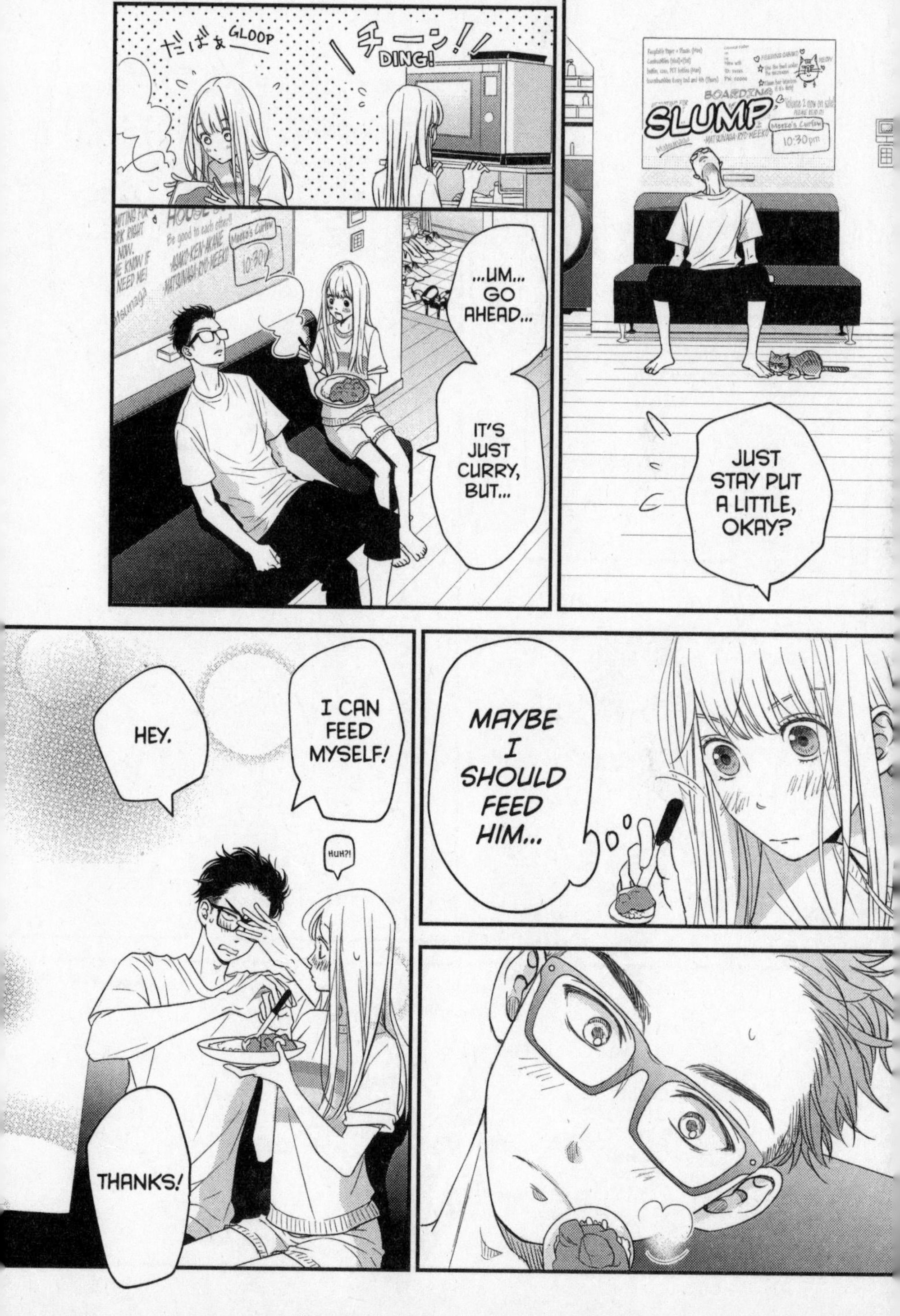
SLUMP
Meeko's Curfew
10:30pm
JUST STAY PUT A LITTLE, OKAY?
だばぁ GLOOP
チーン!! DING!
Be good to each other!!
Meeko's Curfew
...UM... GO AHEAD...
IT'S JUST CURRY, BUT...
MAYBE I SHOULD FEED HIM...
HEY.
I CAN FEED MYSELF!
HUH?!
THANKS!

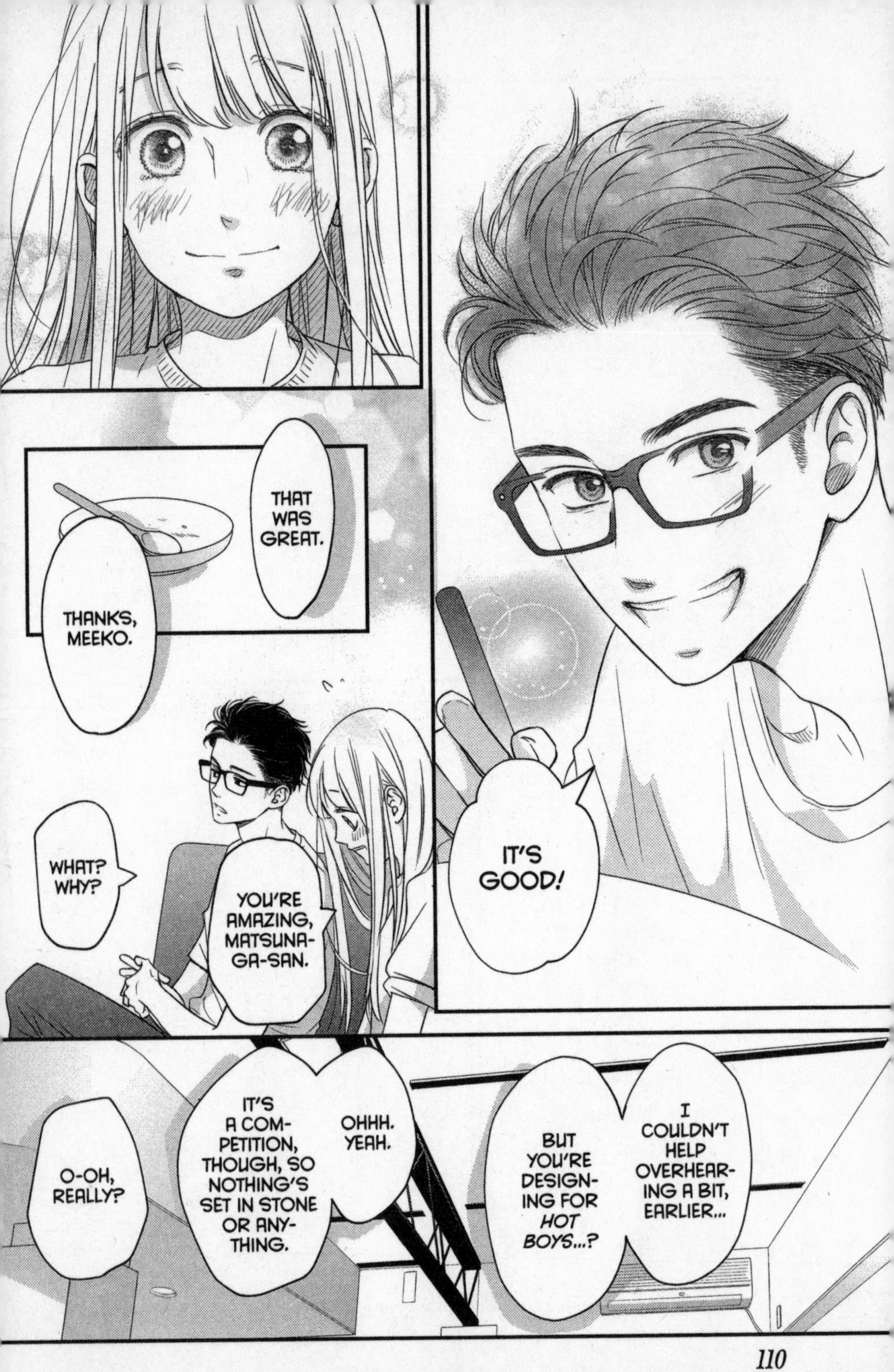

IT'S GOOD!
THAT WAS GREAT.
THANKS, MEEKO.
YOU'RE AMAZING, MATSUNAGA-SAN.
WHAT? WHY?
I COULDN'T HELP OVERHEARING A BIT, EARLIER...
BUT YOU'RE DESIGNING FOR *HOT BOYS*...?
OHHH. YEAH.
IT'S A COMPETITION, THOUGH, SO NOTHING'S SET IN STONE OR ANYTHING.
O-OH, REALLY?

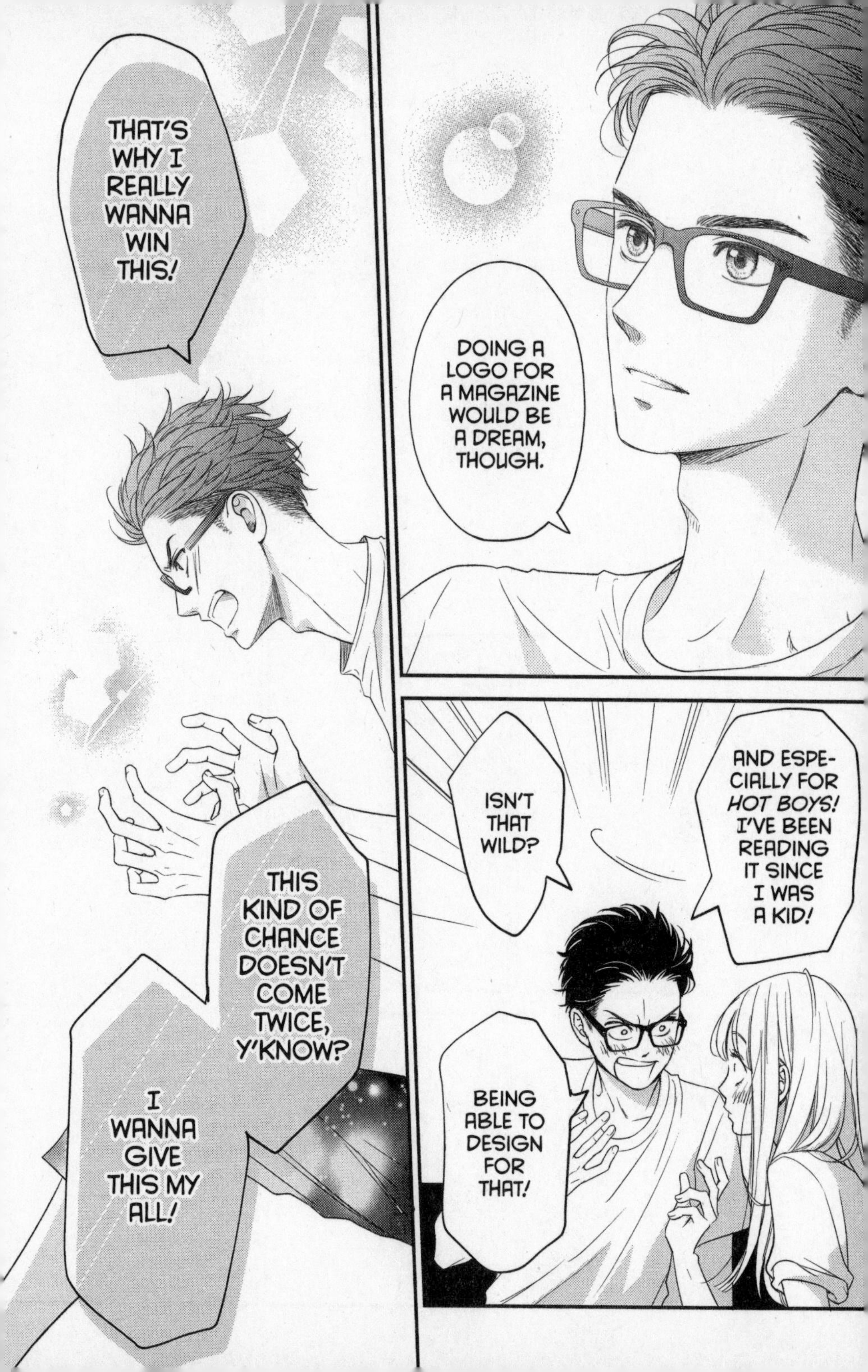
DOING A LOGO FOR A MAGAZINE WOULD BE A DREAM, THOUGH.
AND ESPE-CIALLY FOR *HOT BOYS!* I'VE BEEN READING IT SINCE I WAS A KID!
ISN'T THAT WILD?
BEING ABLE TO DESIGN FOR THAT!
THAT'S WHY I REALLY WANNA WIN THIS!
THIS KIND OF CHANCE DOESN'T COME TWICE, Y'KNOW?
I WANNA GIVE THIS MY ALL!

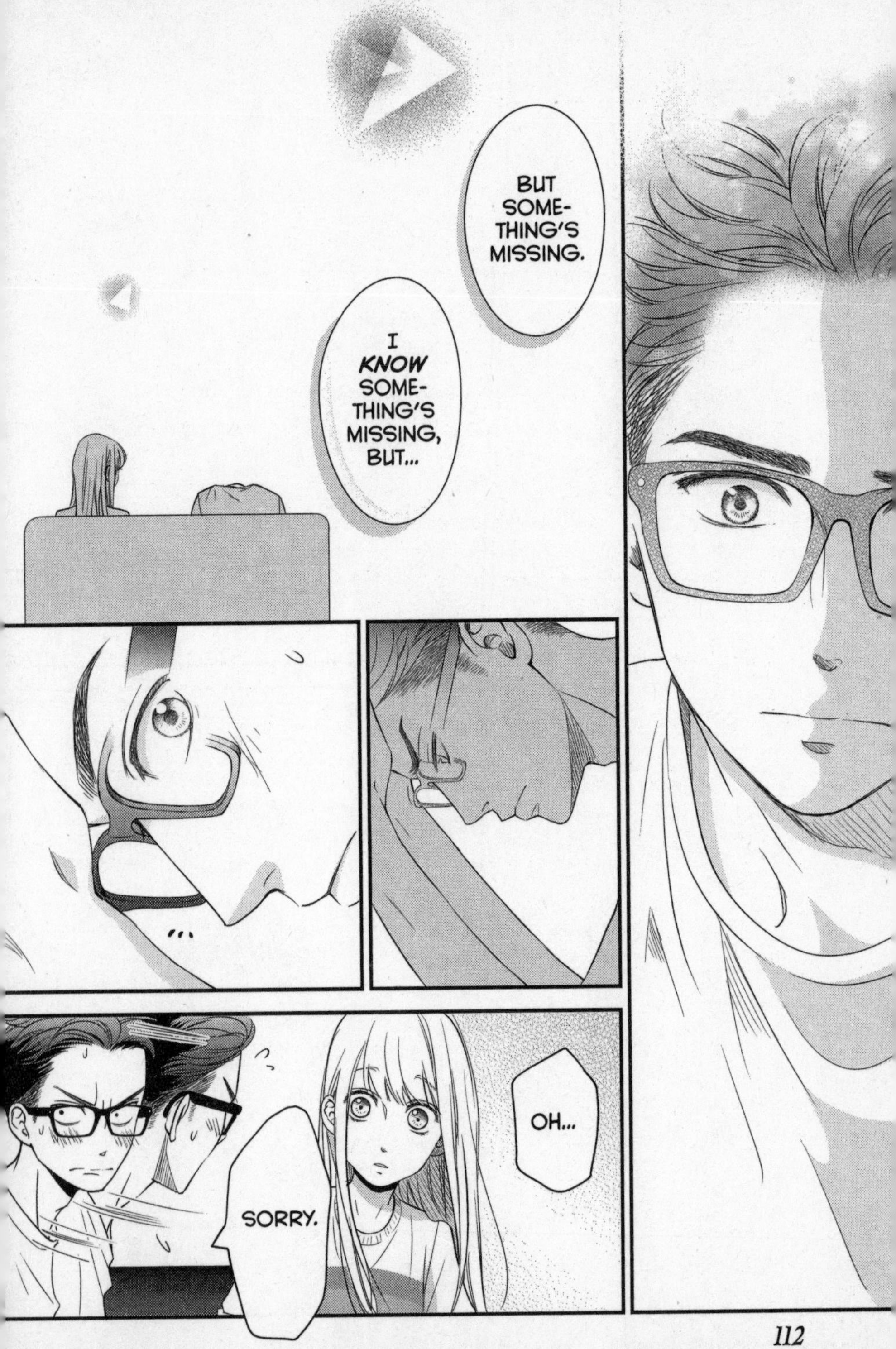
BUT SOMETHING'S MISSING.
I KNOW SOMETHING'S MISSING, BUT...
...
OH...
SORRY.

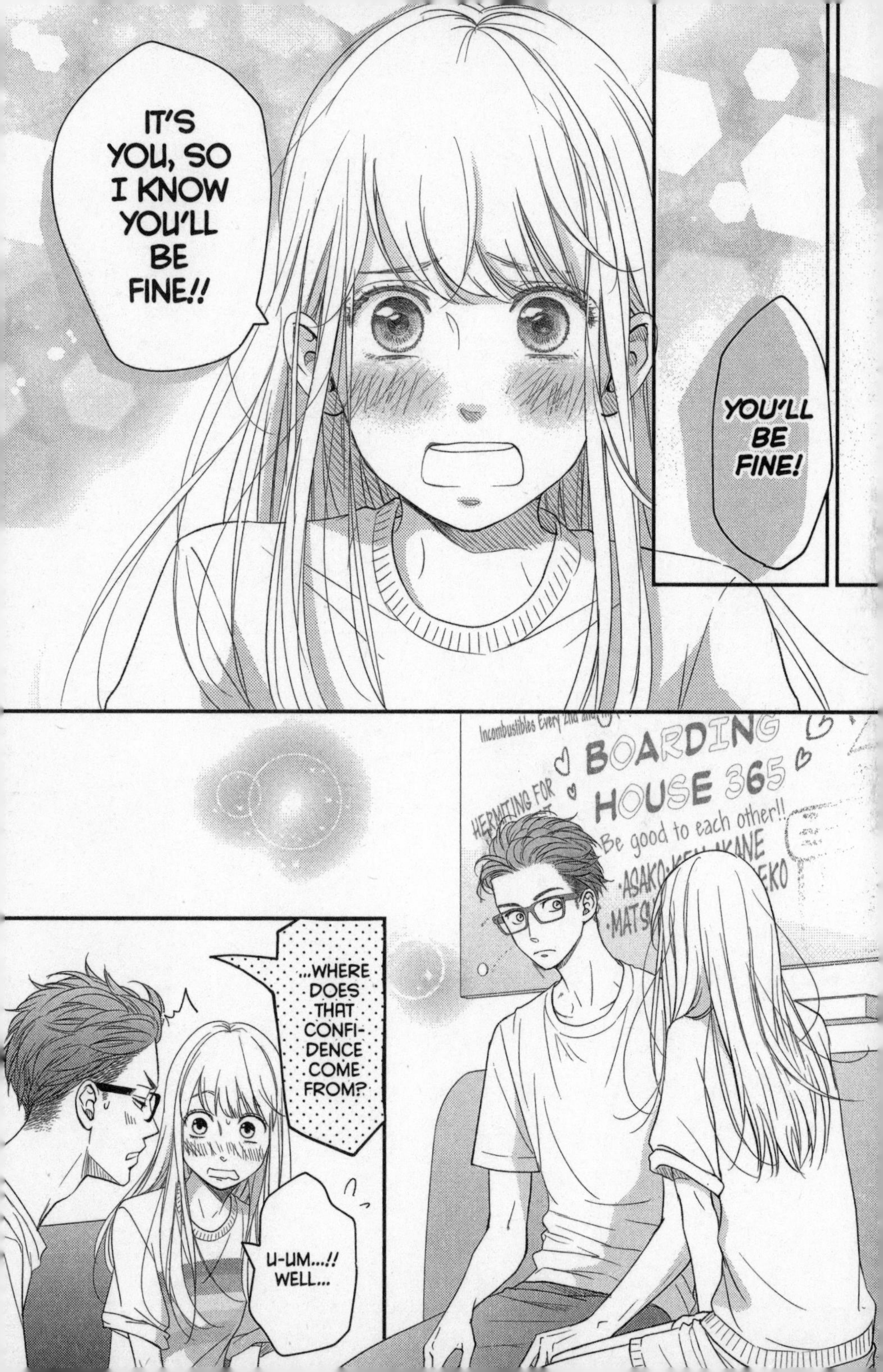
YOU'LL BE FINE!
IT'S YOU, SO I KNOW YOU'LL BE FINE!!
BOARDING HOUSE 365
Be good to each other!!
...WHERE DOES THAT CONFI-DENCE COME FROM?
U-UM...!! WELL...

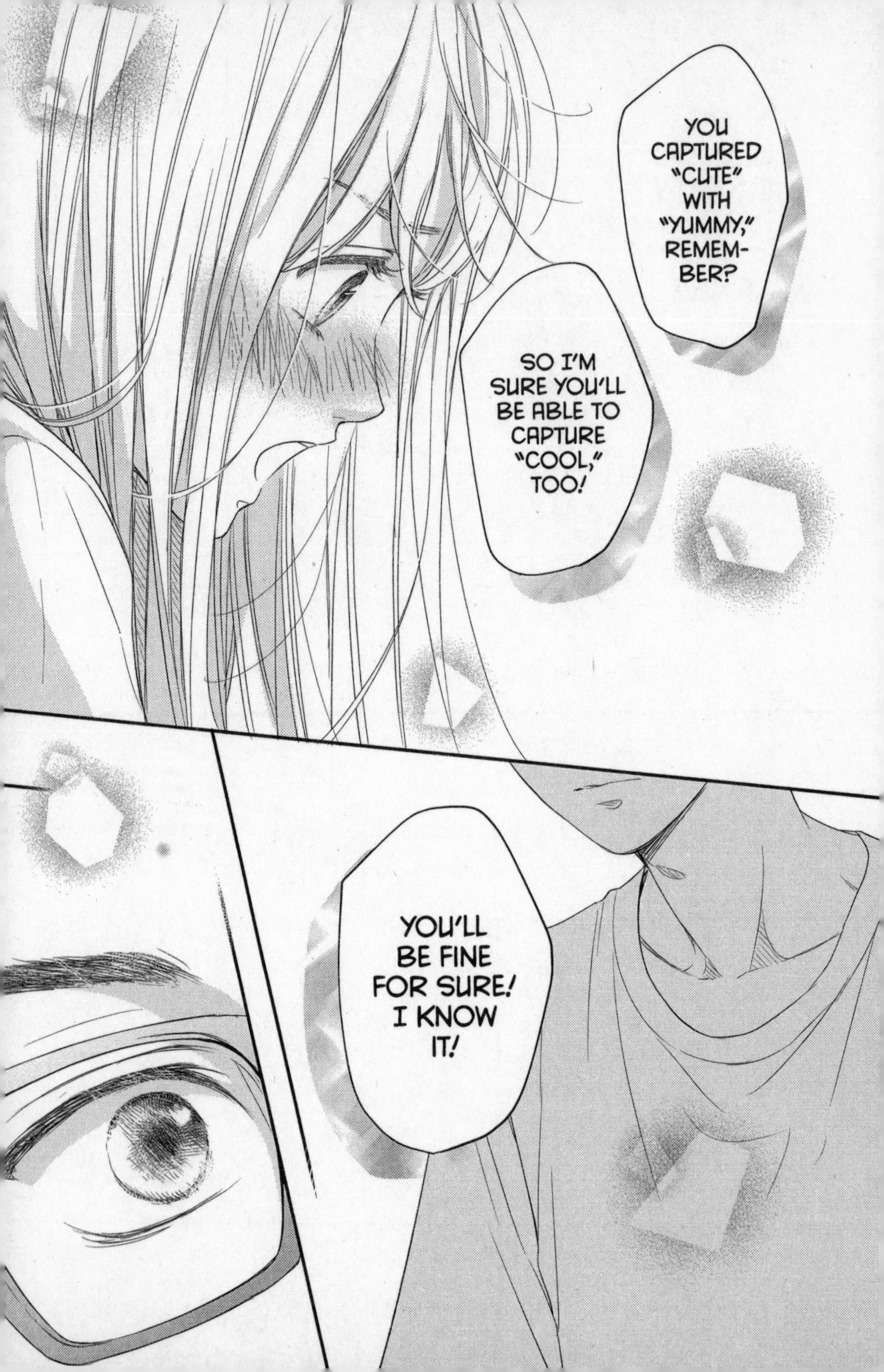
YOU CAPTURED "CUTE" WITH "YUMMY," REMEM-BER?
SO I'M SURE YOU'LL BE ABLE TO CAPTURE "COOL," TOO!
YOU'LL BE FINE FOR SURE! I KNOW IT!

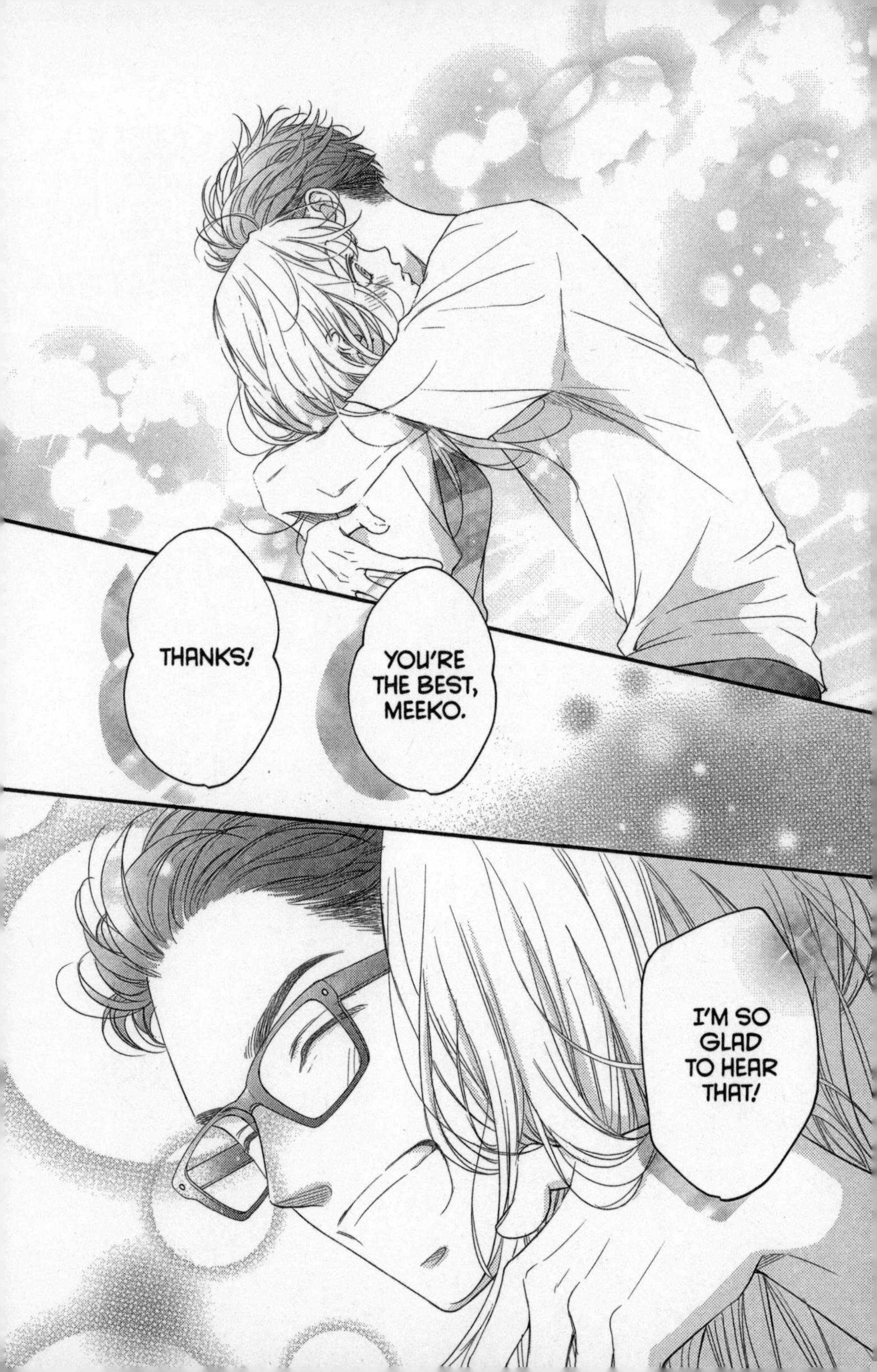
YOU'RE THE BEST, MEEKO.
THANKS!
I'M SO GLAD TO HEAR THAT!

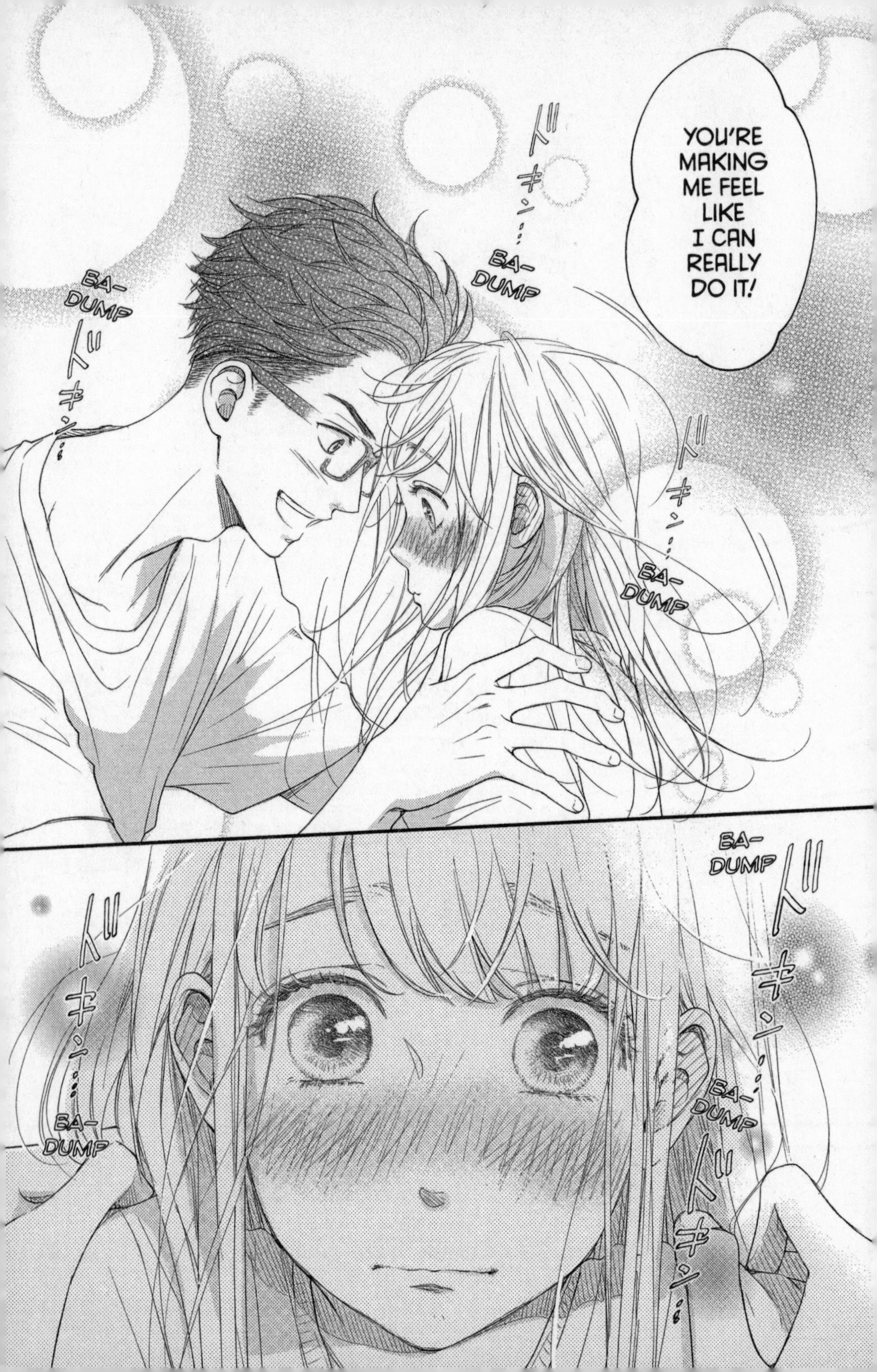
YOU'RE MAKING ME FEEL LIKE I CAN REALLY DO IT!
ドキン…
BA-DUMP
ドキン…
BA-DUMP
BA-DUMP
ドキン…
ドキン…
BA-DUMP
ドキン…
ドキン…
BA-DUMP

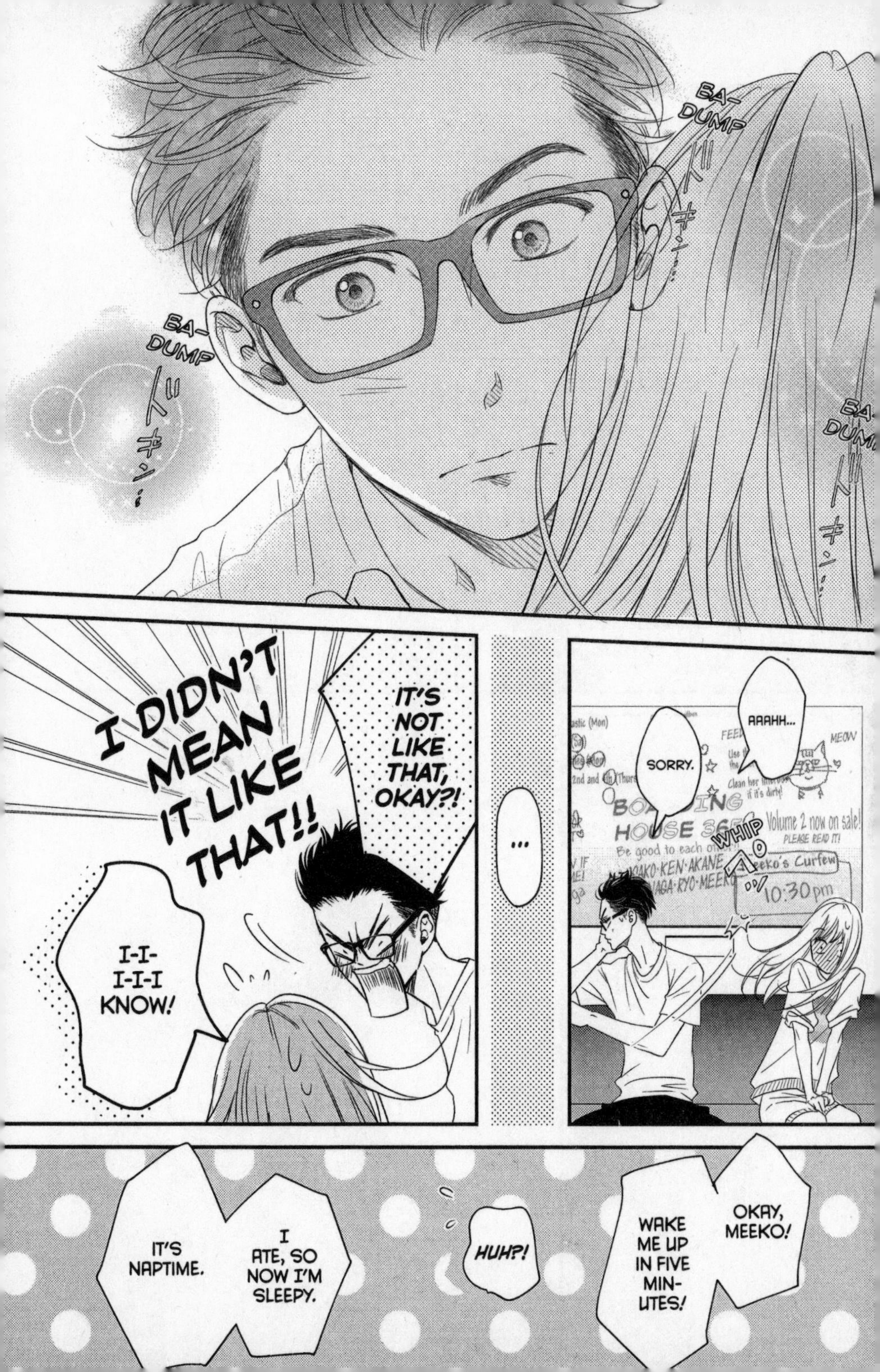
BA-DUMP
BA-DUMP
BA-DUMP
AAAHH...
SORRY.
Volume 2 now on sale!
PLEASE READ IT!
WHIP
10:30 pm
Be good to each other!
MEOW
...
IT'S NOT LIKE THAT, OKAY?!
I DIDN'T MEAN IT LIKE THAT!!
I-I-I-I-I KNOW!
OKAY, MEEKO!
WAKE ME UP IN FIVE MIN-UTES!
HUH?!
I ATE, SO NOW I'M SLEEPY.
IT'S NAPTIME.

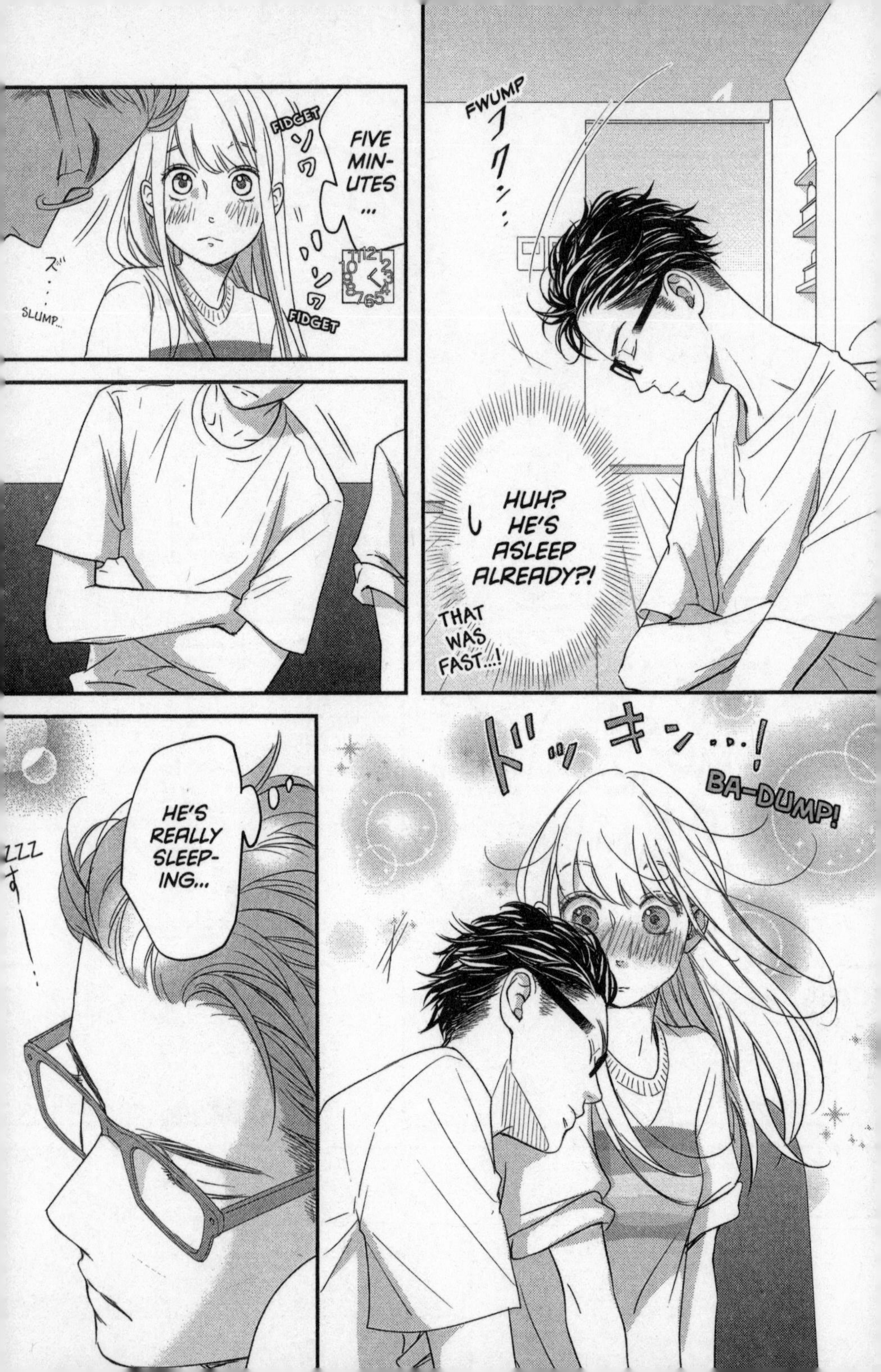
FWUMP
HUH? HE'S ASLEEP ALREADY?!
THAT WAS FAST...!
FIDGET
FIVE MINUTES...
FIDGET
SLUMP...
BA-DUMP!
HE'S REALLY SLEEPING...
ZZZ

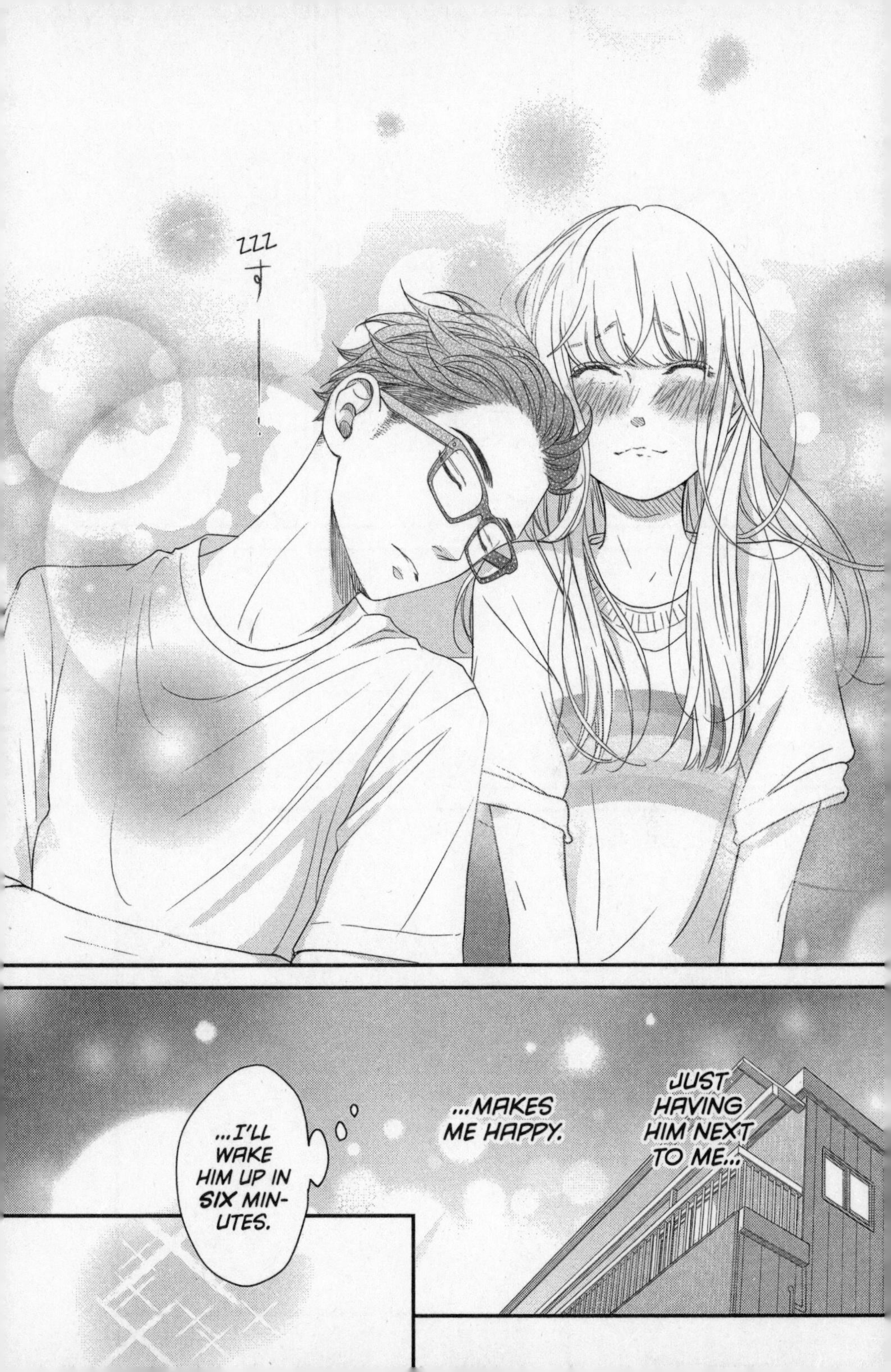
ZZZ
す
JUST HAVING HIM NEXT TO ME...
...MAKES ME HAPPY.
...I'LL WAKE HIM UP IN SIX MIN-UTES.

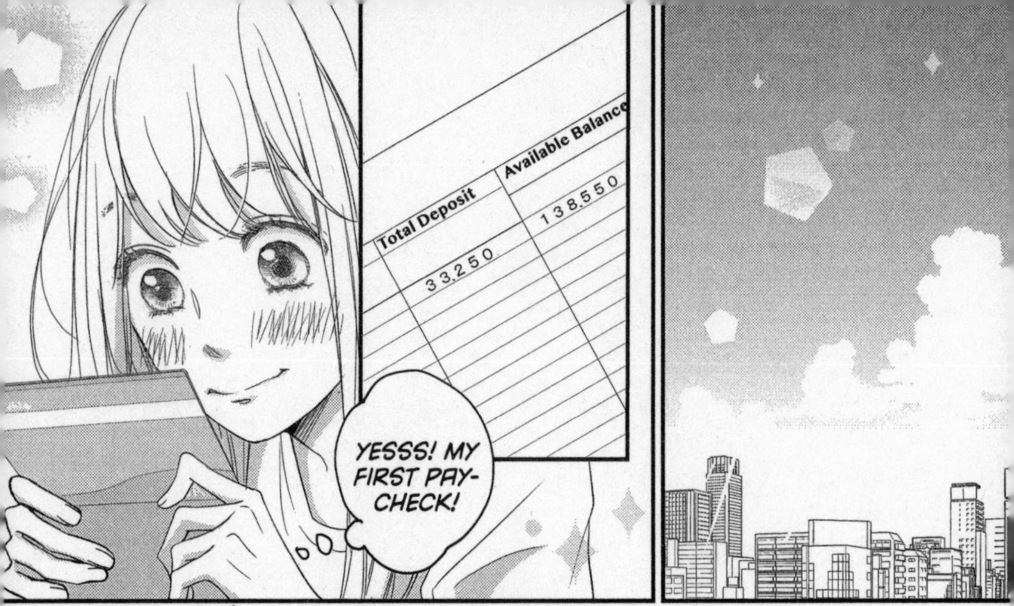
Available Balance
138,550
Total Deposit
33,250
YESSS! MY FIRST PAY-CHECK!

*Approx. $332.50 and $1,385.50 USD respectively

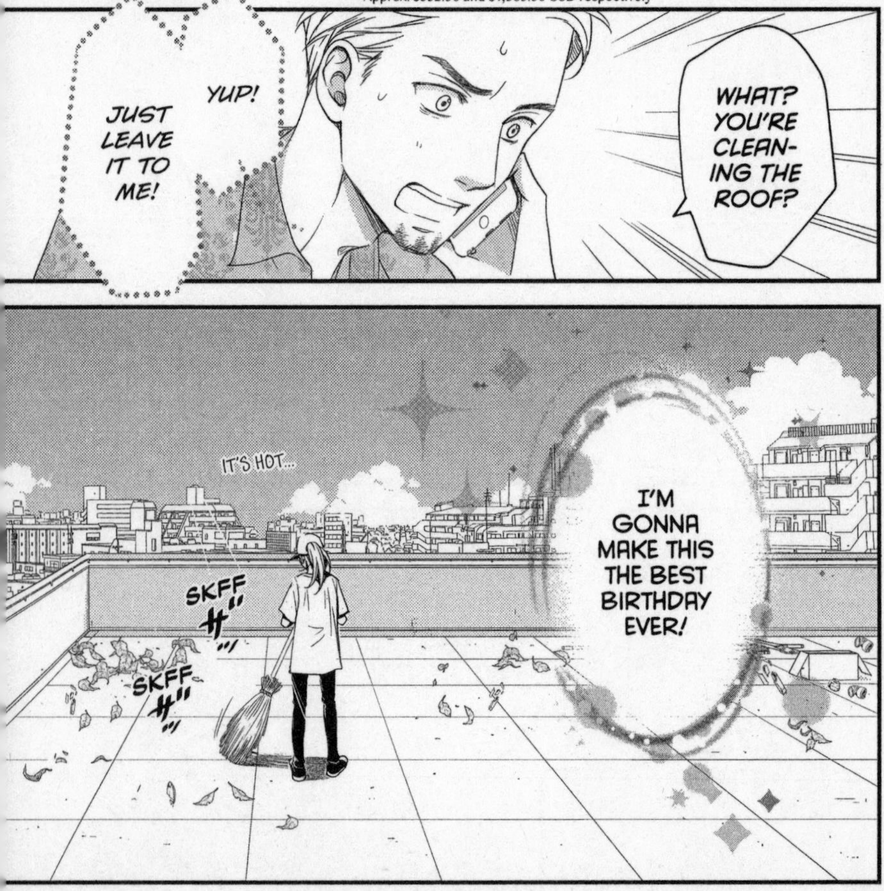
WHAT? YOU'RE CLEAN-ING THE ROOF?
YUP!
JUST LEAVE IT TO ME!
I'M GONNA MAKE THIS THE BEST BIRTHDAY EVER!
IT'S HOT...
SKFF
SKFF

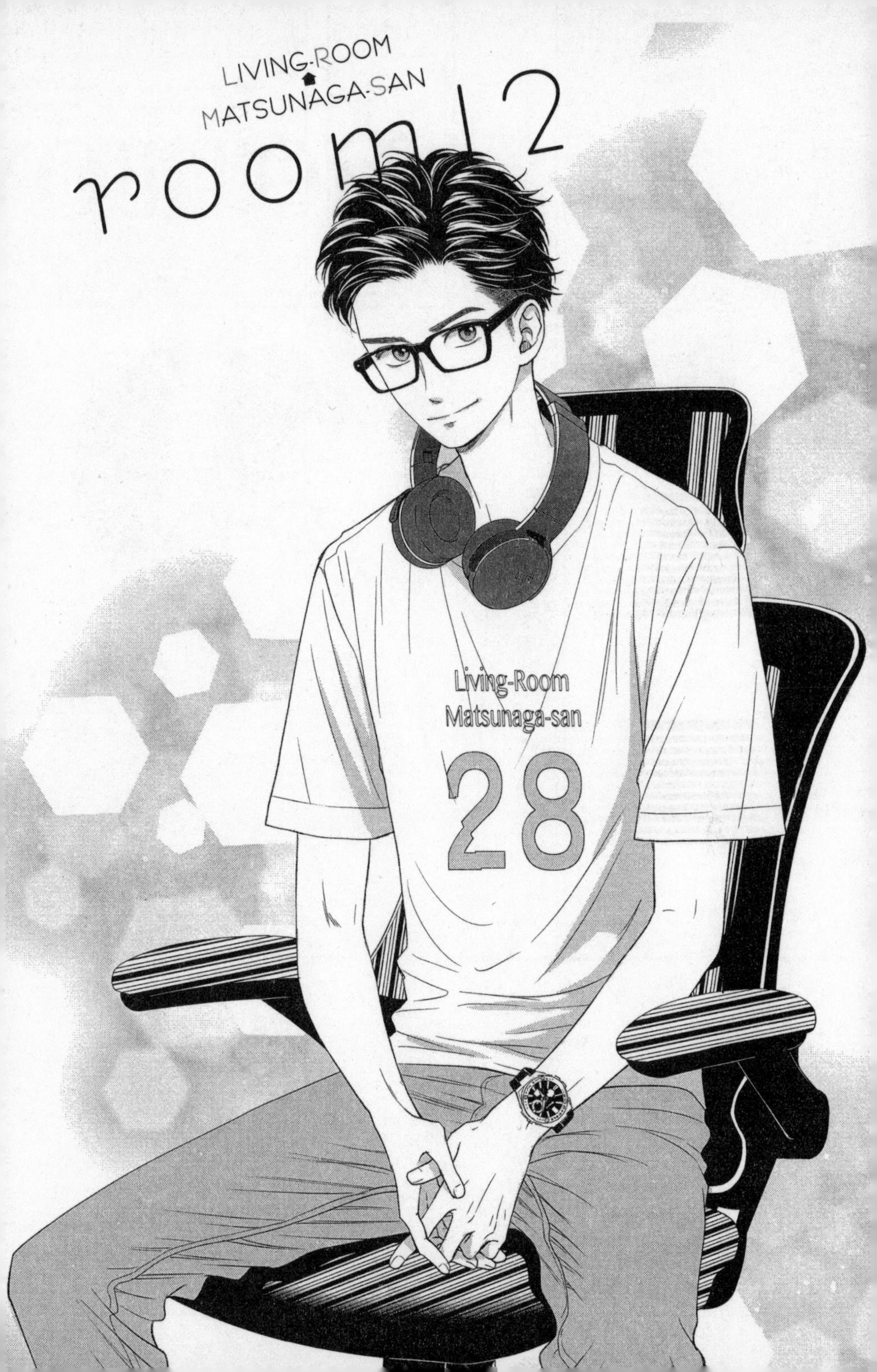
LIVING-ROOM MATSUNAGA-SAN
room 12
Living-Room
Matsunaga-san
28

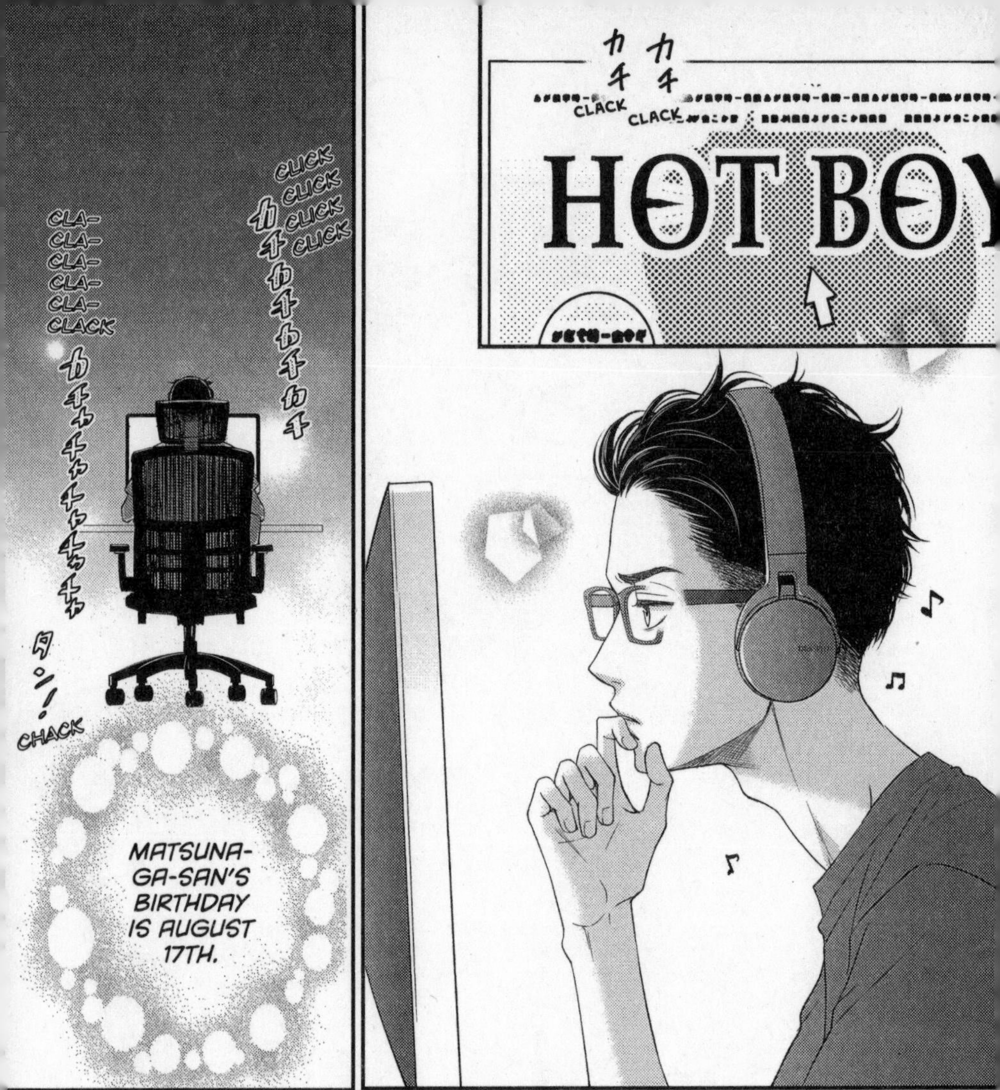
カチ カチ
CLACK CLACK
HOT BOY
CLICK CLICK CLICK CLICK
カチカチカチカチカチ
CLA- CLA- CLA- CLA- CLA- CLACK
カチャチャチャチャチャチャ
タン!
CHACK
MATSUNAGA-SAN'S BIRTHDAY IS AUGUST 17TH.

A DAY IN THE LIFE OF SABAKO

WITH HATTORI-SAN

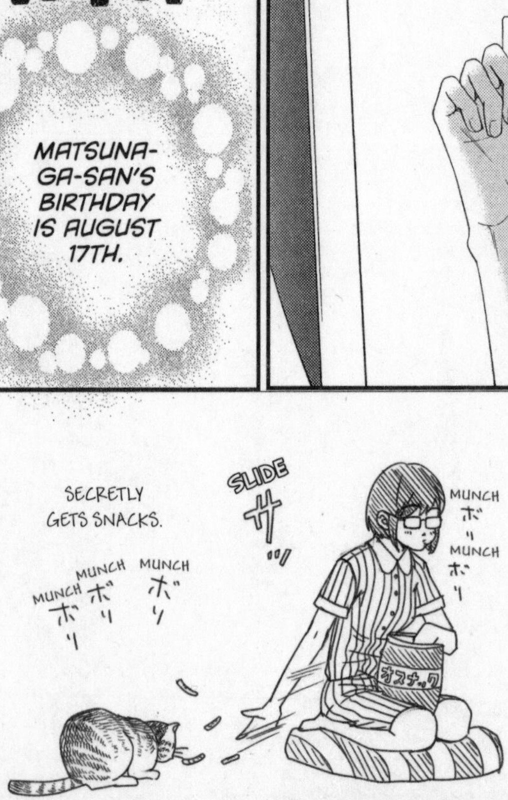
SLIDE
サッ
MUNCH ボリ MUNCH ボリ
SECRETLY GETS SNACKS.
MUNCH ボリ MUNCH ボリ MUNCH ボリ
オスナック

8 August

1	2	3 FIRST JOB	4	5 WORK 10~3
6 WORK 10~3	7	8	9 WORK 10~3	10 WORK 10~3	11	12 WORK 10~3
13 WORK 10~3	14	15 PAY DAY	16 MJ DEADLINE	17 MJB·D	18	19
20 WORK 10~3	21	22	23	24 HOME →	25	26 WORK 10~3
27 WORK 10~3	28	29	30	31	9/1 SCHOOL!

AND I STILL HAVE THE DECORATIONS AND PARTY TO WORRY ABOUT!

OH, NO! I GOTTA PICK UP THE PACE!

EEK! WHAT THE?!

WAIT... AM I NOT GONNA MAKE IT?!

I ONLY HAVE TWO DAYS LEFT...

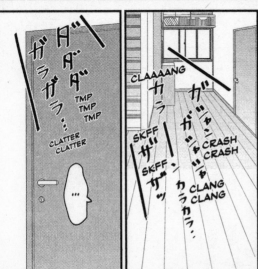

...

123

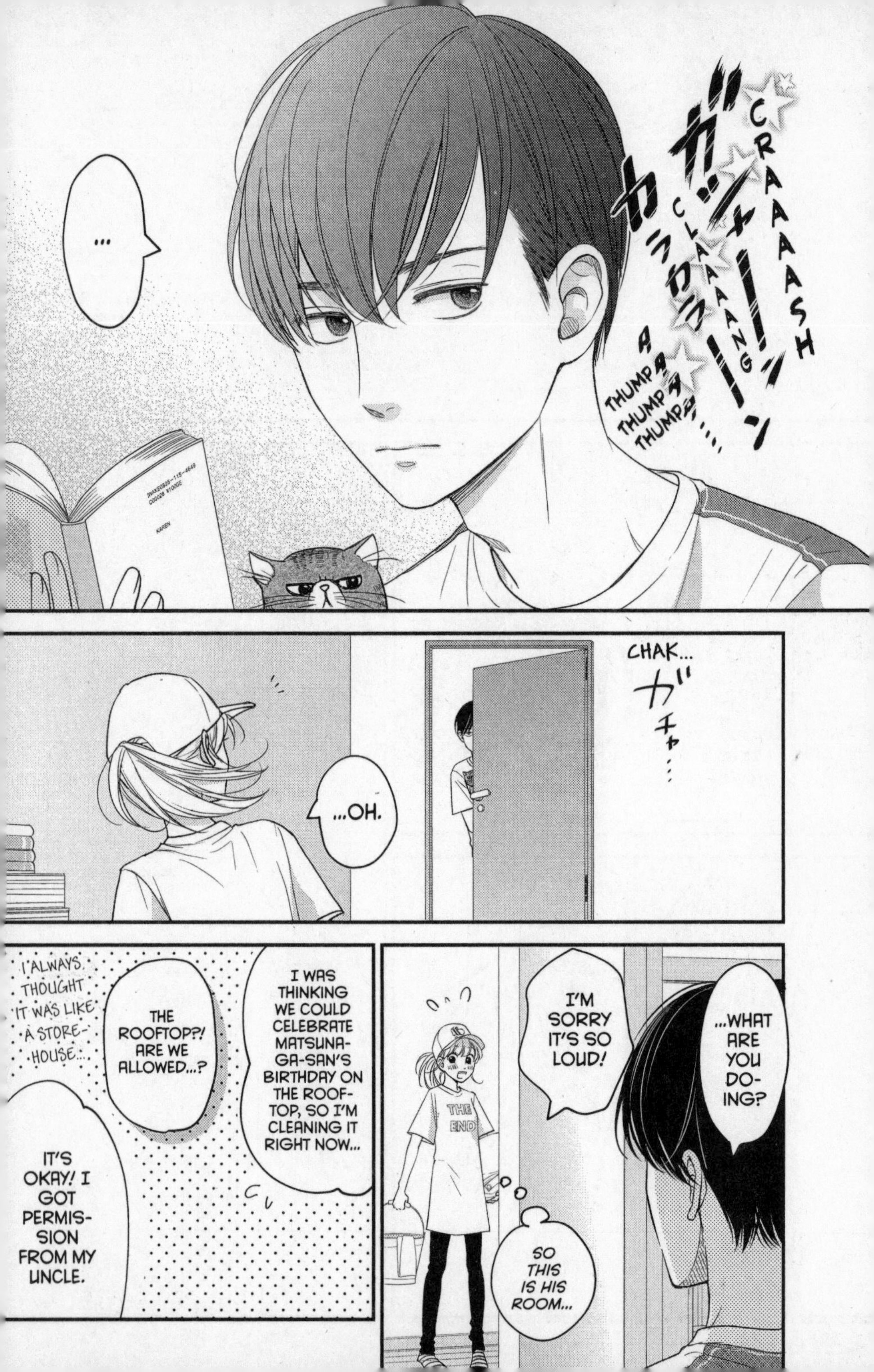
CRAAAASH
CLAAAANG
THUMP THUMP THUMP...
...
CHAK...
...OH.
...WHAT ARE YOU DO-ING?
I'M SORRY IT'S SO LOUD!
SO THIS IS HIS ROOM...
I WAS THINKING WE COULD CELEBRATE MATSUNAGA-SAN'S BIRTHDAY ON THE ROOF-TOP, SO I'M CLEANING IT RIGHT NOW...
THE ROOFTOP?! ARE WE ALLOWED...?
I ALWAYS THOUGHT IT WAS LIKE A STORE-HOUSE...
IT'S OKAY! I GOT PERMIS-SION FROM MY UNCLE.

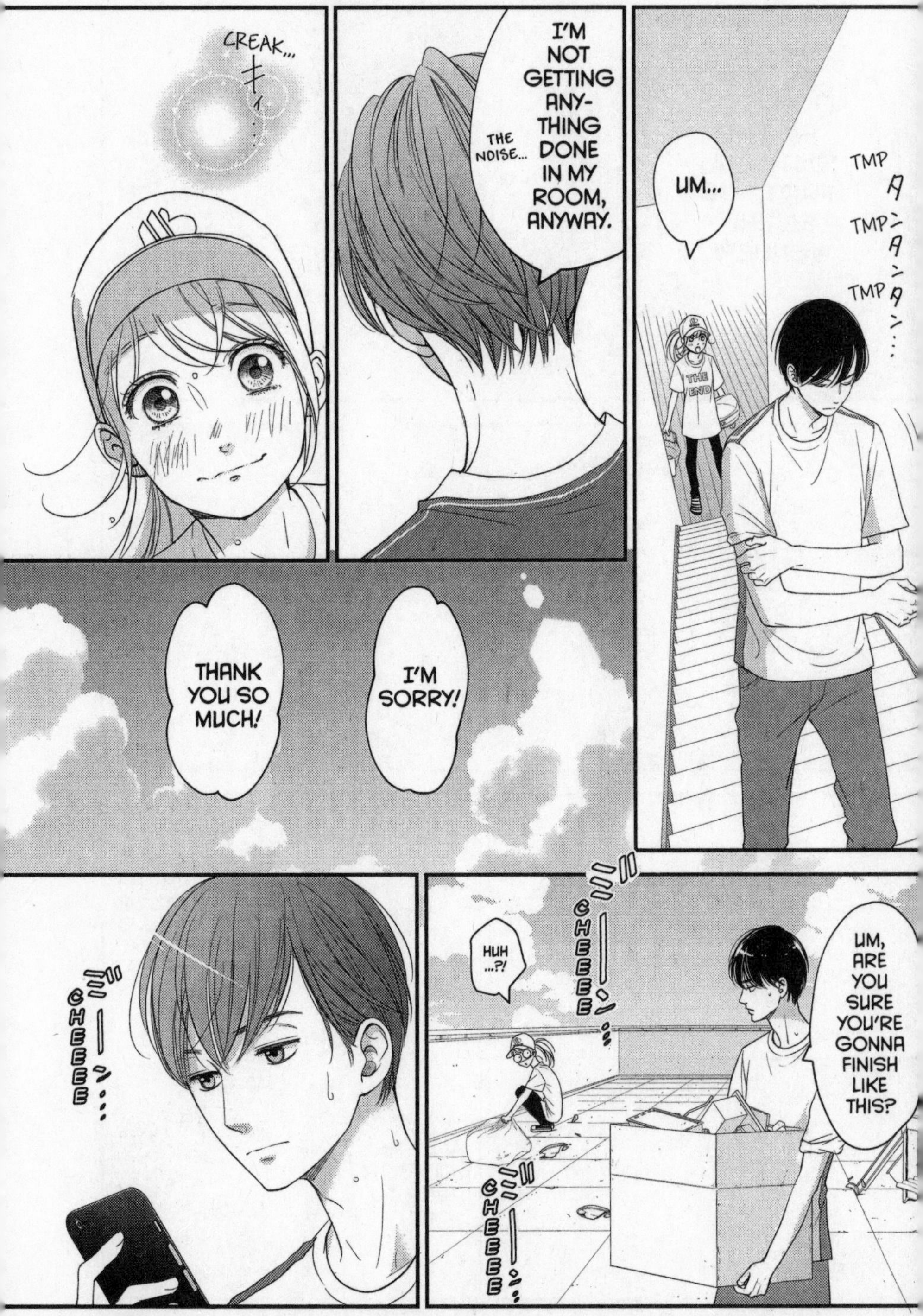
UM...
TMP
TMP
TMP
I'M NOT GETTING ANY-THING DONE IN MY ROOM, ANYWAY.
THE NOISE...
CREAK...
I'M SORRY!
THANK YOU SO MUCH!
UM, ARE YOU SURE YOU'RE GONNA FINISH LIKE THIS?
CHEEEE
HUH ...?!
CHEEEE
CHEEEE

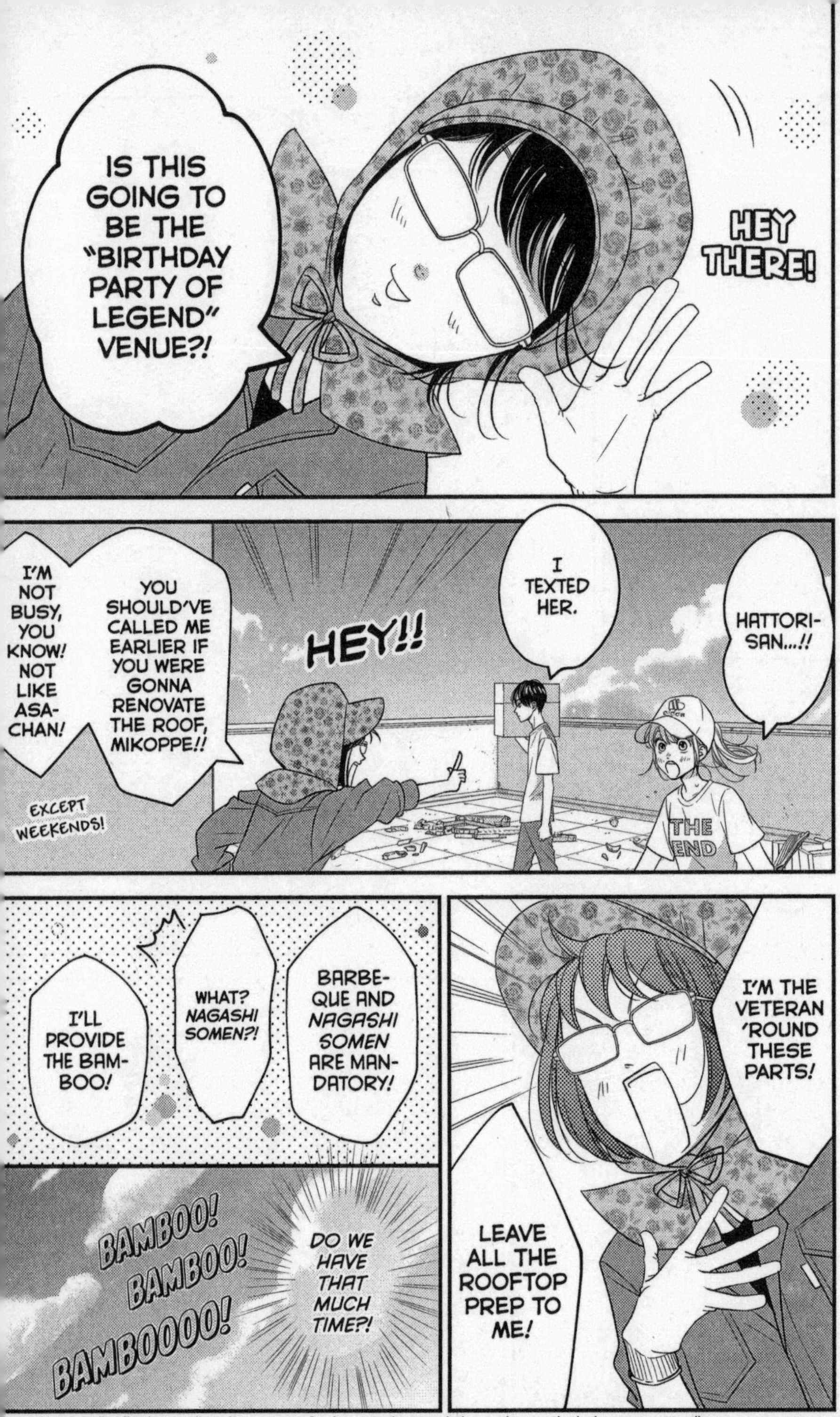
HEY THERE!
IS THIS GOING TO BE THE "BIRTHDAY PARTY OF LEGEND" VENUE?!
HATTORI-SAN...!!
I TEXTED HER.
HEY!!
YOU SHOULD'VE CALLED ME EARLIER IF YOU WERE GONNA RENOVATE THE ROOF, MIKOPPE!!
I'M NOT BUSY, YOU KNOW! NOT LIKE ASA-CHAN!
EXCEPT WEEKENDS!
I'M THE VETERAN 'ROUND THESE PARTS!
LEAVE ALL THE ROOFTOP PREP TO ME!
BARBE-QUE AND NAGASHI SOMEN ARE MAN-DATORY!
WHAT? NAGASHI SOMEN?!
I'LL PROVIDE THE BAM-BOO!
DO WE HAVE THAT MUCH TIME?!
BAMBOO! BAMBOO! BAMBOOOO!

Nagashi somen (lit. "flowing noodles") is a Japanese food commonly eaten during outdoor parties in the summer. Noodles are "flowed" down a long bamboo flume filled with water. The noodles are caught with chopsticks and eaten with dipping sauce.

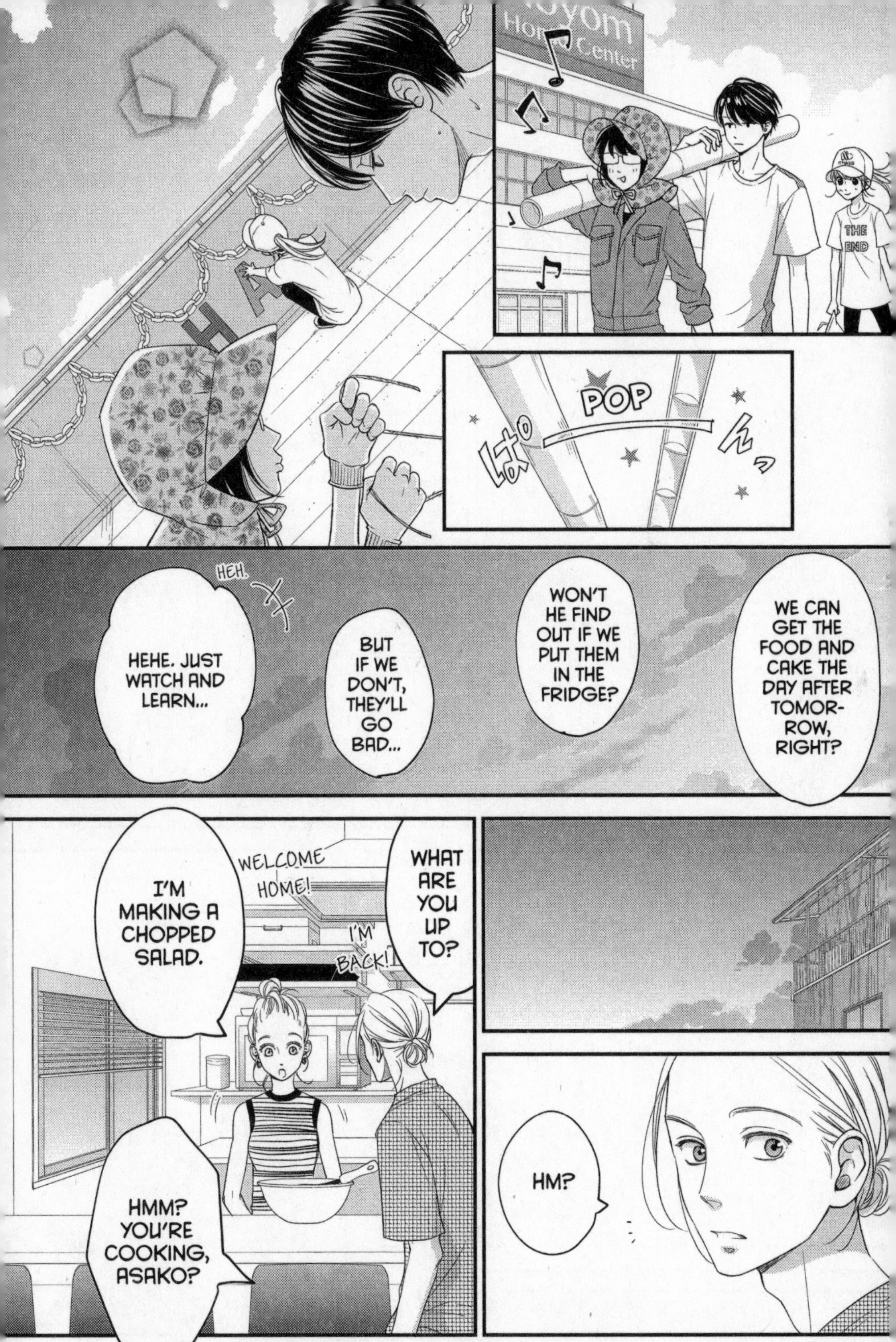

THE END
POP
ぱ
んっ
WE CAN GET THE FOOD AND CAKE THE DAY AFTER TOMORROW, RIGHT?
WON'T HE FIND OUT IF WE PUT THEM IN THE FRIDGE?
BUT IF WE DON'T, THEY'LL GO BAD...
HEHE. JUST WATCH AND LEARN...
HEH.
HM?
WHAT ARE YOU UP TO?
I'M BACK!
WELCOME HOME!
I'M MAKING A CHOPPED SALAD.
HMM? YOU'RE COOKING, ASAKO?

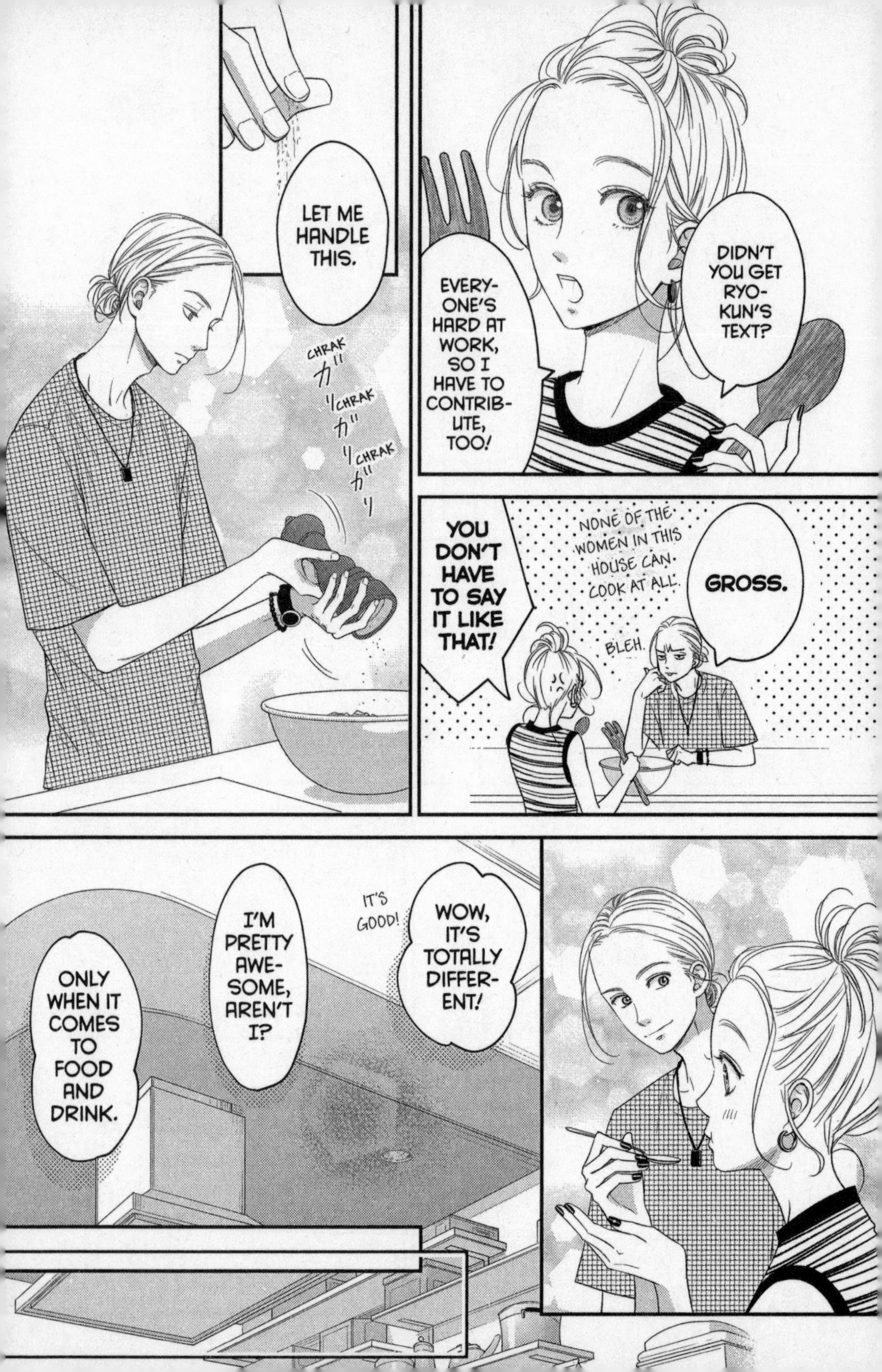
DIDN'T YOU GET RYO-KUN'S TEXT?
EVERYONE'S HARD AT WORK, SO I HAVE TO CONTRIBUTE, TOO!
GROSS.
NONE OF THE WOMEN IN THIS HOUSE CAN COOK AT ALL.
BLEH.
YOU DON'T HAVE TO SAY IT LIKE THAT!
LET ME HANDLE THIS.
CHRAK
CHRAK
CHRAK
WOW, IT'S TOTALLY DIFFERENT!
IT'S GOOD!
I'M PRETTY AWESOME, AREN'T I?
ONLY WHEN IT COMES TO FOOD AND DRINK.

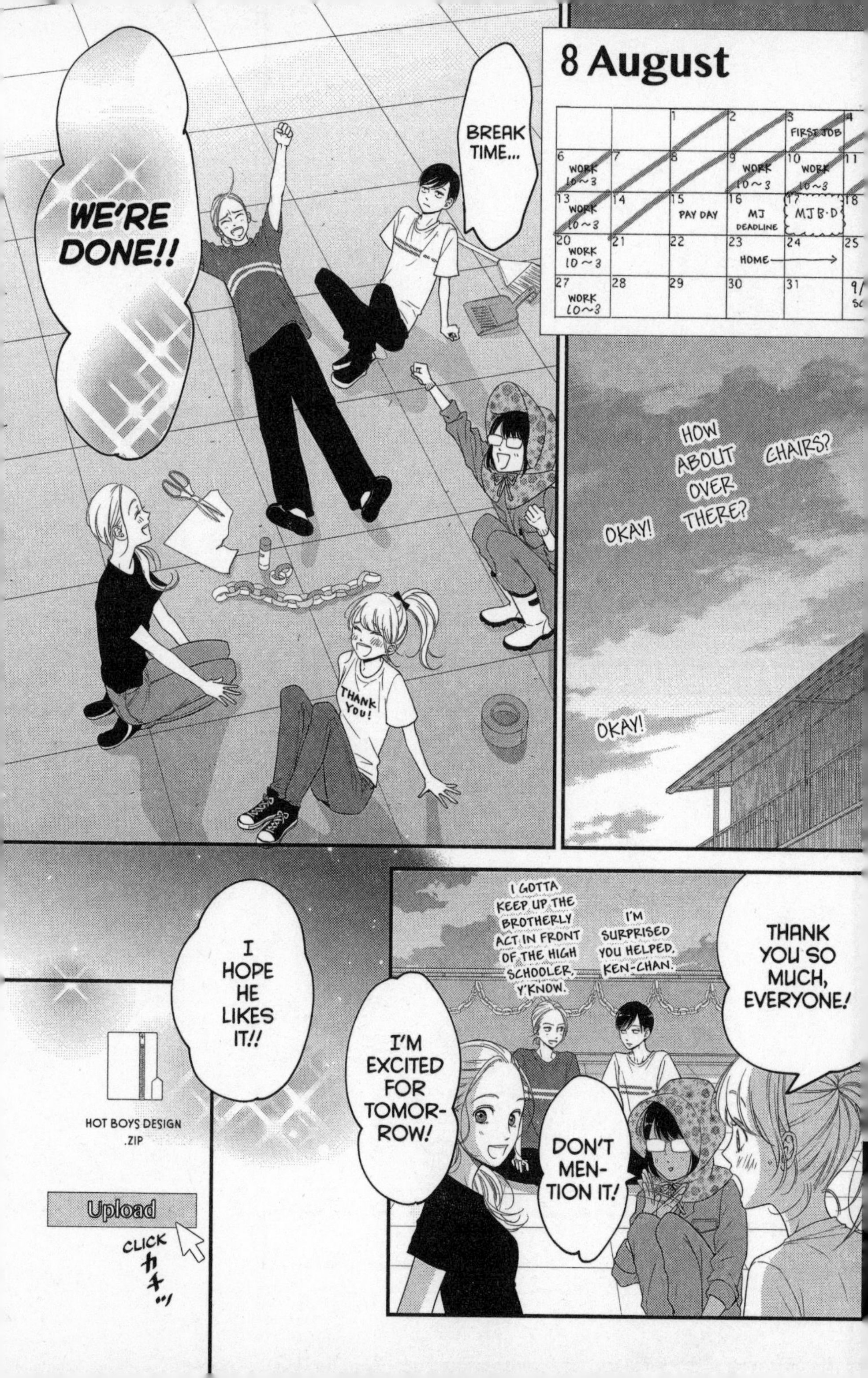
8 August
1
2
3 FIRST JOB
4
6 WORK 10~3
7
8
9 WORK 10~3
10 WORK 10~3
11
13 WORK 10~3
14
15 PAY DAY
16 MJ DEADLINE
17 MJB·D
18
20 WORK 10~3
21
22
23 HOME
24
25
27 WORK 10~3
28
29
30
31
CHAIRS?
HOW ABOUT OVER THERE?
OKAY!
OKAY!
BREAK TIME...
WE'RE DONE!!
THANK YOU!
THANK YOU SO MUCH, EVERYONE!
I'M SURPRISED YOU HELPED, KEN-CHAN.
I GOTTA KEEP UP THE BROTHERLY ACT IN FRONT OF THE HIGH SCHOOLER, Y'KNOW.
DON'T MEN-TION IT!
I'M EXCITED FOR TOMOR-ROW!
I HOPE HE LIKES IT!!
HOT BOYS DESIGN .ZIP
Upload
CLICK
カチッ

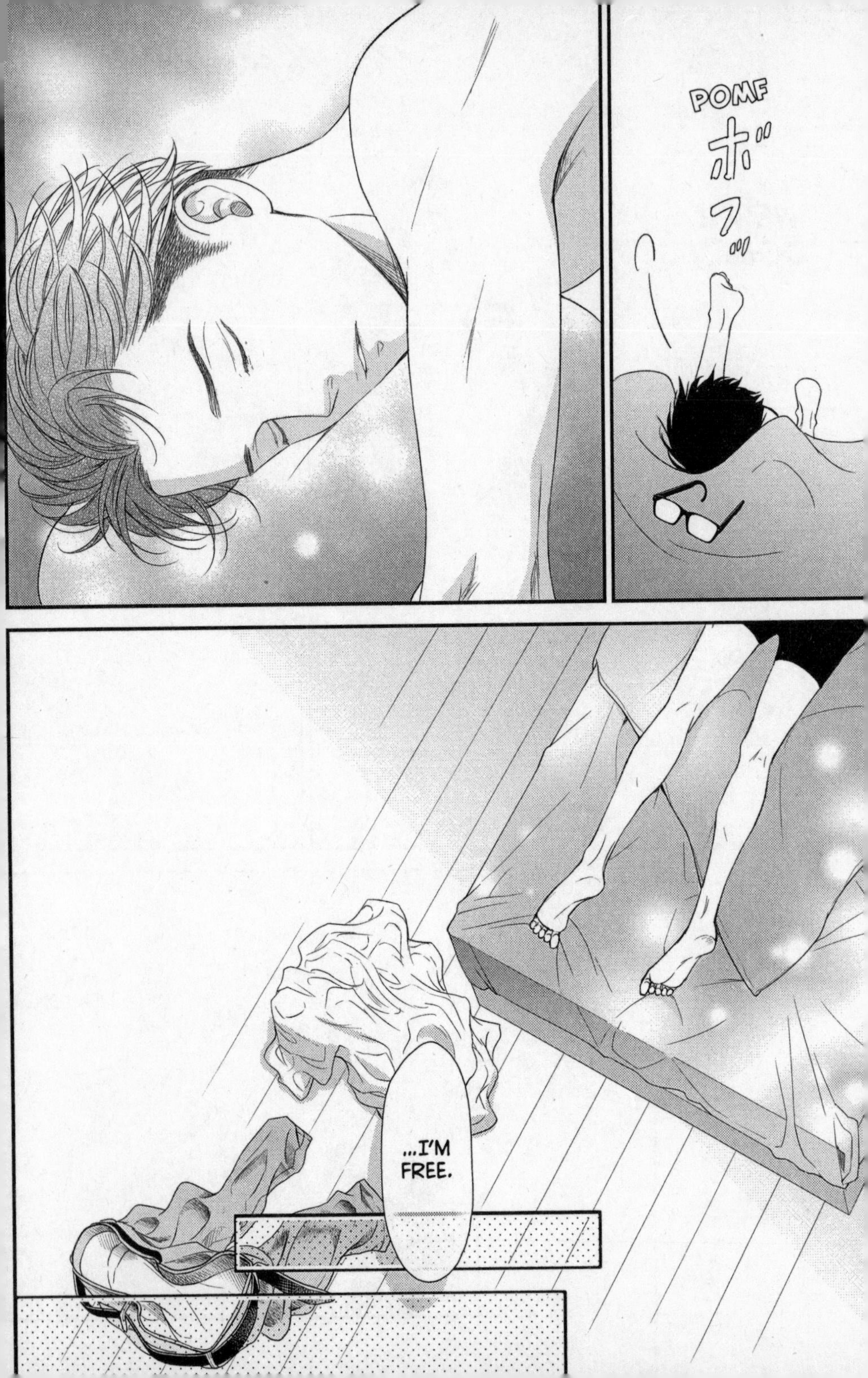
POMF
ボフ
...I'M FREE.

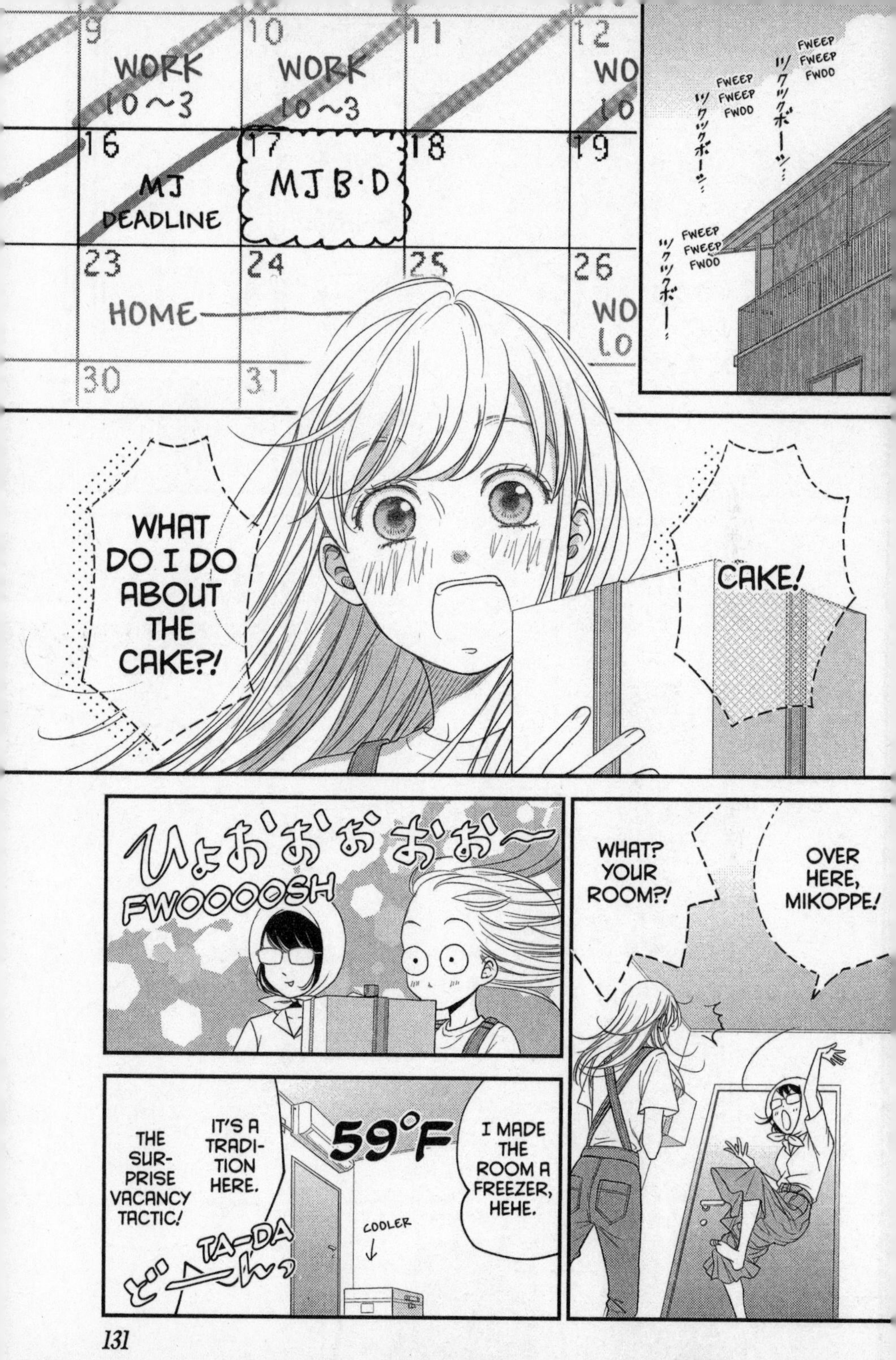
ツクツクボーッ…
FWEEP FWEEP FWOO
ツクツクボーッ…
FWEEP FWEEP FWOO
ツクツクボー…
FWEEP FWEEP FWOO
9
WORK 10~3
10
WORK 10~3
11
12
WO 10
16
MJ DEADLINE
17
MJ B·D
18
19
23
HOME
24
25
26
WO 10
30
31
CAKE!
WHAT DO I DO ABOUT THE CAKE?!
OVER HERE, MIKOPPE!
WHAT? YOUR ROOM?!
ひょおおおおお〜
FWOOOOSH
I MADE THE ROOM A FREEZER, HEHE.
59°F
IT'S A TRADITION HERE.
THE SURPRISE VACANCY TACTIC!
どーーんっ
TA-DA
COOLER

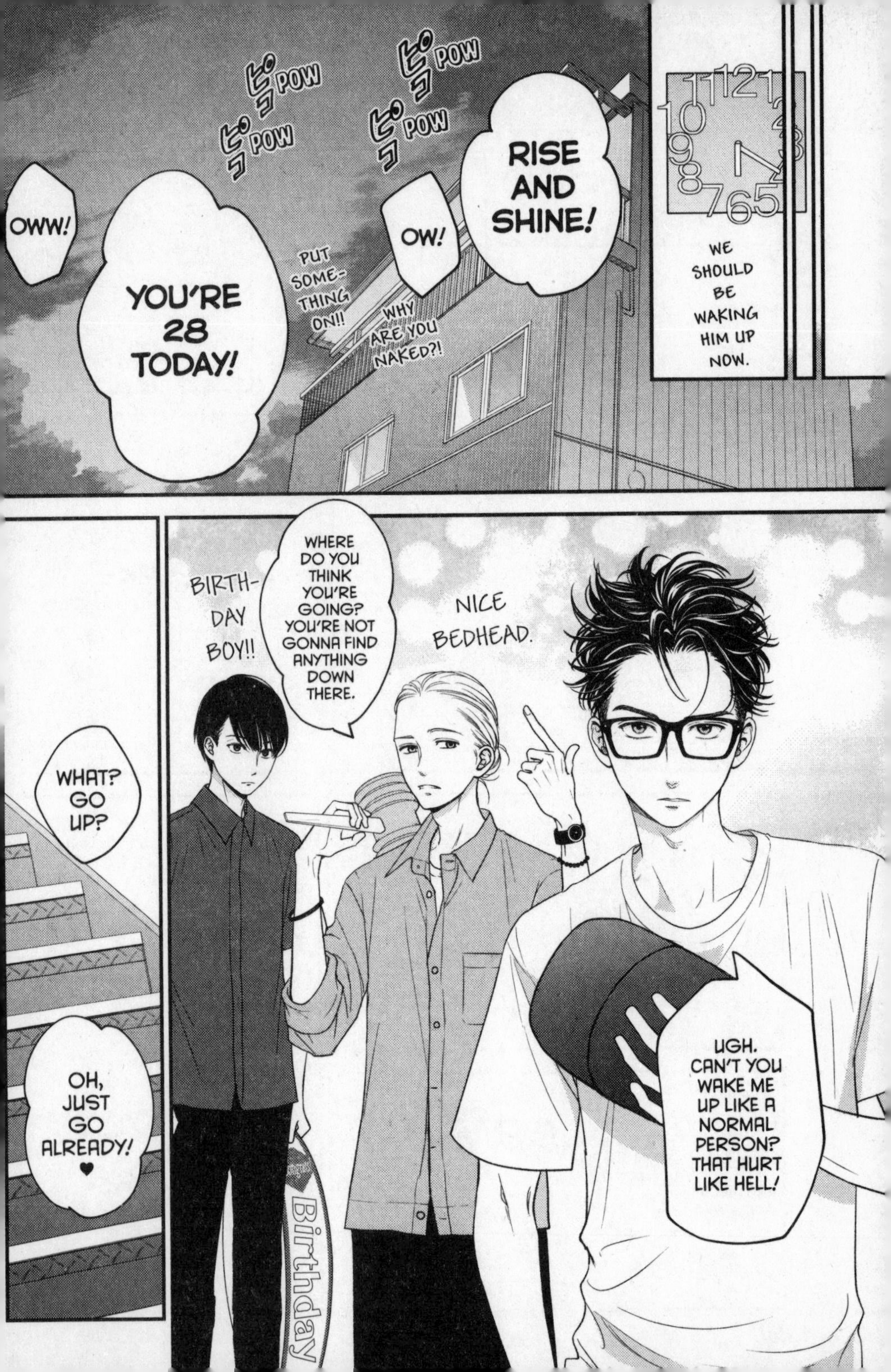
WE SHOULD BE WAKING HIM UP NOW.
RISE AND SHINE!
POW
POW
OW!
WHY ARE YOU NAKED?!
PUT SOME-THING ON!!
POW
POW
YOU'RE 28 TODAY!
OWW!
UGH. CAN'T YOU WAKE ME UP LIKE A NORMAL PERSON? THAT HURT LIKE HELL!
NICE BEDHEAD.
WHERE DO YOU THINK YOU'RE GOING? YOU'RE NOT GONNA FIND ANYTHING DOWN THERE.
BIRTH-DAY BOY!!
Birthday
WHAT? GO UP?
OH, JUST GO ALREADY! ♥

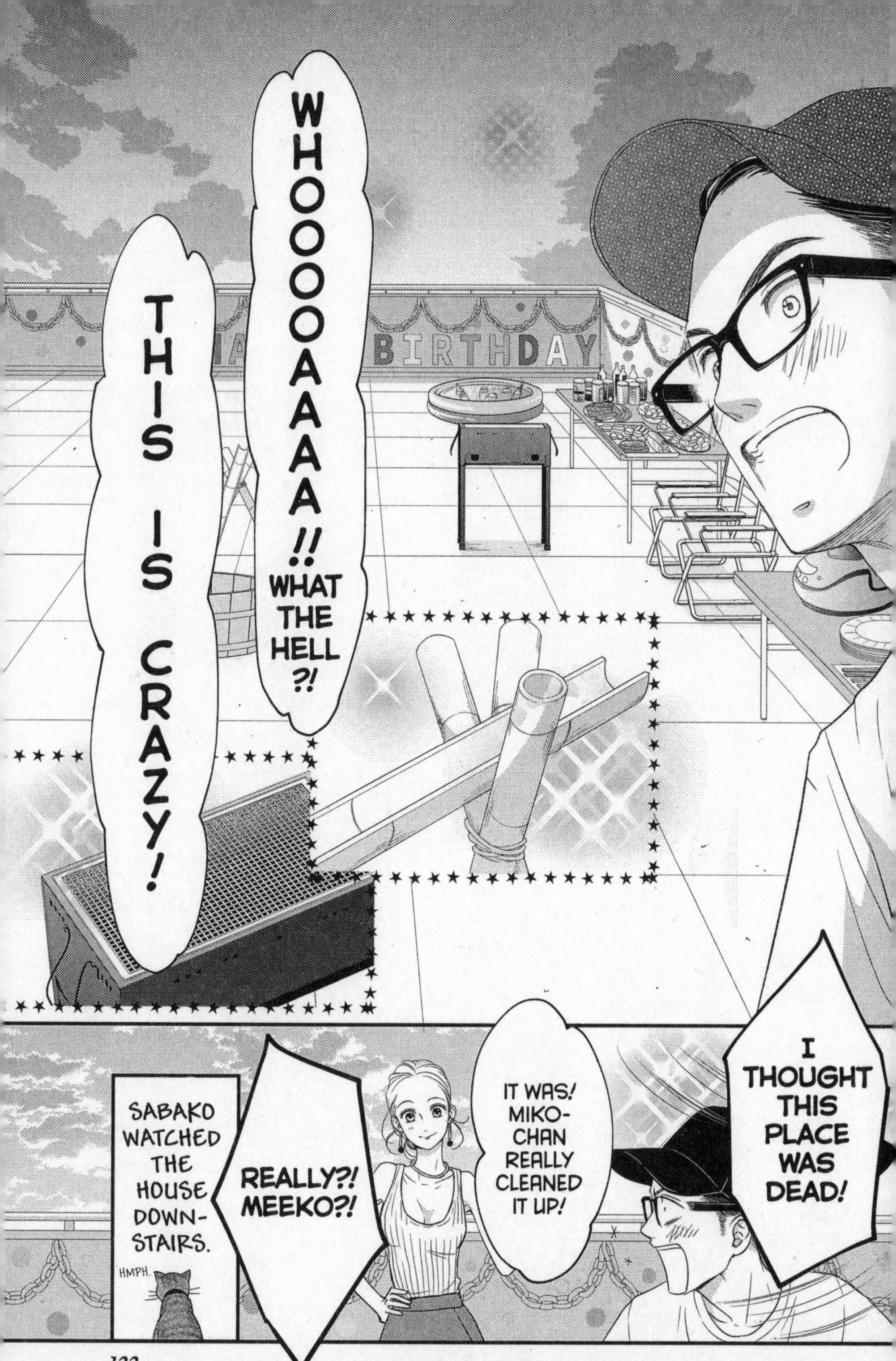
WHOOOOAAAAA!! WHAT THE HELL?!
THIS IS CRAZY!
BIRTHDAY
I THOUGHT THIS PLACE WAS DEAD!
IT WAS! MIKO-CHAN REALLY CLEANED IT UP!
REALLY?! MEEKO?!
SABAKO WATCHED THE HOUSE DOWN-STAIRS.
HMPH.

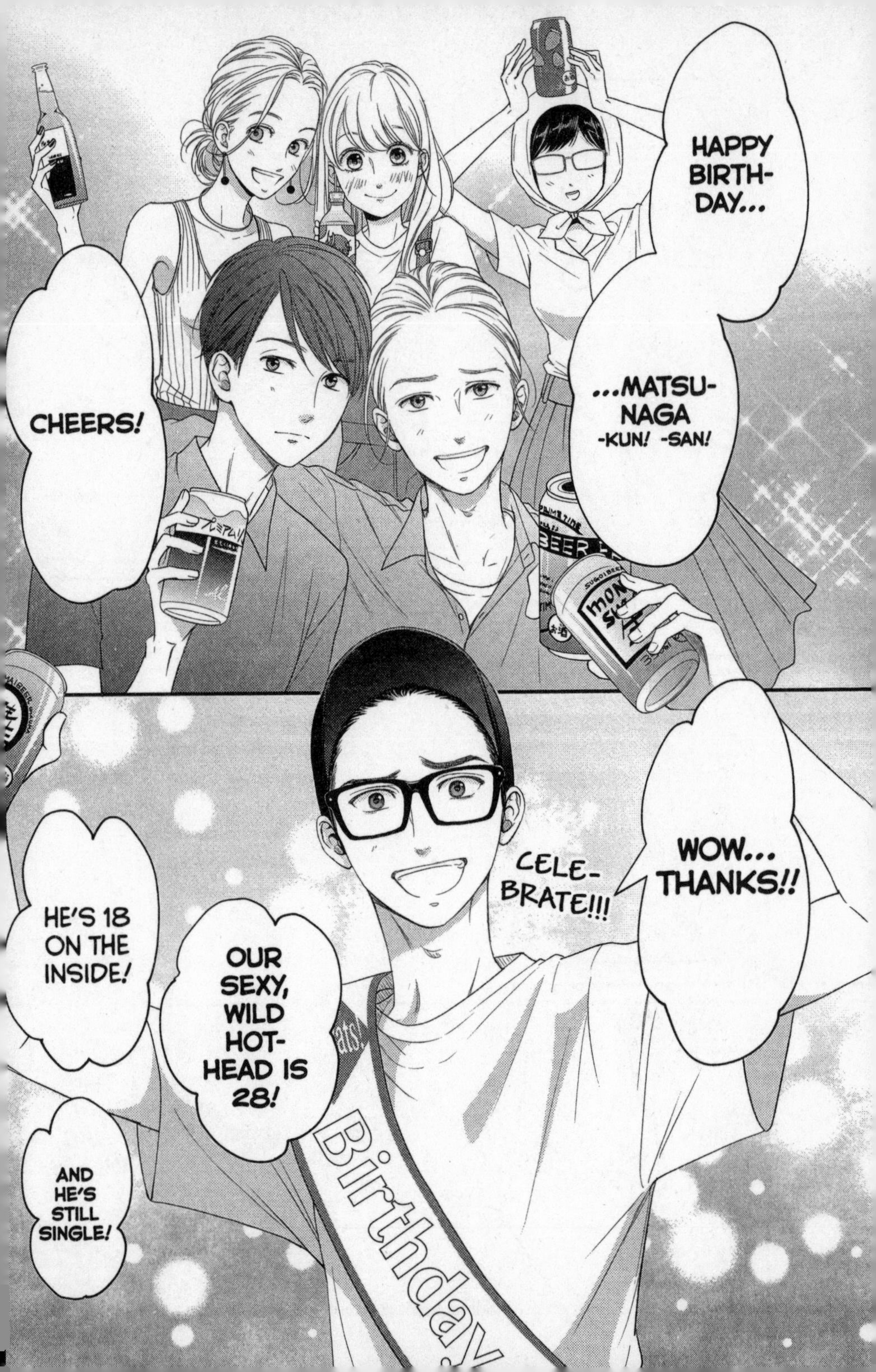
HAPPY BIRTH-DAY...
...MATSU-NAGA -KUN! -SAN!
CHEERS!
WOW... THANKS!!
CELE-BRATE!!!
OUR SEXY, WILD HOT-HEAD IS 28!
HE'S 18 ON THE INSIDE!
AND HE'S STILL SINGLE!
Birthday

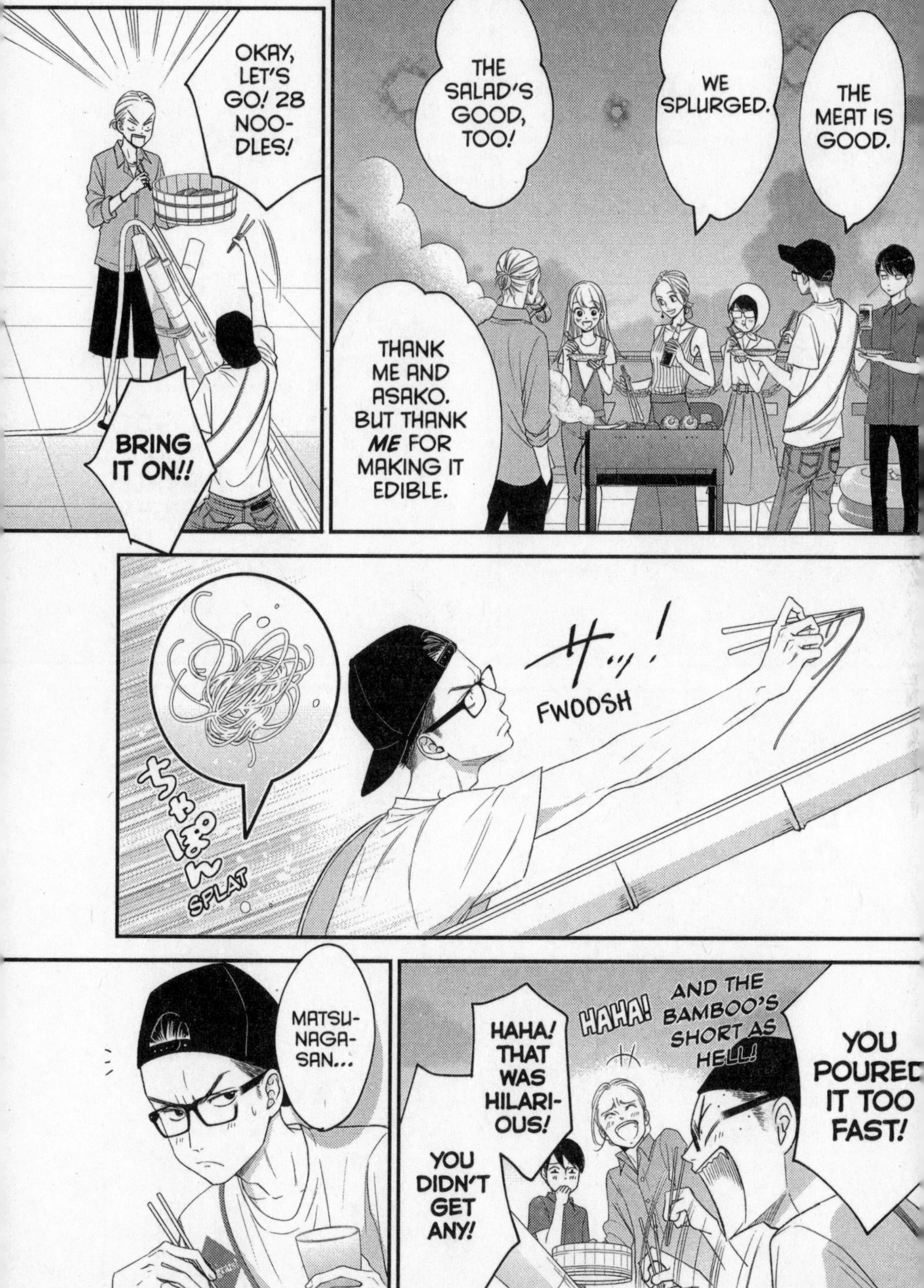
THE MEAT IS GOOD.
WE SPLURGED.
THE SALAD'S GOOD, TOO!
THANK ME AND ASAKO. BUT THANK *ME* FOR MAKING IT EDIBLE.
OKAY, LET'S GO! 28 NOODLES!
BRING IT ON!!
サッ!
FWOOSH
ちゃぽん
SPLAT
YOU POURED IT TOO FAST!
AND THE BAMBOO'S SHORT AS HELL!
HAHA!
HAHA! THAT WAS HILARIOUS!
YOU DIDN'T GET ANY!
MATSUNAGA-SAN...

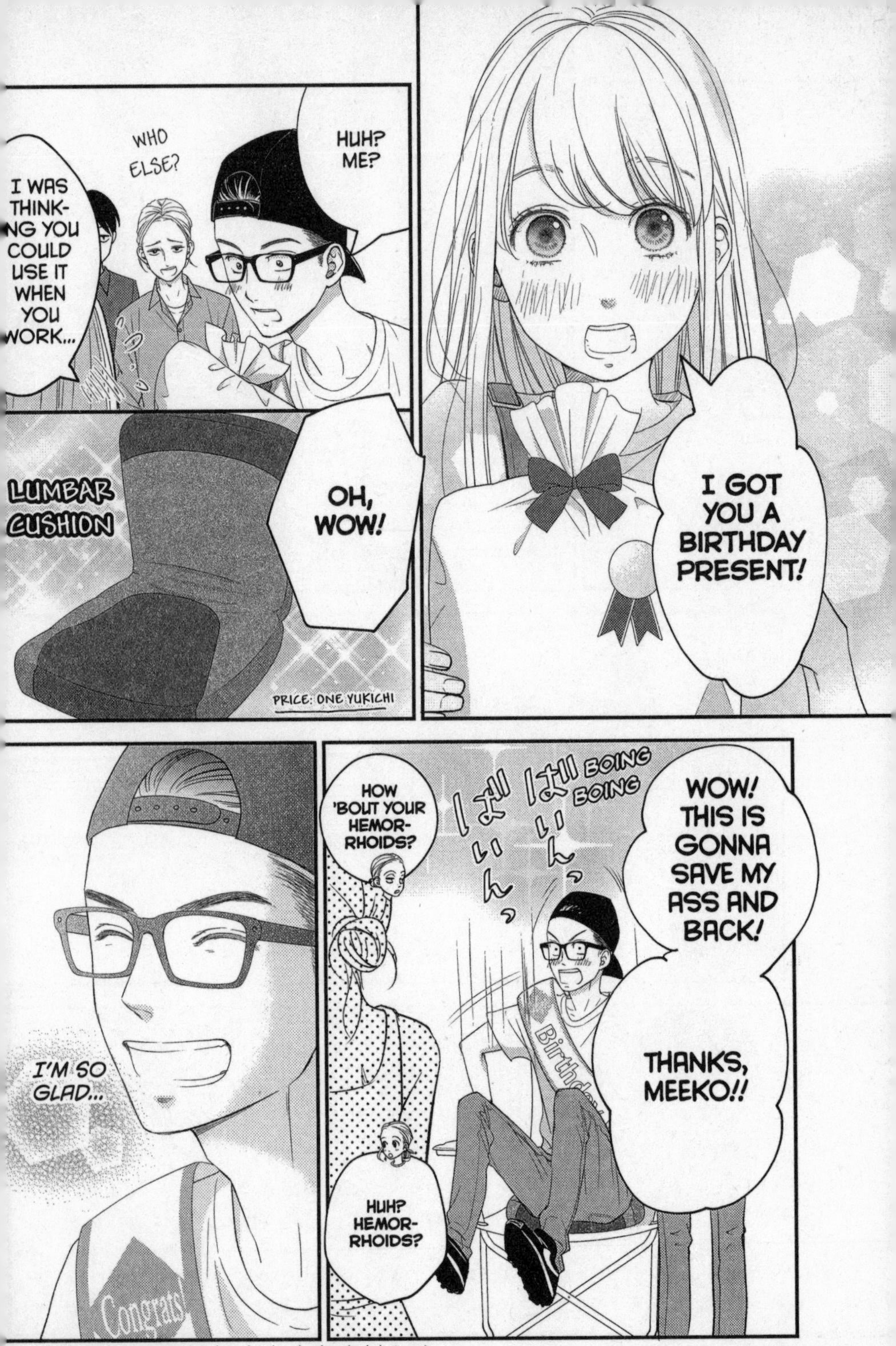
I GOT YOU A BIRTHDAY PRESENT!
HUH? ME?
WHO ELSE?
I WAS THINKING YOU COULD USE IT WHEN YOU WORK...
OH, WOW!
LUMBAR CUSHION
PRICE: ONE YUKICHI
WOW! THIS IS GONNA SAVE MY ASS AND BACK!
BOING BOING
ぱいん ぱいん
HOW 'BOUT YOUR HEMORRHOIDS?
THANKS, MEEKO!!
HUH? HEMORRHOIDS?
I'M SO GLAD...
Birthday
Congrats!

*Yukichi Fukuzawa was a Japanese author who played a pivotal role in Japan's modernization. He is commemorated on the 10,000 yen banknote (approx. $100 USD), and as such, his name has become synonymous with 10,000 yen.

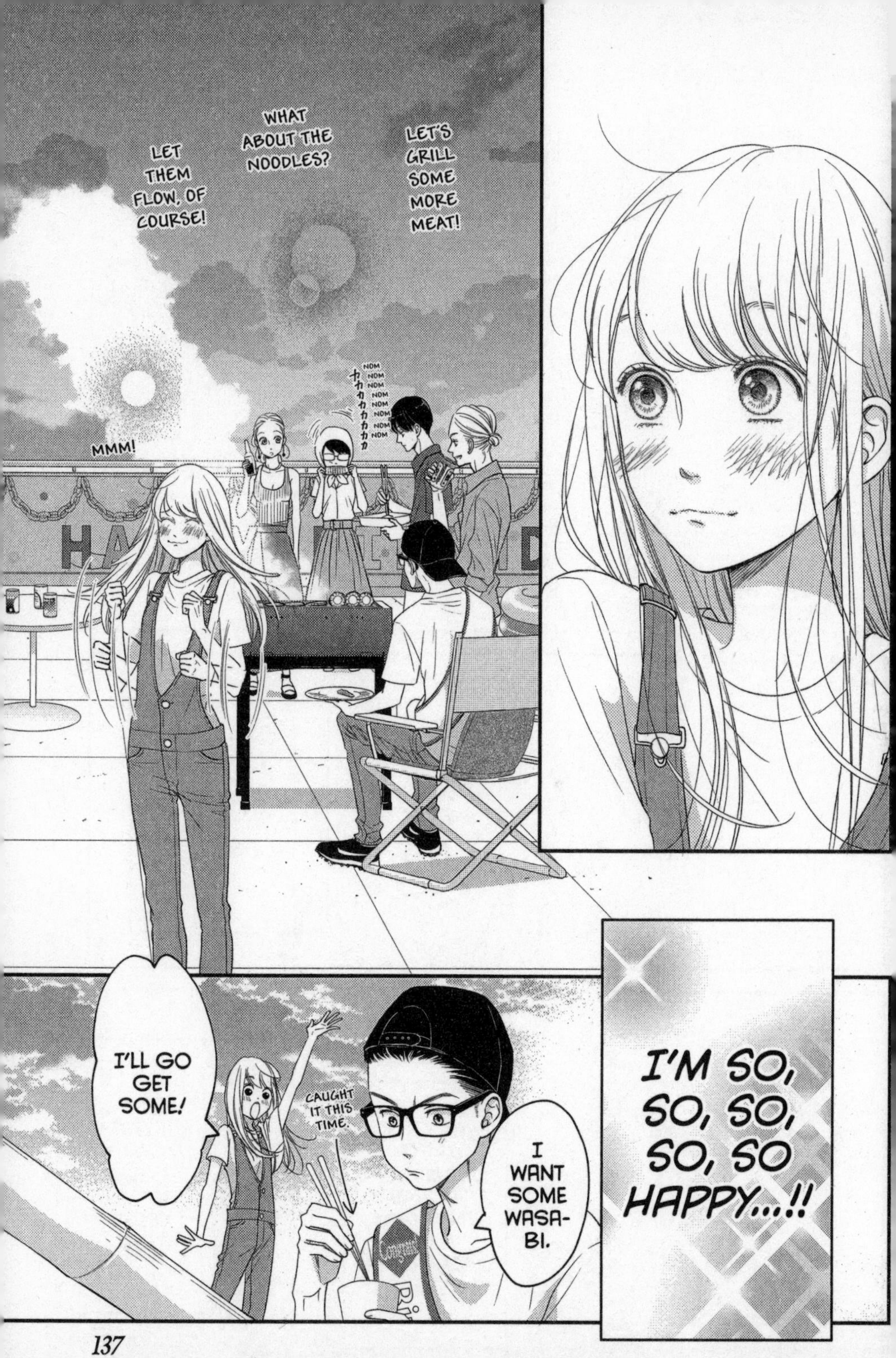
LET'S GRILL SOME MORE MEAT!
WHAT ABOUT THE NOODLES?
LET THEM FLOW, OF COURSE!
カカカカカカカカ
NOM NOM NOM NOM NOM NOM NOM NOM
MMM!
I'M SO, SO, SO, SO, SO HAPPY...!!
I WANT SOME WASA-BI.
CAUGHT IT THIS TIME.
I'LL GO GET SOME!

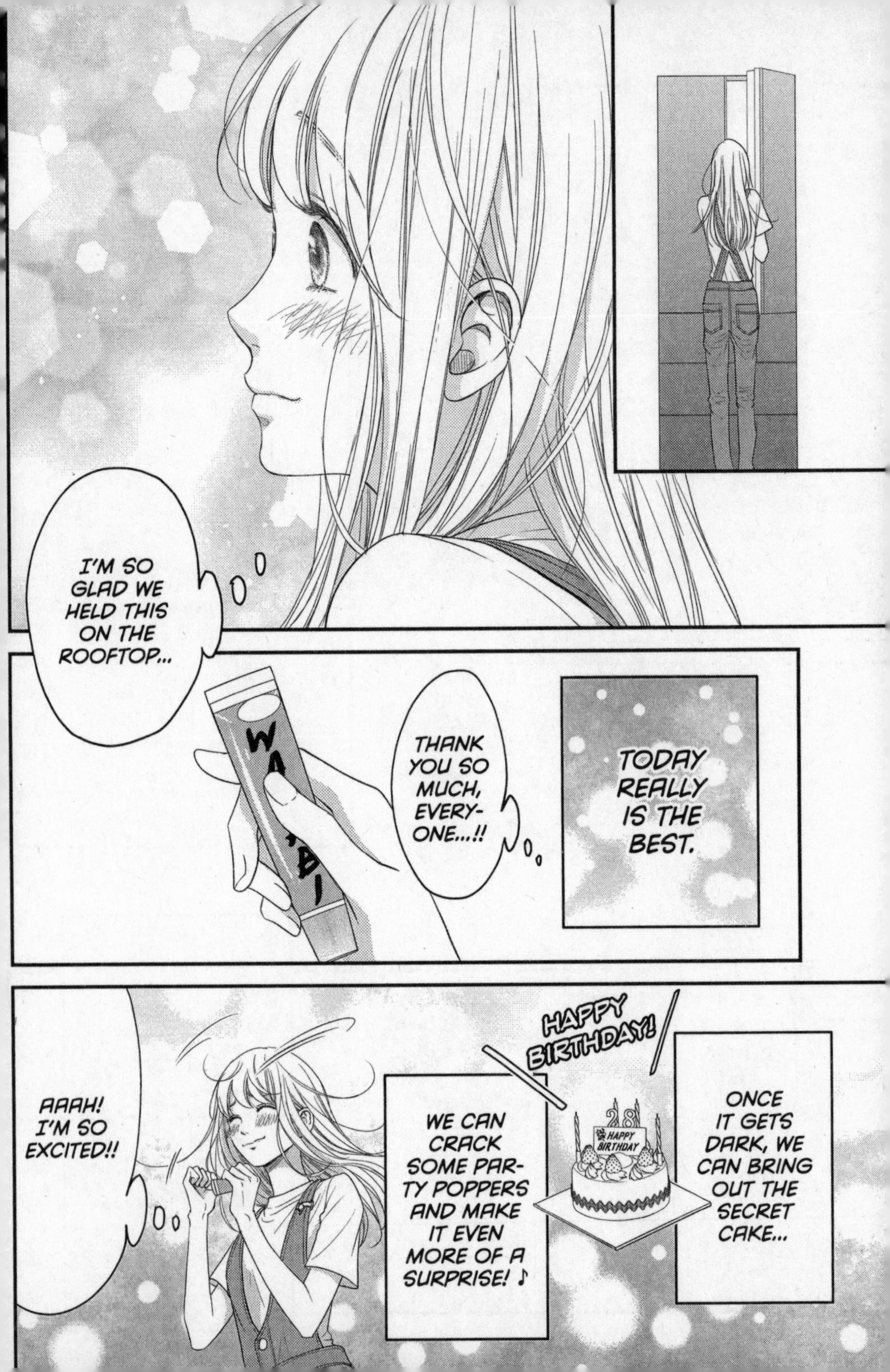
I'M SO GLAD WE HELD THIS ON THE ROOFTOP...
TODAY REALLY IS THE BEST.
THANK YOU SO MUCH, EVERY-ONE...!!
ONCE IT GETS DARK, WE CAN BRING OUT THE SECRET CAKE...
HAPPY BIRTHDAY!
28
HAPPY BIRTHDAY
WE CAN CRACK SOME PAR-TY POPPERS AND MAKE IT EVEN MORE OF A SURPRISE! ♪
AAAH! I'M SO EXCITED!!

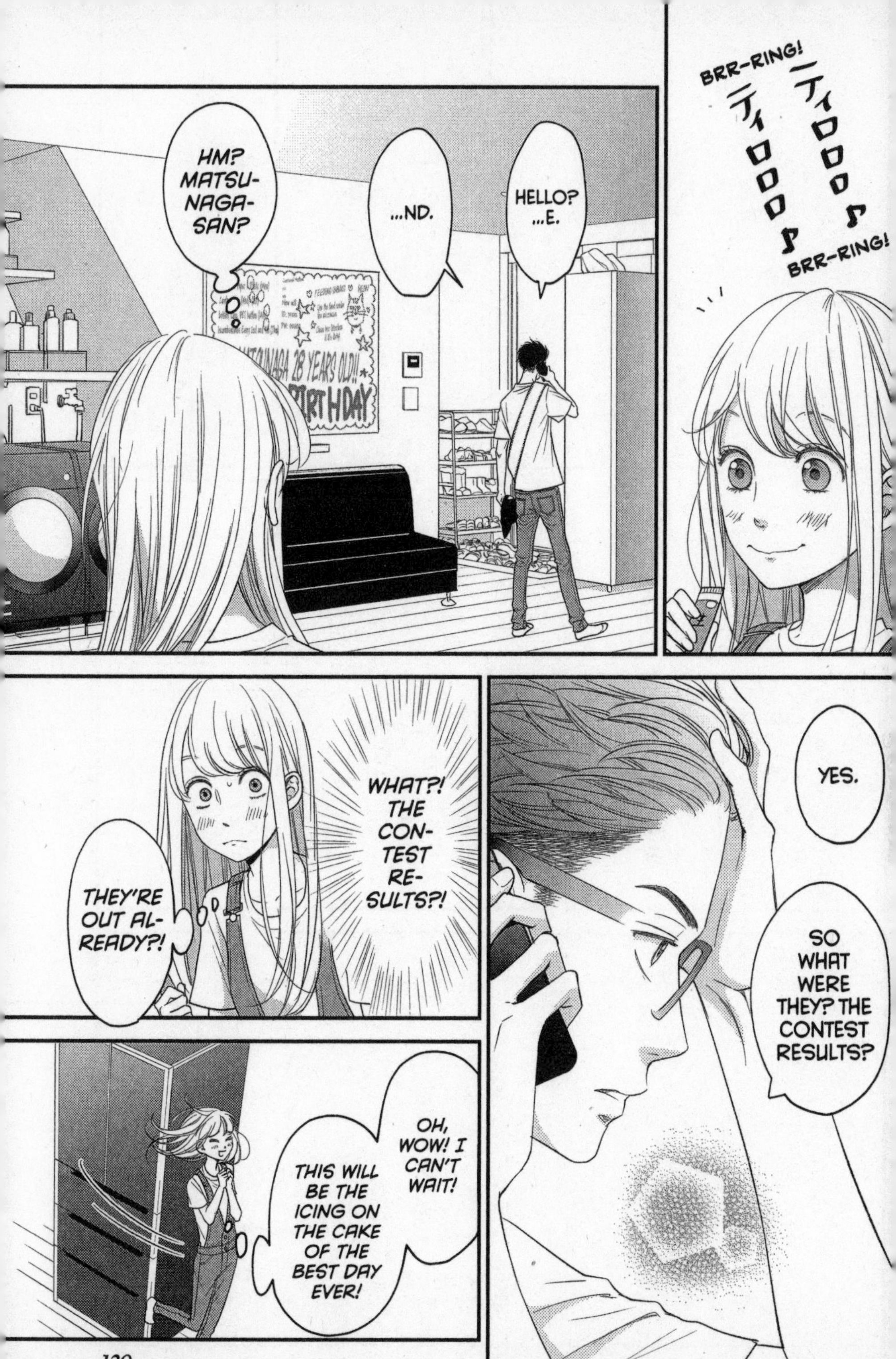

BRR-RING!
ティロロ♪
ティロロ♪
BRR-RING!
HELLO? ...E.
...ND.
HM? MATSU-NAGA-SAN?
YES.
SO WHAT WERE THEY? THE CONTEST RESULTS?
WHAT?! THE CON-TEST RE-SULTS?!
THEY'RE OUT AL-READY?!
OH, WOW! I CAN'T WAIT!
THIS WILL BE THE ICING ON THE CAKE OF THE BEST DAY EVER!

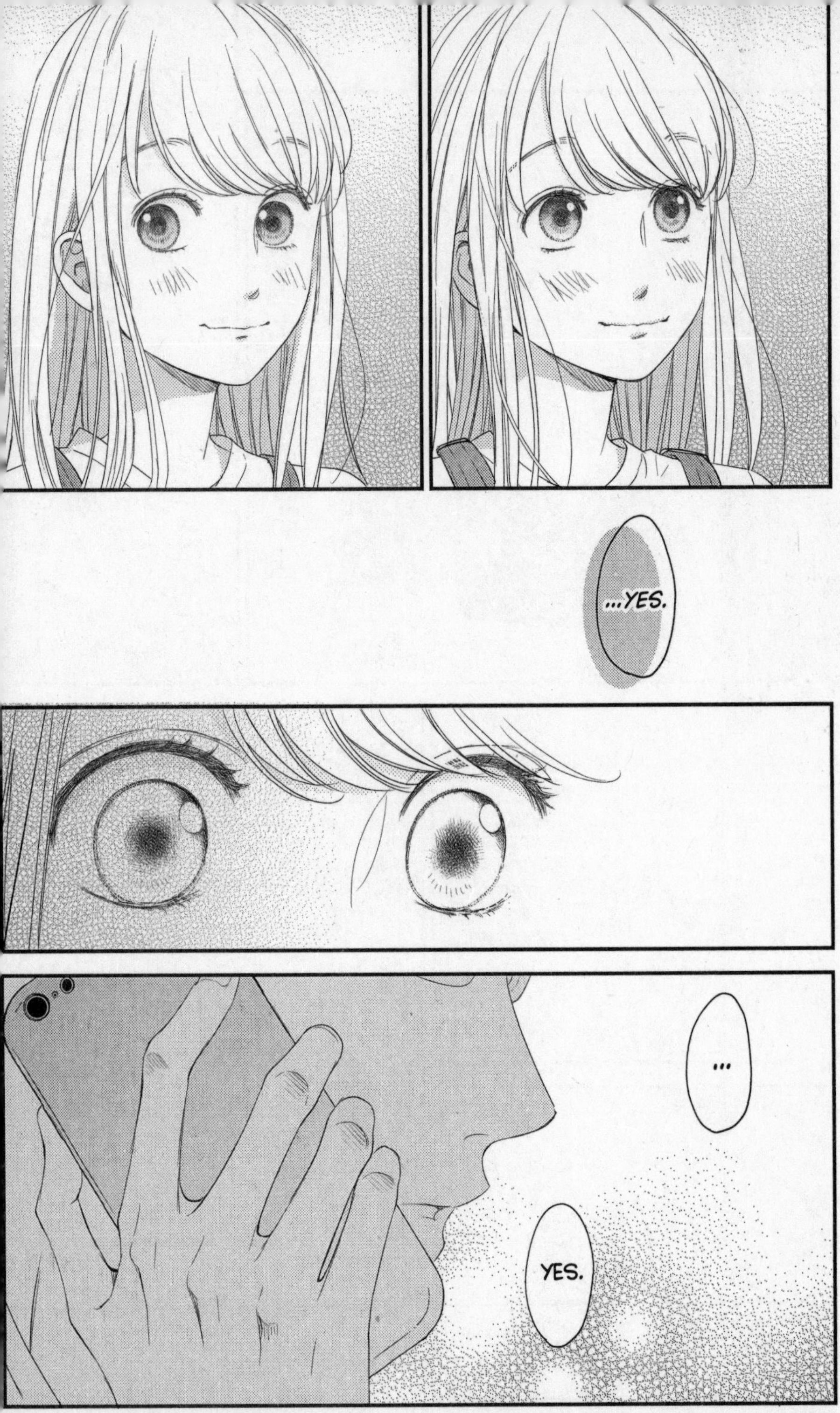
...YES.
...
YES.

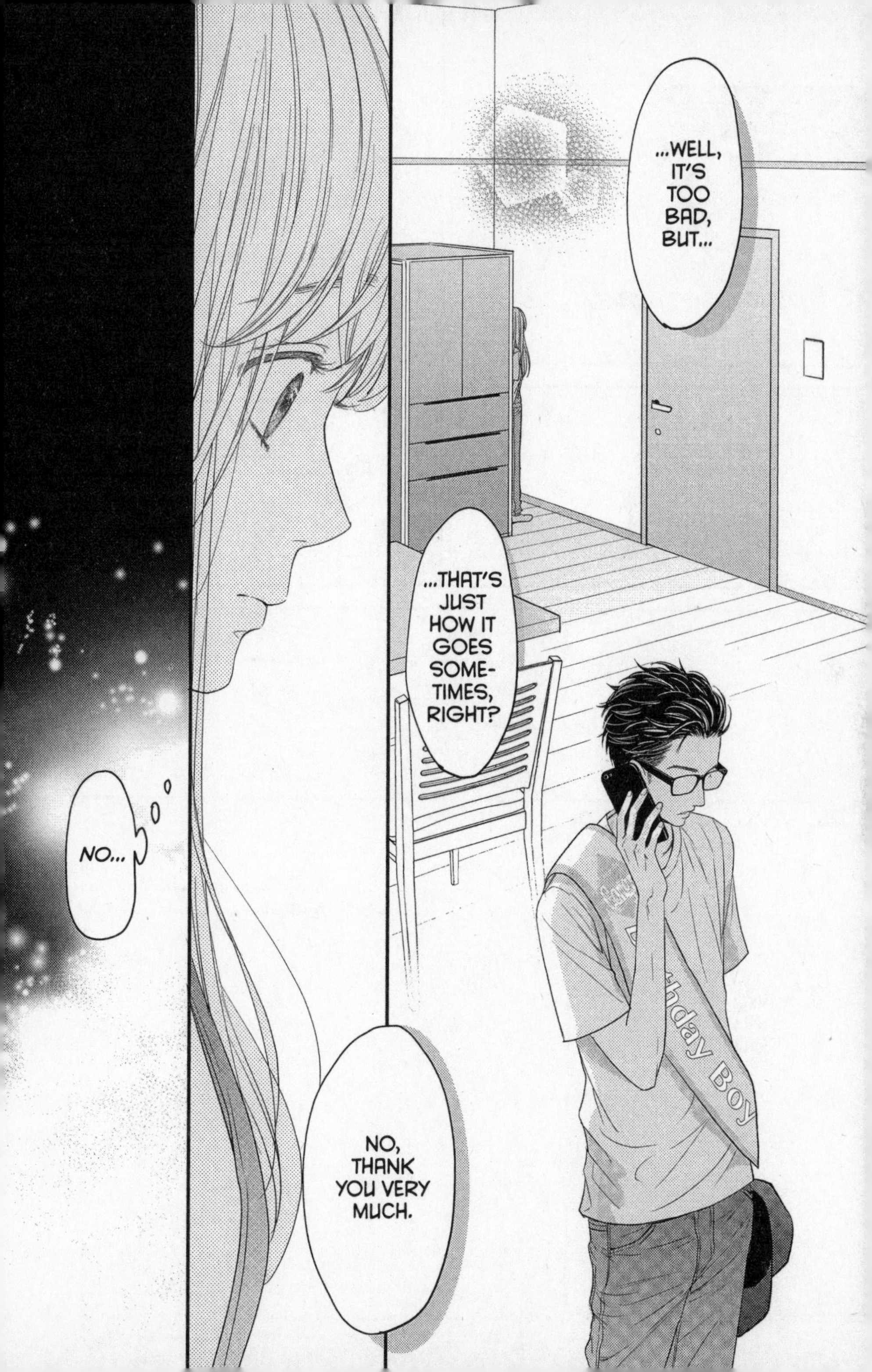
...WELL, IT'S TOO BAD, BUT...
...THAT'S JUST HOW IT GOES SOME-TIMES, RIGHT?
NO, THANK YOU VERY MUCH.
NO...

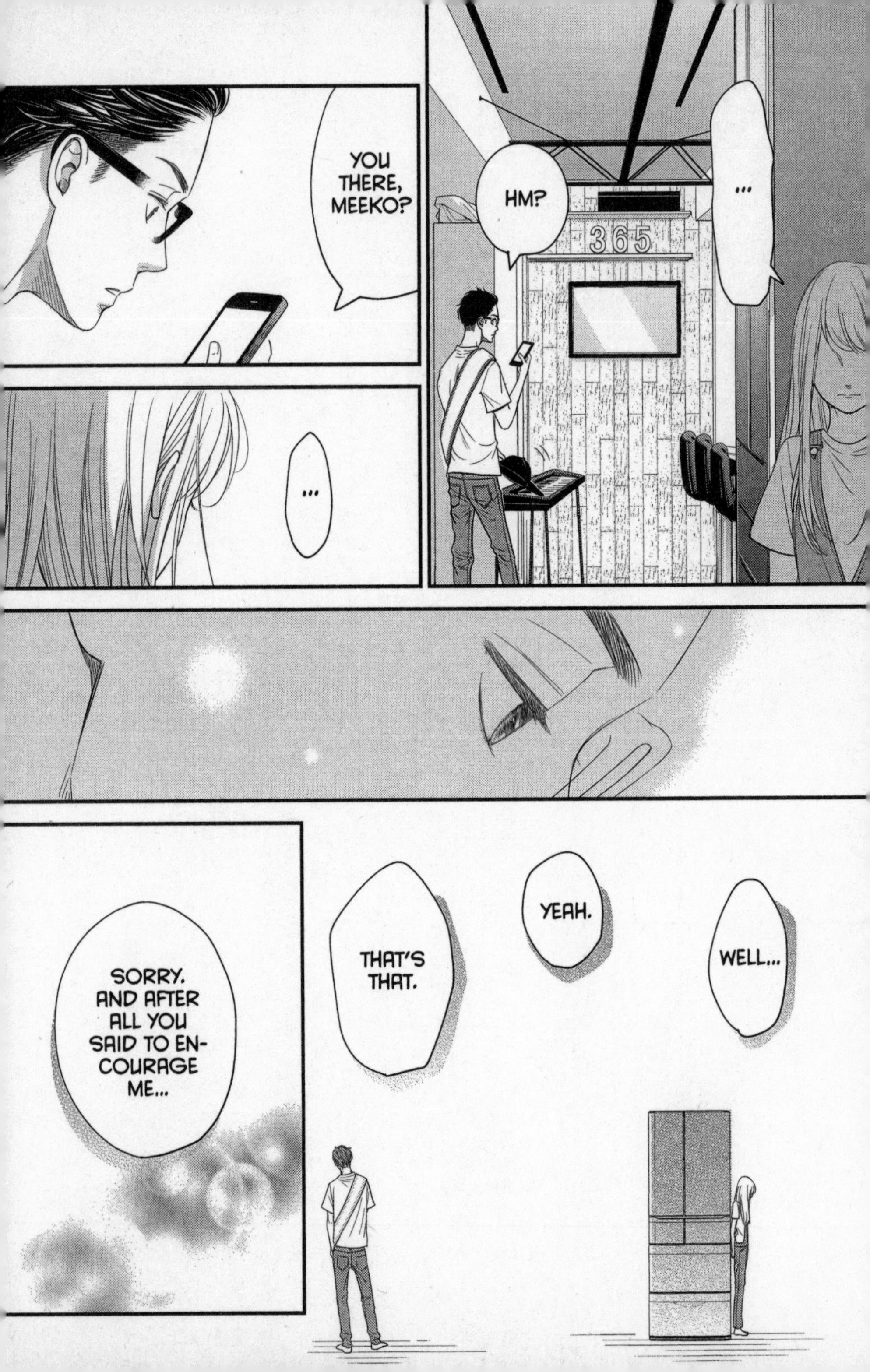
...
HM?
YOU THERE, MEEKO?
...
WELL...
YEAH.
THAT'S THAT.
SORRY. AND AFTER ALL YOU SAID TO EN-COURAGE ME...

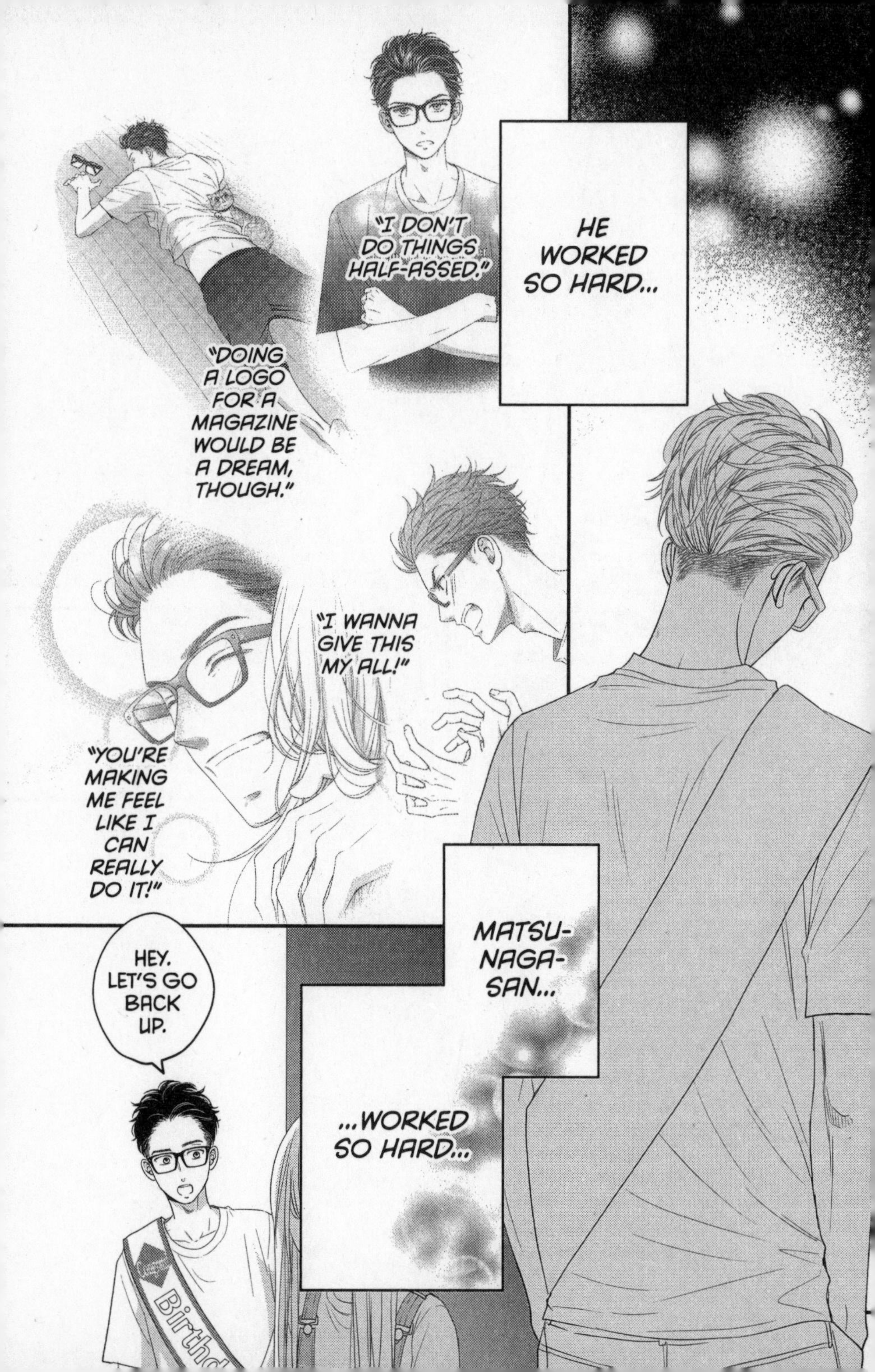
HE WORKED SO HARD...
"I DON'T DO THINGS HALF-ASSED."
"DOING A LOGO FOR A MAGAZINE WOULD BE A DREAM, THOUGH."
"I WANNA GIVE THIS MY ALL!"
"YOU'RE MAKING ME FEEL LIKE I CAN REALLY DO IT!"
MATSU-NAGA-SAN...
...WORKED SO HARD...
HEY. LET'S GO BACK UP.

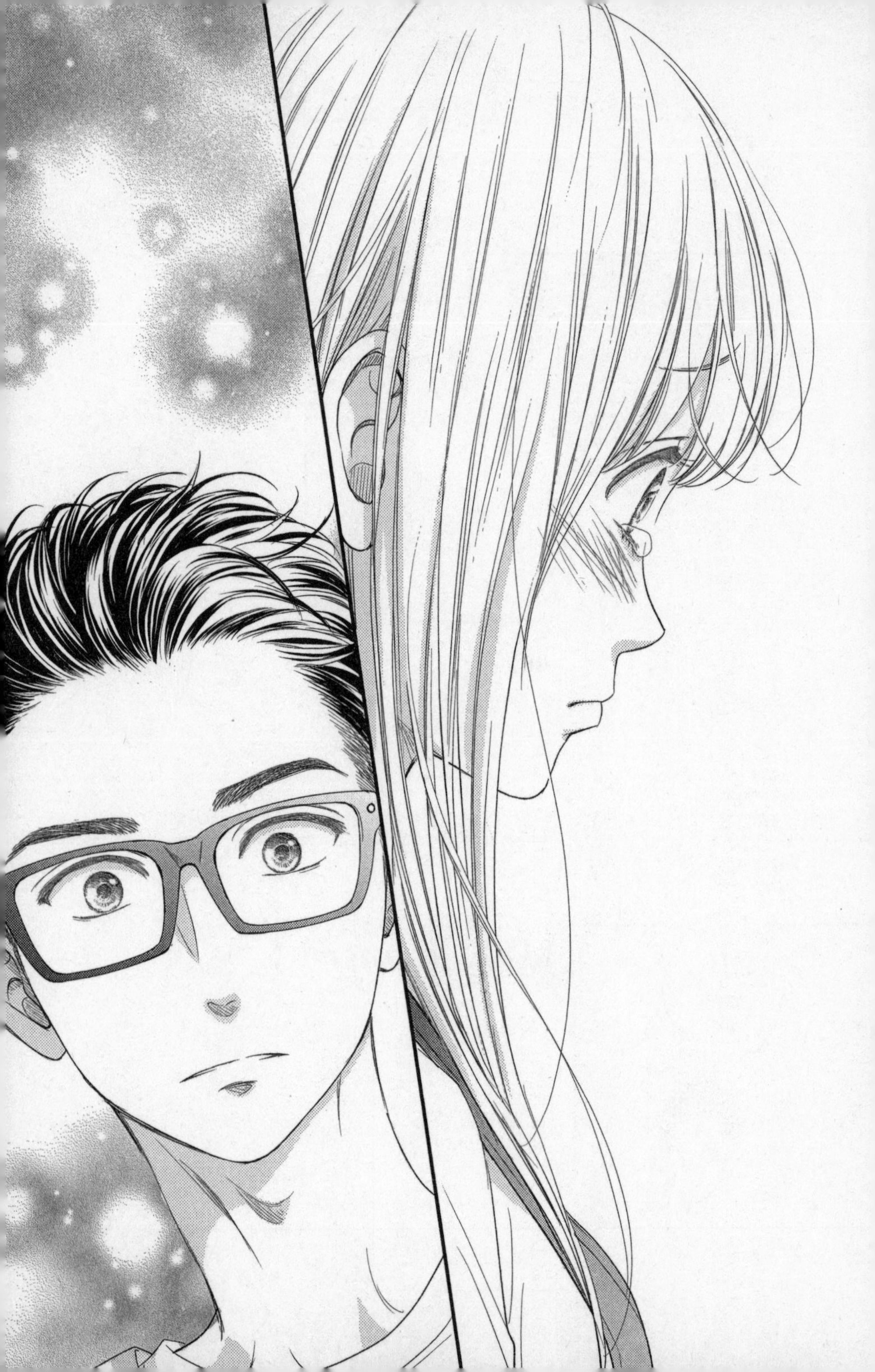

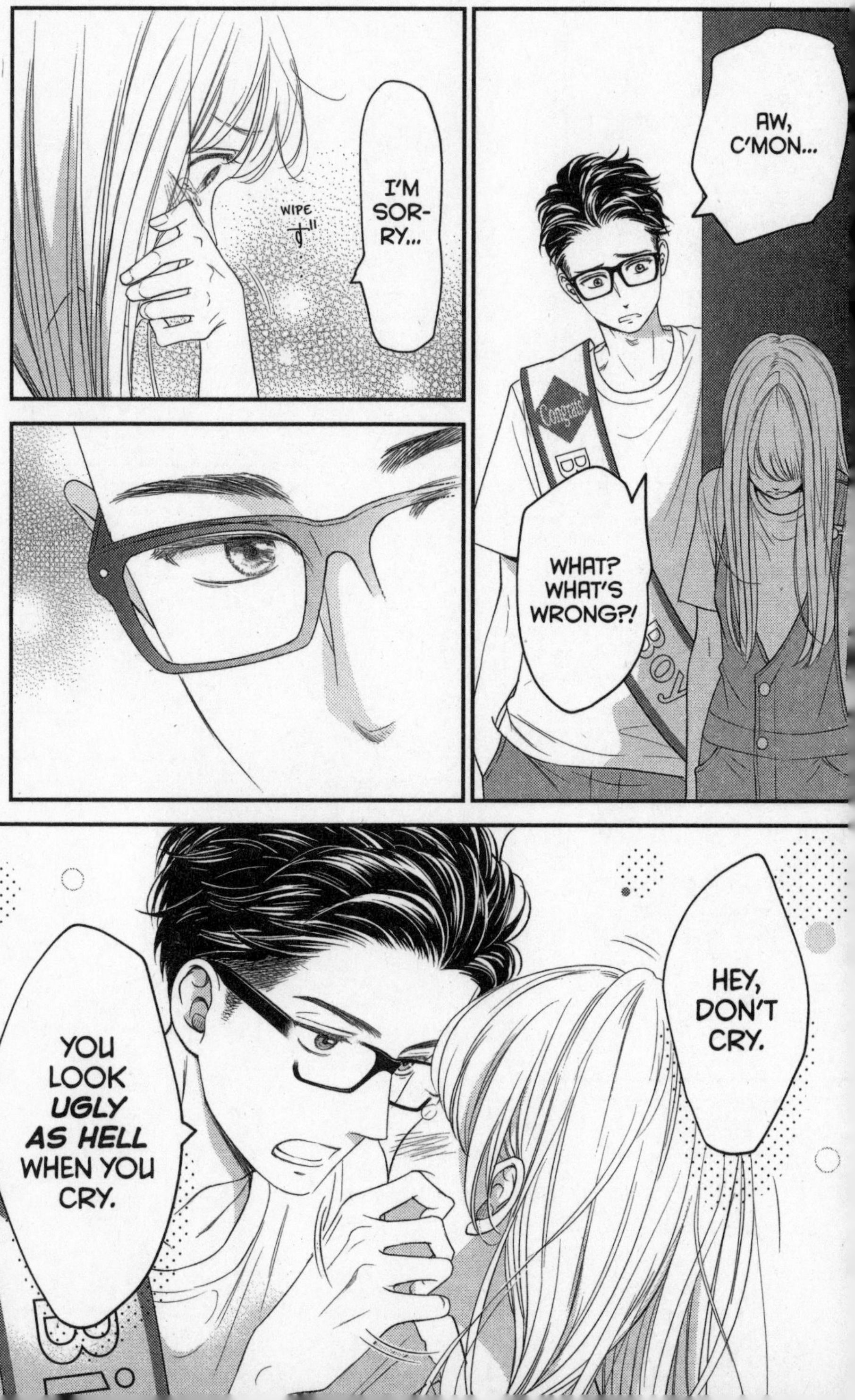
AW, C'MON...
WHAT? WHAT'S WRONG?!
WIPE
I'M SORRY...
HEY, DON'T CRY.
YOU LOOK UGLY AS HELL WHEN YOU CRY.

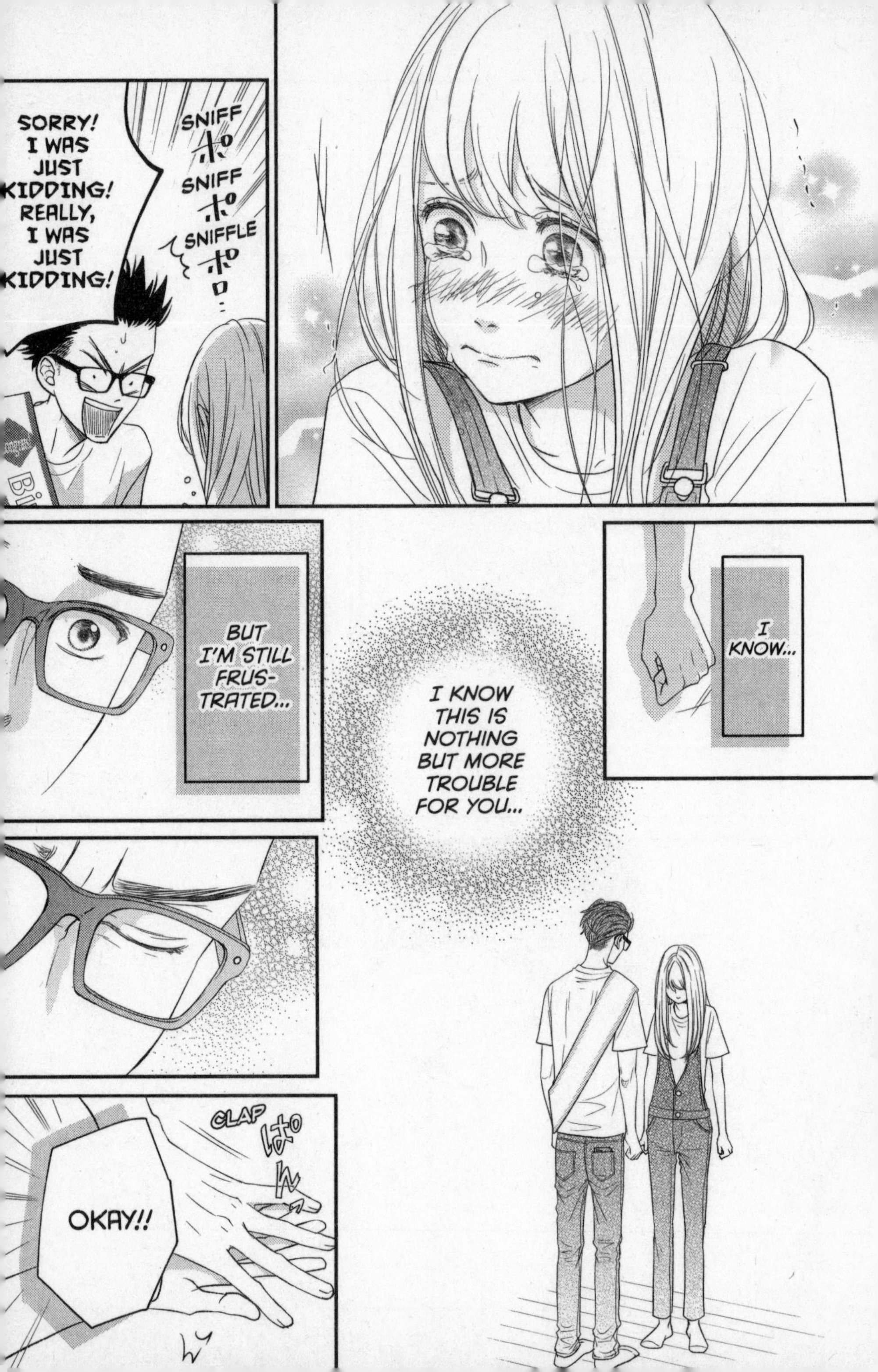
SNIFF
ポ
SNIFF
ポ
SNIFFLE
ポロ...
SORRY! I WAS JUST KIDDING! REALLY, I WAS JUST KIDDING!
I KNOW...
I KNOW THIS IS NOTHING BUT MORE TROUBLE FOR YOU...
BUT I'M STILL FRUS-TRATED...
CLAP
ぱんっ
OKAY!!

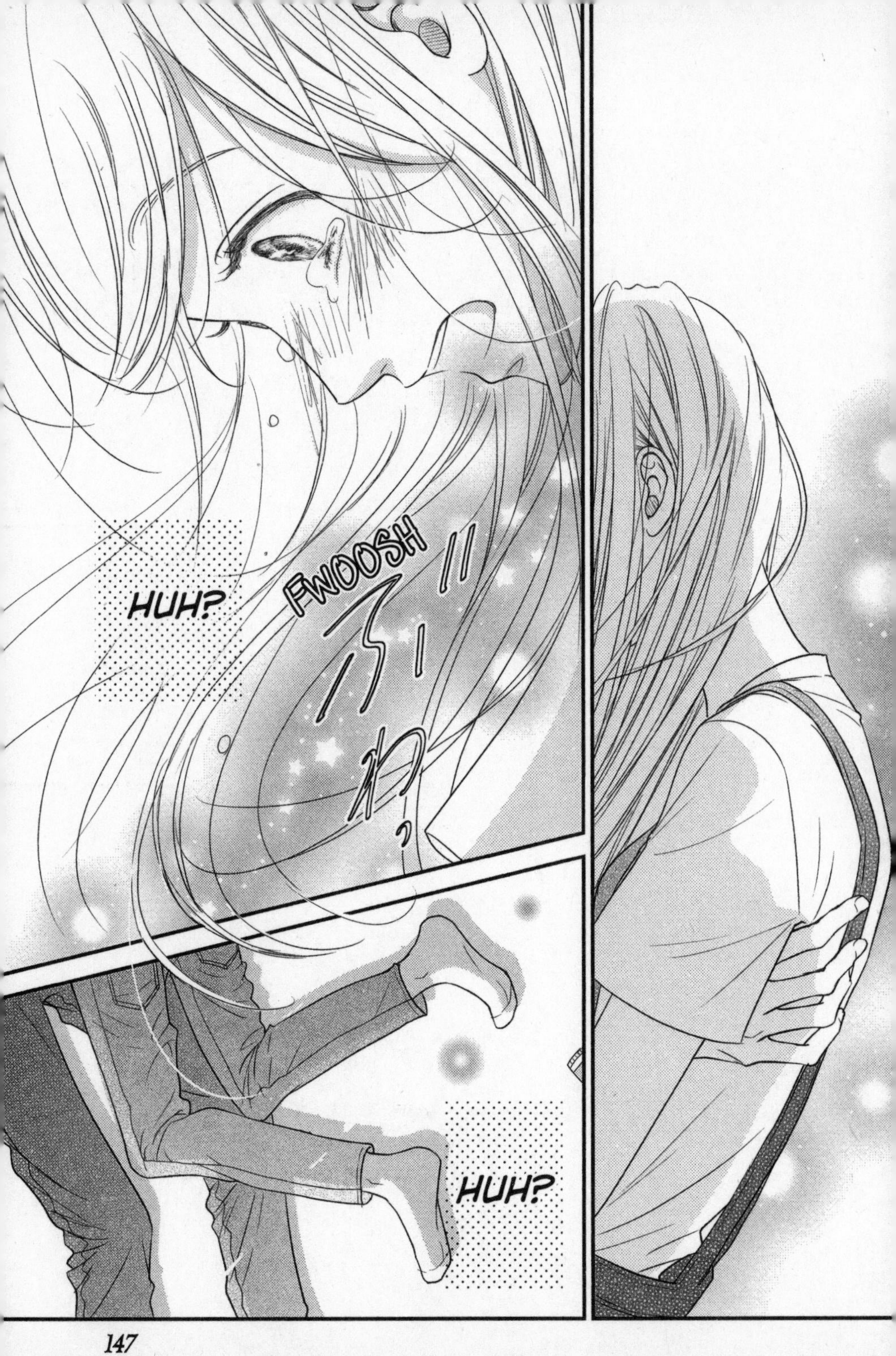
FWOOSH
ふわっ
HUH?
HUH?

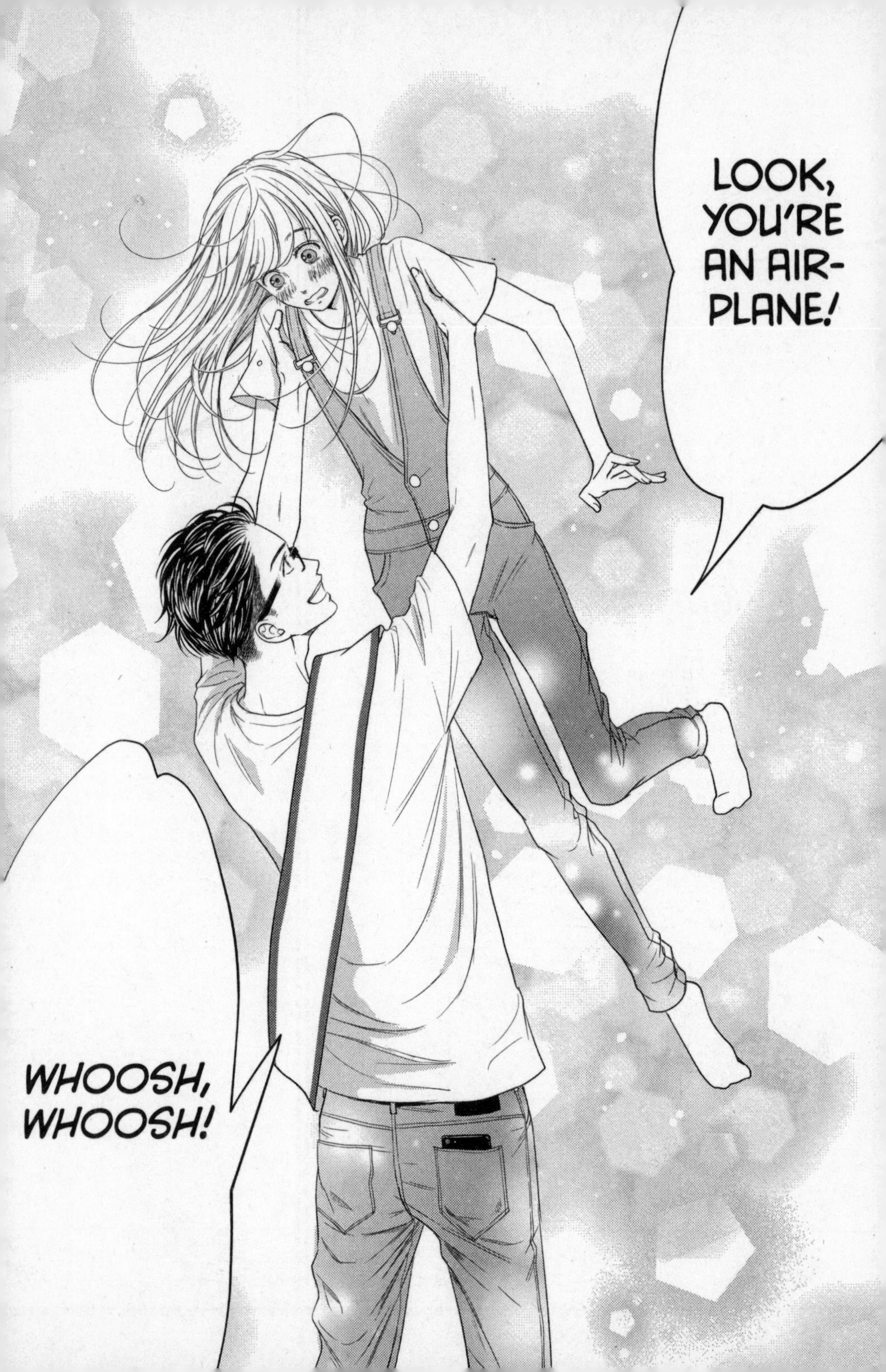
LOOK, YOU'RE AN AIR-PLANE!
WHOOSH, WHOOSH!

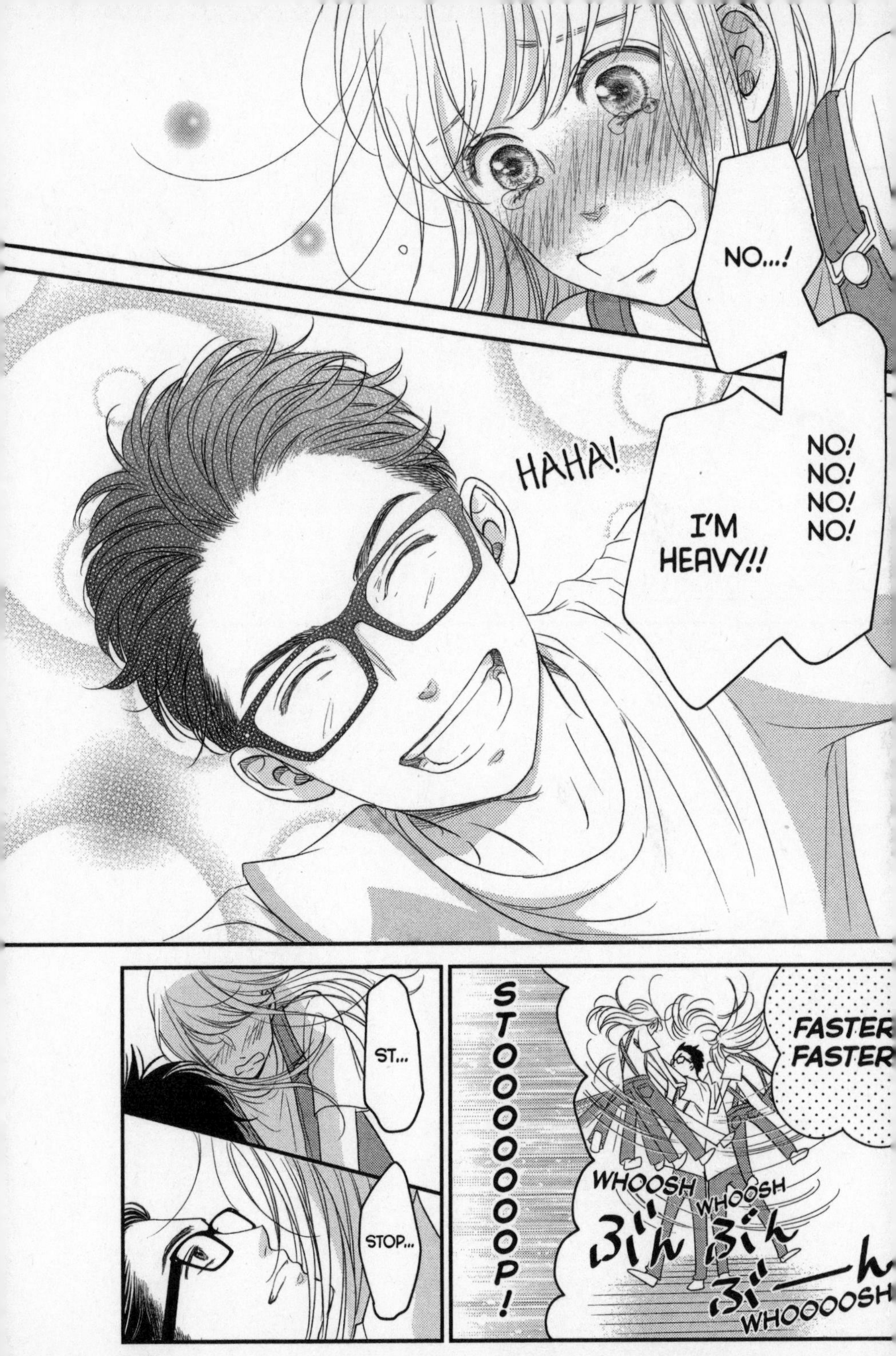
NO...!
NO! NO! NO! NO!
I'M HEAVY!!
HAHA!
FASTER FASTER
STOOOOOOOOP!
WHOOSH
ぶん
WHOOSH
ぶん
ぶーん
WHOOOOSH
ST...
STOP...

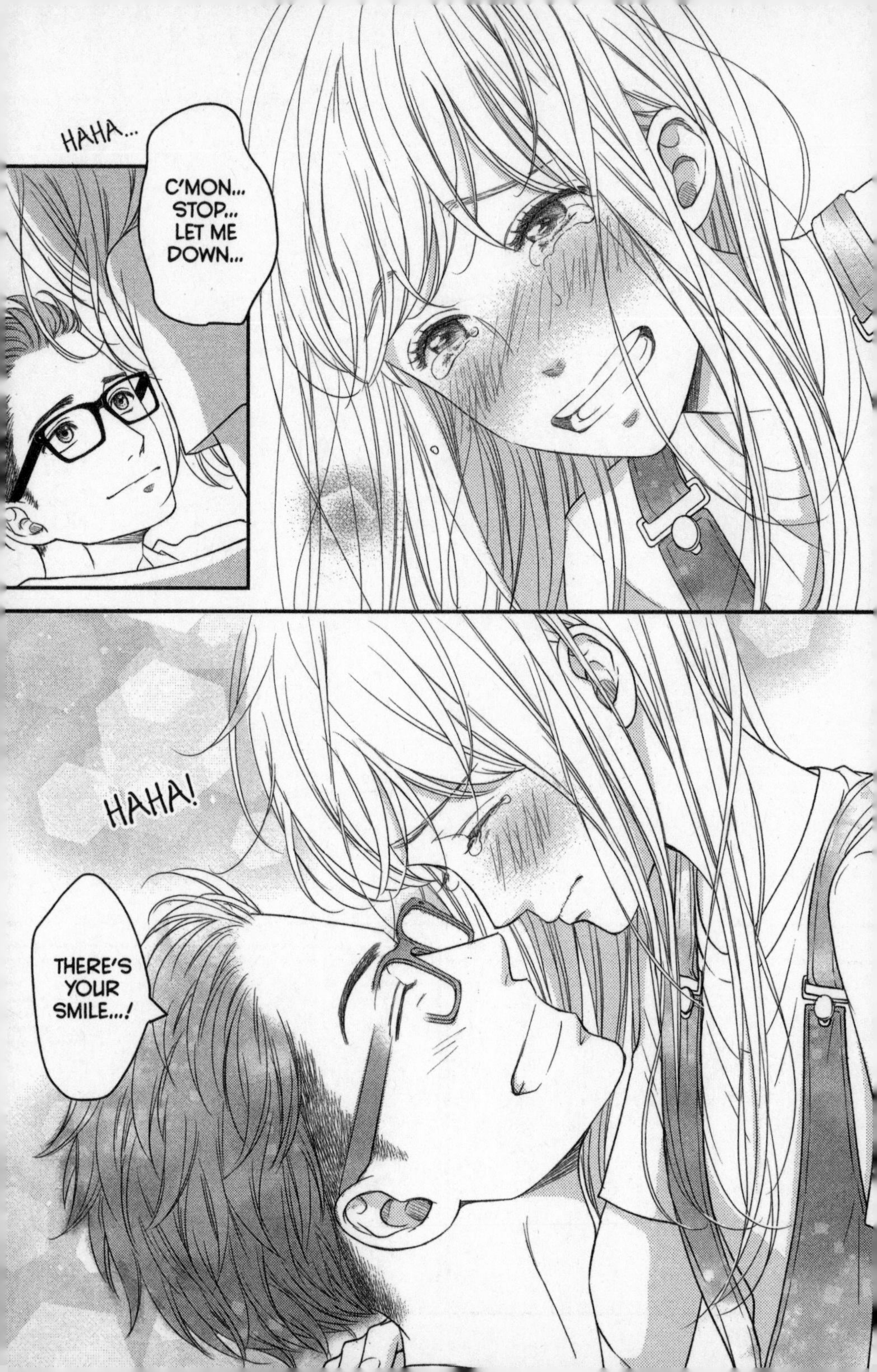
HAHA...
C'MON... STOP... LET ME DOWN...
HAHA!
THERE'S YOUR SMILE...!

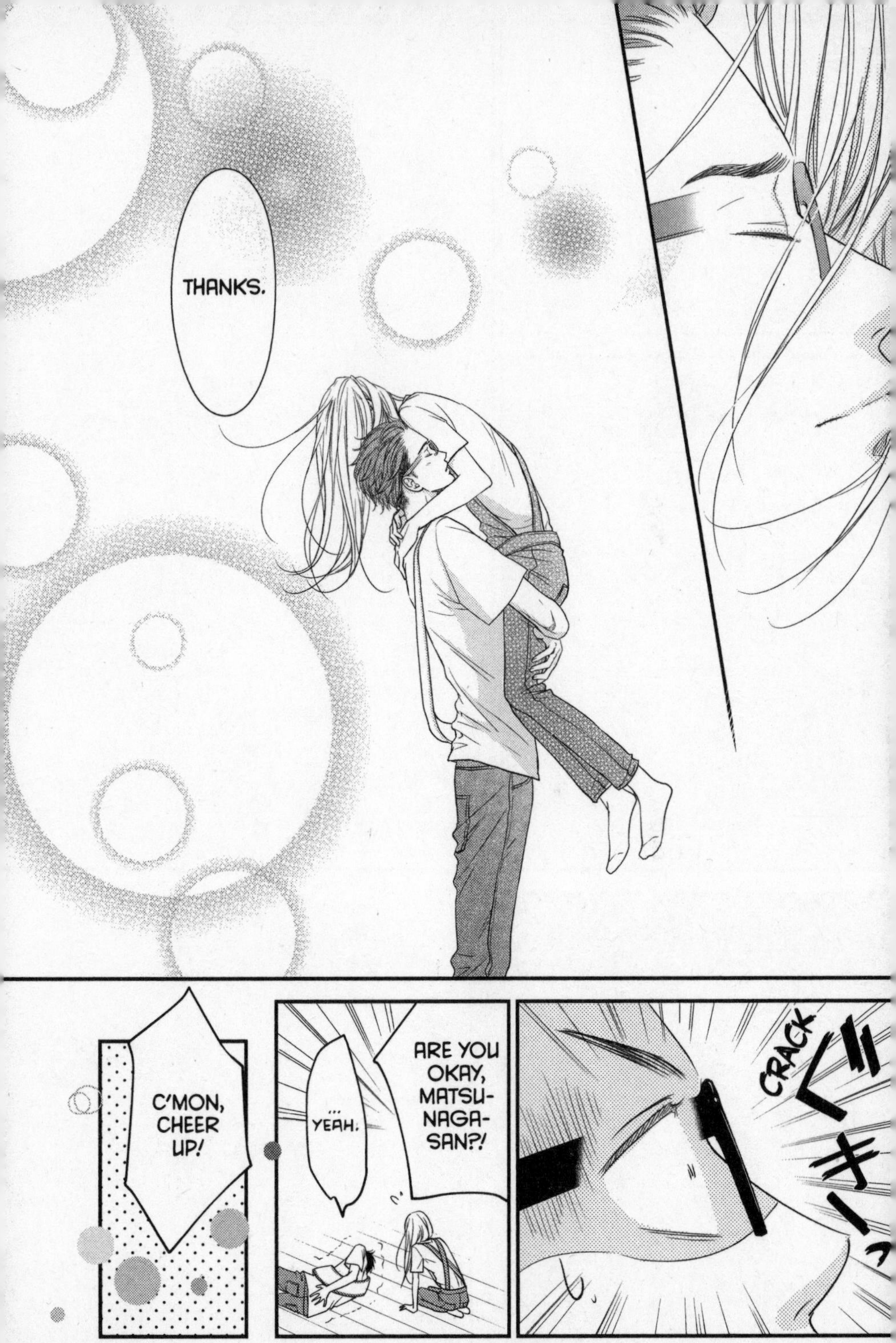
THANKS.
CRACK
ARE YOU OKAY, MATSU-NAGA-SAN?!
...YEAH.
C'MON, CHEER UP!

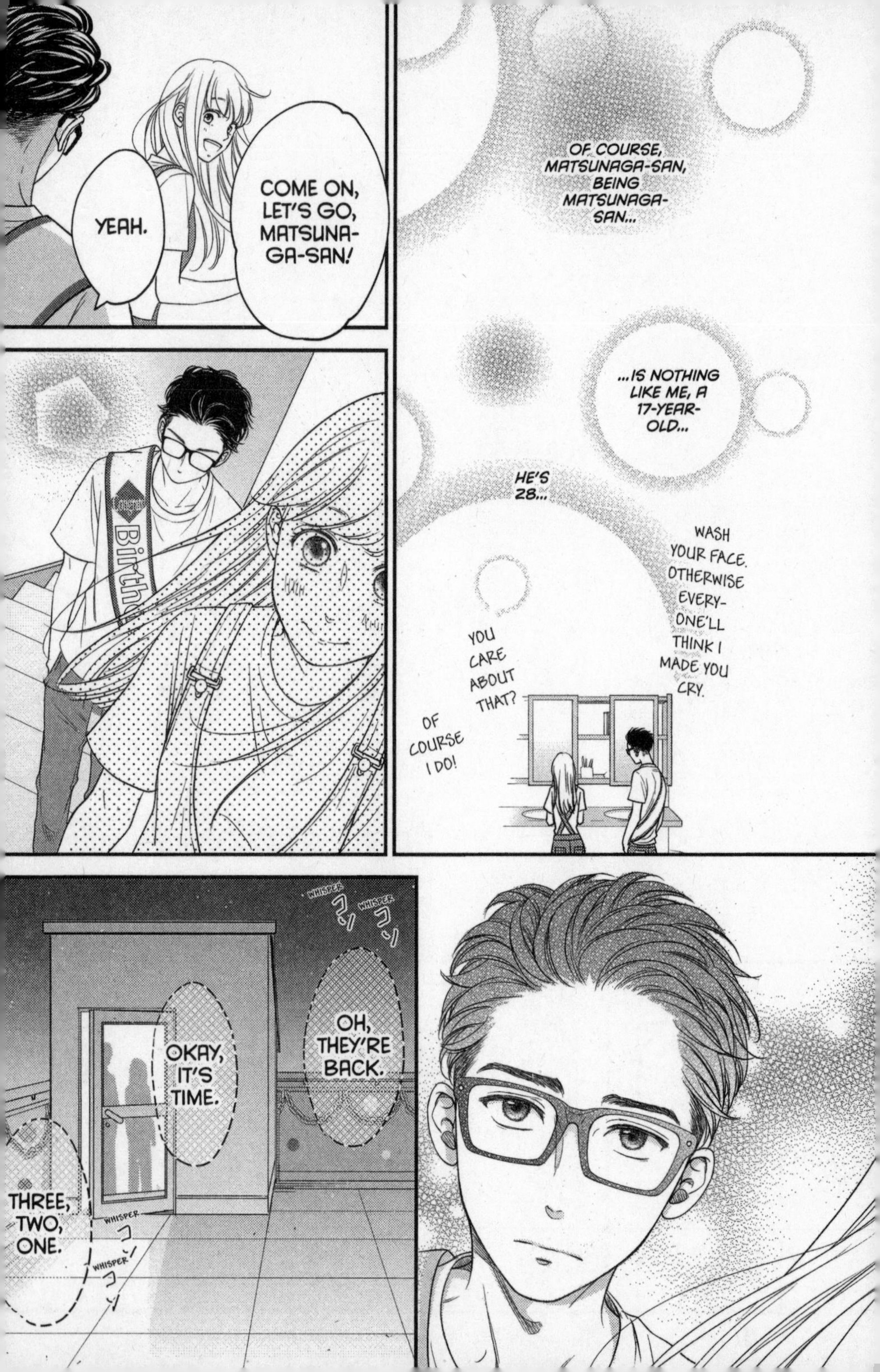
OF COURSE, MATSUNAGA-SAN, BEING MATSUNAGA-SAN...
...IS NOTHING LIKE ME, A 17-YEAR-OLD...
HE'S 28...
WASH YOUR FACE. OTHERWISE EVERY-ONE'LL THINK I MADE YOU CRY.
YOU CARE ABOUT THAT?
OF COURSE I DO!
COME ON, LET'S GO, MATSUNAGA-SAN!
YEAH.
WHISPER
WHISPER
OH, THEY'RE BACK.
OKAY, IT'S TIME.
THREE, TWO, ONE.
WHISPER
WHISPER

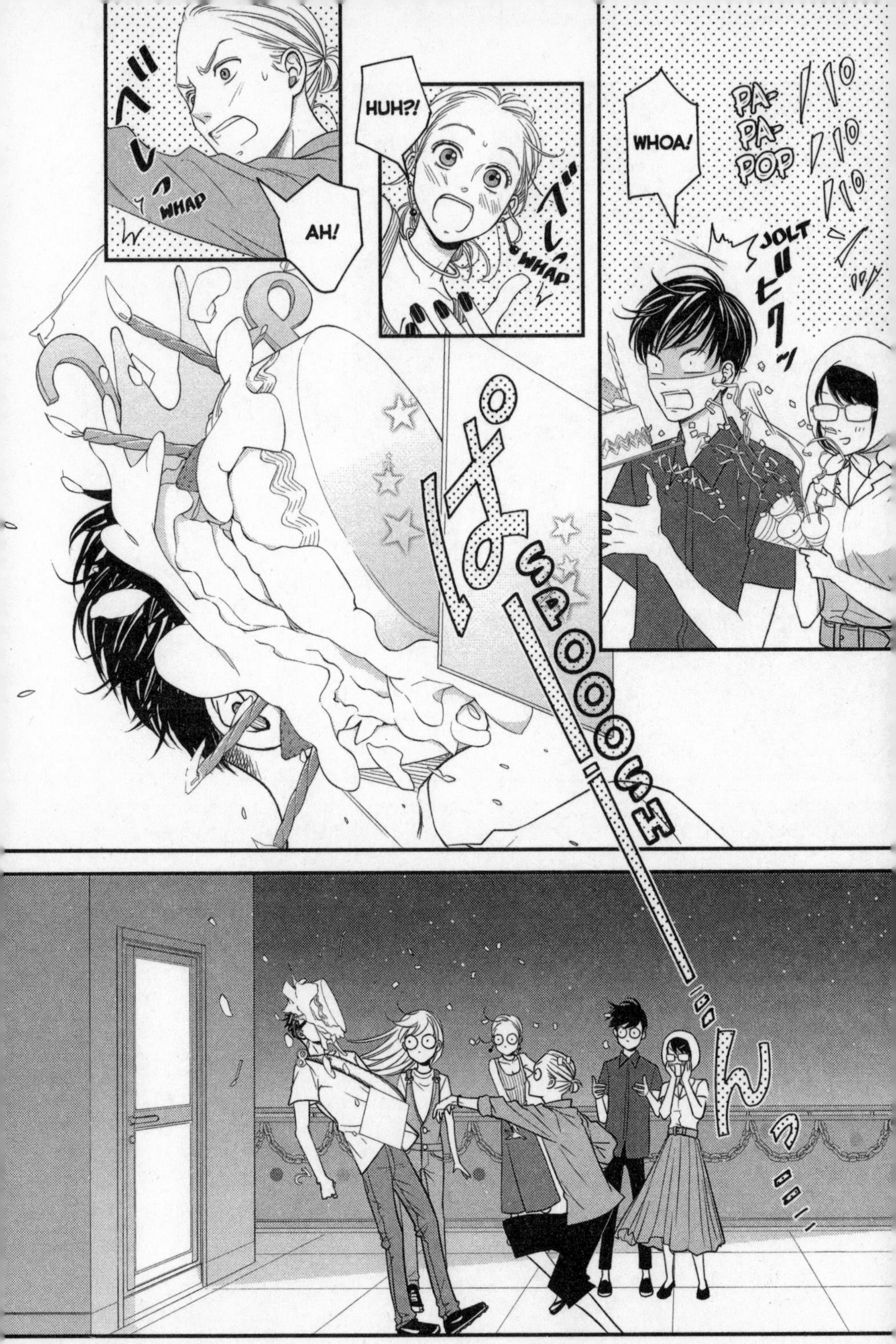
WHOA!
PA-PA-POP
JOLT
HUH?!
WHAP
WHAP
AH!
SPOOOOSH

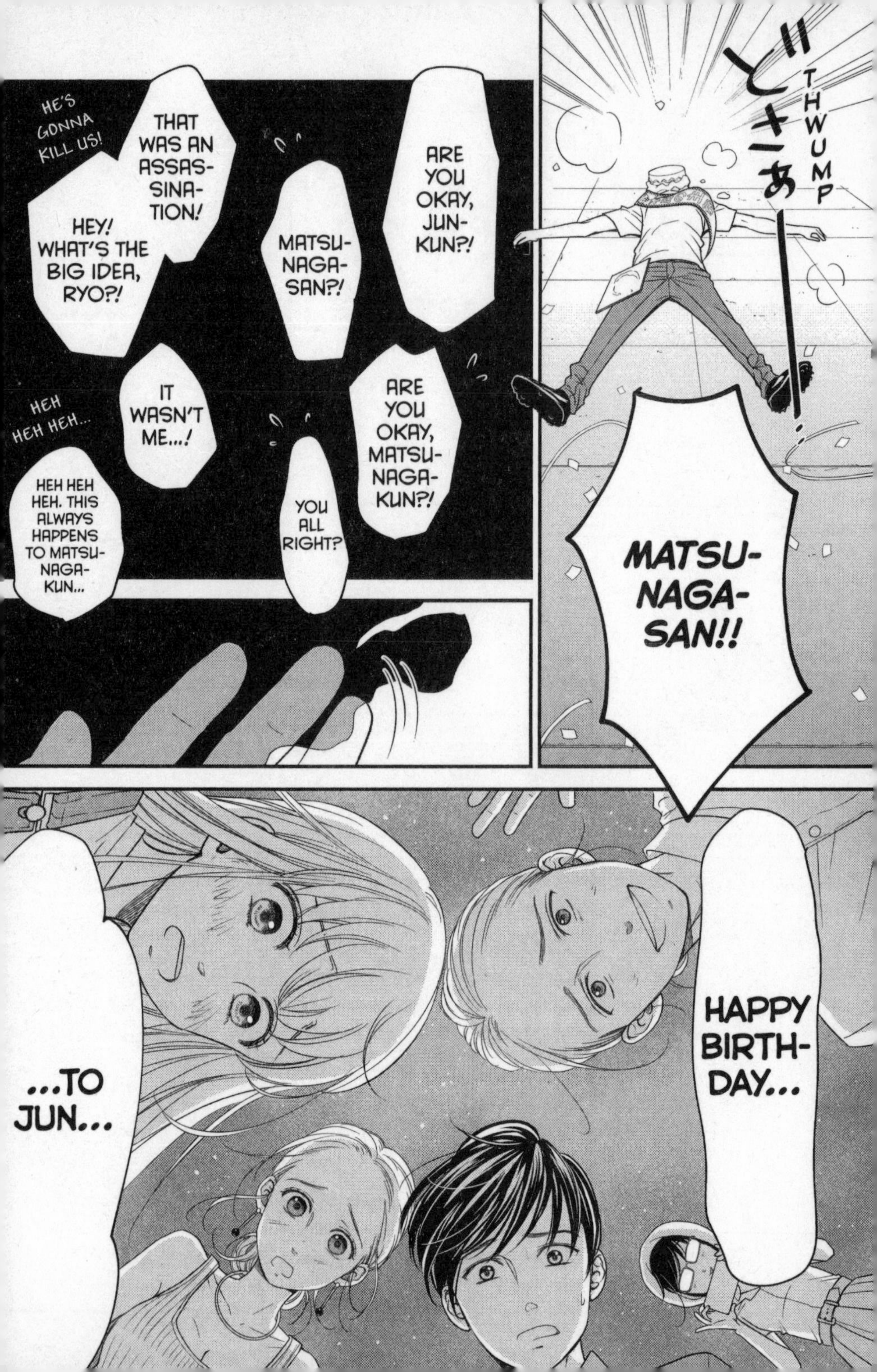
どさあ
THWUMP
MATSU-NAGA-SAN!!
ARE YOU OKAY, JUN-KUN?!
MATSU-NAGA-SAN?!
ARE YOU OKAY, MATSU-NAGA-KUN?!
THAT WAS AN ASSAS-SINA-TION!
HE'S GONNA KILL US!
HEY! WHAT'S THE BIG IDEA, RYO?!
YOU ALL RIGHT?
IT WASN'T ME...!
HEH HEH HEH...
HEH HEH HEH. THIS ALWAYS HAPPENS TO MATSU-NAGA-KUN...
HAPPY BIRTH-DAY...
...TO JUN...

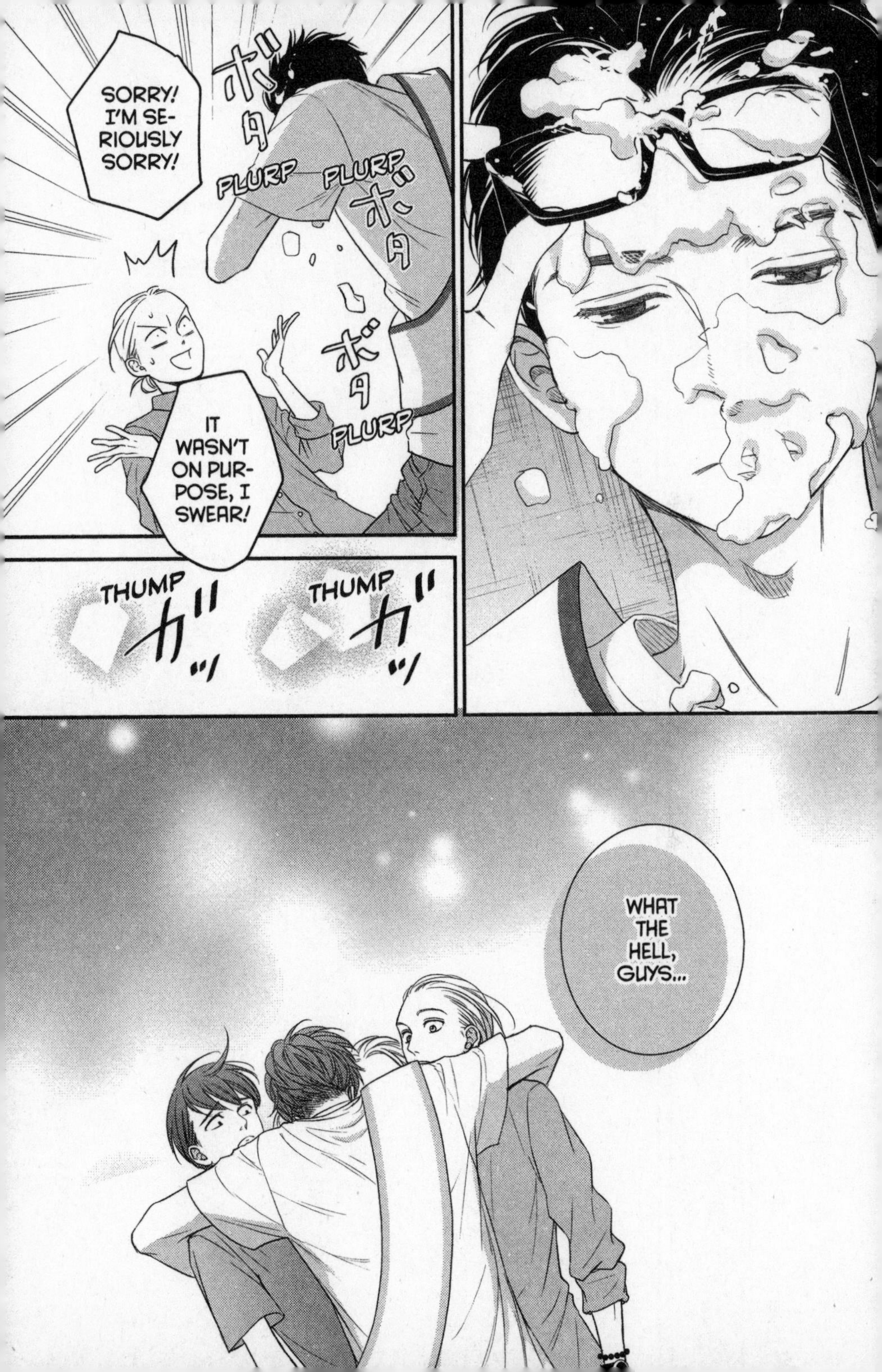
ボタ
PLURP
SORRY! I'M SE-RIOUSLY SORRY!
PLURP
ボタ
ボタ
PLURP
IT WASN'T ON PUR-POSE, I SWEAR!
THUMP
ガッ
THUMP
ガッ
WHAT THE HELL, GUYS...

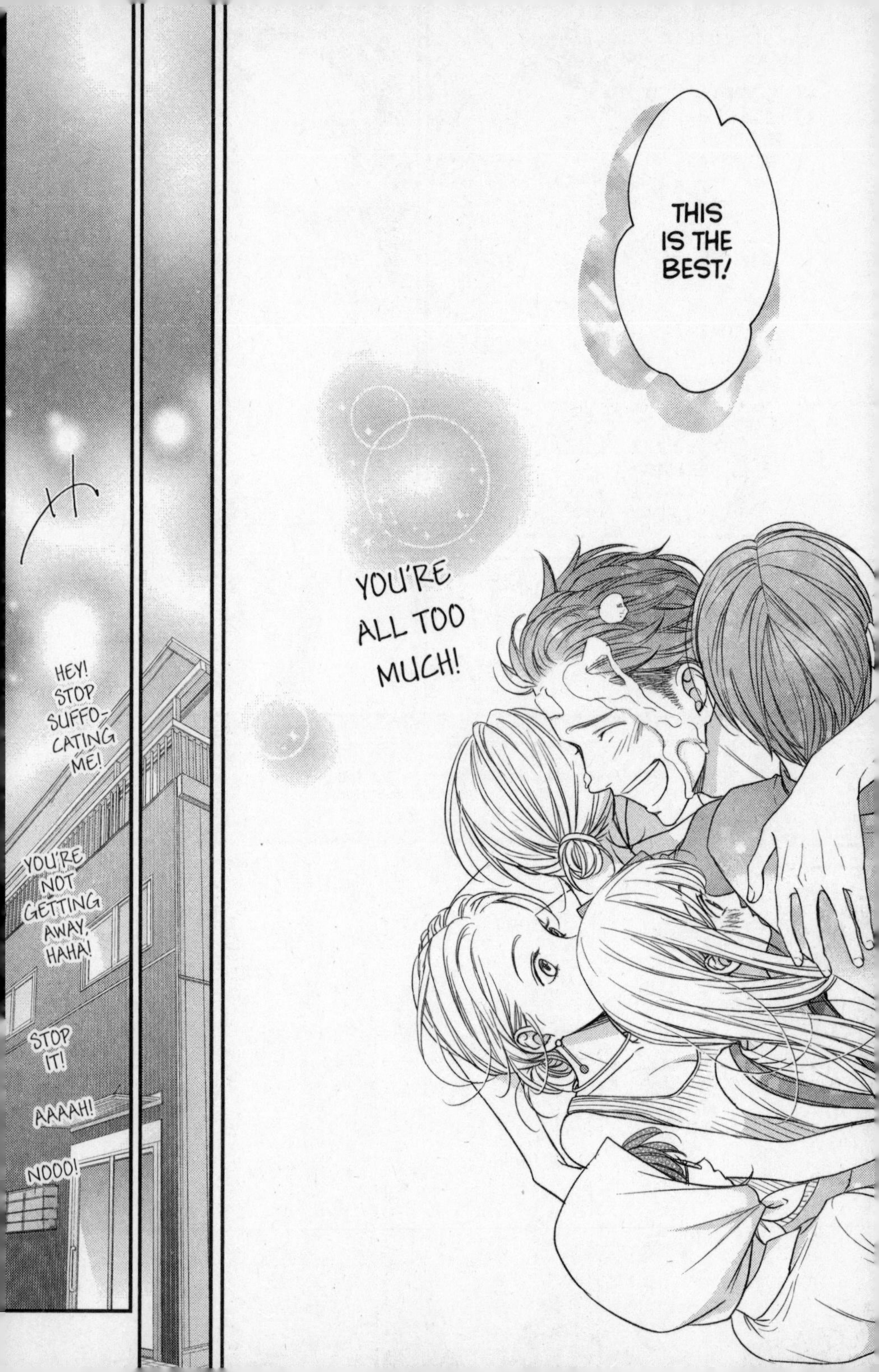
THIS IS THE BEST!
YOU'RE ALL TOO MUCH!
HEY! STOP SUFFO-CATING ME!
YOU'RE NOT GETTING AWAY, HAHA!
STOP IT!
AAAAH!
NOOO!

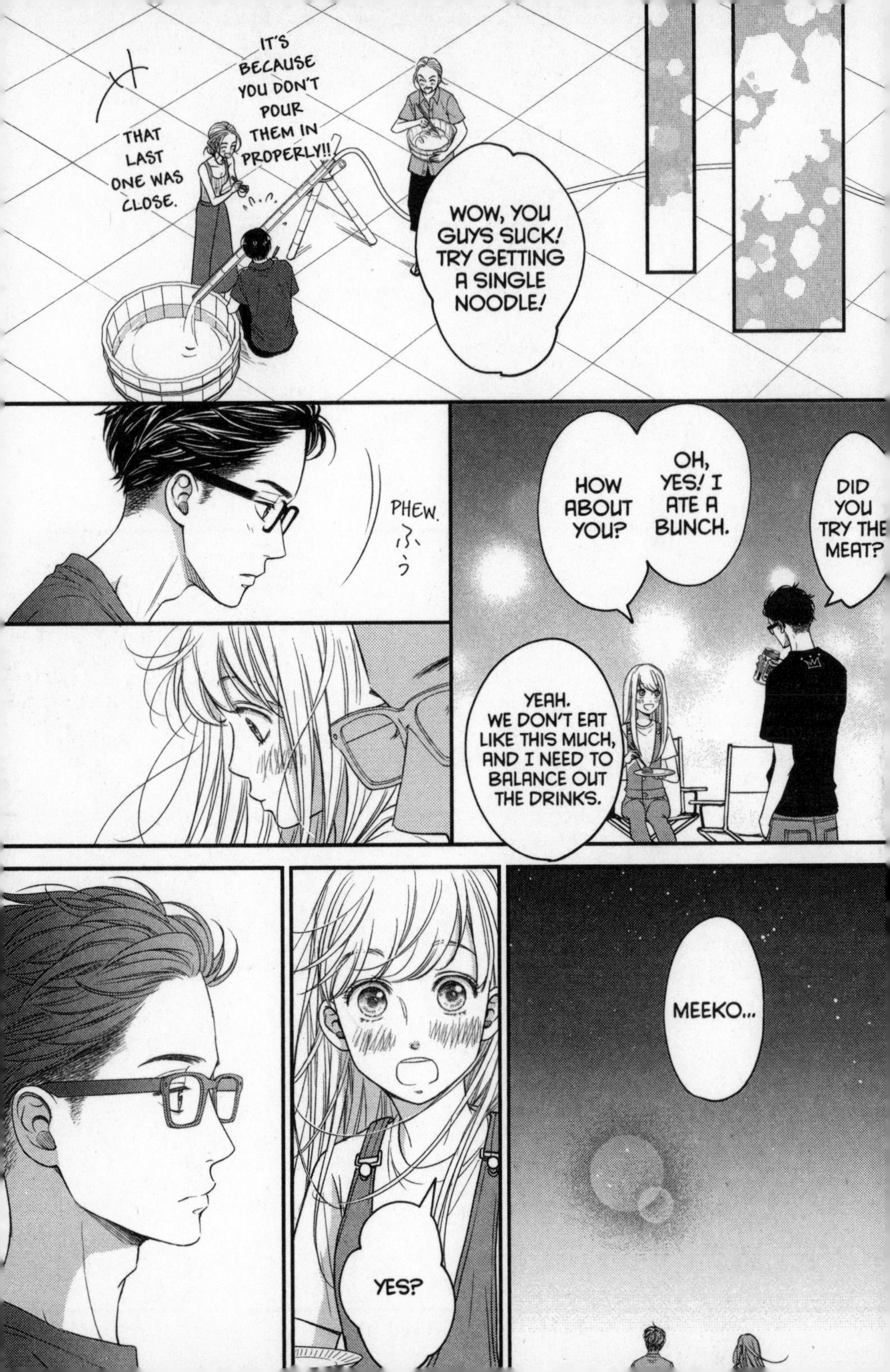
WOW, YOU GUYS SUCK! TRY GETTING A SINGLE NOODLE!
IT'S BECAUSE YOU DON'T POUR THEM IN PROPERLY!!
THAT LAST ONE WAS CLOSE.
DID YOU TRY THE MEAT?
OH, YES! I ATE A BUNCH.
HOW ABOUT YOU?
YEAH. WE DON'T EAT LIKE THIS MUCH, AND I NEED TO BALANCE OUT THE DRINKS.
PHEW.
ふぅ
MEEKO...
YES?

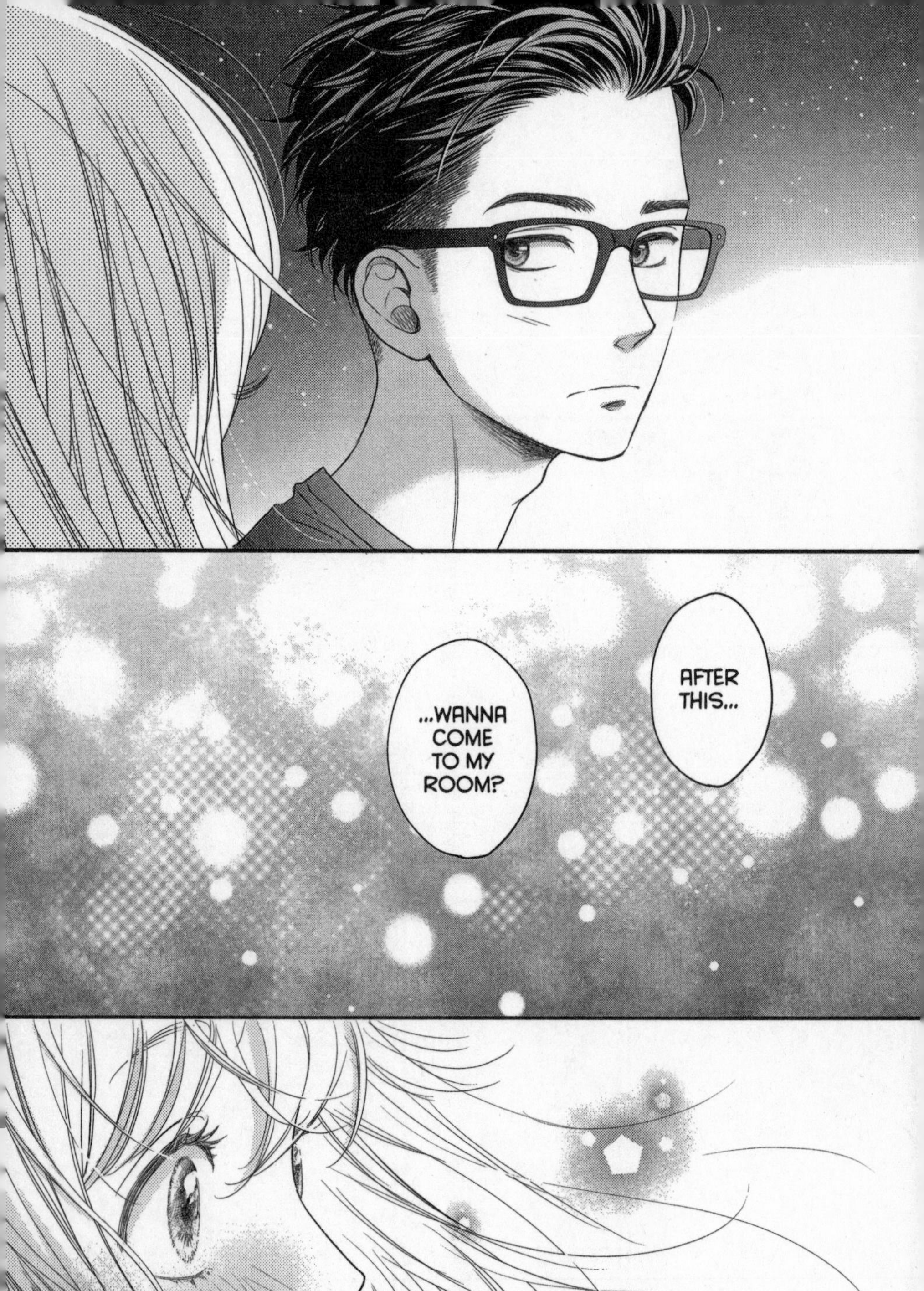
AFTER THIS...
...WANNA COME TO MY ROOM?

TO BE CONTINUED IN VOLUME 4

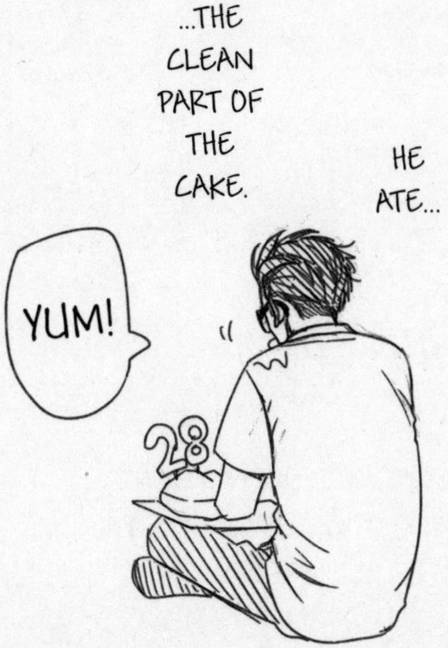
HE ATE...
...THE CLEAN PART OF THE CAKE.
YUM!
28

☆ AFTERWORD ☆

THANK YOU SO MUCH FOR READING *LIVING-ROOM MATSUNAGA-SAN*.
WOW... VOLUME 3!!! MY FIRST EVER VOLUME 3!!
I COULDN'T HAVE DONE THIS WITHOUT THE SUPPORT
OF THOSE AROUND ME AND, OF COURSE, MY READERS.
THANK YOU, FROM THE BOTTOM OF MY HEART!!!
I THINK THERE'S A LOT TO LOOK FORWARD
TO IN VOLUME 4! YOUR SUPPORT IS INVALUABLE. ♡

I LOOK FORWARD TO YOUR FEEDBACK. ♡

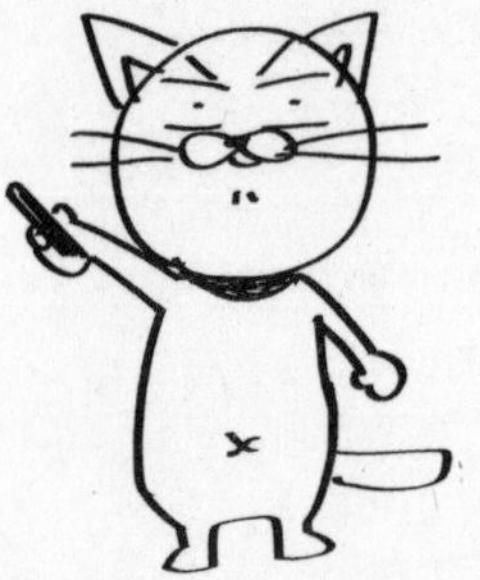

I'M TIRED OF THE COLD! SPRING, COME PLEASE! ♡

"LOOKING AT THIS PANEL OUT OF CONTEXT WOULD MAKE YOU THINK MATSUNAGA-SAN IS A LOT."

MY ASSISTANT TOLD ME THIS WAS THE PERFECT SHOT.

I GUESS... "BA-DUMP BA-DUMP"... IS RIGHT...

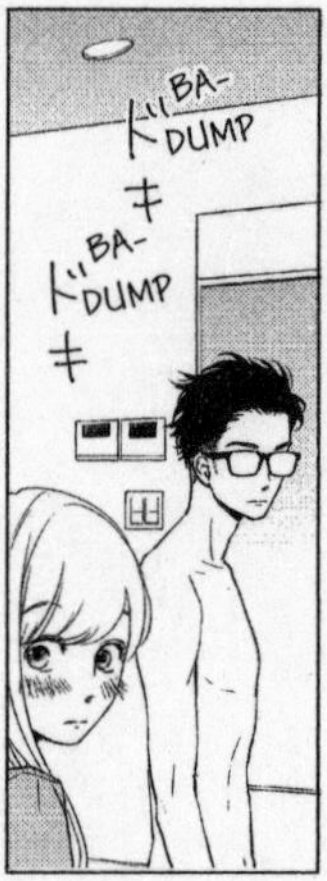
BA-DUMP
BA-DUMP

☆ SPECIAL THANKS ☆

EDITOR KITAHARA,
EVERYONE IN THE DESSERT EDITORIAL DEPARTMENT,
MY ASSISTANTS (EI AND SAKATA), THE DESIGNERS, THE
PRINTER, MY FAMILY, MY FRIENDS, EVERYONE AT
SUNAZUKA CAFÉ WHO LET ME INTERVIEW THEM...
AND MY READERS!!! THANK YOU SO MUCH!!

KEIKO IWASHITA
2018.2.13

BOYS ①

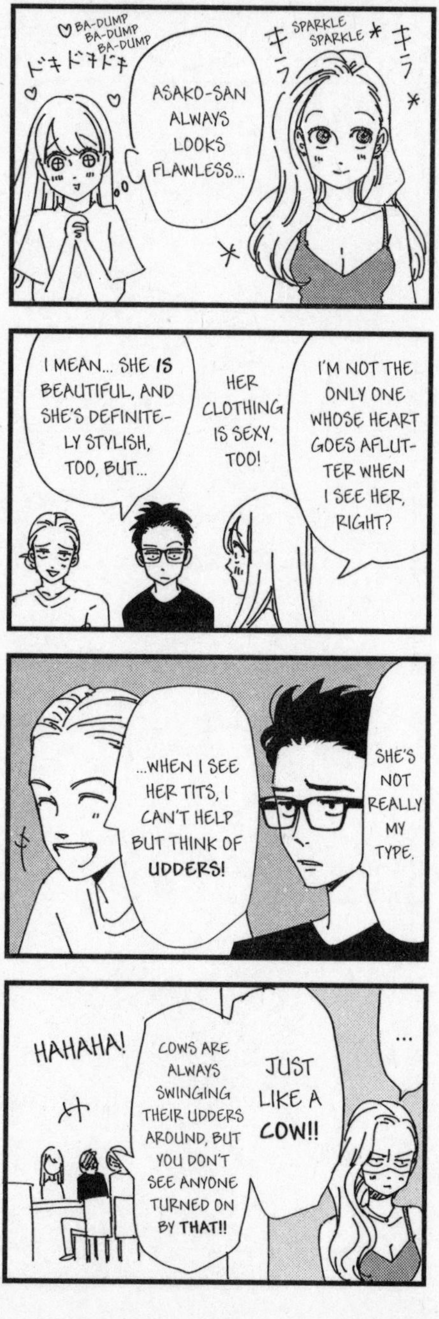
キラ キラ
SPARKLE SPARKLE
ASAKO-SAN ALWAYS LOOKS FLAWLESS...
ドキドキドキ
BA-DUMP BA-DUMP BA-DUMP
I'M NOT THE ONLY ONE WHOSE HEART GOES AFLUTTER WHEN I SEE HER, RIGHT?
HER CLOTHING IS SEXY, TOO!
I MEAN... SHE IS BEAUTIFUL, AND SHE'S DEFINITELY STYLISH, TOO, BUT...
SHE'S NOT REALLY MY TYPE.
...WHEN I SEE HER TITS, I CAN'T HELP BUT THINK OF UDDERS!
...
JUST LIKE A COW!!
COWS ARE ALWAYS SWINGING THEIR UDDERS AROUND, BUT YOU DON'T SEE ANYONE TURNED ON BY THAT!!
HAHAHA!

BOYS ②

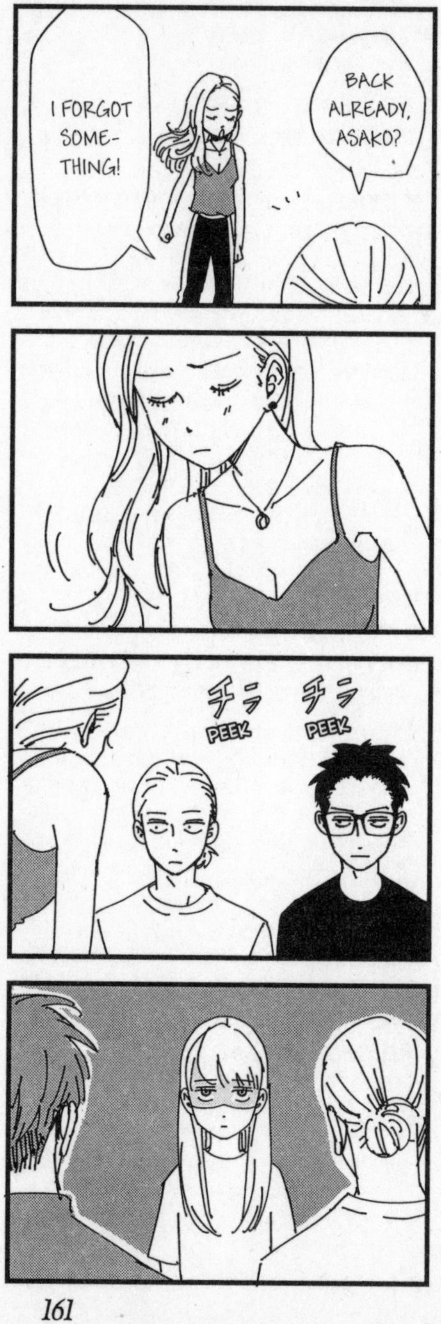
BACK ALREADY, ASAKO?
I FORGOT SOMETHING!
チラ PEEK
チラ PEEK

CHARACTER DATA & INSIDER INFO

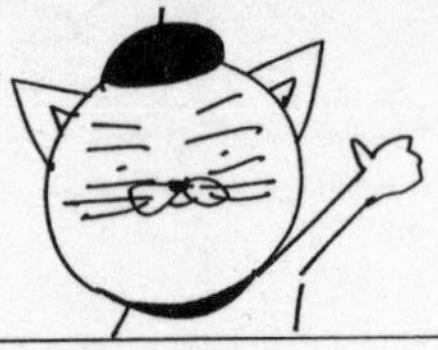
DUE TO ADULT CIRCUMSTANCES, I'VE LEFT SOME THINGS AS QUESTION MARKS. I APPRECIATE YOUR UNDERSTANDING!
(IT'S NOT THAT I HAVEN'T THOUGHT OF THEM. I JUST DON'T WANT TO LOCK MYSELF INTO ANYTHING BY WRITING IT DOWN...)

"THE BIG BROTHER"

JUN MATSUNAGA
(28 IN THIS VOLUME)
GRAPHIC DESIGNER
BIRTHDAY: 8/17 BLOOD TYPE: O
HEIGHT: 180 CM (5'10.9")

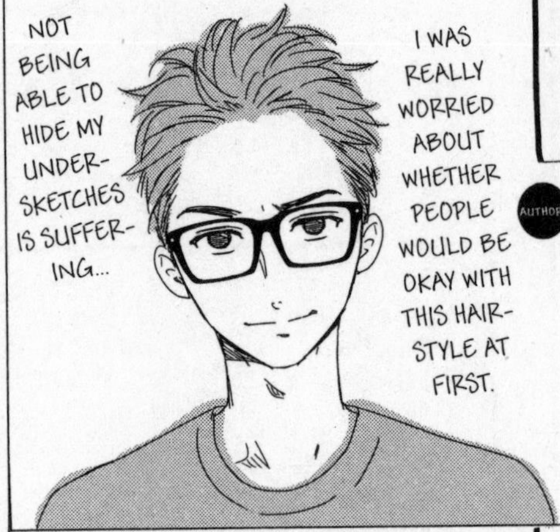
I WAS REALLY WORRIED ABOUT WHETHER PEOPLE WOULD BE OKAY WITH THIS HAIR-STYLE AT FIRST.
NOT BEING ABLE TO HIDE MY UNDER-SKETCHES IS SUFFER-ING...

AUTHOR: I'VE HAD IT UP TO HERE WITH YOU, MATSUNAGA-SAN! WHENEVER I DRAW THE ROUGH DRAFT OF THIS MANGA, HE NEVER DOES ANYTHING I WANT HIM TO DO. IT DRIVES ME CRAZY, BUT I GUESS THAT'S WHAT MAKES ME LOVE HIM SO MUCH. I KNOW HE DOESN'T LOOK OR ACT LIKE THE TYPICAL MALE ROMANTIC LEAD, BUT DON'T WORRY, HE'S ONLY GOING TO HAVE MORE MASCULINE CHARM FROM HERE ON OUT!!!

"THE MIDDLE BROTHER"

KENTARO SUZUKI (26)
BARTENDER
BIRTHDAY: ?/? BLOOD TYPE: B
HEIGHT: 172 CM (5'7.7")

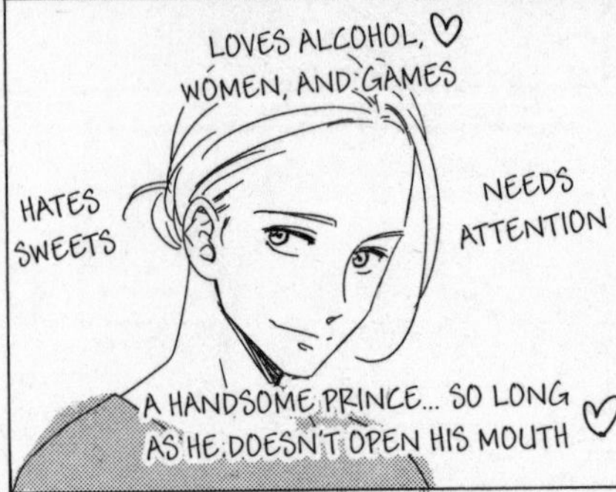
LOVES ALCOHOL, WOMEN, AND GAMES ♡
NEEDS ATTENTION
HATES SWEETS
A HANDSOME PRINCE... SO LONG AS HE DOESN'T OPEN HIS MOUTH ♡

AUTHOR: A (NASTY) PRINCE ON A WHITE STEED. ♡ I WONDER IF HE'LL EVER DROP THAT PART IN PARENTHESES? HE OFTEN PUSHES THE STORY FORWARD, SO I OWE A LOT TO HIM.

"THE THIRD BROTHER"

RYO HOJO (20)
COLLEGE STUDENT (SABAKO'S BOYFRIEND)
BIRTHDAY: ?/? BLOOD TYPE: O
HEIGHT: 175 CM (5'8.9")

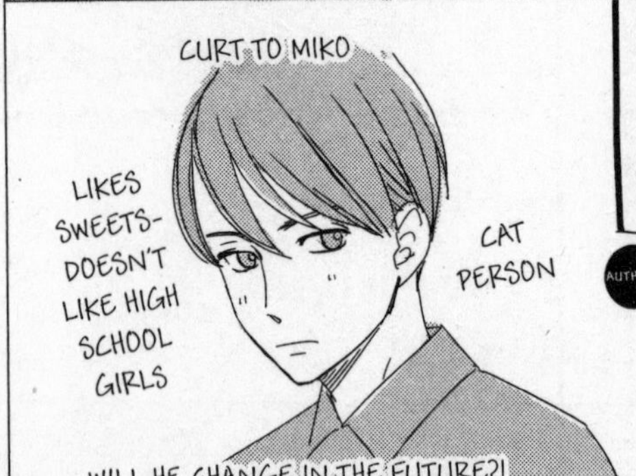
CURT TO MIKO
CAT PERSON
LIKES SWEETS-DOESN'T LIKE HIGH SCHOOL GIRLS
WILL HE CHANGE IN THE FUTURE?!

AUTHOR: RYO FINALLY DID SOMETHING! PEOPLE HAVE BEEN BEGGING FOR HIM TO SHOW UP MORE EVER SINCE BACK WHEN HE MIGHT AS WELL HAVE BEEN AN EXTRA. HE HAS BANGS, SO HE'S EASY TO DRAW. I LIKE HIM.

«THE BIG SISTER»

ASAKO ONUKI (25)
NAIL STYLIST
BIRTHDAY: ?/? BLOOD TYPE: A
HEIGHT: 169 CM (5'6.5")

AUTHOR BEAUTIFUL, STYLISH, KIND...
DRAWING HER IS ALWAYS A PLEASURE.
SHE LOOKS LIKE THE PERFECT WOMAN, BUT
IN REALITY SHE HOLDS A TERRIBLE SECRET...
WILL WE EVER FIND OUT WHAT IT IS?!?!

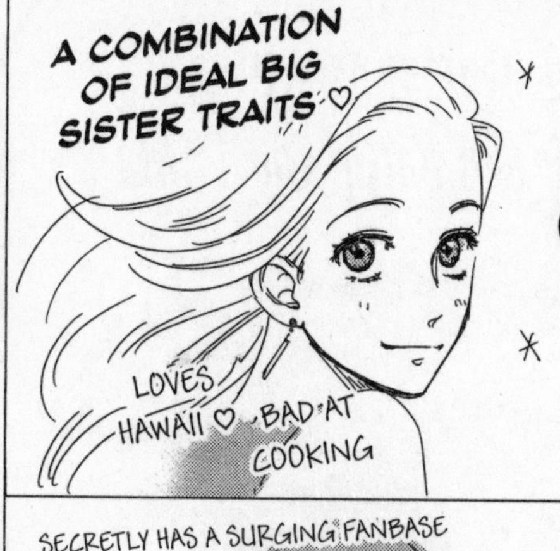
A COMBINATION OF IDEAL BIG SISTER TRAITS ♡
LOVES HAWAII ♡
BAD AT COOKING

«THE MIDDLE SISTER»

AKANE HATTORI (2?)
????
BIRTHDAY: ?/?
BLOOD TYPE: AB
HEIGHT: 156 CM (5'1.4")

AUTHOR THE ENIGMATIC HATTORI-SAN. I'D
ORIGINALLY INTENDED FOR HER TO BE MORE
OF A GLOOMY CHARACTER, BUT SHE ENDED
UP BECOMING 100% SUNNY. I'VE REALLY
THOUGHT ABOUT WHAT HER OCCUPATION IS,
SO IT BUT IT MIGHT SHOW UP SOON...

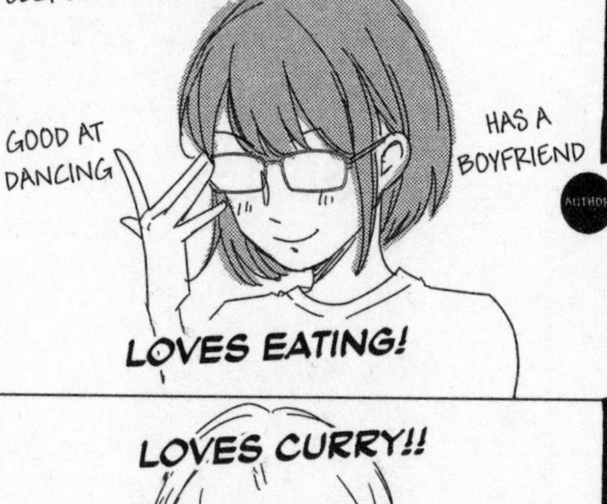
SECRETLY HAS A SURGING FANBASE
HAS A BOYFRIEND
GOOD AT DANCING
LOVES EATING!

«THE BABY»

MIKO SONODA (17)
SECOND YEAR HIGH SCHOOL
STUDENT (ALL GIRLS' SCHOOL)
BIRTHDAY: 5/5
BLOOD TYPE: A
HEIGHT: 159 CM (5'2.6")

AUTHOR IF I EVER HAD A DAUGHTER,
I WOULD HAVE WANTED TO NAME HER
MIKO, BUT NOW I USED IT ON MIKO
THE CHARACTER INSTEAD.
IT LOOKS LIKE I RAISED AN EARNEST
AND IMPRACTICAL HARD WORKER. YUP.
I WAS ORIGINALLY PLANNING FOR HER
TO BE SASSIER.

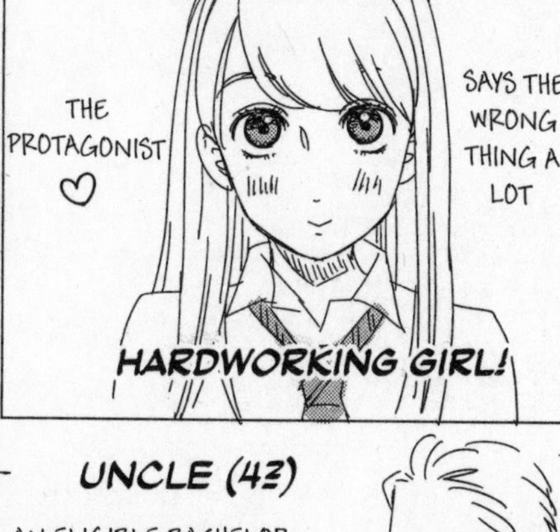
LOVES CURRY!!
SAYS THE WRONG THING A LOT
THE PROTAGONIST ♡
HARDWORKING GIRL!

SABAKO

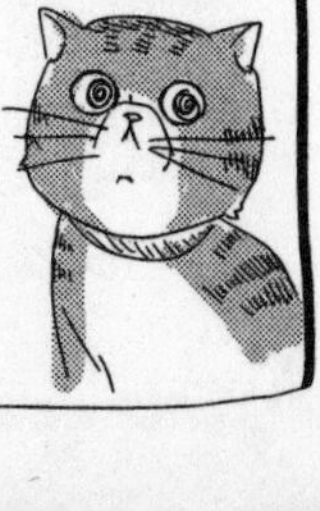
UGLY CUTE ♡

THINKS SHE
IS VERY CUTE.
I HATE HAVING TO DRAW
HER STRIPES OVER AND
OVER AGAIN WHEN I'M
ON A TIGHT DEADLINE!

UNCLE (4?)

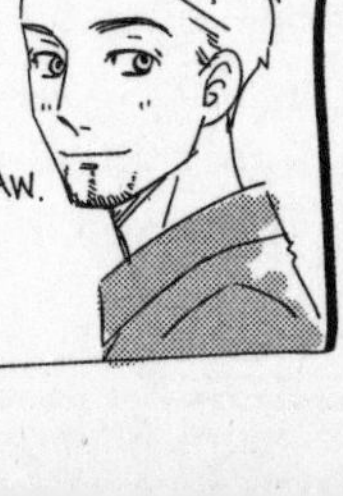

AN ELIGIBLE BACHELOR
WHO LOVES HIS NIECE.
DOESN'T SHOW UP MUCH
ANYMORE, BUT HE'S FUN TO DRAW.
I FORGET TO DRAW HIS BEARD
SOMETIMES. SORRY.

Young characters and steampunk setting, like *Howl's Moving Castle* and *Battle Angel Alita*

A boy with a talent for machines and a mysterious girl whose wings he's fixed will take you beyond the clouds! In the tradition of the high-flying, resonant adventure stories of Studio Ghibli comes a gorgeous tale about the longing of young hearts for adventure and friendship!

One of CLAMP's biggest hits returns
in this definitive, premium, hardcover
20th anniversary collector's edition!

"A wonderfully
entertaining story
that would be a great
installment in anybody's
manga collection."
— Anime News Network

"CLAMP is an all-female
manga-creating
team whose feminine
touch shows in this
entertaining, sci-fi soap
opera."
— Publishers Weekly

Poor college student Hideki is down on his luck. All he wants is a
good job, a girlfriend, and his very own "persocom"—the latest
and greatest in humanoid computer technology. Hideki's luck
changes one night when he finds Chi—a persocom thrown out in
a pile of trash. But Hideki soon discovers that there's much more
to his cute new persocom than meets the eye.

KC/
KODANSHA
COMICS

The art-deco cyberpunk classic from the creators of *xxxHOLiC* and *Cardcaptor Sakura*!

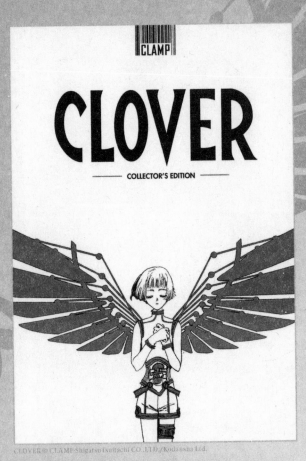

"Starred Review. This experimental sci-fi work from CLAMP reads like a romantic version of *AKIRA*."
—Publishers Weekly

CLAMP
CLOVER
COLLECTOR'S EDITION

Su was born into a bleak future, where the government keeps tight control over children with magical powers—codenamed "Clovers." With Su being the only "four-leaf" Clover in the world, she has been kept isolated nearly her whole life. Can ex-military agent Kazuhiko deliver her to the happiness she seeks? Experience the complete series in this hardcover edition, which also includes over twenty pages of ravishing color art!

KC
KODANSHA COMICS

PERFECT WORLD

Rie Aruga

A TOUCHING
NEW SERIES
ABOUT LOVE AND
COPING WITH
DISABILITY

An office party reunites Tsugumi with her high school crush Itsuki. He's realized his dream of becoming an architect, but along the way, he experienced a spinal injury that put him in a wheelchair. Now Tsugumi's rekindled feelings will butt up against prejudices she never considered — and Itsuki will have to decide if he's ready to let someone into his heart...

"Depicts with great delicacy and courage the difficulties some with disabilities experience getting involved in romantic relationships... Rie Aruga refuses to romanticize, pushing her heroine to face the reality of disability. She invites her readers to the same tasks of empathy, knowledge and recognition."
—Slate.fr

"An important entry [in manga romance]... The emotional core of both plot and characters indicates thoughtfulness... [Aruga's] research is readily apparent in the text and artwork, making this feel like a real story."
—Anime News Network

KC KODANSHA COMICS

MAGIC ★ KNIGHT RAYEARTH

25TH ANNIVERSARY EDITION

CLAMP

A BELOVED CLASSIC MAKES ITS STUNNING RETURN IN THIS GORGEOUS, LIMITED EDITION BOX SET!

This tale of three Tokyo teenagers who cross through a magical portal and become the champions of another world is a modern manga classic. The box set includes three volumes of manga covering the entire first series of *Magic Knight Rayearth*, plus the series's super-rare full-color art book companion, all printed at a larger size than ever before on premium paper, featuring a newly-revised translation and lettering, and exquisite foil-stamped covers. A strictly limited edition, this will be gone in a flash!

KC/ KODANSHA COMICS

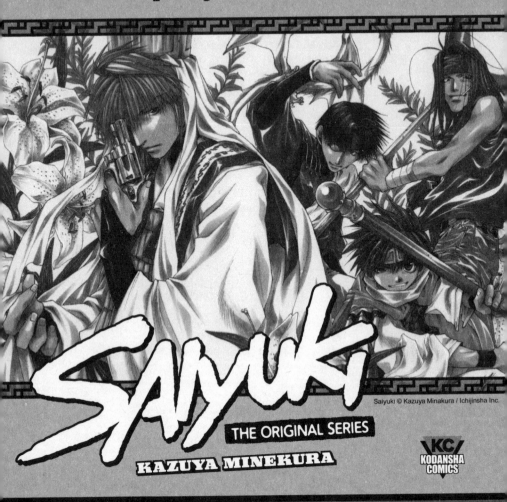

Something's Wrong With Us

NATSUMI ANDO

The dark, psychological, sexy shojo series readers have been waiting for!

A spine-chilling and steamy romance between a Japanese sweets maker and the man who framed her mother for murder!

Following in her mother's footsteps, Nao became a traditional Japanese sweets maker, and with unparalleled artistry and a bright attitude, she gets an offer to work at a world-class confectionary company. But when she meets the young, handsome owner, she recognizes his cold stare...

KC KODANSHA COMICS

The adorable new odd-couple cat comedy manga from the creator of the beloved *Chi's Sweet Home*, in full color!

Praise for Chi's Sweet Home

"Nearly impossible to turn away... a true all-ages title that anyone, young or old, cat lover or not, will enjoy. The stories will bring a smile to your face and warm your heart."

~School Library Journal

Sue & Tai-chan

Konami Kanata

Sue is an aging housecat who's looking forward to living out her life in peace... but her plans change when the mischievous black tomcat Tai-chan enters the picture! Hey! Sue never signed up to be a catsitter! *Sue & Tai-chan* is the latest from the reigning meow-narch of cute kitty comics, Konami Kanata.

KC KODANSHA COMICS

THE SWEET SCENT OF LOVE IS IN THE AIR! FOR FANS OF OFFBEAT ROMANCES LIKE *WOTAKOI*

Sweat and Soap © Kintetsu Yamada / Kodansha Ltd.

In an office romance, there's a fine line between sexy and awkward... and that line is where Asako — a woman who sweats copiously — meets Koutarou — a perfume developer who can't get enough of Asako's, er, scent. Don't miss a romcom manga like no other!

KC KODANSHA COMICS

The beloved characters from *Cardcaptor Sakura* return in a brand new, reimagined fantasy adventure!

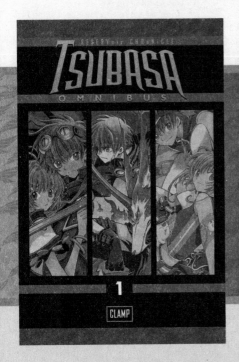

"[*Tsubasa*] takes readers on a fantastic ride that only gets more exhilarating with each successive chapter." —Anime News Network

In the Kingdom of Clow, an archaeological dig unleashes an incredible power, causing Princess Sakura to lose her memories. To save her, her childhood friend Syaoran must follow the orders of the Dimension Witch and travel alongside Kurogane, an unrivaled warrior; Fai, a powerful magician; and Mokona, a curiously strange creature, to retrieve Sakura's dispersed memories!

"Clever, sassy, and original....*xxxHOLiC* has the inherent hallmarks of a runaway hit."
—NewType magazine

Beautifully seductive artwork and uniquely Japanese depictions of the supernatural will hypnotize CLAMP fans!

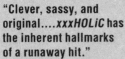

Kimihiro Watanuki is haunted by visions of ghosts and spirits. He seeks help from a mysterious woman named Yuko, who claims she can help. However, Watanuki must work for Yuko in order to pay for her aid. Soon Watanuki finds himself employed in Yuko's shop, where he sees things and meets customers that are stranger than anything he could have ever imagined.

Living-Room Matsunaga-san 3 is a work of fiction. Names, characters, places, and incidents are the products of the author's imagination or are used fictitiously. Any resemblance to actual events, locales, or persons, living or dead, is entirely coincidental.

Published in the United States by Kodansha Comics, an imprint of Kodansha USA Publishing, LLC, New York.

Publication rights for this English edition arranged through Kodansha Ltd., Tokyo.

First published in Japan in 2018 by Kodansha Ltd., Tokyo as *Living no Matsunaga-san*, volume 3.

ISBN 978-1-63236-967-3

Original cover design by Tomohiro Kusume and Hirotoshi Ikewaki (arcoinc)

Printed in the United States of America.

www.kodanshacomics.com

9 8 7 6 5 4 3 2 1
Translation: Ursula Ku
Lettering: Ean Scrale
Additional Lettering: Michael Martin
Editing: Thalia Sutton and Tiff Ferentini
Kodansha Comics edition cover design by Phil Balsman

Publisher: Kiichiro Sugawara
Vice president of marketing & publicity: Naho Yamada

Director of publishing services: Ben Applegate
Associate director of operations: Stephen Pakula
Publishing services managing editor: Noelle Webster
Assistant production manager: Emi Lotto, Angela Zurlo